MISCELLANEOUS PAPERS
RELATING TO INDO-CHINA

Trübner's Oriental Series

SOUTHEAST ASIA
In 7 Volumes

MISCELLANEOUS PAPERS RELATING TO INDO-CHINA

VOL II

REINHOLD ROST

Routledge
Taylor & Francis Group

LONDON AND NEW YORK

First published in 1886 by
Kegan Paul, Trench, Trübner & Co Ltd

Published 2016 by Routledge
2 Park Square, Milton Park, Abingdon, Oxfordshire OX14 4RN
711 Third Avenue, New York, NY 10017

First issued in paperback 2016

Routledge is an imprint of the Taylor and Francis Group, an informa business

© 1886 Reinhold Rost

British Library Cataloguing in Publication Data
A CIP catalogue record for this book
is available from the British Library

Miscellaneous Papers Relating to Indo-China
ISBN 0-415-24552-4
Southeast Asia: 7 Volumes
ISBN 0-415-24295-9
Trübner's Oriental Series
ISBN 0-415-23188-4

ISBN 13 : 978-1-138-99592-5 (pbk)
ISBN 13 : 978-0-415-24552-4 (hbk)

MISCELLANEOUS PAPERS

INDO-CHINA.

REPRINTED FOR THE STRAITS BRANCH OF THE
ROYAL ASIATIC SOCIETY

*FROM DALRYMPLE'S "ORIENTAL REPERTORY," AND THE
"ASIATIC RESEARCHES" AND "JOURNAL" OF THE
ASIATIC SOCIETY OF BENGAL.*

VOL. II.

LONDON:
TRÜBNER & CO., LUDGATE HILL.
1886.

CONTENTS OF VOL. II.

MISCELLANEOUS ESSAYS.

XXXV.

CATALOGUE OF MAMMALIA INHABITING THE MALAYAN PENINSULA AND ISLANDS.

Collected or observed by THEODORE CANTOR, M.D., *Bengal Medical Service.*

["Journal of the Asiatic Society of Bengal," vol. xv. pp. 171-203, 241-279.]

QUADRUMANA.

SIMIADÆ.

Gen. PITHECUS, *Geoffroy.*

PITHECUS SATYRUS, Geoffroy.

SYN.—Simia Satyrus, Linné.
Simia Agrias, Schreber.
Singe de Wurmb, Audebert.
Papio Wurmbii, Latreille.
Pithecus Satyrus, Desmarest.
Simia Wurmbii, Kuhl.
Orang Pandak, Raffles.
Simia Satyrus, ⎫
Simia Abelii, ⎬ apud Fischer.
Simia Wurmbii, ⎭
Simia Satyrus, apud Ogilby.
Satyrus rufus, Lesson.
Pithecus Satyrus, apud Martin.
Simia Satyrus, apud Schinz.
" Orang 'Utan" of the Malays.[1]

HAB.—*Borneo, Sumatra.*[*]

[1] [See above, vol. i. pp. 172-178, and 301-318.]
[*] Localities printed in *italics* signify those from whence the animals of the catalogue were obtained ; in ordinary type those previously given by authors.

The physiognomy and the colour of the face exhibit a marked difference in living individuals from the two localities.*

Gen. HYLOBATES, *Illiger.*

HYLOBATES LAR, Ogilby.

SYN.—Grand Gibbon, Buffon.
Homo Lar, Linné, Mantiss.
Simia longimana, Schreber.
Simia longimana, Grand et Petit Gibbon, Erxleb.
Simia Lar, Linné Syst.
Le Gibbon, Audebert.
Pithecus Lar, Desmarest.
Simia albimana, Vigors and Horsfield.
Simia Lar, apud Fischer.
Hylobates Lar, Lesson apud Martin.
Hylobates albimanus, apud Schinz.
" Ungka étam " of the Malays of the Peninsula.
HAB.—*Malayan Peninsula.*
Siam, Burmah, Tenasserim.

LIGHT-COLOURED VAR.

SYN.—Petit Gibbon, Buffon,
Simia Lar, β Linné.
Pithecus variegatus, Geoff.
Pithecus variegatus, apud Kuhl.
Pithecus variegatus, apud Desmarest.
Hylobates variegatus, Ogilby.
Hylobates leuciscus, apud Cantor (" Ann. and Mag. of Nat. Hist.").
" Ungka putih " and " Wow-wow " of the Malays of the Peninsula.

The colour varies from blackish-brown to light-brown, yellowish- or dirty-white, sometimes uniform, sometimes mottled. The index and middle toes of both or of one foot are in some individuals, of whatever sex or shade of colour, united by a broad web throughout the whole of the first phalanx; in some partially so, and in others not. The ribs vary from twelve (7 + 5) to thirteen pairs (7 + 6) as observed by Mr. Blyth (" Journal 'Asiatic Society," 1841, vol. x. p. 839).

---

* An excellent likeness of a young male Bornean Orang Utan, living in my possession upwards of two years, has lately been taken by Mr. Thornam, one of the artists of the scientific expedition on his Danish Majesty's ship *Galathea.*

HYLOBATUS AGILIS, F. Cuvier.

Var. UNGKA ETAM, Martin.

SYN.—Ungka etam, Raffles.
Oungka, Hylobates Lar, F. Cuv.
Simia Lar, Vigors and Horsfield.
Hylobates Rafflesii, Geoff. apud Ogilby.
Hylobates variegatus, Müller apud Schinz.*
" Ungka etam " of the Malays of the Peninsula.
HAB.—*Malayan Peninsula (Malacca, Purlís, Kéddah, Púngah).*
Sumatra.

The first phalanges of the index and middle toes are in some individuals of either sex partially or entirely united by a web. Sometimes the first phalanx of the middle toe is partially united to the fourth.

An adult male examined had thirteen pair of ribs (6 + 7), an adult female fourteen (7 + 7), a young male on the left side thirteen (7 + 6), on the right twelve (7 + 5). In these three individuals the stomach was constricted at the fundus and the pyloric part, which characters, when compared with specimens of *Hylobates agilis* from Sumatra, will go far to decide the identity of that species and *H. Rafflesii.* On the Malayan Peninsula the latter appears to be less numerous than *H. Lar.* The light-coloured var. of *H. agilis* I have not seen.

HYLOBATES LEUCISCUS, Kuhl.

SYN.—" Wou-wou," Camper.
Simia leucisca, Schreber.
Simia moloch, Audebert.
Pithecus cinereus, Latreille.
Pithecus leuciscus, Geoffroy.
Pithecus leuciscus, apud Desmarest.
Simia leucisca, apud Fischer.
Hylobates leuciscus, apud Ogilby.
Hylobates leuciscus, apud Schinz.†
HAB.—*Borneo* (?).
Java.

Gen. SEMNOPITHECUS, *F. Cuv.*

SEMNOPITHECUS OBSCURUS, Reid.

SYN.—Simia maura (?), Lin.   Lotong, apud Raffles.‡
Semnopithecus leucomystax, Temm. in MSS.

---

* Schinz gives as a synonym, *Pithecus variegatus*, Geoff., which, however, is *Hylobates Lar*, Var.

† Among the syn. occurs *Ungka puti*, Raffles, which is *Hylobates agilis.*

‡ The hab. Pinang and Singapore, in neither of which islands *Semnopithecus femoralis* appears to occur, tends to prove that Sir S. Raffles did not,

Semnopithecus obscurus, apud Martin.
Presbytes obscura, Gray, List of Mamm. B.M.
Semnopithecus sumatranus, Müller apud Schinz.*
Semnopithecus halonifer, Cantor (" Proceed. Linn. Soc.").
" Lótong," or " Lótong etam," of the Malays of the Peninsula.
HAB.—*Malayan Peninsula, Pinang, Singapore.*
District adjacent to Singapore, in the Malayan Peninsula.

SEMNOPITHECUS ALBOCINEREUS, Schinz.

SYN.—Cercopithecus albocinereus, Desmarest.
Simia albocinerea, Fischer.
Semnopithecus dorsatus (young), Waterhouse MSS.† apud Martin.
Presbytes cinerea, Gray, List.
Semnopithecus albimanus, Is. Geoff. (?)
" Ka-ka " of the Malays of the Peninsula.
HAB.—*Malayan Peninsula.*

The young of this species, described by Martin (p. 481), is, from the peculiar distribution of the colours, as easily distinguished from the young of *S. obscurus* as it is difficult to distinguish the adults of these two species.   Both attain to the same size, have in common the shape of the body, the white marks of the face, and the general distribution of colours.   In the adult of the present species the prevailing colours are clear ashy-grey above and white below.   On either parietal bone the hairs form a whorl, and the anterior are directed forward, projecting beyond the eyebrows.   The two whorls are distinct in the young, though the hairs of the head are too short to mingle with the long, erect, divergent black hairs of the eyebrows.   Just below the spot where the two whorls come in contact the skull is naked, thus forming a rather broad, triangular forehead.   The general colour of

as it has been supposed, refer to that species.   His short description indicates *S. obscurus* (Lotong), the most common species in both islands.   Sir S. Raffles evidently did not describe the living animal, or he would not have omitted one of the most striking characters—viz., the white marks of the face, which in preserved specimens become obliterated, so that the face appears uniformly black.   The omission of this character by Sir S. Raffles, and subsequently by later describers of this species, has given rise to confusion.

* Schinz repeats *S. femoralis*, Martin, as a syn. for *S. sumatranus*, and says in a note that Müller, in his monograph of *Semnopithecus*, refers that species to his *S. sumatranus* (Schinz, Syn. Mam. i. p. 39, note).   Were even the two identical, the species should not have been re-named, as *S. femoralis, Horsfield*, not Martin, would take precedence, being the denomination under which Dr. Horsfield described it in the " Appendix to the Life of Sir T. Stamford Raffles," 1830.

† Martin, p. 481, refers the young *S. dorsatus* to *S. femoralis*, but the description is that of the young of the present species.

S. obscurus, both in the young and adult state, is considerably darker. On the upper parts a blackish or brownish ash colour prevails, lighter below, which acquires in some individuals a whitish appearance from the white skin of the stomach, which is but scantily covered with hairs. Of parietal whorls there is no trace; the hairs of the head, directed backwards, originate in a peak as far down as the glabella, and are smoothed down on the top of the head from the occipital crest backward.

SEMNOPITHECUS CRISTATUS, Horsfield.

SYN.—Simia cristata, Chingkau, Raffles.
Semnopithecus pruinosus, Desmarest.
Semnopithecus pruinosus, apud Lesson.
Semnopithecus cristatus, apud Martin.
Presbytes cristata, Gray :* List.
Semnopithecus cristatus, apud Schinz.*
HAB.—*Pinang, Malayan Peninsula.*
Sumatra, Borneo, Banka.

The whitish colour round the eyes and mouth is present, though less distinct in this than in the preceding two species.

SEMNOPITHECUS FEMORALIS, Horsfield.

SYN.—Semnopithecus chrysomelas, Müller apud Martin and Schinz.
HAB.—*Purlis (on the Malayan Peninsula).*
Borneo, Java (?), Sumatra (?).

In a young male of this apparently everywhere difficultly procurable species the face during life was intense black, except the white-haired lips and the chin, which were of a milk-white colour. In the preserved specimen the latter soon changed into the dull brownish-black of the rest of the face. The interdigital membrane, often loosely connecting the first phalanges of the four fingers and toes in *S. obscurus, albocinereus, cristatus,* and other Malayan monkeys, was also present in this individual, in which even the first and second phalanges of the index and middle toe were thus connected. In preserved specimens the interdigital web becomes shrivelled and indistinct, and therefore, being at all times a very questionable if not altogether inadmissible specific character, ought in such state to be least relied upon. On its arrival at Pinang the animal was in too sickly a state to allow of its natural habits being observed.

---

* Gray quotes *S. maurus,* Horsfield, and Schinz *S. femoralis,* Martin, as synonyms, both of which are species—in physiognomy, colours, and, as far as *S. maurus* is concerned, in habits, distinctly different from the present one.

Gen. CERCOPITHECUS, apud *Ogilby*.

CERCOPITHECUS CYNOMOLGUS, Ogilby.

SYN.—Simia cynomolgus, Linné.
Simia aygula, Linné.
Simia attys, Schreber.
Macacus cynomolgus, Desmarest.
Simia fascicularis, Raffles.
Cercocebus aygula, Geoff. apud Horsfield.
Macacus cynomolgus, apud Gray : List.
Macacus cynomolgus, apud Schinz.
" Kra" of the Malays of the Peninsula.
HAB.—*Pinang, Malayan Peninsula.*
Sumatra, Java, Banka, Borneo, Celebes, Timor, Tenasserim, Nicobar Islands.

The first phalanges of the four fingers and toes, and in some individuals also the second phalanges of the toes, are united by a membrane.

Gen. PAPIO, apud *Ogilby*.

PAPIO NEMESTRINUS, Ogilby.

SYN.—Simia nemestrinus, Linné.
Simia platypygos, Schreber.
Simia fusca, Shaw.
Macacus nemestrinus, Desmarest.
Simia carpolegus, Raffles.
Macacus nemestrinus, apud Gray : List.
Macacus nemestrinus, apud Schinz.
" Broh" of the Malays of the Peninsula.
HAB.—*Pinang, Malayan Peninsula.*
Sumatra, Borneo.

The interdigital membrane of the first phalanges of the four fingers and index and middle toe occurs also in this species.

LEMURIDÆ.

Gen. NYCTICEBUS, *Geoffroy*.

NYCTICEBUS TARDIGRADUS, Waterhouse (" Cat. Zool. Soc.").

SYN.—Lemur tardigradus, Linné apud Raffles.[1]
Nycticebus bengalensis, Geoff.
Nycticebus javanicus, Geoff.
Loris tardigradus, Geoff.

[1] [O. Mohnike, l. l. p. 397.]

Stenops javanicus, Van der Hoeven.
Stenops tardigradus, Wagner apud Schinz.
" Kúkang " of the Malays of the Peninsula.
HAB.—*Pinang, Malayan Peninsula.*
Java, Siam, Tenasserim, Arracan, Bengal, Sylhet, Assam.

The sublingual appendage is cartilaginous, of a white colour ; the apex divided in a number of fine points. The new-born is of the same colour as the adult, but paler, and has the dense soft fur mixed with a number of long hairs, grey at the base, white at the point. In a male, measuring from the apex of the nose to the root of the tail one foot two and a half inches, the tail five-eighths of an inch, the dimensions of the intestinal canal were :—

Small intestines	. . . . . .	3 feet o½ inch.
Large ditto.	. . . .	2 „ 3¾ inches.
Cæcum .	. . . .	o „ 3½ „

Gen. GALEOPITHECUS, *Pallas.*

GALEOPITHECUS TEMMINCKII, Waterhouse.

SYN.—Lemur volans, Linn. apud Marsden and Raffles.
" Kubong " or " Kurbong " of the Malays of the Peninsula.
HAB.—*Singapore, Pinang, and other Islands in the Straits of Malacca, Lancavy Islands, Malayan Peninsula.*
Java, Sumatra, Borneo, Pelew Islands, Siam.

Two individuals are never of precisely the same design and ground-colour, which colour varies from clear ashy-grey to greyish-brown or chestnut. The white spots on the back of the anterior extremities appear to be constant in every age. Though there are four mammæ situate in pairs one above the other close to the axilla of a number of females with young, none had more than one offspring, which was carried wrapped in the wide mantle-like membrane. In several shot on the hills at Pinang the stomach contained vegetable matter, but no remains of insects. In confinement, plantains constitute the favourite food, but deprived of liberty the animal soon pines and dies. The anterior margin of the broad smooth tongue has a fringed appearance, produced by a number of rounded papillæ. In a male, measuring from the apex of the nose to the root of the tail one foot four inches, the tail nine inches, the intestinal canal was of the following dimensions :—

Small intestines	. . . . . .	4 feet 4 inches.
Large ditto	. . . . . .	7 „ 7 „
Cæcum .	. . . .	o „ 11 „

Costæ veræ seven pairs, spuriæ six pairs.

CARNIVORA.

CHEIROPTERA—INSECTIVORA.

Gen. Rhinopoma, *Geoffroy.*

Rhinopoma Hardwickii, Gray.

Syn.— Vespertilio (Rhinopoma) Hardwickii, Elliot.
Hab.—*Malayan Peninsula.*
Southern Mahratta country, Calcutta, Allahabad,* Agra,†
Mirzapore.

A single male, in no way differing from Bengal individuals, was obtained by Captain Congalton, H.C. steamer *Diana,* in a cave on an island in Girbee river, in latitude 8° on the Malayan Peninsula.

This species is provided with a true cæcum, the existence of which in all Cheiroptera has erroneously been denied, or restricted to the cardiac cæcum observed in the genera *Vampyrus* and *Pteropus.* The present species and *Megaderma spasma,* also possessing a true cæcum, thus presents a higher organization than has hitherto been attributed to Cheiroptera.

Length of the small intestine . . . . $7\frac{1}{4}$ inches.
    „   „   large ditto 1   inch.
    „   „   cæcum . . . . . . $0\frac{3}{16}$ „

Gen. Megaderma, *Geoffroy.*

Megaderma spasma, Geoffroy.

Syn.—Vespertilia spasma, Schreber.
Megaderma trifolium, Geoffroy.
Megaderma spasma, apud Fischer.
Megaderma spasma, apud Schinz.
Hab.—*Pinang, Malayan Peninsula.*
Singapore, Java, Ternate.

Incis.$\frac{0}{4}$; Canin. $\frac{1-1}{1-1}$; Mol. $\frac{4\cdot4}{5\cdot5}$

Length of the head and body . . . $3\frac{1}{4}$ inches.
    „   „   inter-femoral membrane 1 inch.
Extent of the flying membrane . . . 14 inches.

The five caudal vertebræ project one quarter of an inch beyond the pelvis, but are completely enveloped in the inter-femoral membrane, and therefore not apparent. The inguinal warts are,

---

* Numbers inhabit the subterraneous Hindoo place of worship within the fort at Allahabad.
† In the Taj-Mahal,

as in the Rhinolophi, most developed in the adult female. A true cæcum, though smaller than in *Rhinopoma Hardwickii*, is present in this species.

Length of the small intestines 7   inches.
„   „   large ditto . . . . . $1\frac{1}{16}$ inch.
„   „   cæcum . . . . . . $0\frac{1}{16}$ „

Gen. NYCTINOMUS, *Geoffroy.*

NYCTINOMUS TENUIS, Horsfield.

SYN.—Nyctinomus tenuis, apud Fischer.
Molosse grêle, Temminck.
Dysopes tenuis, Schinz.
HAB.—*Malayan Peninsula.*
Java, Sumatra, Borneo.

Two individuals had the back of a velvety snuff colour, becoming a shade lighter on the under parts. Entire length of the larger, four and four-eighth inches, of which the tail one and a half inch; extent of the flying membrane ten and four-eighth inches. In the size of the ears some difference exists in the two.

Gen. TAPHOZOUS, *Geoffroy.*

TAPHOZOUS MELANOPOGON, Temminck.

SYN.—Taphozous melanopogon, apud Schinz.
HAB.—*Pulo-Tikus, Pulo-Láncavy, Malayan Peninsula.*
Java, Caves of Cannera.

Temminck's description, as quoted by Schinz, is taken from the adult male, the Malayan individuals of which differ in having the black beard surrounded by a broad light-brown band, covering, like a pelerine, the chest and shoulders. The rest of the lower parts are either white or brownish-white. The flying membrane in the adult male is whitish ; in the females and young males it is blackish or brownish between the legs, along the sides of the body, and the arms. The colour of the female and young male is on the back of a more or less brownish mouse-grey, becoming much lighter or whitish beneath, but both are destitute of the black beard, which, out of a number of between forty and fifty from different Malayan localities, occurred but in seven males, although some of the beardless males, in size and extent of flying membrane, equalled or even slightly exceeded the bearded. The entire length of the largest male was four inches, of which the tail measured one inch ; extent of flying membrane, fifteen and four-eighth inches. Dentition :—

Incis. $\frac{0}{4}$; Canin. $\frac{1-1}{1-1}$; Mol. $\frac{4\cdot4}{5\cdot5}$

TAPHOZOUS SACCOLAIMUS, Temminck.

SYN.—Taphozous pulcher, Elliot MSS. apud Blyth.
HAB.—*Pinang*.
  Java, Sumatra, Borneo, Celebes, Southern India.

In two males captured at Pinang, in houses in the valley, the colours somewhat differ from Temminck's description, quoted by Schinz. In the larger, the head and back are of a sooty black, with a few white dashes, the lower parts of a pure white. The flying membrane is black between the legs, along the sides of the body and the arms, and between the index, second, and third fingers; the rest being dull, semi-transparent white. The length from the apex of the nose to the posterior margin of the inter-femoral margin is four and seven-eighth inches, of which the tail measures one inch; the extent of the flying membrane eighteen inches. Dentition as in *T. melanogogon*. The smaller differs in having the chest of a pale brownish white, the abdomen and the pubes light rust-coloured, leaving the sides pure white. Mr. Blyth quotes *Taphozous pulcher*, Elliot, from Southern India, as being " black brown above with white pencillings, and pure white below " ("Journ. As. Soc." xiii. 1844, p. 492), from which, as well as from Mr. Elliot's specimen, at present in the Museum of the Asiatic Society, it appears that the Indian more resemble the Malayan individuals than those of the Indian Archipelago, described by Temminck. The internal surface of the gular sac secretes an odorous oily fluid of a light brown colour.

Gen. RHINOLOPHUS, *Geoffroy;* RHINOLOPHUS, *Gray*.

RHINOLOPHUS AFFINIS, Horsfield.

HAB.—*Pinang*.
  Java.

Of two individuals, the male is reddish-brown above, light greyish-brown beneath; the female is above golden fulvous, which becomes lighter on the lower parts.

Entire length of the male . $2\frac{1}{2}$ inches—female, $2\frac{7}{8}$ inches.
Tail . . . . $0\frac{1}{2}$,, female, $0\frac{5}{8}$,,
Extent of flying membrane . $11\frac{1}{4}$,, female, $12\frac{1}{2}$,,

$$\text{Incis.} \ \frac{2}{4} \ ; \text{Canin.} \ \frac{1—2}{1—1} ; \text{Mol.} \ \frac{5.5}{5.5}$$

The inguinal warts are highly developed in the female.

HIPPOSIDEROS, *Gray.*

A. *Adult male with a frontal pore, with a tuft of rigid hairs.*

HIPPOSIDEROS DIADEMA, Gray?

SYN.—Rhinolophus Diadema, Geoffroy?
HAB.—*Pinang, Malayan Peninsula.*
   Timor.

The Malayan individuals are, according to age and sex, of a more or less intense reddish or greyish-brown above, under certain lights assuming a golden lustre, owing to the whitish points of the hairs ; beneath they are of a lighter greyish-brown.   Individuals occur of a light golden-brown, in colours resembling *Rhinolophus larvatus,* Horsfield.   In the adult male the livid flesh-coloured nasal appendage is larger, more complicated, and somewhat different from the figure given by Geoffroy St. Hilaire (" Ann. du Muséum," xx. pl. 5 and 6), which resembles the female in the simpler appendage and the absence of the frontal pore.   The latter organ in the adult male is large, secreting a yellowish-brown oily fluid, the odour of which resembles that of *Arctictis Binturong,* Fischer.   A female during lactation presented a great inequality in the development of the inguinal warts, of which the right measured one-quarter of an inch in length.   At the time of her capture it was reported that a young one had been "sucking" the right wart. Not having myself observed the young clinging to that organ, I cannot vouch for the correctness of a statement which, if authentic, would tend to explain the use, being to afford support to the young when not sucking.   The size of the Malayan individuals appears to exceed those from Timor, the entire length of the former being five and six-eighth inches, of which the tail measures two inches. Extent of the flying membrane, twenty-one and a half to twenty-two inches.   The extremity of the second phalanx of the fourth and fifth fingers is bifid, or terminating with two minute diverging joints, a structure also existing in the Malayan individuals of the following species :—

$$\text{Incis. } \frac{2}{4} \text{ ; Canin. } \frac{1-1}{1-1} \text{; Mol. } \frac{5.5}{5.5}$$

HIPPOSIDEROS NOBILIS, Gray.

SYN.—Rhinolophus nobilis, Horsfield.
   Rhinolophus nobilis, apud Fischer.
   Rhinolophe fameux, Temminck.
   Rhinolophus nobilis, apud Schinz.
HAB.—*Pinang, Malayan Peninsula.*
   Java, Sumatra, Timor, Amboyna.

The frontal pore is less developed than in the former species, as compared with which the present is of a more slender form, though of a size little less inferior. Entire length, five and four-eighth inches, of which the tail measures two and one-eighth inches ; extent of flying membrane, twenty-one and four-eighth inches. Dentition similar to that of *H. Diadema*. In the valley of Pinang single individuals of both species are at night abroad at all seasons, but during the rains they are particularly numerous.

HYPPOSIDEROS VULGARIS, Gray.

SYN.—Rhinolophus vulgaris, Horsfield.
 Rhinolophus insignis, var. apud Temminck.
 Rhinolophus insignis, Horsf. apud Schinz.
 Rhinolophus vulgaris, Horsf., *female of insignis*, apud
 Schinz.*
HAB.—*Pinang.*
 Java.

Entire length, four inches, of which the tail measures one and three-eighths ; extent of flying membrane fourteen inches.

$$\text{Incis.} \ \frac{2}{4} \ ; \ \text{Canin.} \ \frac{1-1}{1-1} \ ; \ \text{Mol.} \ \frac{4 \cdot 4}{5 \cdot 5}$$

HIPPOSIDEROS MURINUS, Gray.

SYN.—Rhinolophus murinus, Elliot.
HAB.—*Pinang.*
 Southern Mahratta country, Nicobar Islands.

Entire length, two and four-eighth inches, of which the tail measures one inch ; extent of flying membrane, nine and four-eighth inches. Dentition similar to that of the last species.

B. *Forehead simple.*

HIPPOSIDEROS GALERITUS, N.S.

H. prosthematis simplicis membranâ transversâ latâ, altè erectâ, auriculas tangente ; auricularum, latè pyriformium, apicibus laciniâ exsertis, besse postico lobuloque basali villosis ; vellere longo, denso, molli, bicolore ; suprâ saturatè, subtus pallidius-fusco-rufescenti. Latet fæmina.

HAB.—*Pinang.*

Entire length, three inches, of which the tail measures one inch ; extent of the flying membrane, ten and four-eighth inches.

$$\text{Incis.} \ \frac{2}{4} \ ; \ \text{Canin.} \ \frac{1-1}{1-1} \ ; \ \text{Mol.} \ \frac{4 \cdot 4}{5 \cdot 5}$$

* The only individual of *Rhinolophus vulgaris*, Horsfield, observed at Pinang happened to be a *male*.

The livid flesh-coloured nasal appendage is simple but large, occupying the whole upper part of the face and the forehead; the horse-shoe or nasal disc covers the short, rounded, hairy muzzle, which has two leaves on either side; the transversal membrane is concave, as broad and as long as the horizontal horse-shoe, which it joins under a right angle, while its sides are almost in contact with the ears. The latter are sub-erect, broader than long, their breadth equalling the length of the head; the shape is broad, pyriform, narrowing towards the apex, which appears like a small artificially-rounded flap, scarcely elevated above the level of the fur covering the vertex. More than two-thirds of the back of the ear is covered with fur, leaving a narrow naked line along the external margin, which, as well as the singular shape of the ear itself, affords a distinguishing character. The hairs are buff or whitish at the base, the other half of their length brown. The general colour of the upper parts is deep brown, with a slight reddish hue, becoming a shade lighter beneath.

This species somewhat resembles *Hipposideros apiculatus*, Gray (*Vespertilio speoris*, Schneider apud Schreber; *Rhinelophus speoris*, Geoffroy), from which, however, it differs in the absence of the frontal pore, in the shape of the ears, and in colours. A solitary male was captured in the valley of Pinang.

Gen. VESPERTILIO, *Linné;* VESPERTILIO, Gray.

VESPERTILIO ADVERSUS, Horsfield?

SYN.—Vespertilio adversus, Fischer?
Vespertilio adversus, Temminck?
Vespertilio cineraceus, Blyth MSS.
HAB.—*Pinang.*
Java, Calcutta.

This bat, having the characteristic distinction of the upper incisor described by Horsfield, is above greyish-brown, beneath light greyish, measuring in length three and two-eighth inches, of which the tail is one and four-eighth inch; extent of flying membrane, ten and four-eighth inches. It differs from *V. adversus* in having on each side five molars, of which but two are spurious, which character also obtains in *V. cineraceus*, Blyth MSS., and specimen in the Museum Asiatic Society, which (as observed by Mr. Blyth), as well as the present, may prove varieties of *V. adversus*, Horsfield.

KIRIVOULA, Gray.

KIRIVOULA PICTA, Gray.

SYN.—Vespertilio ternatanus, Seba?
Vespertilio pictus, Pallas apud Horsfield.
Vespertilio kerivoula, Boddaert.
Vespertilio kerivoula, apud Geoffroy.

HAB.—*Pinang.*
Java, Sumatra, Borneo, Ceylon.

KIRIVOULA TENUIS, Gray.

SYN.—Vespertilio tenuis, Temminck apud Schinz.
HAB.—*Pinang.*
Java, Sumatra, Borneo.

A single male, in colours slightly differing from Temminck's, being above of a dark greyish-brown, many of the hairs with white points, beneath of a lighter shade. Entire length, three and two-fourth inches, of which the tail one and four-eighth inch; extent of flying membrane, ten inches.

$$\text{Incis. } \frac{2—2}{6} \quad \text{Canin. } \frac{1—1}{1—1}; \quad \text{Mol. } \frac{5.5}{5.5}$$

Trilatitus, Gray.

TRILATITUS HORSFIELDII, Gray.

SYN.—Vespertilio tralatitus, Horsfield.
Vespertilio Gärtneri, Kuhl apud Schinz.
HAB.—*Pinang.*
Java, Sumatra.
Scotophilus, Leach apud Gray.

SCOTOPHILUS TEMMINCKII, Gray.

SYN.—Vespertilio Temminckii, Horsfield.
Vespertilio Belangerii, Isid. Geoff.
Vespertilio noctulinus, Isid. Geoff.
Scotophilus castaneus, Gray.
Nycticeius Temminckii, Schinz.
Nycticeius Belangerii, Temminck apud Schinz.
Nycticeius noctulinus, Temminck apud Schinz.
" Klàwah " of the Malays of the Peninsula.
HAB.—*Singapore, Pinang, Malayan Peninsula and Islands.*
Java, Sumatra, Borneo, Timor, Pondicherry, Calcutta.

As observed by Schinz, this species is very variable in its colours, according to age, all of which variations occur in individuals inhabiting Pinang and the Malayan Peninsula. The following are the specific names attributed to different individuals of this species :—

1. *Vespertilio Temminckii*, as originally described and figured in " Zoological Researches in Java." Back dark brown, greyish-brown underneath. Entire length, four inches six lin., of which the tail one five-eighth of an inch; extent of flying membrane, twelve inches.

2. *Scotophilus castaneus*, Gray.

3. *Nycticeius Belangeri,* Temminck apud Schinz. Hairs of the back brown at the base, chestnut or olive-chestnut at the apex; beneath light yellowish-brown, isabella, or whitish. Entire length, 3$\frac{1}{2}$″, of which the tail 1″ 11‴; extent of flying membrane, 13″.

$$\text{Incis. } \frac{1-1}{6}; \text{ Canin. } \frac{1-1}{1-1}; \text{ Mol. } \frac{4\cdot4}{5\cdot5}$$

4. *Nycticeius noctulinus,* Temminck apud Schinz, is the very young. Above, more or less intense brown or rust-coloured; beneath, isabella or light greyish-brown. Entire length, three to three two-eighth inches, of which the tail seven-eighth to one two-eighth of an inch; extent of flying membrane, eight six-eighth to nine inches. In this state it has frequently been observed clinging to the mother.

$$\text{Incis. } \frac{2-2}{6}; \text{ Canin. } \frac{1-1}{1-1}; \text{ Mol. } \frac{4\cdot4}{5\cdot5}$$

This species is exceedingly numerous, forming large congregations in sheltered situations on the Malayan Peninsula, and in the caves of the numerous islands of limestone which stud the shores from Maulmein to Java, and in such localities large deposits of guano occur. The latter ("Ty Kláwah" of the Malays—*i.e.*, bats' manure) has been tried by agriculturists at Pinang, but has been found much less efficacious than the guano obtained from the swift (*Collocalia*), producing the edible nests.

FRUGIVORA.

Gen. PTEROPUS, *Brisson.*

PTEROPUS EDULIS, Geoffroy.[1]

SYN.—Pteropus javanicus, Desm. apud Horsfield.
Pteropus Edwardsii, Geoffroy.
" Kalong" of the Javanese.
" Klúang" of the Malays of the Peninsula.
HAB.—*Pinang, Singapore, Malayan Peninsula and Islands.*
Java, Sumatra, Banda, Bengal, Assam.

Gen. CYNOPTERUS, *Fred. Cuvier.*

CYNOPTERUS MARGINATUS, F. Cuv.

SYN.—Vespertilio Marginatus, Buchan Hamilton, MSS.
Pteropus marginatus, Geoffroy.
Pteropus titthæcheilus, Temm.
Pachysoma titthæcheilus, Temm.

[1] [O. Mohnike, l. l. pp. 399-402.]

Pachysoma brevicaudatum, Is. Geoff.
Pteropus brevicaudatus, Schinz.
Pachysoma Diardii, Isid. Geoff.
Pteropus Diardii, Schinz.
Pachysoma Duvaucellii, Is. Geoff.
Pteropus pyrivorus, Hodgson apud Gray.

HAB.—*Singapore, Pinang, Malayan Peninsula and Islands.* Java, Sumatra, Southern Mahratta country, Bengal, Nipal.

The colour is very variable, not only individually, but according to age and sex, which has given rise to several supposed distinct species. But they all resemble each other in habits and dentition ; they occupy one common place of rest, and their new-born or very young are of a uniform colour. The ears of the adult are in all more or less distinctly margined with white.

1. *Cynopterus marginatus.* Back reddish or brownish grey; lighter underneath.

2. *Pachysoma titthæcheilus.* 3. *Pteropus brevicaudatus.* Male : back reddish or olive brown ; a tuft of hair on the sides of the neck, the chest, and the sides of the greyish abdomen rusty or orange-coloured. Female : above, yellowish or greyish brown, beneath lighter. In some individuals from Malacca the flying membrane is of a light reddish-brown.

4. *Pachysoma Diardii.* Back greyish-brown, abdomen greyish, brown on the sides.

5. *Pachysoma Duvaucellii :* pale greyish-brown.

The following is a description of a new-born :—The upper part of the head, the nape of the neck, the back and the posterior surface of the humerus and femur were covered with dense, soft, short hairs of a dark greyish-brown ; all the rest of the body was naked, of a greyish-black colour. The eyelids were not yet separated. The joints of the bones of the extremities were cartilaginous. The nails of the thumb and index were developed, but the feet and nails of the toes had already attained the size of the adult. The tongue was considerably extensile. The teeth present were :—

$$\text{Incis. } \frac{4}{4} \text{ ; Canin. } \frac{1-1}{1-1} \text{ ; Mol. } \frac{2.2}{2.2}$$

Entire length, one and four-eighth of an inch, of which the slightly projecting tail two-eighth inch ; extent of the flying membrane, six and four-eighth inches.

In an individual measuring two and four-eighth inches in length, with an extent of the membrane of nine inches, the face and the lower parts, excepting the throat, have become scantily covered with light brownish-grey short hairs. The eyelids were separated. The shoulder, elbow, hip and knee joints had become ossified, the other joints still remaining cartilaginous.

INSECTIVORA.

Gen. TUPAIA, *Raffles.*

SYN.—" Tupai Press," Raffles and Horsfield.
  Cladobates ferrugineus, F. Cuv. apud Schinz.
  Sorex Glis, Diard and Duvaucel.
  Glisorex ferruginea, Temminck.
  Hylogale ferruginea, Desmarest.
  Herpestes, " Calcutta Journ. Nat. Hist."*
  " Tupai tana " of the Malays of Pinang.
HAB.—*Pinang, Singapore, Malayan Peninsula.*
  Sumatra, Java, Borneo.

The young of this very numerous species in hilly jungle is easily
tamed, and becomes familiar with its feeder, though towards
strangers it retains its original mistrust, which in mature age is
scarcely reclaimable. In a state of nature it lives singly or in
pairs, fiercely attacking intruders of its own species. When
several are confined together they fight each other, or jointly attack
and destroy the weakest. The natural food is mixed insectivorous
and frugivorous. In confinement individuals may be fed exclusively on either, though preference is evinced for insects; and
eggs, fish, and earth-worms are equally relished. A short peculiar
tremulous whistling sound, often heard by calls and answers in the
Malayan jungle, marks their pleasurable emotions, as, for instance,
on the appearance of food; while the contrary is expressed by
shrill protracted cries. Their disposition is very restless, and
their great agility enables them to perform the most extraordinary
bounds in all directions, in which exercise they spend the day, till
night sends them to sleep in their rudely constructed lairs in the
highest branches of trees. At times they will sit on their haunches,
holding their food between the fore-legs, and after feeding they
·smooth the head and face with both fore-paws, and lick the lips

---

* Vol. ii. p. 458, pl. xiii¼. The explanation accompanying this figure is
as follows :—" Searching for Col. Farquhar's drawing of *Rhizomys Sumatrensis*,
already referred to, I found in the Society a drawing of a bushy-tailed *Herpestes*,
differing merely from Mr. Hodgson's *Gulo Urva* in having the tail of one uniform colour with the body, without the yellow tip. There is no name or letter
on the drawing to show from whence it came, and to prevent its following the
fate of Colonel Farquhar's *Rhizomys* we here afford a copy of it." Pl. xiii½
represents no *Herpestes :* the elongated muzzle, the proximity of the large eye
to the ear, which is exposed and not hidden by the hairs of the cheek, are
characters foreign to every known species of *Herpestes*. The draughtsman has
very correctly represented a *Tupaia*, and the drawing reappearing as a *Herpestes* in the " Calcutta Journal of Natural History" has by Mr. Blyth been
traced to be the original of pl. ix., " Asiatic Researches," vol. xiv., where it
properly accompanies the description of *Sorex Glis* (i.e., *Tupaia ferruginea*) of
MM. Diard and Duvaucel.

and palms. They are also fond of water, both to drink and to bathe in. The female usually produces one young; she has four mammæ, the anterior pair of which is situated on the lower lateral part of the chest, the posterior on the side of the abdomen. On the lower surface of the tongue the frenum is continued to within a short distance of the apex in a raised line, on either side of which the skin is thickened, fringed at the edges, and thus presenting a rudimentary sublingual appendage, somewhat similar to that observed in *Nycticebus tardigradus*, though in *Tupaia ferruginea* the fringes of the margin only are free, the rest being attached to the tongue, but easily detached by a knife. The lateral raised lines of the palms and soles, the posterior part of the first phalanges, and the third phalanx (second of the thumbs), which is widened into a small soft disc—in fact, all the points which rest upon the ground—are studded with little transversely curved ridges or duplicatures, similar to those observed under the toes of some of the *Geckotidæ*, which fully account' for the precision, the *aplomb*, with which these animals perform the astounding leaps from below, barely touching with the soles the *point d'appui* above. In a cage the tupai will continue for hours vaulting from below, back downwards, poise itself for an instant, continuing back downwards under the horizontal roof, and regain the point of starting, and thus describe a circle—the diameter of which may be three to four times the length of the animal—in far shorter time than is required for the description. In a young male, measuring from the nose to the root of the tail seven and three-fourth inches, the tail six and a half inches, the dimensions of the intestinal canal were :—

Small intestines . . 3 feet 4½ inches ; diameter, ⅛ inch.
Large ditto . . . 0 „ 3¾ „ „ ⅕ „
Cæcum . . . . . 0 „ 0¾ „ „ 1/16 „
Costæ veræ, 8 pairs ; spuriæ, 5 pairs = 13 pairs.

This species* is infested with a tick of the following description :
Ixodes Tupaiæ.—Body suboval, shining dark green olive, scaly plate, palpi casing the pointed sucker, and the legs pale reddish-brown. Length when swollen three-eighth inch.

Gen. Gymnura, *Raffles.*

Gymnura Rafflesii, Vigors and Horsfield.

Syn.—Viverra gymnura, Raffles.
     " Tíkus ámbang búlan," Raffles.
Hab.—*Malacca.*
     Sumatra, Singapore.

---

* Single light-coloured individuals occur, with the back, limbs, and abdomen greyish, whitish, or isabella.

In a district not distant from Malacca the animal is said to be numerous, though not to be seen in other localities.

Gen. SOREX, *Linné.*

SOREX MURINUS, Linné.*

SYN.—Sorex myosurus, Pallas apud Schinz.
Sorex cærulescens, var. Raffles?
" Chincorot " of the Malays of the Peninsula.
HAB.—*Pinang.*
Java.

Dark brownish-grey above ; beneath, light brownish-grey. Feet and tail flesh-coloured in the living animal, changing to cinereous after death. In the young the colour is more of a bluish-grey, slightly mixed with brown on the back. Length of the head and body, five and a half inches ; tail, three inches.

$$\text{Incis. } \frac{2}{2}; \text{ Canin. } \frac{0}{0}; \text{ Mol. } \frac{8.8}{5.5}$$

The present differs from the " musk shrew " of Bengal (" Choochundr ") in its proportionally broader, more developed, and from the head more diverging ear, which characters also distinguish it from *Sorex nigrescens* (gray), which it somewhat resembles in its colours. The smell of musk emitted by the adult animal, and which in the young is barely perceptible, is much less intense than that of the Bengal musk-shrew.

CARNIVORA.

Gen. URSUS, *Linné ;* HELARCTOS, Horsfield.

HELARCTOS MALAYANUS, Horsfield.

SYN.—Ursus Malayanus, Raffles and Horsfield.[1]
" Brúang " of the Malays.
HAB.—*Malayan Peninsula.*
Sumatra, Tenasserim Provinces, Assam, Nipal.

Colour of the young :—Snout and lips pale ferrugineous. Head, back, and outside of the limbs, black mixed with pale rust colour, in consequence of many of the black hairs having the point, or a part next to the point, of the latter colour. Ears, tail, paws, and

---

* The following synonyms are given in Gray's " List of Mam. in British Museum :"—*Sorex myosurus*, Pallas. Geoff. Ann. Mus. xvii. ; *S. Soneratii* and *S. giganteus*, I. Geoff. Mem. xv. ; *S. indicus*, Geoff. Mem. Mus. i. ; *S. capensis*, Geoff. Ann. Mus. xvii. ; *S. Pilorides*, Shaw, Mus. Lever. ; *S. cærulescens*, Shaw, Zool. ; *S. crassicaudatus*, Licht. Säugeth; *S. nepalensis*, Hodgson ; *S. moschatus*, Robinson, Assam. Olivier, Voy. Buffon, H. N. Suppl. vii.

[1] [O. Mohnike, l. l. pp. 417 f.]

C 2

inner side of the extremities shining black. The somewhat woolly hairs of the abdomen are faintly marked with ferrugineous, and are mixed with longer stiff black hairs. As observed by Schinz, the mark on the breast is very variable in its form. It may be compared to a crescent, assuming, according to the smaller or greater breadth of the limbs, the shape of the letter U, of a horse-shoe, or a heart. In the living animal it is of a pale rust or orange colour; in some individuals with a few small blackish spots, fading after death to a yellowish-white. A very old male presented the following dentition :—

$$\text{Incis. } \frac{6}{6} \text{; Canin. } \frac{1-1}{1-1} \text{; Mol. } \frac{4.4\,(2+2)}{6.6\,(3+3)}$$

In a young female three feet in length, the intestinal canal measured fifteen feet. It had neither cæcum nor valve to mark the transition. She had ten grinders in either jaw, of which four were spurious, six true.

Gen. ARCTICTIS, *Temminck.*

ARCTICTIS BINTURONG, Fischer.

SYN.—Viverra ? Binturong, Raffles.
  Paradoxurus albifrons, F. Cuvier.
  Ictides ater, F. Cuvier.
  Arctictis penicillata, Temminck.
  Ictides ater, Blainv. " Calcutta Journ. of Nat. Hist." *
  " Unturong " of the Malays of the Peninsula.
HAB.—*Malayan Peninsula.*
  Tenasserim, Arracan, Assam, Bhotan, Nipal.

Java and Sumatra are quoted by M. Schinz, but neither Dr. Horsfield, nor Sir S. Raffles, nor M. Temminck ("Discours Préliminaire, Fauna Japonica"), mentions the *Binturong* as inhabiting either of the two islands.

The general colour of either sex is black, sprinkled on the body and extremities with pale ferrugineous, produced by some of the hairs having a part next to the point of that colour. In both sexes nearly all the hairs of the head, face, and throat are thus

---

* In the third vol. of " Calcutta Journ. of Nat. Hist.," p. 410, occurs the following passage :—" The *Binturong* was first discovered in Java, but the first notice of its existence on the continent of India will be found in the second volume of this Journal, p. 457 " (sic), &c. Sir Stamford Raffles, who published the first account of this animal, distinctly states that it was discovered at Malacca (not Java, as erroneously stated) by Major Farquhar, and Malacca is situated on the continent of India as well as Tenasserim. The fact of its inhabiting Bhotan was, according to Cuvier ("Règne Animal"), first made known by Duvaucel ; and the author of the article " Ictides " in the " Penny Cyclopædia," 1838, gives Mr. Hodgson's authority of the *Binturong* inhabiting Nipal (Kachar, though they occasionally occur in the central region of Nipal).

marked, which communicates to these parts a whitish or greyish appearance. In the young of either sex there is a faint trace of a white spot over the eyes. The long ear-tufts are always black, the margin of the auricle being either white or pale rust-coloured. The tail is black, but the hairs of the anterior or basal half are whitish at the root, or in some uniformly of that colour. The pupil is vertically contracted by the influence of light: the iris is of a beautiful Vandyke brown. In its habits the *Binturong* is both arboreal and terrestrial, and nocturnal, sleeping until the sun is below the horizon, when it displays great agility in searching for smaller quadrupeds, birds, fishes, earthworms, insects, and fruit. The howl is loud, resembling some of the Malayan *Paradoxuri*. The young are easily tamed, but the old animal retains its natural fierceness. Between the anus and penis is situated a large pyriform gland, exceeding two inches in length, partially divided by a deep naked fossa, commencing from the latter organ. The gland secretes a light brown oily fluid of a peculiarly intense but not fœtid or sickening odour. In a young male, measuring from the nose to the root of the tail two feet three and five-eighth inches, the tail two feet two and a half inches, the intestines were of the following dimensions :—

Small intestines . . . . . 7 feet 11 inches.
Large ditto . . . . . 1 „ 10 „
Cæcum . . . . 0 „ 0½ „

The circumference of the small intestines about seven-eighth inches ; of the large but little more ; but the rectum was thickened two inches in circumference.

The short cæcum is crescent-shaped or lengthened pyriform. The stomach is remarkably lengthened cylindrical ; the parietes much thickened towards pylorus. Œsophagus enters close to the fundus ventriculi, in consequence of which there is but a slight difference between the curvatures.

Length along the greater curvature . . 1 foot 2 inches.
„ „ smaller „ . . 1 „ 1 „

The circumference from cardia round fundus ventriculi measured five and a half inches ; round pylorus two six-eighth inches. Both the gall-bladder and the spleen presented a remarkably elongated shape. The former organ, lengthened pyriform, measured in length two inches ; ductus cysticus two and a half inches. The spleen, tapering to a narrow point, was half an inch broad, and eight and a half inches in length. Costæ veræ, 9 pairs ; spuriæ, 5 pairs = 14 pairs.

Gen. Mustela, *Linné ;* Putorius, Cuvier.

Putorius nudipes, Fred. Cuvier.

Syn.—Mustela nudipes, Desmar. apud Schinz.
"Pulásan" of the Malays of the Peninsula.
Hab.—*Malayan Peninsula.*
Sumatra, Borneo.

The muzzle and the soles of the feet are pale flesh-coloured. The animal is said to inhabit the densest jungle, and is most difficult to obtain.

Mustela, Cuvier.

Mustela flavigula, Boddaert.

Syn.—Viverra quadricolor, Shaw.
Marte à gorge dorée, Desmarest.
Mustela Hardwickii, Horsfield.
Martes flavigula, Hodgson apud Gray.
"Anga Prao" of the Malays of the Peninsula.
Hab.—*Malayan Peninsula.*
Java, Sumatra, Nipal.

The Malayan individuals differ from those from Northern India, originally described, in having the fur shorter and less dense, the head pale brown, the neck and back pale yellowish-brown, becoming darker towards the tail, which, as well as the posterior extremities, is black. The anterior extremities are greyish-brown ; the feet and the streak behind the ear deep brown ; the lips whitish ; the throat and chest yellowish-white, or ochreous ; the scanty hairs of the abdomen pale brownish.

Gen. Lutra, *Storr.*

Lutra nair, Fred. Cuvier.

Syn.—Lutra indica, Gray.
"Anjing Ayer" of the Malays of the Peninsula.
Hab.—*Malayan Peninsula.*
China, Bombay, South Mahratta country.

Lutra barang, Raffles.

Syn.—"Barang Barang," or "Ambrang," Raffles.
Lutra leptonyx, Wagner apud Schinz.
Lutra Simung, Schinz ? *

* In Schinz's diagnosis of *Lutra Simung* is said, "ungvibus robustis falcularibus" ("die Nägel an den Zehen sind stark und gekrümmt"), which, if the passage refers to *Lutra leptonyx*, Horsfield, must be a mistake, as the original diagnosis expressly states "ungvibus brevibus sublamnaribus." As Schinz describes *Lutra Barang* "ungvibus minutissimis obtusis," *Lutra leptonyx* is probably meant, and thus the one species is mistaken for the other.

" Mumrang," or " Amrang " of the Malays of the Peninsula.

HAB.—*Malayan Peninsula.*
Sumatra, Borneo.

The young are very playful, and soon become sufficiently domesticated to roam about the house, and to appear when called. Its
voice is a short shrill whistling, not unlike the sound of the cricket,
but stronger. Its food is not confined to fishes and crustacea;
birds and insects are equally relished. The muzzle is hairy, but
in the old animal the hairs become rubbed off. The Malayan
individuals appear to attain to a greater size than the Sumatran,
described by Raffles. An old male measured from the apex of
the nose to the root of the tail two feet eight and a half inches ;
the tail one foot eight inches. In a young male two feet two
inches, and the tail one foot two-eighth of an inch in length, the
simple intestinal canal measured nine feet and one inch, with a
circumference throughout of about two and two-eighth inches. No
cæcum. Each of the kidneys consisted of ten loosely connected
glands.

AONYX, Lesson.

AONYX LEPTONYX, Gray : List.

SYN.—Lutra leptonyx, Horsfield.
Lutra cinerea, Illiger.
Lutra perspicillata, Is. Geoff.
Mustela Lutra, Marsden.
Aonyx Horsfieldii, Gray.
Lutra Barang, apud Schinz ?
" Anjing Ayer " of the Malays of the Peninsula.
HAB.—*Malayan Peninsula.*
Java, Sumatra, Singapore, Nipal.

This, as well as the two preceding species, inhabits numerously
the banks of the Malayan rivers, and all are at times used by the
Malays in river-fishing.

Gen. CANIS, *Linné ;* CUON, Hodgson.

CUON PRIMÆVUS, Hodgson.

SYN.—Canis primævus, Hodgson.*
Chrysæus primævus, Hamilton Smith.
Chrysæus soccatus, Cantor.
" Anjing útan " of the Malays of the Peninsula.

* Mr. Ogilby considers *Canis Dukhunensis,* Sykes, and *Canis primævis,*
Hodgson, to be identical, and apparently not different from *C. sumatrensis,*
Hardwicke (" Mem. on the Mammalogy of the Himalayahs," apud Royle).
Colonel Sykes, on the contrary, describes *C. Dukhunensis* as being "essentially
distinct from *Canis Quao,* or *Sumatrensis,* Hardwicke."

HAB.—*Malayan Peninsula.*
     Bengal, Nipal.

Some slight differences occur in the Malayan individuals. The inferior surface, the inside of the ears and limbs, and the lips and throat are the same colour as the back, but much paler. A black carpal spot, like that of the wolf, is very distinct in the male, less so in the female. The young animal of either sex has a faint white spot with a few blackish bristles situated nearly midway between the angle of the mouth and the ears. Of the wavy wool of the Buansu, the Malayan wild dog, inhabiting a tropical climate, has but a little on the inner side of and immediately behind the ear; the posterior part of the abdomen is almost naked. The short bristles of the lips, cheeks, throat, and above the eyes are all black. In habits, so fully described by Mr. Hodgson, and in size, the Malayan agrees with the Nipalese. In a young male, from the nose to the root of the tail two. feet eight and a half inches in length, the tail one foot, the intestinal canal was of the following dimensions :—

Small intestines	6 feet	2 inches.
Large ditto	0 „	$10\frac{1}{2}$ „
Cæcum	0 „	4 „

The latter intestine is spiral, much widened at the origin.

Costæ veræ, 8 pairs ; spuriæ, 5 pairs = 13 pairs.

The Malays mention another black wild dog (Anjing útan étam) as also inhabiting the denses, jungle. A hyæna is also reported to occur on the peninsula.

Mongrel curs, " pariah dogs," of every description, infest every village, but apparently not uninhabited places, nor localities far distant from the dwellings of man. As they all may be said to be in a state of half-domestication, and are of forms very different from the wild dog, which shuns the human presence, their origin cannot with certainty be traced to the Malayan Peninsula.

Gen. VIVERRA, *Linné.*

VIVERRA ZIBETHA, Linné.

SYN.—Viverra undulata, Gray.
     Viverra melanurus, Hodgson ⎫
     Viverra orientalis, Hodgson ⎬ apud Gray : List.
     Viverra civettoides, Hodgson ⎪
     Undescribed Civet, McClelland ⎭
     " Tanggallong " of the Malays of the Peninsula.
HAB.—*Pinang, Singapore, Malayan Peninsula.*
     Southern China, Siam, Bengal, Khasyah Hills, Nipal.

Judging by the comparatively few individuals observed in the

Straits of Malacca, this species would appear to þe far less numerous than the following. Of several, the largest, which was a female, measured from the apex of the nose to the root of the tail two feet and eight inches ; the tail one foot eight and a half inches.[1]

VIVERRA TANGALUNGA, Gray.

Syn.—Viverra zibetha, Lin. apud Raffles.
" Tangalung," Raffles.
Viverra zibetha, Lin. apud Horsfield.
Viverra zibetha, apud Fred. Cuvier.
Viverra zibetha, Lin. apud Schinz.*
" Músang jebát " of the Malays of the Peninsula.
Hab.—*Pinang, Singapore, Malayan Peninsula.*
Sumatra, Borneo, Celebes, Amboyna, Philippines.

This species is readily distinguished from *V.* zibetha by a continuous longitudinal black band occupying the upper surface of the tail, the numerous irregular rings being separated only on its inferior half (Gray, " Proceed. Zool. Society," 1832, p. 63). The number and distance of the half-rings on the lower surface of the tail vary in different individuals, some of which have either the entire tail or the anterior half or third of the tail thus marked, the rest being black. The very young animal is generally of a much darker ground colour than the adult, and the black marks are therefore less conspicuous. Under certain lights the colour appears uniformly black. *Viverra tangalunga* and *zibetha*, however similar in habits and general colours, neither live nor breed together. Placed side by side, the living animals present a marked dissimilarity of countenance, which, although obvious to the eye, would be most difficult, if possible at all, to convey in words. The female has three pairs of mammæ, and produces from one to three young. The Malays of the peninsula distinguish by different names the *zibetha* and the *tangalunga*, but as they suppose the civet of the former species to be of better quality, perhaps because it is scarcer, they will frequently offer for sale individuals of the latter exceedingly numerous species, imposing upon it the name of *V.* zibetha—" Tanggallong " of the Peninsula. The largest individual of the present species observed measured in length from the apex of the nose to the root of the tail three feet and one inch ; the tail one foot five and a half inches. In a younger, a female, three feet five and a half inches in length, of which the tail one foot and one inch, the intestinal canal was of the following dimensions :—

[1] [O. Mohnike, l. l. p. 414.]
* The true *Viverra zibetha*, Linné, is quoted by Schinz under the denominations of *V. bengalensis*, Hardwicke (?), and *V. melanura*, Hodgson.

```
Small intestines . . . . . . . 7 feet 5 inches.
Large  ditto  . . . . . . . 0  „  9   „
Cæcum  . . . . . . . . . . 0  „  1   „
Costæ veræ, 7 pairs ; spuræ, 6 pairs = 13 pairs.
```

VIVERRICULA, Hodgson.

VIVERRICULA MALACCENSIS.

SYN.—Viverra malaccensis, Gmelin.
    Viverra Rasse, Horsfield.
    Viverra Gunda, Buchanan Hamilton MSS.
    Viverra indica, Geoffroy.
    Viverra bengalensis, Gray : Illustr.
    Viverra pallida, Gray : Illustr.
    Genetta Manillensis, Eydoux.
HAB.—*Malayan Peninsula.*
    China, Philippine Islands, Java, Singapore, Cochin-China,
        Tenasserim Provinces, Bengal, Nipal, Hindoostan, Duk-
        hun, Bombay.

On the Malayan Peninsula this species appears to be more numerous than *V. zibetha;* less so than *V. tangalunga,* and in size inferior to either. The largest observed was three feet four inches in length, of which the tail was one foot three and a half inches. In a male measuring from the apex of the nose to the root of the tail two feet and three-fourths of an inch, the tail one foot one inch, the dimensions of the intestinal canal were :—

```
Small intestines . . . . . . . 4 feet 0  inch.
Large  ditto  . . . . . . . . 0  „  8 inches.
Cæcum . . . . . . . . . . . 0  „  0¾ inch.
```

The three preceding species have the following characters in common :—The pupil is vertical, oblong ; the iris of a rich brown. They are arboreal as well as terrestrial, preying upon the smaller quadrupeds, birds, fish, crustacea, insects, and fruit. Naturally very fierce, they are scarcely reclaimable except in youth, but with age the original disposition returns. The voice is peculiar, hoarse, and hissing.

Gen. PRIONODON, *Horsfield.*

PRIONODON GRACILIS, Horsfield.

SYN.—Viverra ? Linsang, Hardwicke.
    Felis gracilis, Horsfield.
    Viverra Hardwicke, Lesson.
    Viverra gracilis, Desmarest apud Schinz.
    Linsang gracilis, Müller apud Gray : List, and Schinz.
HAB.—*Malayan Peninsula.*
    Java, Sumatra, Borneo, Siam.

The ground colour is buff, and the dark marks are of a deep snuff colour, inclining to black with purple reflection. Length from the apex of the nose to the root of the tail, one foot six inches, the tail one foot three six-eighth inches.

Mr. Rappa, for many years a dealer in objects of natural history at Malacca, who previously had been supplied with a figure and description of *Prionodon gracilis,* reported in a memorandum accompanying the specimen that it had been captured in the jungle at some distance from Malacca. It was unknown to himself and to the natives. At first the animal was fierce and impatient of confinement, but by degrees it became very gentle and playful, and when subsequently suffered to leave the cage, it went in search of sparrows and other small birds, displaying great dexterity and unerring aim in stealthily leaping upon them. Fruit of every description it refused. Another younger individual was captured about the same time, but contrived to make its escape.

Gen. PARADOXURUS, *Fred. Cuvier ;* PAGUMA, Gray.

PAGUMA LEUCOMYSTAX, Gray : List?

SYN.—Paradoxurus leucomystax, Gray ?
Amblyodon auratus, Jourdan ?
" Músang búlan " of the Malays of the Peninsula.
HAB.—*Malayan Peninsula.*
Singapore, Sumatra.

In a single individual observed the hairs of the body, limbs, and anterior third of the tail are greyish-yellow at the base, next bright rust-coloured, with the apex shining black, which produces a mixture of ferrugineous and black, the latter prevailing on the nape of the neck, middle line of the back, and the anterior third of the tail. The hairs of the vertex and the bridge of the nose are dark at the base, with yellowish points. The large oblique whitish spot in front of the ear, produced by uniformly whitish hairs, is on either side blended with the whitish vertex and ridge of the nose, and is continued down the sides of the neck, forming a large broad arrow-shaped mark. The orbits are dark brown ; the face, lips, and throat pale brown. The long rigid white whiskers are mixed with a few shorter black bristles. The feet are dark brown, the posterior two-thirds of the tail uniformly black. The lower surface and the inner side of the extremities are pale ferrugineous. From the apex of the nose to the root of the tail, two feet three inches ; the tail one foot eight inches.

PAGUMA TRIVIRGATA, Gray : List.

SYN.—Viverra trivirgata, Reinwardt, Mus. Leyd.
Paradoxurus trivirgatus, Gray.
" Músang ákar " of the Malays of the Peninsula.

Hab.—*Malayan Peninsula.*
Singapore, Tenasserim.

The ground colour varies from yellowish or brownish to blackish-grey. Fur short, peculiarly soft, silky. The dorsal streaks are either continued, undulated (the central nearly always), or composed of separate black spots. Some individuals have a short white streak on the ridge of the nose. The largest male measured from the apex of the nose to the root of the tail two feet two and a half inches; the tail two feet three inches.

PARADOXURUS MUSANGA, Gray.

Syn.—Viverra hermaphrodita, Pallas apud Schinz.
Viverra fasciata, Gmelin?
Viverra Musanga, Marsden, Raffles.
Musang bulan, Raffles.
Viverra Musanga, var. javanica, Horsfield.[1]
Ichneumon prehensilis, Buchanan Hamilton MSS.
Platyschista hermaphrodita, Otto ⎫
Paradoxurus Pallassii, Gray ⎪
Paradoxurus Crossii, Gray ⎬ apud Schinz.
Paradoxurus dubius, Gray ⎭
Paradoxurus Musangoïdes, Gray.
Paradoxurus typus, apud Schlegel.
Paradoxurus felinus, Wagner apud Schinz.
" Músang," or " Músang Pándan " (when the tail is with white point: " Músang Búngkwang ") of the Malays of the Peninsula.
Hab.—*Pinang, Singapore, Malayan Peninsula.*
Java, Sumatra, Borneo, Timor.

The ground colour and dorsal marks of this exceedingly numerous species are liable to considerable variations, the principal of which are noted by Schinz; individuals occur (probably of every species) with the apex of the tail white, with elongated white spots on the abdomen, with the tail spirally twisted. In most the dorsal marks become indistinct or invisible in certain lights. The female has from one to three young, of colours similar to the adult, but less distinct; their fur is softer, somewhat woolly, mixed with longer stiff black hairs. The young is tamed without difficulty, and is sometimes kept in houses to destroy rats and mice. The *Paradoxuri* are in habits like the *Civets.* They have an elliptical pupil, vertically contracted by the influence of light. Their glandular secretion is of a peculiar (not civet or musk-like) odour. The largest specimen of a great number measured from the apex of the nose to the root of the tail two feet and half an

---

[1] [O. Mohnike, l. l. pp. 249, 250, 413.]

inch ; the tail one foot four and a half inches. In a male measuring three feet one and a half inches in length, of which the tail was one foot four and a half inches, the intestinal canal was of the following dimensions :—

Small intestines . . . . 5 feet 8 inches.
Large ditto . . . . 0 ,, 5 ,,
Cæcum . . . . 0 ,, 1½ ,,
Costæ veræ, 7 pairs ; spuriæ, 6 pairs = 13 pairs.

PARADOXURUS (?) DERBYANUS, Gray.

SYN.—Paradoxurus (?) Zebra, Gray.
Hemigalea zebra, Jourdan.
Viverra Boiei, Müller.
" Musang Bátu " or " Sángah Prao " of the Malays of the Peninsula.
HAB.—*Malayan Peninsula.*
Borneo.

The ground colour varies from pale ochreous to buff, and the dark marks, in shape and number scarcely alike in any two individuals, from snuff colour to black. The species is apparently not numerous, and is celebrated among the Malays for its great agility. It is said chiefly to feed upon the larger birds, such as the *Argus* pheasant, which it will hunt down, following its prey till the strength of the latter is exhausted, when it falls an easy victim to the indefatigable pursuer. The slender vermiform make, the countenance and distribution of colours, the serrated, flattened false molars, the soles, hairy between and under the toes, and slightly in the centre, the somewhat removed thumb, are characters by which this animal differs from *Paradoxurus*, and forms a link between that genus and *Prionodon* in the same manner that *Viverricula* connects *Viverra* to *Prionodon*. The largest male observed measured from the apex of the nose to the root of the tail two feet ; the tail one foot and four inches.

Gen. CYNOGALE, *Gray.*

CYNOGALE BENNETTII, Gray.

SYN.—Viverra (Limictis) carcharias, Blainville.
Potamophilus barbatus, Kuhl.
Cynogale barbata, Schinz.
HAB.—*Malayan Peninsula.*
Sumatra, Borneo.

The very young, of which two individuals, a male and a female, were found with the mother, differ from the adult in having a very soft, silky, dense fur, mixed with longer hairs, which are black, except on the chest and abdomen, where the apex is silvery. Over the tarsus and on the upper surface of the feet some of the hairs have a subterminal white band close to the black apex. The posterior margin of the ear is hairy and of a silvery colour. This animal appears of rare occurrence on the Malayan Peninsula, and the natives are consequently not acquainted with it. The largest male examined measured from the apex of the nose to the root of the tail two feet three inches ; the tail eight inches.

Gen. HERPESTES, *Illiger.*

HERPESTES JAVANICUS, Desmarest.

SYN.—Ichneumon javanicus, Geoffroy.
Mangusta javanica, Horsfield.
"Garangan," Horsfield.
HAB.—*Pinang, Malayan Peninsula.*
Java.

The species is numerous. The largest male measured from the apex of the nose to the root of the tail one foot four and a half inches ; the tail one foot one and a half inch.

HERPESTES AUROPUNCTATUS, Hodgson.

SYN.—Mangusta auropunctata, Hodgson.
Herpestes nepalensis, Gray.
Herpestes Edwardsii, apud Ogilby (?).
Herpestes javanica, Hodgson apud Gray : List.
HAB.—*Malayan Peninsula.*
Bengal, Nipal, Scinde, Afghanistan.

This species somewhat resembles *H. javanicus*, but the ground colour is lighter, and the lower surface uniformly pale yellowish-grey ; whereas in the former species it is similar to the back, or a shade paler. A single female observed measured from the apex of the nose to the root of the tail one foot one inch ; the tail nine inches.

HERPESTES GRISEUS, Desmarest.

SYN.—Ichneumon griseus, Geoffroy.
Mangouste de Malacca, F. Cuvier ⎫
Mangusta malaccensis, Fischer ⎪
Mangusta grisea, Fischer ⎬ apud Schinz.
Herpestes Edwardsii, Fischer ⎪
Mangusta Nyula, Hodgson ⎭
Herpestes griseus, Nyool apud Ogilby.
Herpestes pallidus, Schinz.
Forsan H. nipalensis, Gray, var. apud Schinz.

HAB.—*Malayan Peninsula.*
Bengal, Hindoostan, Scinde, Nipal.

The present differs from the other species not only by its grey colour, but by its broader head, particularly between the prominent eyes, and by its shorter, blunter nose, which places the eyes comparatively nearer to the muzzle. In a single female, measuring from the apex of the nose to the root of the tail one foot two and a half inches, the tail nine and a half inches ; the intestinal canal was of the following dimensions :—

Small intestines	. . . . .	3 feet	$1\frac{1}{2}$	inches.
Large ditto	. . . . .	0 „	$5\frac{1}{2}$	„
Cæcum	. . . .	0 „	1	„

By a contraction in the middle of the greater curvature, the stomach is distinctly separated into a cardiac and pyloric cavity.

HERPESTES BRACHYURUS, Gray.

SYN.—" Musang Túron " of the Malays of the Peninsula.
HAB.—*Malayan Peninsula.*

The largest male measured from the apex of the nose to the root of the tail one foot six and a half inches, the tail nine inches. It is distinguished from the other species, not only by its colours and comparatively short tail, but by its larger size and much more robust make.

Gen. FELIS, *Linné.*

FELIS TIGRIS, Linné.

SYN.—Tigris regalis, Gray : List.
" Harímau " or " Rímau " of the Malays.
HAB.—*Malayan Peninsula.*
India.

Lieut.-Colonel James Low has communicated the following denominations by which the Malays of the Peninsula distinguish different varieties :—

" Rimau Sípai," reddish coated, striped.
" Rímau Bállu," darker coloured.
" Daun Pínang," reddish coated, without stripes.
" Tuppu Kassau," darkish, without stripes, but with longer hairs than the others.
" Puntong Prun," very dark, striped.

FELIS LEOPARDUS, Schreber.

SYN.—Felis pardus, Linné?
    Felis varia, Schreber
    Felis Panthera, Erxleben
    Felis chalybeata, Hermann   apud Gray: List.
    Felis antiquorum, Fischer
    Felis fusca, Meyer
    Felis Nimr, Ehrenberg
    Leopardus varius, Gray: List.
    Felis Leopardus, apud Schinz.
    " Rímau Bíntang " of the Malays of the Peninsula.
HAB.—*Malayan Peninsula.*
    India.

DARK VAR.

SYN.—Felis melas, Péron apud Gray: List.
    " Rimau Kúmbang " * of the Malays of the Peninsula.

The ground colour is a shining beetle-brown, mixed with white hairs, not, however, sufficiently to impart a grey appearance. The black spots become distinctly visible in certain lights only. The skin of a male killed at Malacca measured from the nose to the root of the tail four feet four and a half inches, the tail two feet ten and a half inches.

The leopards of the Malayan Peninsula appear to attain to a larger size, and to be more ferocious than is generally the case in India. Instances of their having killed and carried off Malays are on record.

FELIS MARMORATA, Martin.

SYN.—Felis Diardii, Fischer apud Schinz.
    Felis Diardii, apud Jardine. Tab. 21 and 22.
    Leopardus marmoratus, Gray: List.
    " Rímau dáhan " of the Malays of the Peninsula.
HAB.—*Malayan Peninsula.*

The ground colour varies from rusty-grey or fulvous to grey, and the black markings are scarcely quite alike in any two individuals, nor is the extremity of the tail constantly black. The adult exceeds the size given in the original description ; a female measured from the apex of the nose to the root of the tail two feet half an inch ; the tail one foot nine inches. The species is numerous.

---

* " Kúmbang " signifies a beetle ; applied *par excellence* to a species of *Oryctes*, resembling *Scarabeus nasicornis*, Linné, which is very destructive to cocoanut plantations. " Rímau Kúmbang," Raffles, is by Schinz referred to *Felis pardus*, Temminck, var. *nigra*, Müller ; *Felis melas*, F. Cuvier, the habitat of which is said to be Java and Sumatra.

FELIS JAVANENSIS, Desmarest.

SYN.—Felis javanensis, Desmarest apud Horsfield.
"Kuwuk," Horsfield.

Felis minuta, Temminck
Felis servalin, Temminck
Felis sumatrana, Horsfield } apud Schinz.
Felis undata, Desmarest

Felis Diardii, Griffith
Leopardus javanensis } apud Gray, List.

"Rímau ákar" of the Malays of the Peninsula.
HAB.—*Pinang, Malayan Peninsula.*
Java, Sumatra?

The ground colour in the Malayan individuals varies from pure grey to greyish-brown or ferruginous. The largest adult male measured from the apex of the nose to the root of the tail one foot eleven and a half inches, the tail ten inches ; another of equal dimensions of the body had the tail eight inches in length. The intestinal canal was of the following dimensions :—

Small intestines	3 feet	8	inches.
Large „	0 „	9½	„
Cæcum	0 „	1½	„

In the scansorial habits of this very numerous species originates its local denomination, "ákar," signifying a climber as well as a root.

FELIS PLANICEPS, Vigors and Horsfield.

SYN.—Chaus (?) planiceps, Gray, List.
"Kúching-útan," or "jálang" of the Malays of the Penin-
sula.
HAB.—*Malayan Peninsula.*
Sumatra, Borneo.

The Malayan individuals of this apparently not numerous species differ from the Sumatran, originally described, in having the whitish throat, chest and abdomen, and the inner side of the limbs undulated with brown, transversal, interrupted bands. In none of the Malayan wild cats is the length of the tail more variable. In a male, measuring from the apex of the nose to the root of the tail two feet one and a half inch, the tail, consisting of twelve gradually diminishing caudal vertebræ, measured five and a half inches ; in another, one foot ten and three-fourth inch in length from the nose to the root of the tail, the latter organ measured two inches, consisting of four slightly decreasing vertebræ, the last one of which was broad, flattened, and rounded at the posterior extremity. It is of most ferocious habits, and untameable. In the smaller individual the intestinal canal was of the following dimensions :—

Small intestines	. . . . .	3 feet	6½ inches.
Large ,,	. . . . .	0 ,,	5⅜ ,,
Cæcum	. . . .	0 ,,	0⅜ inch.

FELIS DOMESTICA, Auct.

" Kúching " of the Malays.

The Malays, like most Muhamedans, are as partial to cats as they are the reverse to dogs. As observed by Sir S. Raffles, some of the Malayan, like the Madagascar domesticated cats, have a short twisted or knobbed tail, others are tailless. Among those of an uniform colour, a light ashy and a bluish (or slaty-grey) variety, with single longer black hairs on the back and tail, are conspicuous. They frequently relapse from a state of domestication, resort to the jungle, and shun the presence of man.

RODENTI.

SCIURIDÆ.

Gen. SCIURUS, Linné.

SCIURUS BICOLOR, Sparrmann.

SYN.—Das javanische Eichhorn, Schreb.* apud Horsf.

Sciurus giganteus, McClelland MSS. ⎱ apud Horsfield,
Sciurus bicolor, Sparrmann ⎰ " Proc. Zool. Soc."
Sciurus madagascariensis ⎱ apud Gray, List.
Sciurus macruroides, Hodgson ⎰

" Chingkráwah étem " of the Malays of the Peninsula.

HAB.—Pinang, Malayan Peninsula.

Java, Sumatra, Borneo, Siam, Tenasserim, Assam, Nipal.

The original diagnosis will prevent misunderstanding as to the species under consideration. " Sciurus supra niger, infra fulvus auriculis acutis imberbibus, palmarum ungue pollicari magno rotundato." (Sparrmann apud Horsfield.) The colour of the head, back, tail, outside of the extremities, and the feet, is intense shining black, the single hairs being blackish-grey at the root, those of the tail blackish-brown at the root. In some individuals the black hairs generally, in others those of the tail, or some part of the back only, have a broad subterminal band of bright cinnamon, or Indian red, which imparts a reddish tint to the general black

---

* Sciurus javensis, Schreber, and bicolor, Sparmann, apud Gray, List, is Sciurus Leschenaultii Desmar. apud Horsfield. Syn. S. hypoleucus, Horsfield.

colour. The mustachios, whiskers, and the superciliary bristles are black ; those of the throat and forearm are black in some, ferruginous, or with the apex of that colour, in others. The under-parts vary from a deep golden fulvous to isabella colour. What-ever be the prevailing shade, it is always most distinct on the lateral line, which, commencing from the cheeks, passes along the sides of the body. The fur of the lower parts of the body and of the inside of the extremities is much shorter, softer, and less dense than that of the back. The single hairs are greyish or blackish at the root, with the apex of the shade of yellow prevail-ing in the individual. Single low bristles, either uniformly or partially black or fulvous, appear on the chest and abdomen. The species, under the present garb, is very numerous in the Malayan forests and hills.

Var. β, Horsfield.

" Sciurus supra fuscus, varians a fusco-nigricante ad sordide fulvum, pilis velleris fulvis et canescentibus intermixtis, subtus fulvus vel pallide flavescens." (Horsfield.)

Syn.—Sciurus auriventer, Is. Geoff. apud Schinz.
      Sciurus aureiventer, Is. Geoff. apud List.
      " Chingkráwah," or " Chingkráwah puteh," of the Malays of the Peninsula.

Single individuals, resembling the Javanese one figured in " Zoological Researches in Java," occur at Pinang, but there, as in Java, tawny of different shades, with a greyish cast, is more frequent. In some the head is of a darker colour, in others large spots of dark appear on the back, or the tail is above barred with black. The upper part of the nose, a ring encircling the eyes, and the ears appear in all individuals to be of a darker brownish colour, and all have a more or less distinct large white spot on the anterior and upper part of the thigh. The back of the feet is either dark brown or fulvous. The palms, soles, mammæ, and genital organs are black in all. The single hairs of the back are greyish-brown at the root, darker than the apex, which imparts the general colour to the back. With the hairs of the tail the reverse is the case, the basal half being isabella or white ; the apical darker. On the lower surface of the distichous tail the roots of the hairs form a white line on either side of the vertebræ, which are covered with short dark brownish or fulvous hairs. The under-parts of the body are of the same colours as those of the black-coated animal, but their roots are yellowish-white. The mustachios, whiskers, and other bristles, are in all of a blackish-brown ; but the single bristles of the abdomen are sometimes fulvous.

The black-coated individuals stand in a similar relation to the light-coloured varieties as that in which the black-coloured

Hylobates Lar stands to the light-coloured. Such differences of colour, wide no doubt, are of no uncommon occurrence among the Malayan Mammalia, and ought to be well considered by zoologists who have not the opportunity of studying the living animals.

This, as well as the rest of the Malayan squirrels, is capable of being tamed to a certain extent, and evinces attachment to those who feed them, but the appearance of a strange person, animal, or even an unusual sound, startles them, and recalls their natural shyness. The largest of a great number measured from the apex of the nose to the root of the tail one foot six inches; the tail one foot nine and a half inches. The intestinal canal was of the following dimensions :—

Small intestines	9 feet	6 inches.
Large „	4 „	9 „
Cæcum	1 „	2 „

SCIURUS RAFFLESII, Vigors and Horsfield.

SYN.—Sciurus rufogularis, Gray.
     Sciurus rufoniger, Gray.
     Sciurus Prevostii, Desmar. apud Schinz.
     " Túpai baláng " of the Malays of the Peninsula.
HAB.—*Malayan Peninsula.*
     Java, Borneo, China* (Canton).

This species, numerous in the Malayan countries, occurs with the following individual variations of colour :—

Cheeks and throat iron-grey, shoulders uniformly or mixed with red. (*Sciurus rufogularis*, Gray : " Mag. Nat. Hist." 1842, p. 263.)

The cheeks are sometimes dark brown, or ferruginous.

* China is the habitat assigned to *Sciurus rufogularis*, Gray. Without doubting the authenticity, it is perhaps as well to observe that skins of the more showy animals and birds of India, Malacca, and the Indian Archipelago, are offered for sale as indigenous productions in the shops of Canton and Macao. Skins of *Halcyon Smyrnensis*, for instance, and other birds from different parts of India, are bought up by the Chinese merchants of our colonies in the Straits of Malacca, who annually, on Chinese junks, ship quantities of considerable value to China, where they are manufactured into fans and artificial flowers. In a list of birds contained in a collection of Chinese productions exhibited in London in 1842, Mr. H. E. Strickland observes, in his communication to the Zoological Society, that some of them appear to have been imported from Malacca. Skins and other parts of a host of animals, from the most distant parts of Asia, form items in the Chinese Pharmacopœia. On my visits to Chinese dispensaries in China and in our Malayan colonies I have been shown horns of rhinoceroses and deer, tusks of the Dugong, heads of Buceri, tortoise-shells, and well-preserved skins of *Trigonocephalus Blomhoffii*, from Japan ; ammonites and other fossils, *cum multis aliis*, all supposed to possess specific virtues, and accordingly prescribed by Chinese medical practitioners.

In some the white lateral line commences from the side of the nose, passing over the cheeks, the sides of the neck, and over the shoulder. The lateral line is either pure white, more or less distinct, or mixed with single longer hairs with black apex.

Some have a short black line immediately below the white; in others there is above the latter a grizzled line, sometimes continued over the outside of the thigh. The tail is seldom uniformly black, frequently partially black, reddish, or grizzled, owing to the apex of the hairs being white. The tuft is frequently reddish or rust-coloured.

The feet are sometimes white or pale ferruginous.

The Museum of the Asiatic Society possesses a specimen from Java, differing from *Sciurus rufoniger*, Gray, in having the tail grizzled instead of black. *Sciurus redimitus*, Van de Boon, is probably another variety of *S. Rafflesii.*

A young male, about a fortnight in confinement, after having finished his usual meal of cocoanut, seized and devoured an *Iora typhia*, which had just been shot and happened to be placed within reach. Sparrows and other smaller birds were subsequently eaten and apparently relished.

The largest male measured from the apex of the nose to the root of the tail eleven and a half inches; the tail one foot two inches.

Sciurus hippurus, Is. Geoffroy.

Syn.—Sciurus erythræus, Pallas?
Sciurus caudatus, McClelland? } apud Gray, List.
Sciurus anomalus, Kuhl
Sciurus rufogaster, Gray.
Sciurus castaneoventris, Gray.
" Túpai Jinjang," " Ummu," or " Jau," of the Malays of the Peninsula.
Hab.—*Malayan Peninsula.*
Java, Sumatra, Assam, China (Canton).

The ground colour of the Malayan individuals differs but slightly, according to the more red or yellow rust colour of the bands of the hairs. The anterior part of the tail above is of the same colour as the back, the rest is either uniformly black, reddish, or with transverse bands, or has the tuft of that colour. The colour of the ears is brownish in some, but generally of the leaden grey, grizzled colour of the head, cheeks, chin, and outside of the limbs. The feet are black or slightly grizzled.

The largest individual of this numerous species measured from the apex of the nose to the root of the tail one foot; the tail one foot and half an inch.

SCIURUS VITTATUS, Raffles.

SYN.—Túpai, Raffles.
Sciurus bivittatus, Raffles, Desmar. ⎱ apud Horsfield.
Ecureuil Toupai, F. Cuvier ⎰
Macroxus Toupai, Lesson, apud Gray, List.
Sciurus flavimanus, Is. Geoffroy apud Schinz.
" Tupai " of the Malays of the Peninsula.
HAB.—*Singapore, Pinang, Malayan Peninsula.*
Sumatra, Borneo, Canton.

This is the most numerous species in the Straits of Malacca, the largest individuals measuring from the apex of the nose to the root of the tail eleven inches ; the tail eleven inches.

SCIURUS NIGROVITTATUS, Horsfield.

SYN.—Sciurus griseiventer, Is. Geoffroy apud Schinz.
HAB.—*Malayan Peninsula.*
Java, Sumatra, Borneo, Canton.

Not numerous ; the largest individual observed, a female, measured from the apex of the nose to the root of the tail nine inches ; the tail eight and half inches.

SCIURUS TENUIS, Horsfield.

SYN.—Sciurus modestus, S. Müller?
HAB.—*Singapore, Malayan Peninsula.*
Java, Sumatra, Borneo, Canton.

Of two individuals observed, the larger, a male, measured from the apex of the nose to the root of the tail six inches ; the tail seven inches.

SCIURUS LATICAUDATUS, Diard var.

SYN.—Sciurus laticaudatus, Diard apud S. Müller?*
HAB.—*Malayan Peninsula.*

The present squirrel differs from the diagnosis of *Sciurus laticaudatus* from the west coast of Borneo (communicated in " Natuur en Geneeskundig Archief," &c. ii. Jaarg. i. Aflev. p. 87), in having neither the first nor the fifth molar of the upper jaw very large. Both are of nearly equal size, and much smaller than the rest. The following is a description of the Malayan animal.

* In the " List of Mammalia in the British Museum " occurs a genus, *Rhinosciurus*, Gray, and a species *R. tupaioides*, Gray, syn. *Sciurus laticaudatus*, Müller ? Generic or specific characters being neither given nor referred to, it is impossible in India to decide whether the specimen in the British Museum thus labelled is identical with the animal here characterized.

The shape of the head is depressed, elongated, conical, gradually attenuated towards the laterally compressed nose. The whole outline, the slender form, and general colours, render the animal strikingly similar to *Tupaia ferruginea*. The eyes are large, brilliant, dark; the ears large, oval, with smooth short hairs; the mouth is small, the upper incisors are very minute, the lower slender, flattened, and almost straight; the black mustachios, whiskers, superciliary and gular bristles, and the few white ones of the forearm, are all shorter than the head; the muzzle hairy, leaving the margins of the small, and at the apex laterally pierced, nostrils naked. The limbs and feet slender; the nailless tubercle of the thumb rudimentary, barely perceptible in the living animal. The claws are small, sharp, compressed, whitish.

The colour of the head, back, outside of the limbs and feet, is a rich rusty red, mixed with shining black, particularly on the occiput, the back and the feet, less on the sides, where the ferruginous prevails; the throat, chest, abdomen, and inner side of the limbs, whitish; in some individuals pale yellowish. The fur is soft and delicate. The separate hairs are leaden-grey at the base, shining black, or with a broad subterminal ferruginous band. The tail is shorter than the body, distichous, broadest in the middle, attenuated at the root, terminating in a thin tuft. It may be compared to a feather, black on each side of the quill, successively ferruginous, again black, margined with buff. Such is the succession of the bands on the separate hairs. This organ is less full and ornamental than in the generality of squirrels. The species is apparently not numerous; the largest out of five examined, a female, was of the following dimensions:—

Length from the apex of the nose to the root of the tail	$10\frac{6}{8}$ inches.
„ of the tail	$6\frac{4}{8}$ „
„ of the head	$2\frac{3}{8}$ „
„ from the apex of the nose to the anterior angle of the eye	$1\frac{2}{8}$ inch.
„ from the posterior angle of the eye to the ear	$0\frac{5}{8}$ „
Breadth above the apex of the nose	$0\frac{1}{8}$ „
„ between the anterior angles of the eyes	$0\frac{7}{8}$ „
„ between the ears	$0\frac{6}{8}$ „
Diameter of the head at vertex	1 „

Its habits in confinement presented nothing remarkable.

Gen. PTEROMYS, *Cuvier*.

PTEROMYS NITIDUS, Geoffroy.

SYN.—Sciurus petaurista, Lin. apud Cuvier?
Sciurus petaurista, Chin Krawa, Raffles?

Pteromys albiventer, Gray, Illustr.

"Túpai Térbang," or "Kúbin," of the Malays of the Peninsula.

HAB.—*Singapore, Pinang, Malayan Peninsula.*
Java, Sumatra, Borneo.

The part of the head anterior to the ears, the cheeks, the chest, and the abdomen, are white in some individuals of either sex, one of which is figured in Hardwick's "Illustrations of Indian Zoology" under the denomination of *Pteromys albiventer,* Gray.

The black or dark-brown eyelids, nose, chin, feet, and tip of the tail appear to be constant characters. The shade and intensity of the red colour is liable to considerable variations.* In the very young there is a short black stripe behind the ears; and the posterior part of the back and anterior half of the tail are shining black, from each separate hair having the apex of that colour. Traces of these characters occur in some adult individuals. This species is very numerous in the Malayan countries. It is not strictly nocturnal, for it is frequently seen abroad during the day. It is particularly fond of the Durian, the fruit of *Durio Zibethinus,* Linné. The flying squirrel has this partiality in common with various other animals, as monkeys, Pteropi and Paradoxuri; nay, the Malays assert that they have to watch this their favourite fruit against tigers.

In a female, measuring from the extremity of the nose to the root of the tail one foot six and a half inches, the tail one foot nine inches, the intestinal canal was of the following dimensions:—

Small intestines	7 feet 4½	inches.
Large „	5 „ 2	„
Cæcum	2 „ 4	„

SCIUROPTERUS, Fred. Cuvier.

SCIUROPTERUS HORSFIELDII, Waterhouse.

SYN.—Pteromys aurantiacus, Wagner apud Gray, List.
HAB.—*Malayan Peninsula.*
Java? Sumatra?

A single skin, brought from Kéddah, measured from the apex of the nose to the root of the tail eight and three-eighth inches; the tail eleven inches.

* In an individual from Malacca the back was very dark Indian red, with a few dashes of pure white. The identity of the species is, however, doubtful.

SCIUROPTERUS GENIBARBIS.

SYN.—Pteromys genibarbis, Horsfield.
" Kechubu," Horsfield.
HAB.—*Malayan Peninsula.*
Java.

Of two, the larger, a male, measured from the apex of the nose to the root of the tail seven and half inches ; the tail seven inches.

MURIDÆ.

Gen. MUS, *Linné.*

MUS BANDICOTA, Bechstein.

SYN.—Mus giganteus, Hardwicke ⎫
Mus malabaricus, Shaw ⎪
Mus perchal, Shaw ⎬ apud Gray, List.
Mus icria, Buchan. Ham. MS. ⎪
Mus nemorivagus, Hodgson ⎭
" Tíkus besár " of the Malays of the Peninsula.
HAB.—*Pinang, Malayan Peninsula.*
Southern Mahratta Country, Bengal, Nipal.

MUS DECUMANUS, Pallas.

SYN.—Mus javanus, Pallas apud Schinz.
Mus norvegicus, Brisson apud Gray, List.
" Tíkus " of the Malays of the Peninsula.
HAB.—*Malayan Peninsula, Pinang.*
Cosmopolita.

MUS SETIFER, Horsfield.

SYN.—" Tíkus virok," Horsfield.
Mus giganteus, Temminck apud Gray.
HAB.—*Pinang.*
Java, Sumatra, Borneo, Van Diemen's Land.

The larger of two individuals, captured in gardens, measured, head and body, ten and one eighth inches ; the tail seven and four-eighth inches.

MUS RUFESCENS, Gray.

SYN.—Mus flavescens, Elliot ⎫ apud Gray, List.
Mus rufus, Elliot ⎭
HAB.—*Pinang.*
Dharwar, Madras, Bengal, Arracan.

In the young the brown bristles are fewer, and leave the lead-coloured under-fur more apparent. The colour of the abdomen is paler yellowish-grey than in the adult. The species is numerous at Pinang in outhouses. In the largest observed, the head and body measured seven and six-eighth inches ; the tail (mutilated) four and two-eighth inches.

Mus musculsus, Linné?

SYN. —" Tíkus rúma " of the Malays.
HAB.—*Pinang.*

In colours this slightly differs from the European mouse, the upper parts being a mixture of shining grey and tawny. The separate hairs are leaden-grey at the base, then tawny with black apex ; some are longer and uniformly dark brown ; beneath, pale ash. The ears are large, more than one-half of the length of the head, with very short hairs, rounded, blackish ; toes, palms and soles whitish ; tail slender, dark grey, with very short appressed brown hairs. Length of the head and body two and five-eighth inches ; tail two and four-eighth inches.

Gen. Rhizomys, *Gray.*

Rhizomys sumatrensis, Gray.

SYN.—Mus sumatrensis, Raffles.
    " Dekan," Raffles.
    Hypudeus de Sumatra, Temm. ⎫
    Nyctocleptes Dekan, Temm. ⎬ apud Gray, List.
    Spalax javanus, Cuvier ⎭
    Rhizomys chinensis, Gray apud Schinz.
    Rhizomys cinereus, McClelland.*
    Rhizomys Decan, Schinz.
    " Tíkus búlow" of the Malays of the Peninsula.
HAB.—*Malayan Peninsula.*
    China, Moulmein, Assam.

Although the animal was first described in Sir Stamford Raffles' catalogue of collections made in Sumatra, the author distinctly

* The description of this supposed species, "Calcutta Journal of Nat. Hist.," vol. ii. p. 456, pl. xiv., states: " There are four toes to each fore-foot, and five to each hind-foot." The draughtsman of pl. xiv., *Rhizomys cinereus,* has at all events observed that all the feet are *five-toed,* however incorrectly he has represented the animal. Another error occurs in the description—viz., " Sir Stamford Raffles describes a species of bamboo rat found in Sumatra by Colonel Farquhar," &c. Sir S. Raffles' words are these :—" Mus sumatrensis.—A drawing and specimen of an animal which appears related to the *Mus Pilorides* was forwarded from Malacca "—*not Sumatra,* as erroneously asserted—" by Major Farquhar, to the Asiatic Society, at the same time with the Binturong. I am informed by him that it is not uncommon at Malacca, and is perhaps to be found in most parts of the Malay Peninsula," &c. (" Transact. Linn. Society," vol. xiii. part ii.)

states that it was forwarded from Malacca by Major Farquhar ; nor does it appear to inhabit Sumatra, although the specific name would lead one to suppose that such is the case. The colour of the adult is liable to individual variations, from grey of different shades to isabella or silvery-buff. The separate hairs are mostly of the colour prevailing in the individual, mixed with single dark-brown hairs with whitish apex, particularly on the vertex, continuing along the centre part of the back. On the nose, anterior part of the head, and on the cheeks, the hairs are of a pale rust colour. On the vertex some white hairs from either a spot or a short line of that colour. The scanty hairs of the abdomen are all of a pale greyish or isabella colour. The mustachios, whiskers, superciliar and gular bristles are either of a pale brown or buff colour. The young are above of a dark grey, with a brown streak on the vertex and back ; beneath, pale grey. The forehead, nose, temples, and cheeks are ferruginous. The adult, like some squirrels and rats, is subject to enlargement of the scrotum. In confinement it is very savage, scarcely tameable. The length of the tail varies from about one-third to little more than one-fourth of the length of the body. It is blackish or brownish ; the apex whitish. The largest male examined measured from the apex of the nose to the root of the tail one foot seven and a half inches ; the tail five and a half inches. The female, in size and colours equalling the male, has ten mammæ—viz., two axillary and three inguinal pairs.

Gen. HYSTRIX, *Cuvier.*

HYSTRIX LONGICAUDA, Marsden.

SYN.—Acanthion javanicum, Fred. Cuvier ?
Hystrix brevispinosus, Schinz.*
" Bábi Lándak " of the Malays of the Peninsula.
HAB.—*Malayan Peninsula.*
Java, Sumatra, Borneo.

Sir Stamford Raffles has pointed out the inaccuracy of Marsden's figure, representing the fore-feet with five toes, instead of with four, and a rudimentary thumb with a flat nail. The figure also has a few mane-like long bristles on the head, whereas the mustachios are situated on the side of the nose, the whiskers below the ear, and one or two bristles above the eye. In colours this species resembles *Hystrix leucurus*, Sykes, from which it differs in the absence of the long mane-like bristles of the head and neck. Although single, scattered, thin, flexible spines, upwards of twelve

---

* In " Nachträge," zum 2ten Bande, this species is supposed to be identical with and substituted for *Atherura fasciculata*, although a very correct description is given of both.

inches in length, occur on the posterior part of the back, the majority of inflexible spines are much shorter than in *Hystrix leucurus* or *H. cristatus,* and are either pure white or with a blackish band in the medial portion. The short, blackish, slightly iridescent spines of the neck, anterior part of the back, the limbs, and abdomen, are generally grooved on the upper surface. The short white pedunculated tubes of the posterior part of the tail are at first closed, terminating in a short spine, which latter wears off, leaving the tubes open. The pubes are disposed in a wreath of stiff bristles, frequently of a deep rust colour. The epidermis of this species, as well as of *Atherura,* is remarkably thin and liable to be torn. Beneath the skin appears a fatty tissue, upwards of an inch in thickness. The anterior molars are slightly larger than the rest. Viewed from above, *in situ,* the crown of the anterior lower molar of either side presents the form of two letters S facing each other (S2). In a fœtus—of which the head measures two and one-eighth inches, the body four and three-eighth inches, the tail one inch in length—the whole of the body and the anterior half of the tail have numerous short hairs, disposed on separate transverse lines of six to eight distant black hairs, becoming longer on the posterior part of the back and sides. The posterior part of the tail has longer and closer hairs. In a female, measuring from the apex of the nose to the root of the tail two feet five inches, the tail four inches, the intestinal canal was of the following dimensions :—

Small intestines	. . . . .	21 feet	6 inches.
Large　　,,	. . . . .	5　,,	10　　,,
Cæcum	. . . .	1 foot	7　　,,

The stomach is of a heart-shaped outline, with thin membranes externally smooth, internally with a few longitudinal rugæ near the narrow fundus.

The species is numerous, and as it is considered a delicacy by the Chinese population, is frequently brought to market.

Gen. ATHERURA, *Cuvier.*

ATHERURA FASCICULATA, Cuvier.

SYN.—Hystrix fasciculata, Lin. apud Cuvier.*
　　　Hystrix orientalis, Brisson apud Gmelin.
　　　Hystrix macroura, Linné.
　　　Porc-epic de Malacca, Buffon.
　　　Hystrix fasciculata, Shaw apud Raffles.
　　　Mus fasciculatus, Desmarest.

* No species of that name occurs in " Systema Naturæ," ed. xiii., Gmelin, 1788; but *Hystrix macroura* is described " cauda longitudine corporis"(?) "apice fasciculo pilorum," &c.

Hystrix fasciculata, Linné apud Gray, Illust.*
Acanthion javanicum, F. Cuv.
Atherurus fasciculatus, Schinz.
Atherurus macrourus, Schinz.
" Lándak " of the Malays of the Peninsula.
HAB.—*Pinang, Malayan Peninsula.*
Java, Sumatra, Borneo.

The nose, lips, forehead, and back of the feet are covered with greyish-brown hairs ; the body and limbs at the root of the spine are covered with dense soft silky hairs, grey on the upper parts and silvery on the abdomen. Single longer flexible spines, white with a dark central band, are scattered over the back ; the anterior part of the tail is, like the back, covered with flat-grooved spines, white at the root, then slightly iridescent brown, and frequently with white apex ; the centre part of the tail is scaly, with very short spines between the scales ; the posterior part is white, with white or silvery, flexible, and in length gradually increasing, spines, which Buffon has aptly compared to narrow slips of irregularly cut parchment ; the pubes are of a deep rust colour.

This species is very numerous in the Malayan valleys and hills. In fretful habits and in its food it resembles the preceding porcupine, like which it is carried to the market at Pinang and Malacca, where as many as twenty to thirty may frequently be seen. In a male, measuring from the apex of the nose to the root of the tail one foot ten inches, the tail ten inches, the intestinal canal was of the following dimension :—

Small intestines . . . . . 19 feet 4½ inches.
Large   „   5   „   3   „
Cæcum . . . . 1 foot 3   „

The stomach is of a general outline, resembling that of *H. longicauda,* but it differs in having an external deep vertical sulcus, dividing the stomach into a pyloric and a cardiac portion, which latter presents six to seven deep oblique sulci. The membranes of the stomach are thick and muscular. Internally the cardiac portion is transversally divided by six or seven ridges, corresponding to the external sulci, intersected by numerous concentric rugæ. The pyloric portion, separated from the cardiac by the rugæ produced by the external vertical sulcus, is much smoother and has but few rugæ.

* In the figure the anterior foot has one toe too many, the animal having four toes and a rudimentary flat-nailed thumb. Nor is the back of the hind foot naked, unless indeed become so by accident.

EDENTATA.

Gen. MANIS, *Linné.*

MANIS JAVANICA, Desmarest.

SYN.—Manis pentadactyla, Lin. apud Raffles.
Manis aspera, Sundeval.
M. quinquedactyla, Raffles apud Gray, List.
" Pengóling " or " Tangling " of the Malays of the
Peninsula.
HAB. —*Pinang, Malayan Peninsula.*
Java, Sumatra, Borneo.

The series of dorsal scales vary in individuals from sixteen to nineteen. The number of central dorsal vary from twenty to twenty-two ; the central and the marginal caudal from twenty-six to twenty-nine : in the young all the scales are finely lineated and the rounded apex only is smooth. With age the lines become obliterated on the exposed surface of the scales, between which appear a few long whitish bristles. The very young animal corresponds to the description of *Manis aspera,* Sundeval. The eyelids, the margins of the ears, and the scaleless parts, except the palms and soles, are scantily provided with short whitish hairs. The two pectoral mammæ are situated at a short distance from the axilla. Its habits present nothing different from those of *Manis cassicaudata (M. pendactyla,* Linné), of which an interesting account is ·communicated by Lieut. R. S. Tickell in " Journal Asiatic Society," vol. xi. 1842, p. 221.

The present species, although numerous in rocky situations, is not often captured, as it is seldom abroad till after sunset. The largest male measured from the apex of the nose to the root of the tail one foot nine and a half inches, the tail one foot eight inches. In a younger male, the entire length of which was one foot eleven inches, the intestinal canal was of the following dimensions :—

Small intestines	. . . . .	8 feet 4 inches.
Large „	. . . . .	0 „ 6 „

Cæcum is rudimentary, indicated by a slight yet distinct widening of the intestines. The stomach is capacious, the pyloric region thickened and gizzard-like. On the external surface, where the greater curvature begins to ascend, is situated a small (one inch in length, one and three-eighths in breadth), triangular, externally gyrated, glandular body, firmly attached to the stomach, but not communicating with the cavity. Its external appearance might be compared to that of a crest of ostrich feathers. The narrowed apex, towards the pylorus, is provided with a small, thick, rounded and wrinkled opening, surrounded by concentric fibres, leading by a common, short, cylindrical duct to the broader cavity, which latter is divided by two longitudinal parietes into three separate portions. If a tube is introduced into the common duct, the air injected will simultaneously fill all three portions of the cavity, but if the tube is inserted into any one of the three separate portions, the air will fill that particular portion, leaving the two others collapsed. The interior surface of this organ secretes a whitish mucus. Adjoining the common opening, from ten to eleven small rounded glands commence, arranged on a line towards the pylorus. Each gland has in its centre a minute wrinkled opening, leading into a small cavity secreting mucus.

The stomach was extended by the remains (heads and legs) of a prodigious quantity of large black ants, inhabiting the hills. The contents of the stomach were involved in mucus, deeply tinctured with bile, and among them appeared five small rounded fragments of granite. Another individual expired after ten days' confinement, during which period it took no food, although it was repeatedly placed among swarms of the black and red ants so excessively numerous in the valley of Pinang. Water it always took when offered, lapping it up with the tongue in the same manner that serpents drink.

Costæ veræ, 8 pairs ; spuriæ, 7 pairs = 15 pairs. The ensiform process of the os sternum is greatly elongated, terminating in a broad, rounded, thin cartilaginous plate.

PACHYDERMATA.

PROBOSCOIDEA.

Gen. ELEPHAS, *Linné.*

ELEPHAS INDICUS, Linné.

SYN.—" Gájah " of the Malays.
HAB.—*Malayan Peninsula.*
India, Burma, Siam, Ceylon, Sumatra, Borneo.

Elephants are very numerous on the Malayan Peninsula. They may be procured at the following rates :—

" For an elephant	4 feet	6 inches high	.	120	dollars.
"	5 "	3 "	.	200	"
"	6 "	0 "	.	220	:,
"	6 "	9 "	.	400	"
"	7 "	6 "	.	420	"

Those exceeding this height are paid for at an advance on the last-mentioned rate of 20 dollars for one foot six inches. If above eight feet and three inches, then an addition of 40 dollars for each one foot six inches is charged. Elephants ten feet six inches in height are taken by the Siamese to the capital, and it is not permitted to sell them. The Keddah chiefs used formerly to breed elephants, a speculation rarely if ever attempted elsewhere. Coromandel native traders were until late years constantly in the habit of loading vessels with elephants for that coast." (Extract from Lieut.-Colonel James Law's "Dissertation," &c.)

ORDINARIA.

Gen. SUS, *Linné.*

SUS INDICUS, Schinz.

SYN.—Sus scrofa, Linné apud Elliot.
Sus indicus   ⎫ apud Gray, List.
Sus scropha, Hodgson ⎭
Sus vittatus, Schlegel.
Sus cristatus, Wagner apud Schinz.
"Bábi útan" of the Malays of the Peninsula.
HAB.—*Malayan Peninsula, Pinang, Singapore, Lancavy Islands.* Bengal, Nipal, Southern Mahratta Country.

The differences between the Indian and the German wild hog (*Sus scrofa ferus*, Lin.) have been pointed out by W. Elliot, Esq. ("Madras Journal," vol. x. 1839, p. 219). The colour of the adult is brownish-black, scantily covered with black hairs, of which few retain the infantile yellowish sub-terminal band. Besides the black recumbent mane of the occiput and back, the whiskers and bristles above and below the eye, there is a bundle of long black bristles on the throat. The hairs of the throat and chest are reversed. The tail is scantily covered with short hairs, the apex compressed, with long lateral bristles like those of the elephant, arranged like the wings of an arrow. The young is more hairy, with the plurality of hairs tawny or fulvous, some with black root and apex, which, as they are more or less mixed with black hairs, produce on the sides of the body saturated fulvous stripes. The hairs of the throat, chest, abdomen, and elbows (in the two latter places very long) are black at the basal and white at the apical half. Wild hogs are exceedingly numerous on the peninsula and most of the Malayan islands. The largest boar examined measured from the apex of the nose to the root of the tail five feet, the tail one foot. The stomach of a young boar, examined shortly after it had been speared, was extended with food, principally consisting of the remains of a very large coleopterous larva, some small seeds of different kinds, leaves, grass, and roots.

SUS SCROFA, var. SINENSIS, Linné.

SYN.—"Babi" of the Malays.
Introduced by the Chinese settlers.

Gen. Rhinoceros, *Linné.*

Rhinoceros unicornis, Linné.

Syn.—Rhinoceros indicus, Cuvier.
Rhinoceros asiaticus, Blumenbach.
Rhinoceros inermis, Lesson.
"Bádak" of the Malays of the Peninsula.
Hab.—*Malayan Peninsula.*
Bengal, Assam, Nipal.

Rhinoceros sondaicus, Cuvier.

Syn.—Rhinoceros sondaicus, Cuvier ⎫
     "Wárak," "Bádak"   ⎬ apud Horsfield.
Rhinoceros javanensis, F. Cuvier apud Schinz.
Hab.—*Malayan Peninsula.*
Java.

This, as well as the former species, appears to be numerous on the Malayan Peninsula.

A *two-horned* Rhinoceros is stated by the Malays to inhabit, but rarely to leave, the densest jungle. The Museum of the Asiatic Society possesses a skull, and also a head with the skin on, of *Rhinoceros sumatranus*, Raffles, from the Tenasserim Provinces, in which locality the existence of the species has been recorded by Dr. Helfer and Mr. Blyth. This fact would seem to corroborate the statement of the Malays, and the habitat of *Rhinoceros sumatranus* may reasonably be expected to be here-after found to extend over the neighbouring Malayan Peninsula. As such it has indeed been enumerated by Capt. Begbie, the author of "Malayan Peninsula," &c., Madras, 1834. In Lieut.-Colonel Low's "History of Tenasserim" ("Journal Royal Asiatic Society," vol. iii. 1836) is figured the head of a young Rhinoceros, which, from the considerable protuberance between the eyes, appears to represent a two-horned (probably the present) species.

Gen. Tapirus, *Linné.*

Tapirus malayanus, Raffles.

Syn.—Tapirus malayanus, apud Horsfield.
Tapirus indicus, Fred. Cuvier.
Tapirus sumatranus, Gray.
Me des Çhinois, Remusat (young?) apud Gray: List.
Tapirus bicolor, Wagner apud Schinz.
"Bádak," "Kúda Ayer," "Tennú" of the Malays of the Peninsula.
Hab.—*Malayan Peninsula.*
Sumatra, Borneo.

The body of a new-born male, found in Province Wellesley in August 1844, was shortly after its death carried over to Pinang. As described by Colonel Farquhar, it was of a beautiful black velvet colour, with purple reflections, with numerous small and other larger irregular spots on the body, arranged in longitudinal stripes, above of a rich gamboge, beneath and on the inner side of the extremities paler yellow. The under-lip was white. The shrivelled remains of the black funiculus umbilicalis were upwards of four inches in length. The fur very short, dense, and velvety ; the separate hairs, of either of the two prevailing colours, slightly curly. Dimensions :—

Length from the apex of the nose to the root
	of the tail	1 foot	10 inches.
,,	of the head	0 ,,	7 ,,
,,	of the tail	0 ,,	$1\frac{2}{4}$,,
,,	of the ear	0 ,,	$1\frac{6}{8}$,,
Diameter of the head from vertex		0 ,,	5 ,,
Height of the shoulder		0 ,,	$8\frac{2}{8}$,,
,, ,, haunch		0 ,,	9 ,,

The animal, from which a sketch was taken on its arrival at Pinang, was the property of the Rev. R. Panting, A.M. The skin, imperfectly preserved, has lately been deposited in the Museum of the Asiatic Society.

On the 16th of May 1845 I obtained a living young female Tapir, captured in Keddah a few days previously. Though still in its infantile garb, it was older than the preceding. The ground colour was a brownish-black, like worn-out velvet; the spots, stripes, and the posterior part of the abdomen were of a dirty-white. The separate hairs were longer and curly; the hairy ears retained numerous white spots on the margins and external surface. The lips were blackish, with numerous short distant bristles, which also appeared round the nostrils, on the ridge of the nose, above and below the eyes, on the cheeks, and on the throat. Two black mammæ were situated between the hind legs, three and a half inches behind the large naked cicatrix of funiculus umbilicalis. Dimensions :—

Length from the apex of the nose to the root
	of the tail	3 feet	$4\frac{3}{8}$ inches.
,,	of the head	1 foot	0 ,,
,,	of the tail	0 ,,	$1\frac{2}{8}$,,
,,	of the ear	0 ,,	$5\frac{4}{8}$,,
Diameter of the head from vertex		0 ,,	$5\frac{4}{8}$,,
Height of the shoulder		1 ,,	4 ,,
,, ,, haunch		1 ,,	6 ,,
Greatest circumference round the body		2 feet	6 ,,
Circumference at the root of the ear		0 ,,	6 ,,

Dentition :—

$$\text{Incis. } \frac{6}{6}; \quad \text{Canin. } \frac{0—0}{1—1}; \quad \text{Mol. } \frac{3 \cdot 3}{3 \cdot 3}$$

From the first, although fresh from its native wilds, this young Tapir showed a remarkably gentle disposition. The daytime it spent in sleeping in a dark recess of the portico of my house, though it would rouse itself if noticed. Towards sunset it became lively, would bathe, feed, saunter abroad, and with its lengthened nose examine objects in the way. Within a few days after its arrival it commenced to exhibit a marked partiality to the society of man, not indeed to its keeper in particular, whom it scarcely had discrimination enough to distinguish, but to anybody who happened to notice or caress it. Towards sunset it would follow a servant on the green in front of the house, and punctually imitate his movements, whether standing, walking, or running. If the man suddenly hid himself, the Tapir would hasten to the spot where it had lost sight of its leader, look about in all directions, and, if unsuccessful in discovering him, express its disappointment by a peculiar loud whistling. On the re-appearance of the man it expressed its pleasure by rubbing its side against his legs, running between them, occasionally giving out a short singular sound, resembling that produced when the larger woodpeckers tap the trees, but more sonorous. When of an evening it heard the voices of people in the verandah above the portico, it exhibited strong marks of impatience till let loose, when of its own accord it would, awkwardly enough, ascend a flight of stairs leading to the verandah. It would then quietly lie down at their feet, and by stretching its limbs and shaking its head, express the satisfaction it derived from being caressed ; and it was only by compulsion that it could be made to leave the company. Its food consisted of plantains, pine-apples, mangustins, jambu, leaves of *Ficus pipul*, sugar-cane, and boiled rice, of which latter it was particularly fond if mixed with a little salt. Its drink was water, and also milk and cocoanut oil, which latter taste the Tapir possesses in common with the Orang-útan. It delighted in bathing, and was otherwise cleanly. When roaming about the garden (its walk was like that of the elephant) it would select a spot with soft earth, and like a cat form with its hind legs a small excavation, and again cover it. The whole body has a peculiar and by no means offensive exhalation, somewhat resem· bling that noted of *Arctictis Binturong*. Indeed, this is so tenacious that although the skin of the individual above described has been preserved more than a twelvemonth, and kept in a strongly camphorated case, the odour is still perceptible.

On the 27th of June 1845 the subject of the preceding notice expired after two days' illness from inflammation of the lungs, brought on by the strong southerly winds prevailing throughout the Straits of Malacca during the season, which in man produce a slight influenza, in animals frequently terminating fatally. The few adult Tapirs which occasionally have been kept in confinement by residents in Malacca have acquired the character of being hardy animals. During the short period that the present lived in my possession no perceptible change appeared in its growth, but a striking alteration took place in its colours. Nearly all the white spots on the head, nape of the neck, and back of the ears gradually disappeared, and the upper part only of the margin of the ears remained white, which colour it retains in the adult animal. On the posterior part of the back and sides the black and white stripes were in a state of progressing obliteration; their hairs had faded to a brownish colour, and were about being replaced by a shorter and less dense fur of the fresh white hairs, which were to form the characteristic permanent white mark, already appearing in outline, when death terminated the unfinished process of nature.

Vertebræ: cervical seven, of which the atlas and epistrophæus the largest; dorsal twenty, lumbar four, sacral seven, caudal three.

Sternum: the anterior extremity cartilaginous, sharply keeled, arched, continued over manubrium, composed of two rounded angularly joined pieces, as far as the second pair of ribs; corpus composed of five pieces, of which the two posterior, in a pair, are connected by cartilage.

Costæ veræ, eight pairs; spuriæ, twelve pairs = twenty pairs. The last spurious rib is rudimentary, and absent on the left side.

Femur, five and two-eighth inches long; the large bony subtrochanteric process, described by Sir Everard Home, is developed, though partly cartilaginous, measuring one inch in length at the base.

Liver of moderate size, each lobe divided into two portions of nearly equal size.

Gall-bladder: none.

Spleen: tongue-shaped, flattened, with cutting margins, seven and half inches in length, one and six-eighths in breadth.

Pancreas: in a state not to admit of accurate examination.

Kidneys: three and six-eighth inches in length, one and six-eighths in breadth.

Renes succenturiati: none.

Urinary bladder: very large.

Stomach: capacious. Its dimensions in the state in which it appeared, distended with food, were—

Length along the smaller curvature	. .	o	foot	$5\frac{2}{8}$	inches.	
,, ,, greater ,,	. .	1	,,	$9\frac{1}{8}$	,,	
Circumference from cardia round fundus		1	,,	o	,,	
,, round pylorus	. . . .	o	,,	$3\frac{1}{2}$	,,	

The internal surface smooth, villous.

Where the duodenum joins the pylorus it is considerably widened. Length of the intestinal canal :—

Small intestines	. . . .	27 feet	7 inches.
Large ,,	. . . .	6 ,,	4 ,,
Cæcum	. . . .	0 ,,	6 ,,
Average circumference of small	. . .	0 ,,	$2\frac{3}{8}$,,
,, ,, large	. . .	0 ,,	$3\frac{1}{2}$,,

Cæcum sacculated, with a longitudinal band on either side. Distended with fæces as it appeared, the greatest circumference close to the fundus was one foot one and a half inch.

In the adult Tapir dissected by Sir E. Home, and which was, according to Mr. Yarrell, eight feet in length, the relative proportion between the length of the intestinal canal and that of the body was as eleven to one. In the present young female the relative length of the intestinal canal is proportionally less than in the adult, being less than as ten to one.

SOLIDUNGULA.

Gen. Equus, *Linné.*

Equus caballus, Linné.

The horse ("Kuda," of the Malays) appears not to be indigenous in the Peninsula. The few ponies, which the wealthier use for ordinary purposes, are imported either from Siam, Burma, or Sumatra. The Malays either travel by water, or prefer the elephant as a locomotive more dignified than the horse.

RUMINANTIA.

Gen. Moschus, *Linné;* Tragulus, Brisson.

Tragulus Kanchil, Gray: List.

Syn.—Chevrotain adulte ⎫ Buffon apud Cray.
      Chevrotain de Java ⎭
      Javan Musk, Shaw.
      Moschus Palandok, Marsden.
      Moschus Kanchil, Raffles.
      Pelandok, Raffles.
      Moschus fulviventer, Gray.
      " Kanchil" or " Pelandok " of the Malays of the Peninsula

Hab.—*Singapore, Pinang, Lancavy Islands, Malayan Peninsula.* Sumatra, Java.

In some individuals the back is nearly black. The colour and distribution of the marks of the chest and abdomen are also liable to individual variations, one of which gave rise to the supposed species, *Moschus fulviventer*. The animal is by the Malays indiscriminately denominated "Kánchil" and "Pelándok;" the latter denomination is sometimes *par excellence* applied to the young, and this circumstance in all probability gave rise to the supposed species *Moschus Pelandok*. The species is astonishingly numerous. In Prince of Wales Island any number may be procured within a short notice, at the rate of one Spanish dollar per dozen. Knowing the partiality of these deer to the leaves of the sweet potato plant (*Convolvolus batatas*), the Malays either use traps baited with this vegetable, or lie in ambush on moonlight nights in fields where it is cultivated, and disable the intruders by throwing sticks at their legs. In confinement, in its native climate, the animal becomes rather delicate, though it occasionally survives, and even breeds. The female has four mammæ, and one or two young at a time. The new-born measures eight and six-eight inches in length, of which the head is three inches, the tail one inch. The skin of the upper parts is of a pale blackish colour, scantily covered with short, fine, brown hairs. The abdomen and inner side of the limbs are pale yellow; the throat and chest have the dark marks of the adult, but paler. The largest adults measure from the apex of the nose to the root of the tail one foot six and a half inches; the tail three inches in length.

TRAGULUS JAVANICUS, Pallas.

SYN.—Moschus javanicus, Gmelin.
    Moschus javanicus, Pallas apud Raffles.
    Napu, Raffles.
    Moschus indicus, Gmelin ⎱ apud Gray.
    Cervus javanicus, Osbek ⎰
    Moschus Napu, Fred. Cuvier.
    "Nápu" of the Malays of the Peninsula.

HAB.—*Malayan Peninsula.*
    Sumatra, Java, Borneo.

On the Malayan Peninsula the species appears to be far less numerous than the preceding. The canines of the female are very small. The four mammæ are situated at the posterior part of the abdomen, a little in front of the hind legs. The anterior pair are half an inch apart; the posterior two-eighths of an inch apart. The two pairs are half an inch distant from each other. In an adult female, measuring from the apex of the nose to the root of the tail two feet four and two-eighth inches, the tail five inches, the intestinal canal was of the following dimensions :—

Small intestines . . . . . 13 feet 6 inches.
Large   ,, ... 7 ,, 10 ,,
Cæcum . . . . 0 ,, 6 ,,

The gall-bladder is very large ; immediately behind it is situated the right kidney.

Gen. CERVUS, *Linné ;* STYLOCEROS, Hamilton Smith.

STYLOCEROS MUNTJAK, H. Smith.

SYN.—Chevreuil des Indes, Allamand.
Cervus Muntjak, Zimmerman apud Horsfield, Sykes and Elliot.
Cervus Muntjak, Boddaert
Cervus vaginalis, Boddaert
Cervus Muntjak, Schreber
Cervus Muntjak, Marsden
Cervus moschatus, Blainville   apud Horsfield.
Cervus subcornutus, Blainville
Cervus Muntjak? Shreb apud Raffles
Cervus Muntjak, Desmarest
Cervus moschus, Desmarest
Cervus aureus, Ham. Smith
Cervus Philippinus, Ham. Smith   apud Gray : List.
Cervus albipes, Fred. Cuvier
Cervus Ratwa, Hodgson
Muntjacus vaginalis, Gray : List.
Cervus Muntiac, Linné apud Schinz.*
" Kídang " of the Malays of the Peninsula.

HAB.—*Malayan Peninsula.*
Java, Sumatra, Banka, Borneo, Tenasserim, Nipal, Assam, Bengal, South Mahratta Country, Dukhun.

In a young male, measuring from the apex of the nose to the root of the tail three feet and one inch, the tail seven inches, the intestinal canal was of the following dimensions :—

Small intestines . . . . . 13 feet 10 inches.
Large   ,, ... 22 ,, 1 inch.
Cæcum . . . . 0 ,, 9 inches.

---

* In Nachträge zum 2ten Bande the author suggests that six distinct species are supposed to lie hid under the denomination of *Cervus Muntiac,* viz.:—
  1. *Cervus styloceros,* Schinz. Syn. *C. Muntiac,* Lin. apud Ogilby. *Hab.* Himalaya.
  2. *Cervus Ratwa,* Hodgson. *Hab.* Himalaya.
  3. *Cervus albipes,* F. Cuvier. *Hab.* India.
  4. *Cervus Muntjak,* Raffles and Horsfield. *Hab.* Java, Sumatra, Banka, Borneo.
  5. *Cervus Reevesii,* Ogilby. *Hab.* China.
  6. *Cervus antisiensis,* Pucheran. *Hab.* Andes.

The right lobe of the liver lies in contact with the right kidney; the spleen with the left.
Gall-bladder: none.

Axis, Hamilton Smith.

Axis maculatus, Hamilton Smith.

Syn.—Axis, Plinius.
Cervus axis, Erxleben apud Gmelin.
Cervus nudipalpebra, Ogilby (black var.) ⎫
Axis major, Hodgson ⎬ apud Gray: List.
Axis minor, Hodgson ⎭
" Rúsa Búnga " of the Malays of the Peninsula.

Hab.—*Malayan Peninsula, Pinang.*
Sumatra, Bengal, Assam, Nipal, Southern Mahratta
Country, Ceylon.

Sir Stamford Raffles thinks it probable that the Axis in Sumatra has been introduced from Bengal. It is numerous in Keddah. and at present in Pinang. But it did not inhabit Prince of Wales Island till one of the last governors of the late presidency took the trouble of importing from Bengal some pairs, which were kept in the park adjoining Government House (Suffolk House). When the Presidency of Prince of Wales Island was abolished, and with it all its paraphernalia, except the titles of as many of its officers as were necessary to the continuance of H.M. Court of Judicature, the deer of the quondam Governor's park found their way into the jungle, where they have multiplied to a prodigious extent.

Rusa, Hamilton Smith.

Rusa equina, Hamilton Smith.

Syn.—Cervus equinus, Cuvier.
Cervus Rusa, Raffles.
Rusa etam or Kumbang, Raffles.
"Rúsa" or "Rúsa étam" of the Malays of the Peninsula.

Hab.—*Malayan Peninsula, Pinang.*
Sumatra, Borneo.

The Malayan individuals correspond with the description given by Sir S. Raffles of *Cervus Rusa.* The lips are whitish; the posterior part of the lower sometimes dark brown. Round the eyes and the lachrymal sinus, on the side of the forehead, root of the ears, and on the throat, the hairs are either uniformly pale ferruginous, or have a subterminal band of that colour, the effect of which is to impart a pale rusty tint to these parts. Normally, each horn has three antlers, of which the lower or anterior, commencing from the burr, is directed outwards till towards the apex, which turns slightly inward. The second and outward turned antler commences at the root of the third, and is the shortest of the three. The third is directed inwards, and is the longest of the three. In the number, direction, and size of the antlers numerous individual variations occur.

According to Mr. Blyth's observations, *Cervus Hippelaphus* has, normally, the third antler much longer than the second; *Cervus Aristotelis* has much larger and more divergent horns, of which the second and third antlers are about equal. Considering the similarity of colours and size of *Cervus equinus, Hippelaphus,* and *Aristotelis,* Mr. Elliot is probably right in considering all three as varieties of the great Indian stag, described by Aristotle under the designation of *Hippelaphus* ("Madras Journal," 1839, p. 220); and *Cervus Peronii,* Cuvier (Cerf du Timor) may probably be added as a fourth variety.

PANOLIA, Gray : List.

PANOLIA ACUTICORNIS, Gray : List.

SYN.— Cervus frontalis, McClelland ?
　　　Cervus lyratus, Schinz ?

HAB.—*Malayan Peninsula.*

A single skull of a stag, killed in Keddah, has the horns so like those of the Munneepore animal, that the species might be taken to be identical, but the Malays assert theirs to be maned, and of a dark colour, with white spots, like the Axis. This stag is further described as being extremely wary, and therefore seldom seen but on heights inaccessible to man. The skull is of an old male, with the teeth (canines in particular) much ground.

Gen. ANTILOPE, *Linné;* NÆMORHEDUS, Hamilton Smith.

NÆMORHEDUS SUMATRENSIS, Hamilton Smith.

SYN.—Kambing utan, Marsden.
　　　Antilope sumatrensis, Pennant apud Raffles.
　　　Cambtan, Fred. Cuvier.
　　　Antilope interscapularis, Lichtenstein apud Schinz.
　　　" Rámbing útan " of the Malays of the Peninsula.

HAB.—*Malayan Peninsula.*
　　　Sumatra, Tenasserim.

It appears to be numerous on the Malayan Peninsula, but exceedingly difficult to obtain, as it frequents the steepest hilly localities, and is very shy and active.

Gen. Bos, *Linné*,

Bos gour, Trail.

Syn.—Bos Gaurus, Ham. Smith.
Bison Gaurus, Ham. Smith.
Bos aculeatus, Wagler.
The Bison : " Hist. of Tenasserim."
Bos (Bibos) cavifrons, Hodgson apud Elliot.
Bos frontalis, Lambert apud Gray : List (?)
" Sápi útan " of the Malays of the Peninsula.

Hab.—*Malayan Peninsula.*
Tenasserim, Hindoostan, Assam, Nipal, Southern Mahratta Country.
Numerous in the Malayan Peninsula.

Bos Taurus, Var. Indicus, Linné.

Syn.—" Sápi " (S. jántan, bull ; S. bétina, cow) of the Malays of the Peninsula.

Although this kind of cattle is plentifully bred in some of the Malayan countries, it is not in general use, and is less numerous than the buffalo.

Bubalus, Hamilton Smith.

Bubalus arnee, Hamilton Smith.

Syn.—Bos indicus, Plinius.
Bos bubalus, Brisson.
Bos arnee, Shaw.
Bubalus ferus Indicus, Hodgson apud Gray : List.
Bubalus Buffelus, Gray : List.
" Karbau " of the Malays of the Peninsula.

Hab.—*Pinang, Singapore, Malayan Peninsula.*
Tenasserim, Southern China.
The wild buffalo is reported, but apparently without proof, to be indigenous in the Malayan Peninsula. Domesticated, it is very plentiful, and is the principal draught cattle employed by the Malays and the Chinese settlers. The black-coloured, apparently the hardier, is preferred by the Malays ; the reddish-white freckled with brown is the greater favourite of the Chinese. Both are very slow, and, as observed by Lieut.-Colonel Low, delicate, and liable to sudden attacks of disease if worked in the sun.

CETACEA.

HERBIVORA.

Gen. HALICORE, *Illiger.*

HALICORE INDICUS, F. Cuvier.

SYN.—Dugon, Buffon.
Trichechus Dugong, Erxleben.
Halicore cetacea, Illiger.
Halicore, Dugong, Cuvier apud Raffles.
Halicore Tabernacularum, Rüppell.
Dugungus marinus, Tiedemann apud Schinz.
" Dúyong " or " Parampúan Laut " of the Malays of the Peninsula.

HAB.—*Singapore, Malayan Peninsula.*
Sumatra, Philippine, Molucca and Sunda Islands, New Holland, Red Sea.

The Duyong appears not to be numerous at Singapore, still less so to the northward, and has but in few instances been observed in Kwála Mùda, the mouth of the river, which forms the northern boundary of Province Wellesley.

ORDINARIA.

Gen. DELPHINUS, *Linné.*

DELPHINUS PLUMBEUS, Dussumier.

SYN.—Delphinus malayanus, Lesson apud Cuvier.
" Parampúan Laut " of the Peninsula.

HAB.—*Coasts of Pinang.*
Malabar Coast.

The species, although very numerous, and rather heavy in its movements, is rarely captured, except by chance in fishing stakes. The stomach, of a single young individual observed, contained remains of small fishes, apparently *Clupeæ*, and *Glyphisodon cælestinus*, Cuvier.

NUMERICAL LIST OF MAMMALIA *inhabiting the Malayan Peninsula and Islands and other localities.*

1	*Hylobates lar*, Ogilby	Malayan Peninsula	Siam, Burma, Tenasserim.
2	*Hylobates agilis*, F. Cuvier	Malayan Peninsula	Sumatra.
3	*Semnopithecus obscurus*, Reid	Malayan Peninsula, Pinang, Singapore.	
4	*Semnopithecus albocinereus*, Schinz	Malayan Peninsula	Tenasserim.
5	*Semnopithecus cristatus*, Horsfield	Pinang, Malayan Peninsula	Sumatra, Borneo, Banka.
6	*Semnopithecus femoralis*, Horsfield	Malayan Peninsula	Borneo, Sumatra? Java?
7	*Cercopithecus cynomolgus*, Ogilby	Pinang, Malayan Peninsula	Sumatra, Java, Banka, Borneo, Celebes, Timor, Tenasserim, Nicobars.
8	*Papio nemestrinus*, Ogilby	Pinang, Malayan Peninsula	Sumatra, Borneo.
9	*Nycticebus tardigradus*, Waterhouse	Pinang, Malayan Peninsula	Java, Siam, Arracan, Tenasserim, Bengal, Silhet, Assam.
10	*Galeopithecus Temminckii*, Waterhouse	Malayan Peninsula and Islands	Pelew Islands, Borneo, Java, Sumatra, Siam.
11	*Rhinopoma Hardwickii*, Gray	Malayan Peninsula	Southern Mahratta Country, Calcutta, Allahabad, Agra, Mirzapore.
12	*Megaderma spasma*, Geoffroy	Pinang, Singapore, Malayan Peninsula	Ternate, Java.
13	*Nyctinomus tenuis*, Horsfield	Malayan Peninsula	Borneo, Java, Sumatra.
14	*Taphozous melanopogon*, Temminck	Pulo Tíkus, Lancávy, Malayan Peninsula	Java, Caves of Kannera.
15	*Taphozous saccolaimus*, Temminck	Pinang	Celebes, Borneo, Java, Sumatra, Southern India.
16	*Rhinolophus affinis*, Horsfield	Pinang	Java.
17	*Hipposideros diadema*, Gray?	Pinang, Malayan Peninsula	Timor.
18	*Hipposideros nobilis*, Gray	Pinang, Malayan Peninsula	Amboyna, Timor, Java, Sumatra.
19	*Hipposideros vulgaris*, Gray	Pinang	Java.
20	*Hipposideros murinus*, Gray	Pinang.	Southern Mahratta Country, Nicobars.
21	*Hipposideros galeritus*, Cantor	Pinang.	
22	*Vespertilio adversus*, Horsfield?	Pinang	Java, Calcutta.

23	*Kirivoula picta,* Gray	Pinang	Borneo, Java, Sumatra.
24	*Kirivoula tenuis,* Gray.	Pinang	Borneo, Java, Sumatra.
25	*Trilatitus Horsfieldii,* Grav	Pinang	Java, Sumatra.
26	*Scotophilus Temminckii,* Gray	Malayan Peninsula and Islands	Timor, Borneo, Java, Sumatra, Calcutta, Pondicherry.
27	*Pteropus edulis,* Geoffroy	Malayan Peninsula and Islands	Java, Sumatra, Banda, Bengal, Assam.
28	*Cynopterus marginatus,* F. Cuvier	Malayan Peninsula and Islands	Java, Sumatra, Southern Mahratta country, Bengal, Nipal.
29	*Tupaia ferruginea,* Raffles	Pinang, Singapore, Malayan Peninsula	Borneo, Java, Sumatra.
30	*Gymnura Rafflesii,* Vigors and Horsfield	Malayan Peninsula, Singapore	Sumatra.
31	*Sorex murinus,* Linné	Pinang	Java, Sumatra.
32	*Helarctos malayanus,* Horsfield	Malayan Peninsula	Sumatra, Tenasserim, Assam, Nipal.
33	*Arctictis Binturong,* Fischer	Malayan Peninsula	Arracan, Tenasserim, Assam, Nipal, Bhotan.
34	*Putorius nudipes,* Fred. Cuvier	Malayan Peninsula	Borneo, Sumatra.
35	*Mustela flavigula,* Boddaert	Malayan Peninsula	Java, Sumatra, Nipal.
36	*Lutra Nair,* F. Cuvier	Malayan Peninsula	China, Bombay, Southern Mahratta Country
37	*Lutra Barang,* Raffles	Malayan Peninsula	Borneo, Sumatra.
38	*Aonyx leptonyx,* Gray	Malayan Peninsula, Singapore	Java, Sumatra, Nipal.
39	*Cuon primævus,* Hodgson	Malayan Peninsula	Bengal, Nipal.
40	*Viverra Zibetha,* Linné	Pinang, Singapore, Malayan Peninsula	Southern China, Siam, Bengal, Khasyah Hills, Nipal.
41	*Viverra Tangalunga,* Gray	Pinang, Singapore, Malayan Peninsula	Amboina, Celebes, Borneo, Philippine Islands, Sumatra.
42	*Viverricula malaccensis*	Malayan Peninsula, Singapore	China, Philippines, Java, Cochin China, Tenasserim, Bengal, Nipal, Hindoostan, Dukhun, Bombay.
43	*Prionodon gracilis,* Horsf.	Malayan Peninsula	Borneo, Java, Sumatra.
44	*Paguma leucomystax,* Gray ?	Malayan Peninsula, Singapore	Sumatra.
45	*Paguma trivirgata,* Gray	Malayan Peninsula, Singapore	Moluccas, Tenasserim.
46	*Paradoxurus musanga,* Gray	Pinang, Singapore, Malayan Peninsula	Timor, Borneo, Java, Sumatra.

47	Paradoxurus Derbyanus, Gray	Malayan Peninsula	Borneo.
48	Cynogale Bennettii, Gray	Malayan Peninsula	Borneo, Sumatra.
49	Herpestes javanicus, Desmarest	Penang, Malayan Peninsula	Java.
50	Herpestes auropunctatus, Hodgson	Malayan Peninsula	Bengal, Nipal, Scinde, Afghanistan.
51	Herpestes griseus, Desmarest	Malayan Peninsula	Bengal, Hindoostan, Scinde, Nipal.
52	Herpestes brachyurus, Gray	Malayan Peninsula	
53	Felis tigris, Linné	Malayan Peninsula	Ceylon, India.
54	Felis leopardus, Schreber	Malayan Peninsula	India.
55	Felis marmorata, Martin	Malayan Peninsula.	
56	Felis javanensis, Desmarest	Pinang, Malayan Peninsula	Java, Sumatra?
57	Felis planiceps, Vigors and Horsfield	Malayan Peninsula	Borneo, Sumatra.
58	Felis domestica.		
59	Sciurus bicolor, Sparrm.	Pinang, Malayan Peninsula	Borneo, Java, Sumatra, Siam, Tenasserim, Assam, Nipal.
60	Sciurus Rafflesii, Vigors and Horsfield	Malayan Peninsula	Borneo, Java, Canton Province.
61	Sciurus hippurus, I. Geoffroy	Malayan Peninsula	Java, Sumatra, Assam, Canton Province.
62	Sciurus vittatus, Raffles	Pinang, Singapore, Malayan Peninsula	Borneo, Java, Sumatra, Canton Province.
63	Sciurus nigrovittatus, Horsfield	Malayan Peninsula	Borneo, Java, Sumatra, Canton Province.
64	Sciurus tenuis, Horsfield	Malayan Peninsula, Singapore	Borneo, Java, Sumatra, Canton Province.
65	Sciurus laticaudatus, Diard. var.	Malayan Peninsula	
66	Pteromys nitidus, Geoffroy	Pinang, Singapore, Malayan Peninsula	Borneo, Java, Sumatra.
67	Sciuropterus Horsfieldii, Waterhouse	Malayan Peninsula	Java? Sumatra?
68	Sciuropterus genibarbis	Malayan Peninsula	Java.
69	Mus bandicota, Bechst	Pinang, Malayan Peninsula	Southern Mahratta Country, Bengal, Nipal.
70	Mus decumanus, Pallas	Cosmopolita.	
71	Mus setifer, Horsfield	Pinang	Borneo, Java, Sumatra, Van Diemen's Land.
72	Mus rufescens, Gray	Pinang	Dharwar, Madras, Bengal, Arracan.
73	Mus musculus, Linné	Pinang	
74	Rhizomys sumatrensis, Gray	Malayan Peninsula	China, Moulmein, Assam.
75	Hystrix longicauda, Marsden	Malayan Peninsula	Borneo, Java, Sumatra.

76	*Atherura fasciculata,* Cuv.	Pinang, Malayan Peninsula	Borneo, Java, Sumatra.
77	*Manis javanica,* Desmarest	Pinang, Malayan Peninsula	Borneo, Java, Sumatra.
78	*Elephas indicus,* Linné	Malayan Peninsula	Borneo, Burma, Siam, India, Ceylon.
79	*Sus indicus,* Schinz	Pinang, Singapore, Lancavy, Malayan Peninsula	Bengal, Nipal, Southern Mahratta Country.
80	*Sus scrofa,* var. Linné	Malayan Peninsula and Islands	China.
81	*Rhinoceros unicornis,* Linné	Malayan Peninsula	Bengal, Assam, Nipal.
82	*Rhinoceros sondaicus,* Cuv.	Malayan Peninsula	Java.
83	*Rhinoceros sumatranus,* Raffles	Malayan Peninsula	Sumatra, Tenasserim.
84	*Tapirus malayanus,* Raffles	Malayan Peninsula	Borneo, Sumatra.
85	*Equus caballus,* Linné	Introduced in the Malayan Peninsula and Islands.	
86	*Tragulus Kanchil,* Gray	Pinang, Singapore, Lancavy, Malayan Peninsula	Java, Sumatra.
87	*Tragulus javanicus,* Pallas	Malayan Peninsula	Borneo, Sumatra, Java.
88	*Styloceros Muntjak,* Ham. Smith	Malayan Peninsula	Borneo, Banka, Java, Sumatra, Tenasserim, Nipal, Assam, Bengal, Southern Mahratta, Dukhun.
89	*Axis maculatus,* H. Smith	Malayan Peninsula, Pinang	Sumatra, Bengal, Assam, Nipal, Southern Mahratta Country, Ceylon.
90	*Rusa equina,* H. Smith	Pinang, Malayan Peninsula	Borneo, Sumatra.
91	*Panolia acuticornis,* Gray ?	Malayan Peninsula	
92	*Næmorhedus sumatrensis,* Ham. Smith	Malayan Peninsula	Sumatra, Tenasserim.
93	*Bos gour,* Trail	Malayan Peninsula	Tenasserim, Hindoostan, Assam, Nipal, Southern Mahratta Country.
94	*Bos taurus,* var. *indicus,* Lin.	Introduced in the Malayan countries.	
95	*Bubalus arnee,* H. Smith	Ditto.	
96	*Halicore indicus,* F. Cuv.	Singapore, Malayan Peninsula	Philippines, Moluccas, Sunda Islands, Sumatra, New Holland, Red Sea.
97	*Delphinus plumbeus,* Dussumier	Malayan seas	Bay of Bengal.

Note to Gen. NYCTINOMUS (p. 9).—A male *Nyctonomus bengalensis,* Geoffroy (syn. *Vespertilio plicatus,* Buchan ; *N. bengalensis,* Geoffroy apud Horsfield ; *Dysopes plicatus,* Temminck apud Schinz), examined after the catalogue had passed through the press, exhibited a true cæcum. The entire length of the animal was 4⅜ inches, of which the tail measured 1⅝ inch. Extent of the flying membrane, 1 foot 0⅝ inch.

Length of the small intestine . . . 9⅛ inches.
„　„　large ditto . . . . . 4⅛ „
„　„　cæcum . . . . . . 0³⁄₁₆ inch.

The cæcum is crescent-shaped, with the concave curvature firmly adhering to the external surface of the small intestine. The convex curvature presents near the apex a sacculated appearance ; the membranes are thickened. Where the cæcum joins, the small intestine and the rectum are narrowed.

FORT WILLIAM, *Dec.* 11, 1846.

XXXVI.

ON THE LOCAL AND RELATIVE GEOLOGY OF SINGAPORE ;

INCLUDING NOTICES OF SUMATRA, THE MALAY PENINSULA, ETC.

By J. R. LOGAN, Esq.

["Journal of the Asiatic Society of Bengal," vol. xvi. pp. 519–57, 667–84.]

THE following paper was sent to the Asiatic Society of Bengal in January 1846. The delay which has taken place in its publication in their Journal enables the writer to append an extract from a letter to Professor Ansted, in which he has given a summary of the result of his subsequent observations made in localities more favourable for geological inquiries than those to which his attention had been confined when the paper was written. It may save the reader some trouble if he be furnished at once with the key to the theoretical discrepancies which may be noticed between the paper and the letter. He thinks it better to do this, and to leave the former as it stands, with all its faults, rather than to alter it in conformity with his more matured but still imperfect views. The geology of every fresh region has to be worked out amidst doubts and errors, and a record of the stages through which its theory, if at all new, passes in its progress towards complete truth, may often serve ultimately as its best demonstration, because it will show that it was not hastily adopted, but gradually grew out of a long-continued and defeated effort to assign to every new phenomenon a place in familiar systems.

The principal result at which the writer had arrived when the paper was written was the opinion advanced hypothetically in it, that the southern extremity of the peninsula, &c., had been ruptured and upraised by subterraneous forces, and that through the rocks so affected ferruginous gases, &c., had been emitted. The action of these gases on the rocks had, amongst other transformations, produced laterite. The paper was written under the impression that the formation of plutonic rocks and plutonic action in sedimentary rocks were confined to deep subterranean levels (see the writings of Mr. Lyell and other English geologists). Hence it seemed necessary to believe that the superficial igneous action with which the paper was mainly concerned was wholly unconnected with the granitic and other plutonic rocks of the district; subsequent investigation of some of the best developments of these led to the conviction that the Tartarean theory was inapplicable to them at least. The disturbed sedimentary rocks were re-examined free from the bias of that theory, and it then appeared that, while the evidence in favour of the metamorphic origin of the laterites, &c., was so strong and varied that it might be now recorded as a demonstrated fact, there were no apparent obstacles to the reception of the simple hypothesis that they were caused by plutonic agency, and that the plutonic rocks of the districts were themselves the agents of the alteration or the effects of one and the same hypogene agency. This hypothesis embraces at once the whole region of elevation in which Singapore is situated, with all the plutonic, volcanic, and metamorphic phenomena which it exhibits. It refers the whole to one cause operating throughout a long period of time, and which has not yet entirely ceased to operate, as the volcanic emission of Sumatra and the vibrations of the whole region, from time to time, and the thermal springs of Sumatra and the peninsula, constantly testify to us. This cause is the existence of an internal plutonic intumescence or nucleus, which has slowly swollen up, fracturing the sedimentary strata, saturating and seaming them with its exhalations, and as it forced itself up beneath them and through the gorges and fissures, at once upheaving them and feeding on their substance, till in many places it pressed and eat through them to the refrigerating surface, and rose, congealing, into the air or sea. It is this latter circumstance that distinguishes the region from all those which have been observed by European geologists, and it is this singularly high level which the plutonic reduction has reached that explains the extraordinary appearances which the unreduced superficial rocks have so often assumed. The metamorphosed rocks of Europe evinced a deep subterranean saturation with plutonic exhalations, and European geologists concluded that plutonic action was necessarily deeply subterraneous. But here, I think, we find a subaërial or subaqueous plutonic activity; and where the plutonic level has not reached that of the pre-existing rocks, a new kind of metamorphism appropriate to the new conditions under which the plutonic exhalations have operated.

The interest which the discussions respecting laterite have given to that rock tends to invest it with undue importance geologically. The ferruginous emissions have affected all rocks indiscriminately, and their action on sandstones, grits, and conglomerates is as well marked as that on clays, marls, and shales, although the latter only produces proper laterite. Even in the clays, laterite denotes one only of many degrees and forms of alteration. To expose the origin of these rocks and its unity, to record the cause of the difficulties which have been presented, and to distinguish them from true metamorphic rocks, I would propose, avoiding any new technical names, to term them simply the *iron-masked* rocks of the Indo-Australian regions. This term will include the principal or plutonically ferruginated rocks, which, without being either completely reduced or metamorphosed, have been either wholly disguised or partially altered by ferruginous emissions, which have saturated them in the mass, or only affected them in fissures and seams, or been interfused between portions of the rocks not actually separated by fissures, but intersected by planes of mere discontinuity, the sides of which have an imperfect cohesion, or having a common border of inferior density and increased porosity caused either by interruptions in the original deposition of the matter of the rock or by unequal stretching or incipient cleavage. The term may be also extended perhaps to those sedimentary beds in which the iron saturation, although coeval with the deposit of the other constituents of the rock, has served to obscure or conceal their true nature as well as the derivation of the beds themselves. These beds appear to have been sometimes formed by superficial layers of gravel, &c., being permeated by iron solutions. With these must not be confounded the broad bands lying over and beside the heads of iron-masked dykes, and which, having been in a loose, gravelly, or fragmentary state at the time when the plutonic emissions passed through them, became cemented into hard, and occasionally scorious, ferruginated conglomerates, &c., and are therefore proper plutonically iron-masked rocks.

Before entering on a detailed account of the mineralogical features of Singapore, it will be convenient to bring into a preliminary paper some discussions of a theoretical nature, which, if not thus separated from the former, might in the sequel occasion frequent interruptions and some confusion. A brief sketch of the topography of the island will suffice as a basis for the remarks which follow it.

The island is of an irregular figure, when correctly laid down (for the published maps, with the exception of Mr. Thomson's, are very incorrect), resembling a bat, the head being at Tanjong Sinoko, in the old strait, the tail at Tullah Blanga, or rather Blakan Mati ; the western wing being fully expanded, and the eastern a little retracted. Its greatest length from Pulo Campong or Point Macalister on the west to Tanjong Changai on the east— *i.e.,* between the tips of the wings—is twenty-one miles. Its greatest breadth from T. Sinoko to T. Blanga coast—*i.e.,* from the head to the tail—is twelve miles. Its superficial extent is roughly calculated at 200 square miles.

The town of Singapore, to start from the best known point, is situated at the south-western extremity of a flat alluvial tract, of which the greatest length in a straight line near the sea-beach is about six miles, and the greatest breadth inland about two and a half miles. Three well-marked deposits occur in this flat. A stiff clay of a greyish hue, becoming in some places darker and even blackish ; a whitish, greyish, or yellowish sand ; and a vegetable deposit, consisting, where most recent, of fragments of wood or masses of aquatic plants more or less decomposed, and, where older, of a soft peaty matter passing into a black mud. The mode in which these beds have been deposited will be described hereafter. The west side of this plain is marked by low rounded hillocks, separated by openings on the same level as the plain. On following these in a north-westerly direction, the former are found to be the extremities of distinct ranges of hills, and the latter the mouths of valleys between them, the principal extending about six miles inland. The largest valley, along which there is a public road, terminates a little to the south of a group of hills called Bukit Temah, the summit of which is 530 feet above the level of the sea, and the highest point in the island. From this group the valley and the stream which drains it borrow their name. The coast of Singapore to the S.W. of this valley also follows a N.W. direction. The intervening space is occupied towards the sea by a prominent range of hills rising abruptly to a height of 300 feet at Tullah Blanga, which has lately been made the signal station. Towards the Bukit Temah valley a broad irregular range of hills is united apparently with the Tullah Blanga range on the N.W., and as it proceeds the S.E. separates from it and gives room for a broad swampy flat, from which the Singapore River flows. Nearer town the range bifurcates, one of the forks terminating in Government Hill and the other in Mount Sophia. These hills approach close to each other, but proceeding inland, the two divisions of the range draw further back, and a secondary valley of considerable breadth and about two miles in length is formed. The range on the N.E. of Bukit Temah valley springs from Bukit Temah, and terminates in a low broad sandy elevation which slopes almost insensibly till it emerges in the plain. It is in some places about one and a half miles broad. The configuration of the range—and most of the others have many features in common with it—may be partially observed in proceeding up the Bukit Temah valley. A succession of low hills present their rounded ends stretching into the valley, which expands into the concave or sinuous hollows between them. The lateral valleys thus formed are of various figures and extent. Many resemble a horse-shoe or amphitheatre. The upper extremities of most are of this shape, and similar indentations occur in the course of the more protracted, at the necks connecting the different hillocks which form their sides. When we strike across the range we are at first confused by the number of hillocks or hollows only partially cleared of jungle; but under patient observation they gradually assume a certain order; about the centre of the range the ground is a comparatively elevated and broad tract, but very irregular in its configuration. All these irregularities, however, it is probable, have relation to the lateral ranges. These are seen to branch off to the north and south in a series of hillocks joined to each other by their sides and sometimes by an elongated neck. Towards the valley they often bifurcate, one limb sometimes taking a direction parallel to the range and then sweeping round and expanding into one of the broad hillocks whose ends approach the public road. The peculiar character of the topography of the country arises from the multitude and individual smallness of the hills, and the circumstance of the valleys which penetrate between the principal ranges and their branches, being, except towards the centres of the ranges, perfectly flat, and very little above the level of the sea, so that the winding outlines of the bases of the hills are nearly as distinctly marked as if they sunk into the level sheet of a lake. We have, in fact, regular mountain ranges in miniature, and so symmetrical, with all the apparent irregularity, that if the highest or summit lines of the ranges and their lateral members were correctly laid down on a map, they would present no remote resemblance to the section of a tree. Beyond the last-mentioned range another long valley occurs.* The stream Balastier, which flows through it, has its rise in Bukit Temah. The further or N.E. side of this valley is formed by the Kallang range of hills, the upper extremity of which is also connected with Bukit Temah : its lower division is penetrated by a long secondary valley. One of its summits rises considerably above the general level of the hills.

* For much information respecting these difficultly accessible valleys I am indebted to Mr. Thomson, the able and indefatigable surveyor to Government for the Straits.

Beyond it the valley of the Kallang River stretches inland. This valley has not been examined up to the top, but it is believed the river rises to the north of Bukit Temah in a continuation of that range. All the preceding ranges terminate in the plain or to the west of it, and the Kallang, Balastier, Bukit Temah, and Singapore rivers all cross the plain, converge towards the town—the three former uniting their waters—and flow through it. The next range beyond the Kallang valley is the central range or backbone of the eastern part of the island. It does not terminate at the line where those already described sink into the plain, but continues its course to the eastward, sending out lateral ranges, the southern and western extremities of which form the boundaries of the plain. This range terminates at the Red Cliffs. All the hills on the east and N.E. sides of the island appear to be expansions of it. The valleys between the lateral ranges are bolder and deeper than those in the ranges first described, owing to the hills being generally higher and steeper. This range is connected with the Bukit Temah range. In its central parts it displays broad undulating tracts on a larger scale than the other ranges. Amongst the multitude of valleys which its branches include there is one on the northern side of some size, in which the Serangoon stream rises. This valley seems to be a peaty swamp. It passes into a broad tract of mangrove jungle, where the stream is lost in a creek which opens into the old straits of Singapore. Other streams fall into the straits from this range. This principal is the Soongie Saletar, which appears to flow through a long valley between a branch of this range and another range proceeding from the Bukit Temah group in a northerly direction. The western side of the island consists of several ranges radiating apparently from the Bukit Temah group, and penetrated by valleys, some of them, such as that of the Kranjee, which flows northward to the old strait, and the Joorong which flows southward to the Salat Samboolan, being of considerable length and terminating in broad creeks intersecting mangrove swamps. Between some of the ranges, the only wide flattish tracts in the island which are not alluvial are found. The lower parts of the valleys are mostly swampy, consisting of sand, clay, and black peaty mud; of the latter there are considerable tracts constantly moist and exhibiting an extraordinary rankness of vegetation. Looking on one of these swamps, covered with tall but slender trees, and dense underwood growing up rapidly, and from the looseness of the deep bed of black vegetable matter—the accumulated remains of their short-lived predecessors—destined soon to fall in their turn, and considering the deposits of clay and sand which accompany and give rise to it, it is impossible to doubt that we see nature repeating the precise process by which the materials of most of the ancient carboniferous strata were brought together. Towards the sea these forest marshes give place to mangrove swamps. An intelligent Chinese Gambier planter compares Singapore, not inaptly, if the eastern part of the island be excluded, to an open umbrella, of which Bukit Temah is the top and the various rivers the ribs. If we suppose the island to have been formed of a somewhat brittle material, and a strong blow from beneath to have struck it at Bukit Temah, from which cracks radiated in different directions, dividing or bifurcating in their progress, a rude idea of the lines of hills may be formed ; or if we view the island from west to east, our old comparison to the section of a tree would serve us best. Bukit Temah and the adjoining hills form the stole from which one main trunk, about twelve miles in length, extends to the Red Cliffs with numerous branches. Several smaller trunks rise on the south side of the main trunk, and extend for about six miles in a S.E. direction, also sending out a multitude of small branches. To the west the roots radiate to different parts of the coast, the tap-root being about seven miles long.

The hills of the first and second ranges in the order in which they are above noticed consist chiefly of sandstone (fine-grained, gritty, and conglomeritic) and shale strata. Towards the eastern extremities of the two next ranges similar rocks are observed. Further on, soft clays of various hues, but mostly mottled white and red or purplish, passing into a soil of different shades of red, yellowish-red, and brownish-red, are observed near the surface, and occasionally protruding blocks of sienite and greenstone occur. The hills of the eastern side of the island seem to be principally sandstone with slight traces of shale. The western side is also for the most part sandstone and shale. At the N.E. extremity granite or sienite appears, and it is also seen at several places along the N. and N.W. coast.

The superficial deposits which occur at various places are very remarkable. On some hills a red stiff clay resembling laterite is found. On many, imbedded in clay of different red and brownish hues, in irregular sheets or in thin seams, occur blocks of a ferruginous clay, rock, or smaller stones and pebbles of various kinds and sizes. These will best be described hereafter by selecting particular localities where they abound.

I now proceed to notice the different hypotheses that have been or may be suggested to account for these appearances. Of the alluvial plains and valleys which ramify through the island in all directions I need say nothing here, as they, in exposed beds at least, have all, or nearly all, been formed subsequent to the hills and their superjacent deposits, and are separated from the latest accessions of matter which these received at a period when they formed a multitude of little bays and long narrow inlets of the sea.

The first class of the hypotheses that may be offered in explanation of the superficial formations of Singapore embraces those that contemplate merely the position, external appearance, and size of the detached rock fragments.

1. ALLUVIAL HYPOTHESIS.

Of these, the first supposes the blocks, gravel, &c., to be the débris of older rocks deposited in the sea before the extrusion of the hills. If it be conceived that the elevation of the hills above the level of the sea was the same act with the protrusion of the strata of which they are composed from their previous horizontal bed to their present inclined position, we are met by the fact that the superficial deposits are not in layers conformable to these strata, but are spread over their uplifted edges. If, again, it be supposed that the hills were formed under water, and that after the accumulation of the gravel, &c., upon them, the platform from which they rise was elevated so as to cause them to emerge from the sea, we are met by other insuperable objections. Of these it is only here necessary to specify one, although looking to single limited localities the gravel deposits appear to be regularly disposed like beds derived from currents ; when we compare one hill with another, we observe far too much irregularity to allow this idea to be tenable.

2. DILUVIAL HYPOTHESIS.

As we extend our observations this irregularity is seen to be so great that we are irresistibly led to conjecture that its causes were diluvial instead of alluvial. In many places rock fragments of all sizes are confusedly intermixed with loose clay or sand, so that if due to aqueous action it must have been of an extraordinary and violent nature thus to have borne along rapidly masses of matter containing large blocks, and deposited them in such confusion, and that often on the summits of hills. A continued diluvial action of variable force might also account for the large quantities of rounded pebbly-looking stones, and the broad thin beds of smaller gravel-like stones that occur. Closer investigation, however, seems to discover an unanswerable argument against a diluvial theory, in the fact that the larger rock fragments, and even the gravel, differ in different localities, often even when these adjoin each other, and that it has always been found that they have a certain correspondence with or relation to the subjacent rocks where these have been exposed. No decided boulder or drift has yet been noticed.

Colonel Low appears to have considered the scoriaceous ferruginous rock as boulders, but he gives no reason for this opinion. The gravel he refers to the concretionary tendency of soils impregnated with iron. I need not stop here to remark upon these evidently hastily formed views.*

3. DECOMPOSITION OF ROCKS IN SITU.

This, which is the hypothesis that next most naturally arises, would embrace many of the facts that are inconsistent with the sedimentary and diluvial suppositions, such as the local character of the rock fragments. The outcrops of the strata, which are generally highly inclined, would under meteoric influence, down to a certain line of depth which would descend with the denudation of the surface, suffer different changes according to the nature of the rock. The harder sandstones and shales would split and break down into irregular fragments. The softer sandstones, clays, and shales—and of the latter especially the finely laminated beds —would, under the combined chemical and mechanical influences of the air, rain, rapid transitions of temperature, &c., lose their distinctive original characters, and gradually become uniform masses of sandy or clayey soils. Every heavy fall of rain would wash away the more superficial particles. According to the declination of the sides of the hills, fragments of rock of different sizes would be carried down by the pressure of water-moved soil and gravelly fragments. Where the hills were steep, larger blocks, from the gradual loosening of their beds, would descend to lower levels by their own gravity, assisted by similar pressure from above. The summits and ridges of the hills would be most exposed to the action of sun and rain, but generally least so to the denuding power of gravity. Where the soil was loose sand, or where there were narrow summits, the process of denudation would be more active than elsewhere. The soil as it was formed would disappear, and only fragments of rock be left where the latter was of a nature to yield with difficulty, slowly and superficially, to decomposition. Where the fragments pulverized more quickly, some soil would generally be found, always drawing additions from the rocks, but always a prey to the rains.

These considerations certainly explain the present appearance of many of the hills, and in every locality phenomena occur evidently due to the forces of which I have been writing. Ridges and summits are often found consisting almost entirely of rock fragments, and it might seem that these forces alone would be adequate causes for their occurrence. But on hills with extensive flattish summits, beds of fragments, sometimes large, sometimes of all sizes mixed, sometimes uniformly small and gravel-like,

---

* I cannot mention Colonel Low, during so many years of official toil almost the solitary votary of science and oriental literature in the Straits Settlements, without expressing the hope that he will not long withhold from this Journal the fruits of his present "learned leisure."

lying under or in the soil at various depths, from an inch to many feet below the surface, are frequently discovered by sections for roads and pits for planting spice trees, &c. It is obvious that the hypothesis which I am now considering will not explain such cases.

There is another phenomenon of frequent occurrence connected with the position of fragmentary rocks which this hypothesis ought to include if it be made the foundation of any general theory. In sections across strata they are almost invariably seen to be more or less curved as they approach the surface. Before reaching it, however, they sometimes gradually, but often abruptly, lose their compact form, and become masses of fragments. In some cases these are almost insensibly mingled with the superincumbent soil till all trace of the stratum disappears. But it is not uncommon to see the curve pass into a line more or less horizontal, and even bent downwards, and the fragments streaming away as it were in a layer of which the direction seems to have no relation to the parent stratum, but which generally possesses or approaches to parallelism with the plane of the surface. It is true that of some of these cases the hypothesis which we are at present pursuing might seem to afford a solution. Thus, suppose a thin layer of hard sandstone to rest on a bed of soft sandy clay or unlaminated shale, both inclined and having their outcrop on the slope of a hill, a certain depth from the surface of the slope, would be subject to the action of meteoric forces which would cause the sandstone to break up into fragments, and the sandy clay to become loose and open. The sandstone rubble, if heavy, might possibly tend to descend or settle in a perpendicular line *through* the upper pulverulent to the lower and more compact soil, and at all events, as the soil below it was carried away, the rubble would descend along the line of the slope, the heavier fragments remaining at and near the point of outcrop, those of medium size streaming further down the slope, and the smallest borne away with the fine sand and clay to lower levels; the possibility of the existence of such lines of rubble, their breadth down the slope from the line of outcrop, and the quantity and size of the fragments being always determined by the texture of the recipient bed of clay or sand, and the declivity of the hill. Where the slope of the hill consisted of a succession of similar layers and beds, the lower layers of rubble would, in course of time and in favourable positions, become covered with soil brought down from above. There are undoubtedly cases which, if taken by themselves, this explanation will satisfy. But when we seek to convert this hypothesis into a general rule we are at once met by numerous discordant appearances. Thus, of the extensive layers of rubble or gravel-like fragments beneath a thick bed of clay which, as before mentioned, are found on broad even summits of hills and ridges, there are many where the clay is too compact and aluminous, or the rubble too fine for the latter to have descended from the surface of the former, and where there are no adjacent higher levels from which the former could have been degraded and superimposed upon the latter. There are other allied cases too which simple atmospherical causes will not account for, and which bring us to the next hypothesis—that of

4. EARTHQUAKES.

The instances alluded to are where the heads of the strata are not merely converted into rubble and bent in the line of slope, but where they are in zigzag, crooked, or sinuous lines; where adjacent layers are differently and irregularly deflected out of their planes; where the rubble is here in large pieces lying in the direction of the proper plane or of a regular curve from it, and there shattered into ·a confused mass of small fragments, sometimes much thicker and sometimes much thinner than the unaltered layer itself; or where fragments of one layer are intermixed with those of an adjacent one, detached pieces of a sandstone layer, for instance, imbedded in a layer of clay above it, or portions of both layers confusedly mingled till all trace of their lines of demarcation is lost.

It is clear that no ordinary mechanical operations caused by atmospherical forces could have produced such results, and that violent convulsive movements of the earth have left these records. In the slight earthquakes felt at Penang in 1843 it was remarked that the residents on the hills described their effects differently from the residents on the plain, or in language more exaggerated. In Belmont House, which is situated on the summit of a peaked hill rising freely out of the Pentland chain, the tremor was particularly strong. Upon general mechanical principles it is evident that the shocks will be most severely felt wherever the rocks acted on are freest. Through a dense homogeneous mass extending uniformly in all directions, equable undulations and vibrations may pass without disturbing the internal arrangement, because the motive force will meet with an equal resistance throughout. But where the mass acted on suddenly changes from a dense to a lighter rock, fractures and other internal disturbances will follow according to the intensity of the force, and where the mass of rocks is met externally by the rare elastic mass of the atmosphere, the resistance in that direction being removed *per saltum*, the general centrifugal tendency which will be impressed by the nether forces, even when their proper direction is more horizontal than vertical, will cause the upper rock to a certain depth to be fractured, loosened, and expanded, the external fragments and particles being perhaps quite free, and even projected. In this condition the whole superficial mass will readily yield to continuing vibratory action, and any or all of the phenomena above described may be the result. It is a further argument in favour of mechanical convulsions of considerable violence and irregularity, that although the general dip of the strata of Singapore be from westerly to easterly, cases are found on a hill resting on the same apparent base, with an adjoining one where the general rule operates, having its strata inclined from east to west, and even in the same hill particular sides or outlying ridges or spurs present deviations both in the direction and in the angle of the dip.

5. Volcanic Action.

Hitherto we have remarked no phenomena that may not be referred to the ordinary mechanical or chemical forces acting at the surface of the earth, or to critical mechanical disturbances: But I have now to notice a large and varied class of facts which require different forces to be introduced. These facts are so numerous, so constant in their occurrence over every part of the island which is open to examination, and not less than elsewhere in those parts from which the observations of writers on the geology or mineralogy of Singapore have been drawn, that it is difficult to conceive through what fatality they have hitherto for the most part escaped notice or been passed over as unimportant. The most obvious of these facts are dykes and veins of igneous rocks, masses *in situ* and scattered fragments of rocks, such as sandstone, clays, shales, granite, &c., altered by the action of fire ; rocks in veins and joints often highly indurated, whereby sandstone has acquired sometimes a cellular structure, and at other times externally a honeycombed appearance ; congeries of curved, zigzag, and radiating veins in sandstone, clays and shales, filled with crystallizations, and both from their own appearance and the alteration in the rock in which they are found showing chemical or electrical action of a volcanic nature ; the presence of sulphur accompanying anthracite in shales denigrated and rendered fuliginous by fire ; the slaggy appearance of many rocks and fragments which are often covered externally by a shining black, bluish-black, or dull iridescent varnish or glaze; the scorious appearance of others, many being mere cinders; the abundant presence of oxides of iron, and particularly their intensity in those places where the other evidences of igneous action are most marked, and their absence where these are entirely wanting. It is impossible to refer these facts, and others of an analogous character which will be mentioned in a future paper in the description of particular localities, to any but volcanic causes. The reddish, reddish-brown, and reddish-black rocks which are found so abundantly have been noticed by Lieutenant Newbold, Colonel Low, and others. The general name of laterite has been sometimes applied to them. Colonel Low uses the terms "iron-clay," "iron-stone," and "iron-ore." The red soils have been in like manner called laterite or iron-soils. Both terms appear to be objectionable. Laterite is a particular species of ferruginous clay which indurates on exposure to the atmosphere, like many other rocks ; it ought to be restricted to the clay to which it was assigned by Dr. Hamilton, and not indiscriminately applied to every new rock strongly marked by oxides of iron. With respect to the term iron-clay or clay-iron-stone, it has not yet been shown that any of the proper argillaceous iron-ores, into the composition of which carbonic acid enters so largely, are found in Singapore. If there are any, they have been disguised and changed by heat, decomposing into peroxides. The fact, however, is, that these so-called laterites and iron-ores, externally as to colour and form differing little if at all, prove often on examination to be only fragments of the common stratified rocks, sometimes calcined, sometimes indurated, and sometimes partially fused by heat. We cannot, therefore, resort to a prevalence either of laterite or iron-ores to explain the geology of the island, and are by the rocks, which have been so designated, led back to volcanic causes.*

Such a comparatively small portion of Singapore has yet in any way been laid bare, and of the accessible parts, with certain

---

* *Laterite.*—Many of the clayey hills here appear to me to be decomposed sienite, sometimes unaltered by supervening volcanic action, but generally partaking in the metamorphism which the matter of most of the elevated land has suffered from that cause. May I venture to suggest that the hypothesis which is developed in this paper for Singapore might, if applied to the laterite of India, perhaps explain its origin, and in doing so to a certain extent also reconcile the conflicting opinions that have been maintained regarding it ? All that I have read of the great laterite formations of the south of India, and which extend to the heart of Bengal, where they are described by Dr. Buchanan, leads to the conclusion that they do not consist of purely volcanic, sedimentary, or decomposed matter, but what I have termed semi-volcanic. The same formation is found at Malacca and analogous deposits at Singapore, and both inseparably associated and evidently contemporaneous with altered rocks of the kind previously noticed. If we conceive an area with trap, granite, sandstone, shale, &c., exposed at the surface (in the atmosphere or in the sea), and partly decomposed or disintegrated, to be subjected to a peculiar species of minor volcanic action like that which is described in this paper (*the distinctive phenomenon probably of one and the same geological epoch*), the result would be that, with the occasional exception of matter ejected from no great depth, and some dykes and veins, the previous soft surface rocks would be merely altered or metamorphosed by heat and impregnated with iron, derived perhaps from the basaltic and other ferriferous rocks through which the discharged steam, gases, and water had passed in their ascent. Whether the action took place under or above the sea would be determined by the presence or absence of the ordinary marks of oceanic denudation.

When clays strongly ferruginous, and soft from saturation with water, are dried, the iron previously held in solution by the water is deposited between the particles, and cements them into a hard compact rock. Hence the induration of laterite clays on exposure to the atmosphere.

exceptions, so little is open to inspection save the mere surface, that had my examination of the most favourable localities of the latter been much more minute and careful than it has been, I should still have hesitated to combine the results into any general hypothesis. But as such an hypothesis has been forced upon me while following up my inquiries, and no facts have hitherto been noticed to which it is irreconcilable, I shall endeavour to explain it, leaving to future observations to build it into a theory or reject it as a fancy. And as I shall proceed in subsequent papers to furnish detailed accounts of different localities, the reader will be enabled to draw his own conclusions.

The general direction of the elevatory force to which the hills of Singapore and the neighbouring islands owe their origin, was from W. by S. to E. by N., since their dip is generally in or near that direction. Although the undulations or upheavings had this general tendency, the causes to which they were due must have been of a somewhat irregular nature, at one time producing a superficial effect, either uniform in its character or small in degree, and at a another time increasing in violence, and at particular points causing convulsive elevations of the rocks in the form of hills, frequently in undulating ridges and chains, the linear directions of which were, it may be, determined by a pre-imposed tendency to fracture, as will be noticed in the sequel. This force was apparently of a volcanic, or what, to distinguish it from concentrated well-developed volcanic action, may be called a semivolcanic nature, producing great heat at particular places, which sometimes merely indurated or calcined the softer strata and reddened the superjacent soil, but often in steam or gases, and occasionally in mud or semi-fused rock burst through them, or found a vent in fissures caused by ruptures during the process of elevation. When the heat was most intense, fused rocks or semifused fragments were cast up through these vents. As its intensity decreased fragments less altered and masses of clay and sand were ejected. The volcanic steam, gases, or fluids were charged with iron, which left strong marks of its presence wherever these were most active, rendering most of the fused and semi-fused rocks, in dykes or ejected above the surface, highly ferruginous and impregnating all the softer adjacent rocks.

In some places the force, although of unusual violence, was at the surface chiefly mechanical, rending solid sandstones and tossing up and mingling the fragments with masses of soft clays and shales. Thus in some parts of Government Hill and the adjoining hill (Mt. Sophia) large angular blocks of solid sandstone, some from 600 to 800 cubit feet in bulk, are found at the surface, and at various depths beneath it, in a confused mass of clays and shales. In the same hills, however, there were also subsequently formed volcanic fissures, through which torrified rocks were ejected into the air, and strewed over the surface, so as in some places to form a thick bed over the disrupted sandstone, &c.

This extreme degree of local mechanical violence, unaccompanied by simultaneous igneous action reaching the surface, is, however, rare, and may have been in some measure caused by a greater thickness and compactness in the resisting rock. But in general the unheaving of the hills has been attended with a violent agitation or tremor, producing the phenomena alluded to in a former page as due to concussion.

From what has been said it will be seen that the volcanic forces were not concentrated at one or two points, and of comparatively great power, so as to form regular craters of eruption or to elevate rocks to a great height, but that they extended over a considerable area, and that their intensity and mode of action varied greatly at different places.

Amongst the most common volcanic products is one, small in size, and varying in its character from common indurated argillaceous and lithomargic to porcellanous and jaspidious, which occurs in very singular forms—vermicular, pseudo-coralloidal, columnar,* and frequently resembling pieces of ginger-root, externally smooth, granulated, corrugated, reticularly fibrous, &c. These are the compact forms, but there often occur vesicular, or rather rudely ramose cavities descending between the short thick irregular branches towards the centre, the branches being themselves also sometimes perforated.

Another product is a small smooth faintly shining black stone like a fine gravel.

At other places a gravel similar in shape, but with a brownish or chestnut-coloured coat or enamel, occurs. These latter products may readily be mistaken for water-worn gravel, especially as they often occur in broad thin beds, but on closer examination it is clear they are of volcanic origin.

All the various forms of ejected substances met with are due, I conceive, in some degree to differences in the original mineral ingredients of the rocks, but chiefly to the inequality of torrefaction, and the circumstance of the heated, fused, or semi-fused substances cooling in the air or in mud or loose sand or clay.

At an early stage in my inquiries I was led to think that the causes of the eruptions were in part what have been called pseudo-volcanic, and if coal shall be discovered it will then become a question whether many of the geological phenomena of Singapore are not due to volcanic action giving rise to and accompanying

---

* Amongst the common large slags, which are generally of irregular rounded shapes, I have occasionally seen one agreeing in form with those small columnar stones and externally rugose and roughly fibrous.   In fact, one may say it is the same as one magnified in bulk from a few cubic inches to 10 or 15 cubic feet, and with all its characters rendered coarse in proportion.

the conflagration of coal-beds. This would account for the paucity of proper volcanic products at the surface, and the abundance of merely altered fragments agreeing in character with the existing superficial strata, and of slaggy and scorious rocks, of which the materials, with the exception of the oxides of iron, might have been derived from similar strata at no great depth. The iron might, on this supposition, have been supplied by beds of ore occurring amongst the carboniferous rocks.

At present this view is inadmissible; and it would still remain so even if no other hypothesis derived from analogy were probable. But there have been many volcanoes without streams of lava, from which earth and altered rocks, gases, steam, water, or mud have been ejected, and there are abundant marks of igneous action throughout the series of stratified rocks, proving how frequently volcanic forces have operated from beneath, often without reaching the surface at all, and at other times producing mechanical, igneous, or electrical changes in the superficial rocks, unaccompanied by the more marked phenomena of proper volcanoes.

But the absence of such products in Singapore is not universal, nor are there wanting proofs of the direct connection of the superficial igneous action with a great nether fountain of volcanic power. It is clear that the action reached below the stratified rocks, for in some of the hills near town I have discovered fragments of unaltered sienite, and on one, a large block of sienite passing into basalt, which may either be an ejected fragment, or the protruded summit of a continuous mass, is now being quarried by Chinese. In the Bukit Temah group solid masses of sienite are exposed, and appear to compose a large part of one of the hills. At some places I found it passing into basalt. That the elevation of the sienite and basalt was contemporaneous with the production of the ordinary volcanic or igneous phenomena of Singapore (if the basalt itself was not also then formed) is, to say the least, highly probable. Not only the sides in general, but the summits of the hill, consist of a thick mass of soft ferruginous clay or mould, holding large quantities of the common igneous rocks found elsewhere, but often bearing marks of a more intense igneous action. Thus on the same side of the hill where the sienite and basalt are laid bare, I found, in contact with soft sandstone, a piece of compact, dull, igneous rock of a light yellowish-brown colour, with veins of a violet colour and vesicles whose sides were similar. At the plane of contact the rock changed into a dark green translucent glass, which included some small opaque white specks. Within the glass the igneous rock for a narrow space was finely vesicular, and violet-coloured like veins and some grains of the sandstone were scattered through this band. The opaque spots in the glass were evidently included grains of sand semi-fused at their edges. This specimen is identical in character with some products of proper volcanoes. In the slopes to the west of Bukit Temah, which are covered with thick beds of clays and sands, included layers, composed of fragments of torrified granite, occur.

Many of the islands and rocks near Singapore exhibit most decisive proofs of volcanic convulsions. Thus in a reef of sandstone rocks lying between the island of Blakan Mati and Pulo Sikijang, a black ferruginous rock has been obtruded as a lava through seams and fissures in the sandstone, and at some places has spread over that rock and boiled up above it, assuming fantastic shapes; the sandstone is altered by heat in the same manner as the rock is often seen to be in Singapore.* Basalt and greenstone are found on Pulo Ooban, which lies close to the north-east coast of Singapore. Similar rocks of various structure and character, compact, vesicular, &c., with claystone, porphyries, and other volcanic minerals, are brought from islands in the neighbourhood to Singapore to be used for the foundations of houses. The original production of the latter rocks must of course be referred to an epoch long anterior to that of the former, which undoubtedly corresponds with that of the Singapore semi-volcanic rocks.

We are therefore, I think, justified in considering Singapore and the neighbouring islands to have been the seat of volcanic convulsions spread over a considerable area, if nowhere of great intensity. There are many reasons, but not strictly local, to believe that their date was in a late era of geological time. The subject, however, is a difficult one, and there is not room for its full discussion in this paper. I may here only mention, amongst the local facts tending to the above conclusion, the softness of some of the rocks which have not been altered by volcanic action, but have been elevated and greatly stretched or drawn out, contorted or compressed, in the process; the absence of any superficial changes not due to atmospherical causes since the time of their elevation, and the very moderate effects of these causes; the apparent continuity of some of the hill beds of sand and clay in adjacent hollows, having a ferruginous and torrified appearance in the former, while in the latter they are not distinguishable from soft modern alluvium; and lastly, some remarkable cases of the elevation of soft alluvial and vegetable deposits agreeing in their character with beds now forming in the island or along its shores.†

* Mr. Thomson describes to me an analogous injection of a reddish-black substance, lateritic in its appearance, into the fissures of a block of *granite* on the north coast of Buitang. This I shall describe on procuring a specimen, if I do not visit the locality.

† It is to be remarked, however, that in a climate like that of Singapore, clay rocks and aluminous sandstones at or near the surface, unless highly indurated, are liable to become soft. The age of the elevation of the island will be more fully considered in the paper on the Straits, in connection with several

Unfortunately the non-observation hitherto of any organic remains, while it is perhaps a reason for assigning a higher antiquity to the soft rocks above mentioned than their general appearance seems to claim, renders it very difficult to compare them with the observations of European geologists, or to ascertain whether they can be made to occupy any determinate place in their systems. This last inquiry is, however, of the least importance for the present, and if entered upon before the phenomena of this locality (so far removed from any of which the geology is in any considerable measure understood), have been minutely and faithfully studied by themselves, is more likely to mislead than to aid research. I may state, however, that in the present state of our knowledge the only European system with which the rocks of Singapore, notwithstanding the apparently recent origin of some of them, can be mineralogically compared, is the new red sandstone. The sandstones, clays, marls (non-calcareous), and shales, in many respects resemble the same rocks of that system. The rareness, if not the absence, of fossils, is a striking circumstance, and even if the two formations be remote in time from each other (for no chronological conclusion can be drawn from merely lithological characters), points to the existence of analogous conditions during the periods of their respective accumulation.

If we now recur to the present superficial igneous and ferruginous deposits of Singapore, the only remaining question under our hypothesis would be, whether their superposition on the hills (to which they are confined) took place before or after the emergence of the latter from the sea. In other words, was the present configuration of the island assumed under the level of the sea, and then the whole tract of land from which the hills spring elevated by one movement, or is it more probable that before the hills were upraised the general level of the land was the same or nearly the same as it now is, and the hills consequently obtruded from that level in whole or in part in the air? The action of the waters of the sea in spreading out the materials brought to the surface by volcanic forces might seem an obvious explanation of some of the facts formerly noticed. But if this cause be admitted at all, its operation must have been transient and limited, otherwise the surface accumulations on the different hills and parts of the same hill would not have retained their striking local characters.* If the agency of the sea is to be admitted, the most probable hypothesis, with our present information, would be, that when the process which dislocated and pushed up the strata in different places into hills began to operate, the general level of the sea-bed was much lower than it now is, and that the same

instances of recent elevation occurring along its borders, where the evidence is of a more satisfactory nature, being derived from organic remains.

* See ante, page 71, *Diluvial Hypothesis.*

action caused its general elevation. In this way the surfaces of the hills may have emerged so gradually from beneath the sea as to admit of a partial action of its waters on their summits and sides during and subsequent to the eruptions of matter, and yet not so slowly as to give time for such extensive denudation as to obliterate the local peculiarities of the ejected substances. My own opinion at present is, that all the phenomena may be accounted for by purely volcanic succeeded by ordinary meteoric causes. At one time rock fragments and semi-fused matter would be voided, heaped up at particular places, or ejected into the air and showered over the surface. At another time, when the heat was less intense or when steam or gases, not ignifluous or melted matter, burst out, masses of soft clays and sandstone might be disembowelled and spread over the bed of fragments. At other places the rocks might be broken and pulverized *in situ*, and receive a considerable vertical pulsion so as transiently to form an incoherent and agitated mass, especially towards the surface, but without the fragments or sand being freely projected into the air.*

One of the most common features of the hills is the occurrence of a bed of igneous stones—at one place large (30 to 60 cubic feet) slaggy and often scorious or amygdaloidal, and gradually but irregularly diminishing in size until they become a coarse and then a fine gravel, in some places dwindling into a seam of minute grains. The beds are of various thickness—from three or more feet to a few lines—and so, often, is the same bed at different places. They may consist of a uniform aggregate of stones, or of stones mingled with loose clay, sand, &c. Over this deposit there is generally a bed of soft clay or sandy clay. Sometimes more than one bed of gravel occurs. Layers of unaltered angular fragments are occasionally, but rarely, found beneath these beds. Layers of the small porcellanous, jaspideous, and varnished stones before noticed, and of large grains of quartz, are more common. All these layers sometimes appear in the same section, but this seldom happens. The localities where the large scoriform rocks abound are often at or near the summits of hills, or where thick dykes of igneous rock come to the surface, and probably in every case they mark the places where the largest fissures or vents were opened. Where they are most abundant they appear at the surface, and that not only in spots exposed to denuding influences, but in flattish and gently sloping tracts. There appears in

* Whether the mechanical action by which the hills were upraised long preceded, or was accompanied or soon followed by, semi-volcanic action in the most intense degree which it here attained, or rather whether the semi-volcanic emissions and eruptions continued during a long period to find vent through the fissures formed when the hills were elevated, is a question that must lie over for the present. It is probable that they originated on, but lasted, or were from time to time repeated, for some time after the elevation of the hills.

many cases to be a connection between the direction of the dykes and fissures, and that of the hills or their spurs. Where good sections of the summits of dykes have been obtained fragments of the rock of which they are composed, not angular but scoriform, can generally be traced as a horizontal layer on the surface, or disposed beneath a bed of clay, &c., to a considerable distance from the head of the dyke. When the dyke is vertical these stones are accumulated over and strewed on both sides of it. When it is inclined they are spread out in the direction towards which the inclination is. Two dykes adjoining each other at the surface have sometimes beds of scoriæ diverging from them in opposite directions, owing to their dips being opposed. The above and other observable facts are all, I think, explicable by the species of volcanic action which I have suggested, susceptible as it is of various modifications, without resorting to oceanic agency. At all events, no fact has yet come under my notice unequivocally attesting the abrading, sorting, or transporting operation of a large body of water, or which could not be referred to some known form of volcanic agency. It must also be borne in mind that the convulsive mechanical action which enters so largely into the general hypothesis, would be most powerful in shattering compact and loosening soft rocks, when the stratified masses were ruptured and raised into highly inclined, vertical, or reversed positions. In such cases the exposed basset edges, in their fragmentary or pulverized state, and before they were protected by any vegetation, would be more acted on by meteoric causes than at present.

The system of hills, with their dykes and veins, affords an interesting field for the application of the principles of mechanical science; but it would be premature to enter on this subject before the country is better opened up, as it will soon be by the lines of road now in progress. There can be little doubt, however, that the directions of the hills agree with the ramifications of fissures which in those places where the intensity of the elevatory force caused their extension to the surface have formed vents through which the superficial volcanic deposits were expelled. The principal ranges, we have seen, are nearly parallel, and have directions approximating to N.W. and S.E. The lateral hills are placed on lines at right angles to these, and the secondary lateral hills again on lines parallel to the principal ranges.

My remarks have been hitherto confined to facts entirely local, and inferences or hypotheses strictly deduced from or applicable to them. Before concluding this paper, however, let us extend the limits of our observations, and see whether a wider geological area presents phenomena repugnant to the large influence which has been assigned to volcanic causes.

That the movements which elevated the central mountains of

the Malayan Peninsula had an intimate relation with those that elevated the mountains of Sumatra, seems evident, whether we regard the hypothesis of De Beaumont, the more recent observations and theories of Mr. Darwin, or the mechanical researches of Mr. Hopkins. Both form long chains which pursue parallel lines not more than three or four degrees distant. But we must probably take in a much wider geographical range if we would seek a general geological theory for the region which they traverse. The mountain chains of the peninsula of India are parallel, or approximately so, to the Malayan, and, like them, spring from the great central system of Asia. The chain of the peninsula of Malaya is directly continued to this region, and from it descend nearly parallel chains through Burmah, Siam and Cochin China. These ranges determine the general direction of the sea-coasts wherever these are exposed to waves sufficiently strong to prevent the formation and extension of alluvial plains. The western coasts of India and of the Tenasserim Provinces, Siam, the Gulf of Siam, and the eastern coast of Cochin China, are thus fixed. A wide and interesting field of inquiry is opened up by the probable geological connection between the regions of these ranges and those of the Indian Archipelago generally, Australia and the archipelagos of the Pacific, evidenced by the prevalence of parallel lines of elevation, and perhaps also by organic remains, such as the fossil elephant and some of the carboniferous plants of New South Wales. The former existence of a great Australasian continent, an extension probably of the present continent of Asia, which seems to result from Mr. Darwin's theory of atolls, would be an inference in accordance with these facts. Viewing the whole region, interspersed with peninsulas and islands, from the Indian Ocean to the heart of the Pacific, as one, it appears that De Beaumont's theory of parallel rectilinear or oblong areas of elevation and subsidence, which Mr. Darwin has applied to the eastern tracts, requires modification, and that if we conceive curvilinear lines, or systems of parallel curvilinear lines, proceeding from centres and often meeting similar lines or systems from other centres, and again lateral and secondary lines diverging from the principal, the arrangement of the observed ranges will assume greater symmetry, and be found perhaps to accord with the hypothesis that one widely extended mechanical pulsion, accompanied by local foci of intense development from weakness in the rocks or increased plutonic or volcanic action, gave the first direction to all the main lines of elevation. Thus let us conceive such a centre to be situated in the western half of New Guinea— and we have some independent warrant for doing so in the circumstance that the mountains of its unexplored interior appear to attain a magnitude unusual in the achipelago—from this focus we may trace one great curvilinear fracture or band of rupture of the earth's crust through the Sunda Islands to Chittagong; a second through the mountainous volcanic islands of Ceram and Bouro, and along the southern coasts of Celebes and Borneo (Gunong Ratos), Billiton, Banda, the Malay Peninsula, &c.; a third through the Philippines, Formosa, Japan, &c.; a fourth along the southern coast of New Guinea, and through the Solomon Islands, New Hebrides, New Zealand, &c.; a fifth along the southern coast of New Guinea, across Torres Straits, and along the eastern coast of Australia; and a sixth perhaps through the north-western division of Australia. Other principal lines probably proceed across the Moluccas and Celebes, through Borneo and the islands of the China Sea (now a subsiding tract), and join the mountain chains of Cochin China and Siam; but the geography of Borneo is not sufficiently known to allow of our positively ranking these as seventh and eighth lines. The intermediate areas may be occupied by numerous other lines, but the subsidence of various tracts renders it difficult or impossible, particularly to the eastward, to trace the original courses of vertical movement until the soundings of the Polynesian seas are ascertained. Subsequent shifting subterranean action would cause many other fractures in various directions; but it would not, at least until the lapse of a long geological epoch, obliterate the primary lines. It would often cause cross fractures, of which many instances might be pointed out. It is no objection to this hypothesis that many of the lines seem to proceed from the central table-land of Asia. Because if at the time these fissures were being extended southward, a great local action took place at or near New Guinea, they would, according to the mechanical laws examined by Mr. Hopkins, diverge from their original direction towards that point, or to meet the lines radiating from it. Thus we observe the two least broken lines to pursue a southerly direction till they reach the parallel of 8° N.L., when, at the Nicobars in the one and at Junk-Ceylon in the other, they are deflected to the S.E. When they cross the meridian of 106° E. they make a more decided bend to the eastward. If we follow these lines and the chains of Siam and Cochin China northward we may trace them upwards to the Bayan Khara mountains, and thence to the vast central mass of Kulkun, from whence great ranges are said to proceed towards all the points of the compass. But in the north-western part of the province of Yunnan and north-east of Burmah and Assam their continuity is interrupted, and we seem to have ascertained another central region whence radiate not only the lines which afterwards converge to New Guinea, but various other curvilinear ranges proceeding S.E., E., N.E., and N. through China, and N. and N.W. through Thibet; and lastly, the Himalayas and a minor range proceeding south-eastward on the south of the valley of Assam, and continued perhaps in the Vindyas—for a subsequent line of subsidence passing down the plain of the Ganges and through the Bay of Bengal, of which there is some evidence, may have destroyed the pre-existing continuity. Many of these ranges proceeded primarily from the Kulkun, but it is remarkable that they converge towards the region indicated. The region where the Himalayas attain their sublimest proportions and give birth to rivers that embrace them and all India in their courses, is another grand focus. From this centre the range proceeds on the one side to the eastward, and on the other to the N.W. To the north of the former a secondary and approximately parallel range also proceeds eastward, and includes with it the valley of the Sampao, and to the south another and smaller secondary parallel range traverses upper India. To determine the original centres of maximum intensity and directions of the forces that elevated the great connected mountain system that forms the skeleton of the Asiatic continent, is a problem beyond the present reach of geology.*

The Malayan chain I have mentioned as a series of groups, and from the breadth of country which their members occupy compared with their height and apparent bulk, and their general appearance as viewed from the Straits, I am led to believe that they consist of connected systems, each analogous to that of the Singapore hills, or of principal undulating masses from which parallel ranges proceed in a N.W. and S.E. direction. The rivers probably have their sources at the heads of the valleys included between these ranges, and turn seaward at the extremities of the ranges. The most southern rivers, such as the Johore, Sakadai, &c., which flow southward, would also bend to the east and west, where the last system of the continent terminates and that of Singapore begins, did they not meet with a depression so low as to be accessible by the sea.

Singapore is merely separated from the mainland by this depression, which forms a narrow tortuous river-like arm of the sea, and is in fact sunk into the continent and embraced by it on three sides, so that its southern shore seems to be the proper continuation of the southern coast of the peninsula. Its geogra-

---

* There can be little doubt that an extensive knowledge of the physical and mineralogical constitution of mountain ranges will form the true basis of the highest department of the science, now only dawning—the Mechanism of the Earth. But the day is probably not far distant when the geologist, like the astronomer, will need to be thoroughly indoctrinated with the principles of mechanical science in its widest sense. Fortunately for the worshippers of Nature of humbler acquirements, geology is so immersed in matter, so wrought into every inch of the earth, that its priests have need of a whole tribe of Levites. Wherever a man finds himself placed he has but to employ his eyes to become a useful labourer, and so far will a little knowledge be from proving dangerous to him that it may be safely said, that while even entire ignorance is not a bar to the collection of facts, every little accession of knowledge from any of the sciences becomes an instrument of observation.

phical connection with it is therefore complete. When we cross the strait, no difference in the topography is observable. And the low hills, which give the surface an undulating appearance like that of Singapore, probably resemble those of the latter in their internal structure as much as they do in the superjacent soils and in the stunted jungle. The interior of the peninsula is almost wholly unexplored. In coasting along its western shore from Pinang to Cape Rachado, a high chain or rather series of ranges of mountains is observed inland nearly the whole way, which from their generally sharp-peaked summits, the nature of the detritus brought down from them by the rivers, and the evidence afforded by the few points where they have been reached, we are justified in believing to consist in great measure of plutonic rocks. In front of this range we observe a broad tract of country, often appearing to be perfectly flat and very little above the sea-level for miles together, but from which sometimes low hills rise like islands out of the sea. These hills are frequently quite solitary, and at a great distance from the central mountains, or near the coast. Further inland they seem to be generally in groups, and towards the mountains the country at some places appears hilly and undulating. At Malacca these low hills are so much grouped as to resemble some parts of Singapore, and they are covered by gravel and fragments precisely similar to those found on some of the Singapore hills. In some of the hills opposite Pinang I observed similar fragments. In both cases, the soil had a deep red ferruginous aspect.* That most of the hills scattered along the western plains of the peninsula were islands in the sea at no remote date, there can be no doubt. The plains from which they spring are flat, generally only a few feet above the sea-level, alluvial, and at some places abounding in marine shells of the same species that at present inhabit the Straits. The rivers of the peninsula, although generally small, are exceedingly numerous, and bring down large quantities of sediment. In March last, off the mouth of the Salangore River, the steamer in which I was passed through a bread tract discoloured by the sediment. Extensive mud-banks have been formed in the straits and are constantly increasing. For evidence on this subject, I must refer to a separate paper, containing some remarks on the Straits of Malacca and the alluvial tracts along its sides. It is not therefore unreasonable to conclude that the whole chain of these hills, from Pinang to Singapore, has a strict geological connection. At Malacca hot springs exist, and the hills nearest to them are of the nature before mentioned. We naturally resort to the mountain chain of the interior for the seat of that central volcanic force of which the manifestations on these outskirts are of so peculiar a character, so

---

* Cape Rachado is described by Crawfurd to consist of quartz rocks interspersed with frequent veins of clay iron-ore.

wide in their extent, yet so devoid of intensity. But we find that there is no evidence whatever of any volcanoes ever having existed in this chain. If there ever were any, their fires have long been quenched.

If we now direct our attention to the southward of Singapore, we find that it is but one of an extensive archipelago of islands, stretching to the south-east, and which, after a slight interruption, is continued in Banca. That the geological chain continues to the latter island, is clear from the account which Dr. Horsfield gives of it. According to him, the elevated parts of Banca consist principally of granite, but in the secondary elevations " red iron-stone " is extensively distributed in single rocks, or in veins of many united together, covering large tracts of country.* This circumstance and the general topography of the island, as described by Dr. Horsfield, assimilate to Singapore. The paucity of tin-ore in the latter arises from the want of granitic hills. Bukit Temah, the only hill yet explored in which sienite abounds, contains tin, and in fact derives its name from the circumstance, as it literally signifies " Tin Hill." We thus find that what we may call the semi-volcanic band of the Straits of Malacca may, to a certain extent, be disconnected from the peninsula, and viewed as a chain of islands extending probably from Junk-Ceylon to Banca, and including the existing islands and numerous rocks and reefs in the Straits of Malacca. It appears, therefore, that its southern extremity is almost in contact with Sumatra,† and the question arises whether its volcanic connection be not with this great island rather than the peninsula. May it not be reasonably presumed that, if the origin and partial elevation of the Sumatra chain was contemporaneous with that of the peninsula, the line of greatest intensity of the subterranean forces, in whichever it was originally, was ultimately determined to the latter chain, and that at some now ancient era the former was left to comparative repose? The height of the plutonic mountains of the peninsula is greatly inferior to that of the mountains of Sumatra. But all the elevated peaks of the latter appear to be volcanic, and perhaps the purely granitic ranges are not more elevated than those of the peninsula. The elevation of the two plutonic ranges, and the shallow bed of the strait between

---

* See "Memoirs of Sir S. Raffles," p. 150. Major Court, in his account of Banca, notices the gravelly nature of the soil (Gourt's Palembang). Professor Jameson, in Murray's " Encyclopædia of Geography," mentions the circumstance of the primitive mountains being immediately bounded by a formation of red ironstone doubtingly, and adds, "Crawfurd, who makes this statement, gives no description of the formation." From Crawfurd's meagre notice of Banca, I presume he does not write from personal observation, and, like Sir S. Raffles, he probably derived his information from Dr. Horsfield's manuscript.

† It will appear, however, in the paper formerly referred to, that this approximation is due to modern external, not to ancient internal forces.

them, may have been contemporaneous and antecedent to the period when volcanoes burst out along the Sumatra chain. These volcanoes, from their number and power, would arrest the rise of the region, or cause any subsequent elevatory movement to be rare and of small amount. Until the interior of the peninsula is explored, these inquiries to a large extent must be merely speculative ; but it is certain that the Sumatra chain has in recent eras been the seat of great volcanic energy, and that it is still subject to convulsive movements, the tremors or undulations of which are transmitted as far as what I have termed the semi-volcanic band of the Straits on the one side, and which are felt much more severely in the less distant chain of islands on the west coast of Sumatra.

Marsden states that a number of volcanoes exist,[*] and describes one which opened in the side of a mountain about twenty miles inland of Bencoolen, and which, during his residence at that factory, scarcely ever failed to emit smoke. To the S.E. the three volcanic peaks of Gunong Dempo, Lumut, and Berapi, rise to the height of 12,000 feet. Gunong Dempo was ascended by Mr. Church, the present resident councillor at Singapore, with the late Mr. Presgrave, in 1818. An interesting account of the ascent is inserted in Raffles' Memoirs (p. 323). Mr. Presgrave states that he had frequently seen smoke issuing from the mountain, and the natives informed him that, within their memory, it had emitted flames attended with a loud noise. In the upper region of the mountain the party found the trees dead, and externally burned quite black. Further north is the great central volcanic region, partially at least included in the ancient kingdom of Menang Kabu. This is described by Raffles (Memoirs, p. 347) as being exclusively volcanic. The rocks are mostly basaltic. Two lofty volcanic mountains rise near the large lake of Sincara. From one of these, Gunong Berapi (Fiery Mountain), which is above 13,000 feet high, smoke issued. Hot springs also exist here. To the east of the lake the rocks consisted of felspar, granite, quartz, &c., mixed with a great variety of volcanic productions in the greatest confusion. Iron-ore of various kinds lay in the path of the travellers. To the west of the lake were found granite, marble, great varieties of limestones, masses of calcareous spar, and many other substances. On the N.E. of the lake, near Pageruyang, numerous stumps and trunks of trees in a state of petrifaction protruded from the ground. The limits of the region on the north and south are not ascertained. About sixty miles south of Mount Talong, another Gunong Berapi occurs. Near Mount Ophir, a volcanic mountain is marked in Marsden's map, and Mount Ophir itself is probably an extinct volcano. Further north still lies another of the

---

[*] " History of Sumatra," p. 24.

ascertained volcanoes, Mount Batagapit. Mr. J. Anderson, who visited the east coast in 1823, mentions* a native tradition of an engagement having taken place between two of the mountains in the interior of Delli (Sebaya and Senaban), when part of them fell into the valley. From these mountains, sulphur is procured, which if it does not prove that they are formed of volcanic materials, as Mr. Anderson conceives, at least leads to the inference that they have been the seat of volcanic action. At Acheen, abundant supplies of sulphur for internal consumption and exportation are obtained from a volcanic mountain in the neighbourhood.† Lastly, one of the western chain of islands, Si Beero, according to Marsden, possesses a volcano. Earthquakes are of frequent occurrence. Marsden notices one of unusual severity, which occurred in 1770.‡

Sir T. S. Raffles mentions that on the east coast they are said to happen every five or six years.§ The Malays on the east coast represented to Mr. Anderson that slight shocks were occasionally felt,‖ and the same information was received by Lieut. Crooke at Jambi.¶ In the interesting memoir on this state by that officer appended to Mr. Anderson's work it is likewise mentioned that a violent earthquake was stated to have been experienced about twenty years or more previous to his visit in 1820, and to have been preceded by a period of great heat and drought, which ruined the crops and occasioned a distressing scarcity of food. It is not improbable that this earthquake was simultaneous with one which happened in 1797, of which the effect on the opposite coast is mentioned by Raffles. " It is stated that the vibratory shocks continued for three minutes, and recurred at intervals during the space of three hours, till the shock completely ceased. At Padang, the houses of the inhabitants were almost entirely destroyed and the public works much damaged. A vessel lying

---

* " Mission to the E. Coast of Sumatra," p. 199.   † Marsden, p. 313.

‡ " The most severe that I have known was chiefly experienced in the district of Manna, in the year 1770. A village was destroyed by the houses falling down and taking fire, and several lives were lost. The ground was in one place rent a quarter of a mile, the width of two fathoms and depth of four or five. A bituminous matter is described to have swelled over the sides of the cavity, and the earth, for a long time after the shocks, was observed to contract and dilate alternately. Many parts of the hills far inland could be distinguished to have given way, and a consequence of this was, that during three weeks, Manna River was so much impregnated with particles of clay, that the natives could not bathe in it. At this time was formed, near to the mouth of Padang Goochie, a neighbouring river, south of the former, a large plain, seven miles long and half a mile broad, where there had been before only a narrow beach. The quantity of earth brought down on this occasion was so considerable that the hill upon which the English Resident's house stands, appears, from indubitable marks, less elevated by fifteen feet than it was before the event." (*Id.* p. 25.)

§ " Memoirs," p. 295.

‖ Anderson, *ut supra*, p. 199.   ¶ *Id.* p. 402.

at anchor was thrown by the sudden rise of the tide upwards of three miles on shore. The number of lives lost there amounted to above 300; of these, some were crushed under the ruins of falling houses, some were literally entombed by the earth opening on them, and others were drowned by the sudden irruption of the waters of the ocean."

On April 18, 1818, another violent earthquake was experienced on the west coast. Sir T. S. Raffles, who arrived at Bencoolen the day after, found that every house was more or less shattered, and many in ruins. In the island of Pulo Nias, on the west coast, earthquakes appear to be felt very severely. The same remark may possibly apply to the other islands in the same chain, for our knowledge of these phenomena in the native countries has been hitherto almost entirely accidental, and our information regarding Pulo Nias arises from the connection of Europeans with it. Marsden mentions that in 1763 a village in that island was swallowed up by an earthquake, and a recent shock, which will be immediately noticed more at large, was still more disastrous in its effects. That the undulations in most cases extend across the straits to the semi-volcanic line is highly probable. Although our connection with the Straits now extends over a period of sixty years, unfortunately no connected records have been preserved of the critical geological and meteorological phenomena that have been experienced during that time. In Pinang during the last twelve years several shocks have been felt. These occurred in November 1833, August 1835, September 1837, and January 1843.*

Those of 1837 were the most violent, and the undulations appear to have been from south to north, and to have lasted a minute and a half.† The shocks in 1843 happened about half an hour after midnight on the morning of January 6, and at half-past two P.M. on the 8th. The first shock was more severe than the second, but both were slight, producing no other mechanical effects than a tremor of the ground, which caused articles sus-

---

* *Pinang Gazette* of January 7, 14, and 28, 1843.

† "It is said that on that occasion several herds of cattle in the neighbourhood were observed running in the utmost confusion in all directions, that lamps and picture frames oscillated, that the Roman Catholic church bell rang of its own accord, that quantities of large shot piled up in the fort were thrown down and scattered about, that a stone wall of a substantial building in town was rent, and that the whole inhabitants were thrown into a state of consternation. The shipping in the harbour did not experience this shock, nor did the sea appear agitated. Five days subsequently, however, another smart shock was felt, and was followed by a very heavy squall from the N.W., and great agitation and rise of the sea in the harbour. The tides overflowed the northern beach, and flooded the compounds and lower rooms of the houses in the neighbourhood. This convulsion was experienced about the same time at Acheen, and along the Pedier coast, and it is said that these places sustained considerable damage."—*Pinang Gazette* of January 28, 1843.

pended to oscillate, stopped a clock, and occasioned in some persons a giddiness in the head. The first shock, although only felt by a few persons in the plain who happened to be awake, caused the residents on one of the hills to spring from their beds, under the apprehension that robbers had attacked their houses, so violent was the noise of rattling venetians, bolts, &c. The undulations on this occasion, as in 1837, appeared to be from south to north. The shock on the morning of the 6th was experienced precisely at the same instant at Singapore* and at Malacca.† The undulations at Singapore are said to have been from east to west, very slight, and to have lasted eight or ten seconds. About half a year afterwards it was first learned in the Straits that a most violent earthquake had devastated Pulo Nias, commencing about midnight between January 5 and 6, or nearly the same time when the undulations were felt along the western coast of the peninsula. The shocks were at first from the west, shifting to the north ; but as they increased in violence they appeared to lose any fixed direction and became a complete trembling of the earth, which lasted nine minutes ; houses were destroyed, trees uprooted, a portion of a mountain fell, and the ground opened in wide fissures, from which a " black frothy liquid trickled." After a brief interval of inaction, the undulations recommenced, and the sea suddenly rose in a vast wave, which rolled in from the south-east, overwhelming a considerable tract of country and sweeping away whole villages and their inhabitants. The shocks were felt at intervals of two minutes until half-past four in the morning, when another paroxysm even more violent than the first took place, lasting about six minutes. The shocks were from the west, veering to the north, but changing directly to the south. Tremors of the ground were experienced for several subsequent days. Thus the latest earthquake that has occurred in this region was experienced in its greatest violence a little to the west of the volcanic chain of Sumatra, and the undulations were transmitted or induced so widely and so rapidly as to reach Penang, Malacca and Singapore simultaneously and at or about the same time when the first shock was felt at Pulo Nias.

It appears, therefore, that the volcanoes of Sumatra still communicate with an internal igneous sea, and from time to time emit smoke and gases ; that to this day the island is subject to frequent earthquakes ; that several of those that have occurred within the last hundred years have been of great force, rending the ground, and at least on two occasions giving vent to liquid volcanic matter ; and that their operation extends, though with diminished violence, to the western coast of the peninsula. When we consider the height and bulk of the crateriform volcanic

* *Singapore Free Press* of January 12, 1843.   † *Id.* February 2, 1843.

mountains, even viewed only relatively to the level of the hilly country above which they rise, and the large belts of volcanic rocks which exist in the neighbourhood of some of those that have been explored, if they do not connect the whole chain, we are carried back to a period in the history of Sumatra during which its volcanic phenomena were on the grandest scale. If at this day, when the fires of her mountains have ceased or are dormant, the coast of the peninsula is agitated by the comparatively feeble shocks which disturb the repose of the island, it is reasonable to believe that when her volcanoes, whether simultaneously, successively, or alternately, were in full activity along a line of nearly a thousand miles, the neighbouring regions to the distance of 100 to 200 miles must have been subject to earthquakes of great violence, and accompanied, according to the degree of their intensity, by volcanic emissions and eruptions in greater or less abundance. That portion of the volcanic belt where the evidences of violent igneous action are most striking appears to be Singapore and the neighbourhood, although it is not improbable that the whole tract, from Cape Rachado to Banca, exhibits more extensive and continuous disturbance than the northern part of the belt. That region of Sumatra which, so far as observation has extended, may be termed the principal volcanic tract, is about three degrees distant from Singapore, and lies in a parallel about a degree and a quarter to the south of this island. The direction of the Singapore strata is across or approximately at right angles to parallel lines forming the sides of a plane connecting the island with this part of Menangkabu, and the dip of the strata, although, as formerly observed, exhibiting much irregularity, is generally from the point of the compass where Menangkabu lies.

There seems, upon the whole, to be strong grounds for the opinion that the hill system of Singapore has its volcanic* connection with Sumatra, and not with the mountain chain of the peninsula. If this view shall be found to be borne out by further

---

* Our meagre information regarding the formations of Sumatra does not admit of our instituting a comparison between them and the rocks of the opposite coast of the Peninsula. The central mountains are chiefly plutonic and volcanic. The granite or sienite of the southern regions would appear from Marsden's slight notice to resemble that of Singapore. The lower tracts of the west coast, as described by him, possess a remarkable resemblance in their configuration to the surface of Singapore. Like the latter, they consist of rounded elevations of no great height, separated by winding flat swamps penetrating for miles between them. The hills "not unfrequently exhibit the appearance of an amphitheatre." A coincidence in a configuration so uncommon when other analogies are also considered, can hardly be viewed as accidental. The soil he describes as a stiff reddish clay. The rock exposed in sea cliffs and in some places at the bottoms of rivers is a species of clay called by the natives "nappal," which is common in Singapore. The country between the mountains and the eastern coast of Sumatra is little known, but what information has been obtained respecting its geological features I have collected in the paper before alluded to.

observations, we must conceive that the old granite mountain chain of the peninsula (which, as is shown in the paper before mentioned, terminates apparently between Parcelar Point and Pulo Varela, although a few minor groups exist in the interior to the southward) had its extremity in this direction washed by the sea. The region below, which operated the expansive volcanic fluids or gases whose effects we are considering, extended from Sumatra to the peninsula, and probably a little to the westward of the one and considerably to the eastward of the other, for the whole vast platform or partially emerging and partially subsiding continent that rises out of the depths of the Indian Ocean and stretches eastward far into the Pacific, rests on one region of connected though shifting subterranean excitement. The line of most intense force would be the ordinary one, the volcanic chain of Sumatra. Thence the waves of the volcanic sea would travel in parallel lines to the north-eastward, causing a tension of the region and a tendency to split in the direction of those lines. That portion of the region intermediate between the western and eastern mountain chains which had not been disturbed and fractured during the process of elevation like that from which the chains were obtruded, or of which the fractures had not reached the surface, would offer most resistance. But on arriving at the western limit of the old fractures caused during the elevation of the Malayan chain, the space so fractured would yield in various points of weakness. The old fractures at the southern extremity of the chain would by the tension be prolonged in the same direction, that is to the S.E., and cross fractures being established and the volcanic forces sufficing to elevate the rocks and produce eruptions at different places along the line of fissure, the system of semi-volcanic hills extending from the termination of the Malayan plutonic chain to Banca would be produced. Whether we admit the notion of a translation of waves, or suppose that under the region a general volcanic pressure was in operation, producing an expansive tendency whose superficial manifestations varied according to the mineral structure and composition of the rocky crust and particular local intensity of force, the same results would follow under the assigned conditions.

Having in the above paper had occasion to bring together several scattered notices of recent volcanic action in Sumatra and the west coast of the peninsula, it may be remarked that some general facts appear which it may be useful to separate from the local matters with which they are mixed up.

1. The advance of a great wave upon the land is a circumstance common to most earthquakes on sea-coasts. Mr. Darwin considers it to be caused by a line of fracture beneath the sea. If there is a consequent sinking of the sea-bed along the line, the

rush of waters on both sides to restore the level would occasion first the retirement of the sea from the shore, and then the production of a wave rolling in upon the shore. But might it not also be caused without any sinking or even rending of the sea-bed? A strong blow beneath the earth's crust, imparting a momentary centrifugal tendency, would cause the sea above the point or line of impact to rise violently to a height proportioned to the force of the concussion. But this wave would necessarily be partly above and partly below the general level, or have a hollow on each side towards which the neighbouring waters would rush, and thus the same effect be produced along the adjacent coast as in the former case. Mr. Darwin also mentions that places situated on shallow bays suffer great damage from these waves, while those seated close to the edge of profoundly deep water escape. In the same manner the waves of the Indian Ocean, on reaching the shallow coast of Sumatra, rise as they advance until they acquire a great height. This is probably attributable to the friction of the bottom retarding the waves, while a constant succession press on from the sea behind. When bays are narrow, the wave will have a greater tendency to rise owing to its progressive lateral contraction, as is seen more markedly in bores.

2. The opening of fissures and evacuation through them of black fluid matter. The spasmodic expansion and contraction of fissures continued after the shock.

3. The disruption of portions of mountains or landslips.

4. The elevation of tracts of land.

5. The greater violence of earthquakes on hills. This was observed at Pinang in 1843. Marsden remarks that houses situated on a low sandy soil are least affected, and those which stand on distinct hills suffer most from the shocks.

6. The connection between earthquakes and the condition of the atmosphere. To what is stated by Lieut. Crooke respecting the great drought which preceded the earthquake at Jambi, the following extract from Marsden relative to Sumatran earthquakes in general may be added :—" Earthquakes have been remarked by some to happen usually on sudden changes of weather, and particularly after violent heats ; but I do not vouch this upon my own experience, which has been pretty ample." The earthquake of 1843 occurred during one of the longest and severest droughts that had ever happened in Pinang. This drought, which was attended with oppressive heat and occasional hot winds, never before experienced within the memory of the residents, appears to have extended over the northern part of Sumatra.

NOTE.

When the foregoing paper was written I had not seen the talented and elaborate memoir on Indian earthquakes by Lieutenant R. B. Smith, which I received by the *Hooghly.* The portions at which I have had time to glance suffice to show that it contains a mine of wealth. The above notices of Malayan earthquakes, however meagre, may serve to connect his researches with the Indian Archipelago respecting the general geology and recent volcanic disturbances of which I am collecting information. Meantime the subjoined account which has been furnished me by my brother, abridged from the official report of the Alcalde Mayor of the province of Cagayan in the island of Luzon, of an earthquake attended by the subsidence of two hills and by a violent hurricane which occurred there on the night between October 7 and 8 last, may prove interesting. It will appear in the *Singapore Free Press*, but I presume that will form no objection to its being put on record in the more permanent pages of the Journal.

" The Casa Real of Lallo, a brick building, and one of the most solid edifices in the province, was destroyed. The rector's house was destroyed, and the roof of the church suffered much damage, and many other of the public edifices were more or less injured. The Tribunal stood it out well, and will only require a new roof. All the wooden houses were levelled with the ground. None of the attap houses escaped, and the greater part were blown over with many of their unhappy owners in them, and their little stores of paddy. The people, notwithstanding, had been since occupied in repairing the serious injuries which the Renta de Tabacos had suffered, and the wages, which were paid daily, served as some consolation to them in the midst of so much misfortune. Five persons are reckoned to have been killed and eleven wounded. In Calamaningan, the church and rector's house were entirely destroyed, and the priest was living in the Royal Tribunal, which had escaped injury, and in which he had erected an altar. The wooden houses suffered more than those of Lallo. The attap houses were all destroyed. The people experienced the misfortune of being caught by the hurricane with the greater part of their grain still on the ground, the whole of which was destroyed. Eleven persons were killed, and twenty seriously injured. At Aparri, the majority of the houses in the district are of wood, which were mostly all destroyed. The Royal Tribunal, a new and solid building, was overthrown ; the rector's house destroyed, and the church much injured. Nearly all the wooden houses were destroyed, and none of the attap ones escaped, the greater part going to block up the river or into the sea, which rose into the village and contributed to make the night more frightful, and to augment the number of victims, who amounted to twenty-seven killed and fifty-three wounded. All the harvest that had been gathered in perished, being carried into the sea with the houses. The destruction of buffaloes, horses, cows, and other property was excessive. In Buguey nearly all houses and buildings were destroyed; one man killed. The convent of Abulog was entirely demolished, the church lost its roof and belfry, and nearly all the houses were levelled with the ground : eight persons were killed. To the north of this village, at the distance of six miles, there is a high hill on the top of which dwelt a number of natives who pay allegiance to Her Majesty. These people relate that on the evening preceding the hurricane they felt great and frequent tremblings of the earth ; that at nightfall they began to hear in the midst of it a frightful noise, which impelled them to abandon their abode, and fly, full of fear, to a creek for shelter from the fury of the tempest, which was increasing. On the ceasing of the storm, on the morning of the 8th, they returned to their dwelling, when they found that it, and the hill on which it stood, had sunk ; there appeared in its place a large lake of black water, of a fœtid odour, and smoking. In Pamplona, the churches and Tribunal were destroyed, as well as the rest of the houses, with the exception of the church of the division of Masi, which being of very solid construction, escaped with trifling injury : five persons were killed. At the entrance of the river of this village there was a hill sixty feet high separating the sea from the river, which, having disappeared, the two waters are now joined, and a wide and practicable passage opened : five victims are reported. Within the boundaries of all these districts Nature presents a most sombre picture ; not a single green tree is to be seen, the thickest trunks alone remaining, and these as if only left at last to show that vegetation had ceased; which is no doubt owing to the great quantity of electricity with which the atmosphere was charged during the hurricane."

Extract from a letter to Professor Ansted, Vice-Secretary of the Geological Society of London, dated Malacca, February 4, 1847.

Subsequently to the date of the above paper, finding that but a slow and unsatisfactory progress could be made by land, I availed myself of the natural vertical sections afforded by the shores of Singapore, and the smaller islands into which the southern extremity of the peninsula range is broken, and was thus soon in possession of a body of facts which gave a certainty and consistency to the above views. I minutely examined the islands of Púlo Bráni, Blákan Mátí, Sikúkúr, and Sikíjáng on the one side ; and Púlo 'Ubin, Púlo Tíkong Besár, Púlo Tíkong Kechíl, Sejáhát Besár and Kechíl, &c., on the other side. I also explored the neighbouring coasts of the peninsula and the banks of the Johore River. The result was, that I found the foregoing hypothesis, so far as it had been developed, to be substantially an expression of the facts. It had, however, given too much prominence to some modes of the volcanic or semi-volcanic action, and too little to others. Thus, although there has been a certain degree of eruption in some cases where the gases in forcing their way to the surface have excited an unusual mechanical force, their action has, in general, been limited to a partial reduction and metamorphosis of the rock in the zones or dykes through which they have passed up [or in those larger tracts beneath which the surface of the plutonic sea has risen to such high subterraneous levels that the whole superincumbent matter has been saturated by its exhalations. I have also noticed several facts which appear to require us to believe that some portions at least of Singapore were under water at the time when the gaseous action first reached the surface. The vast abundance of hydrated peroxide of iron, and the mode in which ancient ferruginated breccias and conglomerates sometimes occur, would be most simply explained by this hypothesis. The circumstances adverted to in the paper on this subject must be borne in mind. In some places a considerable quantity of matter derived from the hills has been deposited in the intervening valleys, probably at or soon after the time of elevation, and been subsequently covered up by modern sea mud, on which mangroves have rooted and spread].

The most difficult branch of the inquiry has been the relation between the volcanic action to which the sedimentary rocks have been subjected, and the crystalline rocks which are associated with them. But, disregarding this for the present, and considering the volcanic action apart from any hypothesis of its origin or its relations, and reasoning from its visible effects, we may lay down this position absolutely, that the whole region in question (and a much wider one, as it will be found, extending to the lower ranges of the Himalayas, a large part of Australia, a part of Africa, &c.) has been exposed to a well-marked and peculiar, perhaps a unique,*

---

* This I had been very slow to believe, because although there may be places where a fossil fauna or flora altogether peculiar is found, it is scarcely conceivable that any plutonic action should have an entirely local character, or that one repeated over so many parts of an extensive region in Asia, should not hitherto have been observed by geologists in Europe or America. I have, however, read nearly every English work on geology without meeting a description of any considerable development of rocks in those quarters of the globe resembling our laterites, and have consequently been obliged to work out their true theory with little help from books, and by dint of patient and minute observation. A few months ago I was led to think that English writers were too much occupied in establishing their own opinions to present a full view of those of continental geologists, and that the latter were leaving them behind in the science of rocks of injection, reduction, and eruption. It appeared necessary, therefore, to gather their views from their own explanations of them. In

igneous action. It has varied in its intensity and mode of operation, but everywhere certain prevailing characters demonstrate its unity. These are both chemical and mechanical, the first depending principally on the never-failing presence of iron, and the latter evinced by the extraordinary uniformity in the shapes, ramifications, and even sizes of the ranges in which the rocks affected have been raised. Whatever be the nature of the original sedimentary strata, this mighty agent has impressed them with the same marks, and the more powerful its grasp has been the more have their native peculiarities been confounded. But between the effects of this intensest force, and that so weak that we barely detect its touch, the degrees are almost infinite. Still, the only way in which I can render this slight immethodical sketch at all intelligible will be to note a few of the better marked disguises which the rocks assume under this potent influence. I say disguises, because the geology of the Malay Peninsula almost wholly resolves itself into the identification of the original rock under its multiplex transformations. Without a key to this, derived from a minute examination and comparison of the modes of alteration, the whole is a dark riddle, or our geology becomes a congeries of bewildered gropings and sheer mistakes.

The first or lowest degree of alteration, let us say in a clay, is the formation of isolated blotches of a reddish colour in the rock, but unaccompanied by any other apparent change.

Second, a slight comparative hardness in the blotches.

Third, in addition a grittiness—they may now be termed nodules or concretions, and we may include in this catalogue all degrees from an incipient grittiness to a hard compact character, which gives the nodule the appearance of an imbedded pebble. [The nodules are sometimes hard and compact without being gritty or quartzose, and they are gritty in their nascent state where the rock is originally arenaceous in any degree.]

the first work which I ordered, and which I received two days ago by the overland mail, I found an allusion to a district in Europe which has been described by an eminent French geologist, and which, if I may judge from the few lines in which it is referred to, must be in many respects analogous to the lateritic tracts of the Malay Peninsula, and consequently of India, &c., also. In a few months I hope to have the means of ascertaining whether this is the fact, and also whether in the writings of other continental geologists any similar tracts are noticed. A few days ago Mr. Balestier put into my hands a letter which he had received from one of the gentlemen attached to the recent French embassy to China, a pupil of the celebrated chemist Dumas, in which he explains the views of himself and another member of the embassy on the geology of Singapore. His theory of the origin of the laterite had occurred to me when I first began to suspect its real nature. As my observations extended and became more minute, I found that such a theory only explained a small part of the phenomena, and that which I have now held for about two years gradually developed itself, growing clearer and simpler in proportion as it embraced wider ranges of facts.—J. R. L., March 16, 1847.

Fourth, the nodules bulge out at different points, and the preceding three degrees may be repeated in nodules of this shape.

Fifth, the arms or branches unite so that the rock is pervaded by a complete congeries or ramification of red, rounded, but irregularly shaped branches. The form of these branches varies very much, but is generally uniform for a considerable space. Very frequently it is as if ginger roots were continued in all directions. At other times the spaces between the ramifications are narrow sinuous perforations or isolated vesicles or deep straight tubes, or chambers in tubes. This structure is sometimes the result of an allied or predisposing structure in the rock affected, and at other times it appears to be wholly superinduced by the altering agency. In this last form the red portion is found of various degrees of hardness, but not so soft as the first degree. In general it possesses a medium degree of hardness, so as to be cut with an axe.*

Sixth. In this class we may include the products of all degrees of heat that has been suddenly applied in sufficient force to produce calcination, and this distinguishes it from all the preceding, in which the rock has been merely impregnated with hot ferruginous gases or vapours—where the calcination has not been great the original structure of the rock is better preserved than in the merely impregnated rock, because in the latter the indurating action of the iron, the different degrees of its oxidation when it comes within the influence of water and air, and the washing out of the softer portions in the hollows, often give it an amygdaloidal or vesicular structure totally different from that of the original rock ; a slight roasting on the other hand preserves the latter, and saves it from meteoric destruction. The limit of this preserving power is soon reached, and every higher degree of heat and larger infusion of iron exerts in each rock a corresponding destructive or altering power, and approaches nearer that point where the original differences in the rocks cease to be distinguishable. The extreme limits of this class appear to be where the rock is merely scorched on the surface, preserving its original character beneath, and where it is thoroughly reduced to a cinder. This class of rocks very frequently present mamillated and botryoidal surfaces. It occurs in dykes and on the sides of fissures through which hot blasts appear to have rushed. It also occurs in an outer layer or thick crust over rocks of the fifth class, in which case it would appear that the different effects produced by the same gas arose from the upper crust being exposed to the air and consequently burnt. In the same way the calcination to some depth on the sides of fissures may have arisen in certain cases, not from the gas that rushed through them being hotter than that in the body of

---

* It hardens on free exposure to the atmosphere and is used in building.

the rock (though this was most likely the fact in general), but from the presence of air producing combustion. Between dykes of this last class, rocks altered in the above fifth degree are common ; but dykes of the fifth degree also occur. The difference in every case will depend on the relative intensity of the heat and degree of ferrugination of the gas, and the fact whether there was air to support combustion or not.

The preceding remarks are applicable chiefly to rocks either composed of clay or in which there is a basis of clay. But a very small proportion of clay suffices for the exhibition of the above modes of action. When the rock is wholly arenaceous, nodules are not formed. The rock is reduced to a dry incoherent or friable mass where the action has been slight. Where it has been greater, a network of cracks pervades the rocks, and the seams have either a thin plate of blackish ferruginous crust included between them, or their sides have a similar thin coating which is often covered with an exceedingly minute mamillation. In some cases the matter between the seams or ferruginous walls has been dissipated, and the rock appears as a black honeycomb. In all instances of high calcination the sandstone is greatly indurated. It is sometimes converted into a crystalline rock.

Friable shales, again, are sometimes changed into a dry powdery matter resembling volcanic ash.

Where the bodies of the strata are not altered, their planes of junction are sometimes slightly indurated and mamillated. The gas in every case has taken the readiest channels to the surface, and where fissures have not assisted its emission, it has forced itself through the planes of least cohesion, such as the junction planes of different beds, cleavage planes, &c. It thus often exposes the internal structure of the rock where it would otherwise appear compact. The composition of the rock has often had a great influence in determining the channel of emission, so that its action sometimes is chiefly confined to one or more strata, the adjoining beds appearing to be little if at all affected.

Quartz frequently accompanies the ferruginous change, but rarely to a considerable extent.

The above are the most common modes of alteration, but there are others approaching nearer to true metamorphism. Clay is converted into a porcellanous or jaspidious substance—sandstone into a hard siliceous flinty substance. Conglomerates and breccias have frequently a base of this nature.*

The mechanical force accompanying the evolution of the hot ferruginous gases or vapours has been great, but it has been exerted within narrow limits. Thus the strata are often vertical,

---

* I have since found on the eastern coast of Pulo Krimin Kichil (the little Carimon) great masses of clays and conglomerates transformed into a perfect crystalline chert as hard as flint.—J. R. L.

and generally rise at high angles, but the dip varies much, and even in adjacent hills of the same connected range is sometimes reversed. Yet they are never raised more than a few hundred feet above the common basal level, and the majority of the almost innumerable hillocks which compose the ranges of Singapore are probably rather under than above 100 feet. At the southern extremity of the western St. John's (Púlo Sikíjang) two adjoining hills have been formed by strata being bent into a convex shape, rising only a few feet above the level of the beach. There is a remarkable approach to uniformity in the strike of all the strata and in the direction of the hill ranges. Speaking generally, it may be said to approximate to N.W.—S.E. The hills have commonly mamillary surfaces. The ranges may be said to consist of distinct hills bulging out and united at their sides. The central hills are generally the more bulky. Lateral hills ramify on each side to a short distance. The whole connected system is disposed in a symmetrical ramose manner, indicating a wonderful uniformity in the mode of operation of the dynamical forces which produced them. The investigation of the forms of these hills, and of the laws of the mechanical forces of which they are the result, assumes a high interest and importance when we find that these forms are not confined to Singapore, but are repeated in low hill ranges over large portions of the peninsula, Sumatra, Southern India, Northern India, Northern Australia, &c., and accompanied, as I believe, by volcanic phenomena of exactly the same nature as those which I have described. I do not say that the phenomena are identical at all points. In Singapore itself they vary almost infinitely. But they are always analogous, frequently the same, and to my mind are undoubtedly the product of one well-marked species of volcanic* action.

I should not omit to notice the frequent occurrence, in those ranges which have been most burnt, of mounds or monticules of scorious blocks, sometimes on the summits, and sometimes bulging out from the sides of hills. The ridges and angles of hills appear frequently to present scorious blocks.

The valleys between the long hill ranges are in Singapore perfectly flat, so that they display the outlines of the bases of the ranges almost as well as if they still remained what they were at no very remote period, long narrow inlets of the sea. This circumstance also is not confined to Singapore.

I will now briefly notice the nature of the sedimentary rocks

---

* In reference to the igneous changes which the rocks have undergone, I use the words volcanic and plutonic indiscriminately, because a minute examination of some of the best marked developments of crystalline rocks (graduating from basaltic to granitic types) at the extremity of the peninsula, has led me to think that though the distinction is useful and appropriate in some regions, the theory which it expresses is not sound as a general one—at least as expounded by many geologists.

which have been more or less altered and elevated in the modes
I have mentioned. If you think it worth while, you can, I dare
say, procure a copy of Mr. Thomson's chart of Singapore Straits
from the Admiralty for reference. It would scarcely be advisable
at present to attempt to make a geological map. The southern
portion of the island (including the town, the adjacent district to
the N.W.; the ranges between the road from the town to Búkit
Tímáh, the central and highest hill, and the sea to the S.W.), and
the islands of Blakan Mátí, Púlo Brání, St. John's, &c., are composed of shales, clays, sandstones and conglomerates, the shales
predominating. It is impossible to refer these rocks to any place
in your European systems, as no organic remains have yet been
discovered, and the only rocks with which they are associated are
hypogene. In their general appearance and mineralogical characters they agree with the aluminous and arenaceous beds of the
new red sandstone. Between the parallel of strike passing
through the town and the steep Tulloh Blangan range there is an
area about a mile in breadth, stretching from the sea inland over
the Tanjong Pagar and Tanghir districts, and of course in a
direction approaching to N.W., and in the opposite direction,
including Púlo Bráni and the eastern portion of Blakan Mátí,
composed in great measure of shale strata, although a few of
sandstone also occur. The prevailing colours of the shale beds
are dull violet, liver brown, and chocolate. Beds of the most
lively variegated colours sometimes occur molted, striped,
damasked, &c.; the colours are white, yellow, orange, red, violet,
purple, green, bluish, and blackish, in addition to the dull violet
and chocolate. To the N.E. of this tract sandstone is more
frequently interstratified. To the S.W. sandstones, grits, and
coarse conglomerates prevail; and these are continued, interstratified, however, with some shales, from the range along the coast of
Tulloh Blangan through the western portion of Blakan Mátí, and
through Sikúkúr and Sikijang (St. John's), in a south-westerly
zone. I have not yet pursued this zone farther across the strait,
but the island of Sámbo, on the other side, is a continuation of
the same parallel of elevation, and may consist of the same rocks.
To the N.E. of the town a large alluvial plain sweeps into the
country. The hills around it are principally arenaceous. The
arenaceous band, however, on the N.W. of the plain merely
skirts it. Beyond this band (and succeeding the sandstone
ranges to the N.E. of the shale tract first noticed) a broad zone
of clayey hills, of which the boundaries are irregular, but which
may be from three to four miles in breadth, stretches through the
heart of the island of Búkit Tímáh, and thence across to the Sálát
Támbroh, or old Strait of Singapore, behind the island. The tract
to the S.W. of this, stretching from the parallel of the S.W.
boundary of the shale band to the S.W. point of the island

(Tanjong Gúl), is composed principally of sandstone and shale, but granitic bases and ranges also occur. The great clay tract I believe to consist in large measure of decomposed hypogene rocks—sienitic and granitic chiefly (it has only, however, been partially examined or laid open). Blocks of these rocks are seen at the surface in some of the hills, and the sections made by roads so exactly resemble decomposed crystalline rocks, that I have no doubt the whole of the clay hills are at bottom hypogene rocks. Their structure and composition I believe to be very variable. This tract is continued over a considerable part of the rest of the island to the N.E., but a large tract of sandstone (accompanied by a very little shale) stretches into it. The coast boundary of this tract is a line of about four miles, extending along the south-eastern shore of the island from Síglap to beyond Tánáh Merá Besár (the Red Cliffs). It insulates the granitic N.E. projecting portion of the island at Changy, embraces the northern coast from the inner extremity of this promontory to the inner extremity of that of Púngal, and then proceeds inland. The line of its junction on the N.W. with the granitic tract that surrounds it I have not yet ascertained, but it is probably irregular. On the S.W. it connects itself with the arenaceous band surrounding the plain previously mentioned, and indeed forms the larger portion of the boundary of the plain. It then stretches inland for some distance, having the S.E. projection of the great granite tract interposed between it and the arenaceous and shaley bands, first above noticed. P. 'Ubin is entirely hypogene, varying from granitic to compact types. Hornblende is largely developed. The structure of the rocks is highly curious and interesting. I have given much attention to this island, and in the beginning of September last sent a full account of it, and of the geological views to which it seemed to lead, to the Bataviaasch Genootschap van Kunsten en Wetenschappen, in whose Transactions, the president writes me, it will appear. In this paper I had been led to some views with which I find Mr. Darwin had been occupied, and which are developed in the chapter on plutonic and metamorphic rocks in his geological observations on South America, of which, though bearing the same date as my paper, I did not receive a copy till about a fortnight ago. The germ of his ideas is, however, contained in his "Volcanic Islands," which I have referred to in my paper. As I have also considered the subject from some other, and, as I believe, new points of view, I shall send you a copy of the paper in English, the "Batavian Transactions" being in Dutch.* The coast of the mainland

---

* In a general descriptive sketch of some portion of the Straits of Malacca which I sent to the Geographical Society some time ago, I mentioned the singular grooved rocks at the Chinese Quarries on P. 'Ubin, and hazarded some conjectures respecting their origin; when I wrote that paper I had made only

behind P. 'Ubin consists of rocks some of which would be called plutonic and others volcanic, like those of Púlo 'Ubin, but the whole are undoubtedly of the same contemporaneous origin. At Runto, in the estuary of the Johore River, sandstone similar to that of the Singapore Red cliffs, and, like it, remarkable for being nearly horizontal, is exposed. Farther up the river the rocks exposed are of a decomposed felspathic character, and exactly resemble some of those of the hypogene tract of Singapore. At one place a hard ferruginous crust about nine inches thick overlaid a decomposed felspathic rock. Púlo Tikóng Besár and Kechil consist chiefly of sandstones and in part of shales, often greatly altered by volcanic action. On the coast to the S.E. near Johore Hill, or at Tanjong Pingrang, are found within a small compass soft shale or clay—clay indurated so as to resemble chert—conglomerate highly indurated and partially transformed —quartz rock, and traces of blackish brown slags, indicating various degrees and even some difference in the mode of the volcanic action.

The connection between the crystalline and sedimentary rocks of the district is susceptible of two explanations. We may either consider the former in their fluid or viscous state as having been the immediate agents of the volcanic and mechanical forces to which the latter have been subjected, or we may consider the former as the product of the first plutonic action beneath this region ; the latter as sedimentary rocks subsequently accumulated [over them] during a period of quiescence, and their fracture, upheaval, and alteration as the effects of a new excitement to activity in the plutonic sea below, in which the old plutonic crust, with its sedimentary covering was broken and upheaved, and ferruginous or ferro-siliceous gases copiously emitted through the lines of fracture. On either supposition the ferruginous character of the emissions would be accounted for, because the upper granites, &c., contain much iron in their hornblende, and whether the mass below the granite crust had remained in its fluid state during the deposit of the sedimentary rocks, or had been wholly solidified and subsequently melted down anew, the gases given off from it, when vents were formed, would probably preserve the same character as those given off from its original surface before any granitic crust had been formed. I cannot stop now to explain how the prevailing plutonic theories, as applied to the phenomena of the district, seemed, at the time when the paper first mentioned was written, to require the adoption of the

one flying visit to the quarries and was under the impression that the deep channels were confined to this locality. My first geological visit subsequently at once undeceived me. In the paper forwarded to the Batavian Society I have shown how these channels have resulted from the original structure of the rock under ordinary decomposing and eroding influences.

opinion that the granites, &c., were in existence when the volcanic action took place.   Even under the influence of these theories I considered the point as very doubtful, and although it involved consequences irreconcilable with these theories, I ventured to hazard the conjecture that the upper hypogene rocks had been the immediate agents of the changes.   The examination of Púlo 'Ubin shook my faith in these theories as expounded by some of their principal advocates, and the conjecture assumed a high degree of probability.   Latterly I had all but embraced it, but still supended its complete adoption in the hope that I would discover some phenomenon amounting to ocular proof of its truth.

I have only another point to advert to before I come to Malacca. If you have taken any interest in Indian geology, you are doubtless acquainted with the rock called laterite which prevails so largely in Southern India, and is also found in Bengal, &c., and which to this day remains the most fertile subject of discord amongst Indian geologists, although the general opinion appears of late to have settled down in favour of its being a sedimentary deposit.   In the paper first alluded to in this letter I made the following remarks with reference to laterite :—" Many of the clayey hills here [in Singapore] appear to me to be decomposed sienite, sometimes unaltered by supervening volcanic action, but generally partaking in the metamorphism which the matter of most of the elevated land has suffered from that cause."

May I venture to suggest that the hypothesis which is developed in this paper for Singapore, might, if applied to the laterite of India, perhaps explain its origin, and in doing so to a certain extent also reconcile the conflicting opinions that have been maintained regarding it ?   All that I have read of the great laterite formations of the south of India, and which extend to the heart of Bengal, where they are described by Dr. Buchanan Hamilton, leads to the conclusion that they are not purely volcanic, sedimentary, or decomposed matter, but what I have termed semi-volcanic.   The same formation is found at Malacca, and analogous deposits occur at Singapore, and both are inseparably associated and evidently contemporaneous with altered rocks of the kind previously noticed.   If we conceive an area with trap, granite, sandstone, shale, &c., exposed at the surface (in the atmosphere or in the sea), and partly decomposed or disintegrated, to be subjected to a peculiar species of minor volcanic action like that which is described in this paper* (*the distinctive phenomenon, pro-*

* Whether the upper plutonic rocks were the direct sources of the igneous action, or were themselves, together with the sedimentary rocks acted on by a lower plutonic sea, does not affect my explanation of the formation of laterites ; for whether I adopt the one or the other view of *the source* of the injections and impregnations which produced the laterites, or remain in doubt on the subject, *the fact*, deduced from the actual examination of these rocks, that they have been so produced, is not at all rendered doubtful.

bably, of one and the same geological epoch), the results would be, that with the occasional exception of matter ejected from no great depth, and some dykes and veins, the previous soft surface rocks would be merely altered and metamorphosed by heat and impregnated with iron, derived perhaps from the basaltic and other ferriferous rocks through which the discharged steam, gases, and water had passed in their ascent. Whether the action took place under or above the sea would be determined by the presence or absence of the ordinary marks of oceanic denudation. When clays strongly ferruginous and soft from saturation with water, are dried, the iron previously held in solution by the water is deposited between the particles, and cements them into a hard compact rock. Hence the induration of laterite clays on exposure to the atmosphere." My opinion therefore was that, though proper laterite was nothing more than one of the forms of alteration produced by plutonic ferruginous gases—that which, in the arbitrary scale formerly given, I have called the fifth degree—and that any rock in which a sufficient quantity of clay was present, whether it were purely sedimentary or a decomposed crystalline or compact rock, or whatever its origin or character in other respects was— would, on being exposed to certain degrees of impregnation by such gases, and under the conditions before adverted to, become *laterized.* This opinion was abundantly confirmed by later observations, but these also proved that iron alone was capable of producing rocks of a lateritic form. The result therefore was that, although proper laterite is produced in the mode which I have mentioned, yet that mode is not essential to the formation of a lateritic structure. The only essential thing is the diffusion of iron in ramifications throughout a clayey rock. Get the iron so diffused, and it is of little consequence by what door it was introduced. The only distinctive quality of proper laterite is that it has not merely got the iron, but has been in various degrees baked in the process of impregnation, and close examination can always discover traces of this. On the other hand, iron may be introduced by aqueous saturation, and if the soft rocks so saturated have planes of inferior cohesion, as many rocks have, the iron will there accumulate. If the iron solution pervade a homogeneous clayey rock as water does a sponge, the segregating or concre tionary quality of iron so diffused may gradually draw it into connected nodules or ramifications ; and indeed it is probable that in all cases of volcanic gaseous impregnation of the compact parts of rocks the ferruginous matter remained for a time diffused throughout the rock, and that this segregating tendency subsequently superinduced its contraction into ramifications and blotches. Where the gaseous impregnation was weak, it would speedily draw into isolated blotches ; where stronger, into isolated concretions ; where strongest, and the heat not too great, into ramifications. Again, the iron may be laid up in the heart of a crystalline rock solidified from a plutonic fluid holding iron, and the essential condition for the production of the laterite structure may be found in decomposed hornblendic or even black mica- ceous granites that have not been subjected to any supervening volcanic action. The oxidation of iron solutions in clays on exposure to the air, and the combustion of rocks by heated ferruginous gas, are chemically related, and the product of these two processes, geologically so widely sundered, is sometimes difficultly distinguishable by the eye. Ancient conglomeritic and brecciated laterites and ferruginous rocks appear to have been formed in many localities at or soon after the period of the ferruginous emissions by fragments or pebbles settling down in a sandy or clayey base saturated with ferruginous water. Similar conglomerates, breccias, and sandstones are at present forming along the coasts where the hills or banks above contain much iron ; but all these are very obviously distinguishable from the original plutonically laterized sedimentary rocks.

When I visited Malacca about two years ago I had paid very little attention to these subjects, and had not formed the preceding views. When an opportunity occurred at the beginning of last month of revisiting the place, I eagerly seized the occasion of testing these views in a new locality, and one which had been decribed by geologists, such as Captain Newbold and Dr. Ward, familiar with the much-vexed laterites of Southern India. Captain Newbold, in his work on the Straits, describes the Malacca hills "as being generally of granite, with the exception of a few near the sea-coast, which are of laterite overlying the granite. Speci- mens of hornblende rock have been brought to me, he continues, from a hill a little south of Malacca ; the islets on the coasts are of granite of various kinds, with white, red, and green felspar. In all, the felspar appears to be predominant, and mica deficient." Dr. Ward says of the Malacca laterite : "In all its properties it agrees exactly with the rock common on the Malabar coast, and described by Dr. Buchanan under the name of laterite." I was now therefore, for the first time, in a position to bring my theory to the strongest test, for I had not seen any specimen of Indian laterite, and could only compare some of the apparently analogous Singapore rocks with it from descriptions. Captain Newbold, in one of the latest of his numerous papers on the geology of Southern India, describes very minutely the often-mentioned laterite of Beder, and makes some remarks on the long-debated question of origin. He combats the idea that it is a contem- poraneous rock associating with trap, or a product, like trap, of igneous fusion. He also casts doubt on the theory advocated by several geologists, of the laterite being "nothing more than the result of the recent disintegration of the granitic and trappean rocks *in situ,"* and, without giving a decided opinion, says : " The beds of lignite discovered by General Cullan and myself in the laterite of Malabar and Travancore, and the deposits of petrified wood in the Red Hills of Pondichery, in a rock which, though differing in structure, I consider as identical in age with the laterite, and other facts too long for enumeration here, points rather to *its detrital origin like sandstone."* * (" Journal of the Asiatic Society of Bengal," vol. xiii. p. 995, 1844.) Mr. Darwin, I may mention in passing, seems to lean to a similar opinion with respect to analogous rocks noticed by him. " The origin of these superficial beds," he says, "though sufficiently obscure, seems to be due to alluvial action on detritus abounding with iron." (" Volcanic Islands," p. 143.)

The first lateritic locality which I visited on my arrival here was the island of Púlo Upa, from which much laterite has been removed for building purposes, and where it continues to be cut. The first fragment which I knocked off the rock at once satisfied me that my theory was correct. It was a rock totally different in its original character from any which I have found at the southern extremity of the peninsula, but which, by the same agency that altered the ordinary sedimentary rocks there, had been transformed from a common argillo-micaceous schist into a rock undistinguishable, save on minute inspection, and, where the alteration has been great, absolutely undistinguishable from some of the altered sedimentary shales and clays of Singapore. Upon careful examination I found, as I expected, in the sections afforded by the coast of this little islet, the original unaltered micaceous rock with great bands or dykes, and overlying masses, exhibiting abundant varieties of transformation from a rock slightly discoloured by the ferruginous action through several lateritic types, to the calcined slaggy form in which the original composition and structure are wholly obliterated. I cannot enter into further particulars. My subsequent examination of about fifty miles of the coast from Púlo Arang Arang (P. Arram), southward, and of a portion of the interior of Malacca, has proved that the whole of this region has been originally composed in a great measure of the same argillo-micaceous schist. I shall hereafter give its mineralogical characters, for I have not time nor means at present to ascertain them carefully. It is soft and glistering like silk, and leaves a powder on the fingers which exactly resembles in appearance the fine glistering powdery down from a butterfly's wing. In some cases it is less dry and more argillaceous. With the exception of Cape Rachado† it has almost everywhere been more

---

* I have read all Captain Newbold's papers with the attention which they deserve, and I think every fact which he notices in his notes on laterite tracts is reconcilable with the theory which I maintain.

† Where the plutonic action has been of a silicifying more than a ferruginating nature.

or less penetrated in bands (and broad spaces occasionally) by ferruginous gas, which has transformed it into one or other of the forms before described, or some intermediate forms. Dykes and veins of pure quartz and of quartz with numerous fissures filled with an iron crust are frequent in some localities, while in others they are wanting. Wherever these dykes and veins occur the foliation of the schist is much contorted. In some localities the surface is covered with black shining mamillated scorious blocks passing down into a lateritic mass, in which the schist is often not greatly altered, but is penetrated by ramifying dykes and veins of a ferruginous, quartzose, or quartzo-ferruginous character. Isolated pseudo-crystals and isolated plates of quartz occur in the schist in some places, and, on the other hand, patches of the schist are found in the hearts of large pieces of quartz. But it would require other twenty pages to give even an outline of the varied and irregular manner in which the rock has been altered. If we did not everywhere come upon portions of the original rock unaltered, or find traces of it in the altered tracts, it would be almost impossible to believe that all the varieties of the latter have had a common origin. I must briefly allude to Cape Rachado. This is a bolder and higher range than any found elsewhere along the coast, and projects far into the Straits. It is the only locality which I have yet seen where the quartzose has predominated over the ferruginous action of the plutonic gases. The rock everywhere exhibits unequivocal evidence of its having been originally the same argillo-micaceous schist which prevails over the rest of the region. In some places the cliffs are almost wholly quartzose ; in others the rock is a congeries of quartz veins and foliæ ; in others the seams between the quartz foliæ have a coating of the original mica ; in others the original mica predominates, and the quartz is more sparingly scattered through it. Broad dykes of compact quartz, of quartz mixed with a ferruginous crust, of numerous parallel veins with quartz crystals springing from their sides, and the interstices filled with a black ferruginous substance, sometimes dull and sometimes shining (apparently hydrated oxide of iron), and of quartz holding a similar substance in seams also occur. One of the largest and boldest cliffs has been converted into a compact siliceous rock pervaded by numerous quartzose and ferruginous dykes and veins. In some places a complete network of fissures ramifies through the rock, and it is evident that quartzo-ferruginous gas or vapour has been injected through these fissures and the large veins and dykes, and metamorphosed the rock.

At the Water Islands south of Malacca, and at Tanjong Panchur and Budewa to the north, I carefully examined some large developments of granitic rocks. In the former I found some dykes composed of quartz felspar and a ferruginous substance similar to that already noticed. In decomposed felspar, and also in solid quartz in those dykes I found much both of decomposed and of undecomposed iron pyrites. Although these dykes seem to countenance the idea that the plutonic agency which has so greatly affected the superior rocks was exerted after the formation of the upper granite, I have from all my observations come to a different conclusion. I cannot now state its grounds, and I do not positively bind myself to an opinion which perhaps I cannot demonstrate beyond doubt to be correct ; but the result of my constant consideration of the subject in all its relations, and with reference to every new locality that I have explored, is as follows :—The whole region has been subjected to plutonic reduction. The plutonic fluid by its pressure has caused fractures in N.W.-S.E. lines, and it has swollen up in ramifying bands having that general direction. Its pressure and heat have varied at different portions of its surface. In some places the heat has been so intense as to reduce all the superincumbent rock up to the very surface into its own substance, and it has swollen up into mountains in the interior and hills in the exterior lateritic tracts of the peninsula.*

The transformed and partially transformed sedimentary hill ranges rest, I conceive, upon granite bubbles† where the plutonic action has been less intense. The fissures and cracks formed by the pressure of these bubbles have been the channels, the gases given off from their surface the immediate agents, of all the alterations. The tracts where only granite now appears swelling above the surface had previously passed through the same stages. In other words, laterite is one of the earliest stages in the reduction

* This is opposed to prevalent theory, and it may be asked whether in that case it would not have flowed over? But I have found it impossible to apply the prevalent plutonic theory—I mean that of a necessarily Tartarean origin of granite, &c.—to the granites of the south of the peninsula, considered even *per se*, and I would ask in return whether there is any proof or probability that granite prior to solidification ever exists in the upper crust of the globe in any other form than as a viscid cohesive mass. I believe that granitic bubbles always swell up with exceeding slowness, and that the centre of the bubble (if its base be of great size) may remain for centuries, or even longer, in a viscid state, while a thick solid crust of granite has formed on the sides and summit, and that the central part will still exert a slow upward and outward pressure as it solidifies, and may itself be subject to a long-continued elevatory pressure from the sea below. In other words, the summits of granitic mountains and minor masses may go on rising above the base, after the latter with the whole surface has solidified, and when the base has no further upraised movement, save what it may possess in common with the plutonic sea below. Great dislocations in the upper crust must necessarily result, but does not every plutonic mountain range bear witness to such dislocations? I must refer to my paper on Púlo 'Ubin for the facts on which these views are based.

† I do not mean that each base or hill range has a corresponding protuberance on the surface of the plutonic base, but that the whole system of hills and hillocks has been produced by inequalities in that surface, and by the directions which the principal and divergent lines of fracture have taken.

of the upper rocks superincumbent on a plutonic sea into the substance of which that sea is composed. Where the heat has been least intense the upper rocks have merely been raised; where greater, lateritic, scorious, and other partially altered hill ranges have been produced. A higher degree of plutonic action has produced quartzo-ferruginous ranges like that of Cape Rachado. The highest degree has transformed or reduced the whole into granite and allied crystalline rocks ; from the mode in which the granites, &c., come to the surface at Singapore, we see that the whole region there has been broken up by the plutonic sea below. I can proceed no further, however, at present, and must close this rough draught of my ideas.[1]

XXXVII.

CATALOGUE OF REPTILES INHABITING THE MALAYAN PENINSULA AND ISLANDS.

Collected or observed by THEODORE CANTOR, M.D., *Bengal Medical Service.*

["Journal of the Asiatic Society of Bengal," vol. xvi. pp. 607–656, 897–952, 1026–1078.]

CHELONIA.

FAM. ELODIDÆ, or MARSH TORTOISES, *Dum. and Bibr.*

SUB-FAM. CRYPTODERINÆ, *Dum. and Bibr.*

Gen. GEOEMYDA, *Gray.*

HEAD covered with thin continued skin ; chin not bearded. Legs strong, not fringed behind. Toes 5–4, strong, short, free, covered above by a series of shields ; claws short. Tail tapering ; shell depressed, three-keeled ; hinder edge strongly toothed. Sternum solid, broad truncated before, notched behind ; gular plate linear, band-like, small ; axillary and inguinal plates small.

---

[1] [See also the following papers by the same author: "The Rocks of Pulo Ubin," in vol. xxii. (1846) of the "Verhandelingen van het Bataviaasch Genootschap;" "Notices of the Geology of the Straits of Singapore," in the "Quarterly Journal of the Geological Society," vol. vii. (1851), pp. 310–344, and reprinted in the "Journal of the Indian Archipelago," vol. vi. (1852), pp. 179–217; and "Journal of an Excursion from Singapur to Malacca and Pinang," in vol. xvi. of the "Journal of the R. Geogr. Soc." pp. 304–331.]

GEOEMYDA SPINOSA, Bell.

SYN.—Emys spinosa, Bell apud Dum. and Bibr.
Emys bispinoso, Schlegel.
Testudo emys, Müller?
Geoemyda spinosa, Gray.

Shell oblong, subquadrate, keeled, flattened above, chestnut coloured, front and hinder edge strongly serrated; vertebral plates broad, first suburceolate; costal plates with a posterior subsuperior areola, with a slight subconic tubercle; beneath yellow, brown-rayed; *young* depressed, pale brown, bluntly keeled, with a distinct spine in the areola of each discal plate.

HAB.—*Pinang Hills.**
Sumatra.

Two individuals were observed by the Hon. Sir William Norris, late Recorder of H.M. Court of Judicature in the Straits of Malacca, on the Great Hill at Pinang, at a distance from water. The colour of the shell is a dirty brownish ochre, here and there with sooty rays, which numerously intersect the concave sternum. The keel, the marginal spines, and the costal tubercles are nearly obliterated, and the shell presents frequent marks of corrosion. The larger individual is of the following dimensions:—

Length of the head . . . . 1⅝ inches.
„ „ neck . . . . 1⅝ „
„ „ shell . . . . 8 „
„ „ tail . . . . 1⅞ „

A large tick was firmly adhering to the throat of one of these tortoises, the presence of which, however, does not indicate an exclusively terrestrial life, as one species at least of the *Riciniæ* (*Ixodes ophiophilus*, Müller?) occurs on aquatic as well as terrestrial serpents. The following are the characters of *Ixodes geoemydæ*. The short sucker is depressed, slightly widening towards the bifid apex, and encased by the palpi. Above and at a short distance from the latter are two minute rounded fossæ. The cephalic, tetragonal plate is of a reddish-brown colour, with a yellow spot at the posterior angle. The oval body is dark pearl-coloured. On each side, close to the articulation of the posterior leg, appears a small rounded horny plate. The legs are reddish-brown, with a yellow spot at each of the joints, except the last. Swollen as the

---

* Localities printed in *italics* signify those from whence the animals of the catalogue were obtained; in ordinary type those previously given by authors. The descriptions are in most cases taken from life; in the few in which it is expressly noted, shortly after death; in none from specimens preserved in spirits of wine.

tick appeared, it measured six-eighths of an inch in length, half an inch in breadth.

Gen. EMYS, *Brogniart.*

Head moderate, covered with a thin hard skin; chin not bearded. Feet short, covered with scales; toes 5–4, strong, shielded above, webbed to the claws. Tail moderate. Shell, depressed. Sternum solid, broad, truncated before, notched behind, affixed to the thorax by a bony symphysis, covered by the ends of the pectoral and abdominal plates; axillary and inguinal plates moderate, distinct.

A. *Vertebral plates lozenge-shaped.*—Gray.

EMYS CRASSICOLLIS, Bell, MSS. apud Gray, apud Horsfield : " Life of Raffles."

SYN.—Emys crassicollis, Bell apud Dum. and Bibr.
Emys Spengleri, var. Schlegel.

Shell ovate, oblong, rather convex, revolute on the sides and deeply toothed behind, black, slightly three-keeled; keels close; first vertebral plate elongate, six-sided; sternum flat, pale, and keeled on the sides; head and neck thick, black.

HAB.—*Malayan Peninsula, Pinang.*
Sumatra, Java.

In Malayan individuals, numerously inhabiting rivulets and ponds in the valleys, the throat is whitish, and a small white spot appears on each side of the occiput. The vertebral keels and the lateral spines become obliterated with age. The largest individual observed was of the following dimensions :—

Length of the head	. . . .	$1\frac{6}{8}$	inches.
„	„	neck	$1\frac{6}{8}$ „
„	„	shell	9 „
„	„	tail	$1\frac{1}{8}$ „

It feeds upon frogs, and also upon shell-fish and animal offal. Old Malay women, who may be seen after every heavy fall of rain, spending hours, rod in hand, over the overflowing ditches, out of which their huts rise, are often ludicrously disappointed on perceiving this tortoise on the hook.

B. *Vertebral plates broad, six-sided.*—Gray.

EMYS PLATYNOTA, Gray.

SYN.—" Kátong " of the Malays of the Peninsula.

Shell ovate, convex, yellow dotted, with the centre of the back quite flat, as if truncated; shields striated, nucleus central ; vertebral shields broader than long, six-sided, fifth keeled; the front and hinder margin strongly toothed; sternum flat, truncated before and slightly notched behind; tail moderate, tapering.

HAB.—*Malayan Peninsula, Pinang.*
Sumatra.

Mr. Gray's description refers to the young animal, of which the length of the shell is given in "Proceed. Zoolog. Soc." 1834, p. 54, as 9 inches. The representation of *Emys platynota* in "Illust. Ind. Zool.," from its size and the strongly toothed flat front and hind margins of the shell, also appears to be a young animal. The penultimate (the fourth) vertebral shield is represented as divided in two pieces, which if so in the original, must be accidental, as normally the fourth vertebral shield is six-sided, and in size nearly equalling the preceding. The nuclei of the costal shields are more central than represented in the plate.

In the living adult animal the head, neck, shell, tail, and feet are of a dirty yellowish or greenish brown, which becomes paler on the sternum. The nuclei of the vertebral shields are slightly raised. The costal shields are depressed, their sides sloping towards the nuclei, thus forming as it were very shallow hexagonal basins. The front and hind margins are broadly revolute, their toothed appearance worn off. The sternum is slightly concave in the centre. The largest individual was of the following dimensions:—

Length of the head	. . . .	o foot	3	inches.
,,	,,	neck	. . . .	o ,,	3	,,
,,	,,	shell	. . . .	1 ,,	$7\frac{4}{8}$	,,
,,	,,	tail	. . . .	o ,,	$2\frac{4}{8}$	,,

It lived in my garden at Pinang upwards of a twelvemonth, apparently without food, and it was never observed to enter a tank. The shell bears deep white marks of corrosion, in appearance like that observed in Testacea inhabiting stagnant water. The animal suffered itself to be touched with impunity, never offering to scratch or bite. This tortoise inhabits the valleys, but is apparently not numerous.

EMYS TRIVITTATA, Dum. and Bibr.

Shell smooth, entire, subcordiform, arched, yellowish-green, and with three broad longitudinal black bands; jaws toothed.

HAB.—*Malayan Peninsula, Pinang.*
Bengal.

It inhabits rivers and ponds on the Malayan Peninsula, but appears not to be numerous. In the Malayan adult animal there is a large black spot situated at the anterior lower angle of the marginal shields; there is no trace of a keel in the centre of the vertebral shields, and the very minute nuchal shield is triangular, with the apex towards the vertebral shields. The shield is rather oval than subcordiform. The sternum is slightly arched, of a pale whitish yellow. The largest individual was of the following dimensions :—

Length of the head . . . . 0 foot 3 inches.
„   „   neck . . . . 0 „ $2\frac{4}{8}$ „
„   „   shell . . . . 1 „ 6 „
„   „   tail . . . . 0 „ $2\frac{5}{8}$ „

Gen. CISTUDO, *Fleming.*

Head moderate, covered with a thin hard continued skin; toes 5–4, webbed to the claws; web thick, with a small intermediate lobe between the claws; tail short; shell convex, ovate, or hemispherical; sternum broad, rounded before and behind, completely closing the cavity of the thorax, affixed to it by a ligamentous symphysis, and divided by a cross suture between the pectoral and abdominal plates; sternal shields twelve; inguinal and axillary plates very small, but distinct; marginal plates 23–27; nuchal plate small or wanting.

CISTUDO AMBOINENSIS, Daudin.

SYN.—Testudo amboinensis, Daudin.
Emys amboinensis and couro, Schweigger.
Tortue à boite d'Amboine, Bosc.
Terrapene amboinensis. Merrem.
Kinosternon amboinense, Bell.
Cistuda amboinensis, Gray.
Terrapene couro, Fitzinger.
Emys couro, apud Wagler.
Terrapene bicolor, Bell.
Emys couro, var. Schlegel apud Gray.
"Báning" of the Malays of the Peninsula.

HAB.—*Malayan Peninsula, Singapore.*
Java, Amboina, Philippine Islands, Tenasserim provinces.

Shell hemispherical, slightly three-keeled, blackish; margin broad, expanded; nuchal shield linear; sternum black and yellow-varied; animal blackish, varied with yellow; head dark, with two broad yellow streaks on each side.

The dorsal keels become obsolete with age, and the margin of the shell, particularly the posterior part, becomes revolute. This species appears to be numerous in the valleys, in ponds, rivulets, and paddy fields. It is very timid, withdrawing its head and limbs when handled, though it neither bites nor scratches. The largest individual observed was of the following dimensions :—

Length of the head	. . . .	2 inches.
„ „ neck	. . . .	2⅛ „
„ „ shell	. . . .	7 „
„ „ tail	. . . .	1 inch.

Gen. TETRAONYX, *Lesson.*

Toes five; nails 4–4; sternum solid, broad, with six pairs of shields; 25 marginal shields.

TETRAONYX AFFINIS, N.S.

Young.—Shell orbicular, its breadth exceeding its length; the back sharply keeled longitudinally, slightly arched, laterally depressed; costal shields with a tubercular nucleus at the posterior margin; greyish-green olive, minutely spotted with brown; edge sharply toothed, pale greenish-yellow. Sternum truncated in front, angularly indented behind, narrow, yellow; laterally keeled, compressed, pale yellowish-green.

HAB.—*Sea off Pinang.*

The outline of the shell and its composing shields strikingly resemble the young of *Cyclemys orbiculata*, Bell.*

The nuchal shield (wanting in one individual) is small, subrectangular or subtriangular, with the base directed backwards. The vertebral shields are strongly keeled, laterally sloping, hexagonal, broader than long, which, however, with the first is less the case than with the rest; the second, third, and fourth are the broadest, and of nearly equal size; the fifth assumes a broadly truncated triangular shape. The costal shields are nearly all as broad as long; the first, second, and third have each a tubercular nucleus in the centre of the posterior margin; the fourth is smooth, and a little smaller than the preceding. The first pair of marginal shields are truncated triangular; the second and third subrectangular; the fourth, sixth, and eighth pentagonal; the rest subrectangular. In all, the posterior external angle forms a more or less sharp spine, directed over the anterior external margin of the next shield. From the first to the sixth the shield gradually increases in size, the sixth being the largest and broadest, from which the following gradually decrease towards the twelfth pair, and their angular spines become obsolete. The sternum consists of two parts, one central and two lateral, formed by the sterno-

---

* SYN.—*Emys dentata,* Illust. Ind. Zoolog. ; *Emys dhor,* Gray ; *Emys Hasseltii,* Boie ; *Emys Spengleri,* var. Schlegel ; *Cistudo Diardii,* Dum. and Bibr.

costal processes of the two central pairs, sharply sloping towards the marginal shields. The central part is longitudinally a little concave, narrowing towards both extremities, truncated in front, angularly indentated behind. The gular pair of shields is very short, broadly subtriangular, with the posterior margin concave, curved backwards. The second and fifth pairs are of nearly equal size, subquadrangular; their external margins forming a sharp ridge. The central part of the third and fourth pairs is subrectangular, broader than long, their margins forming a sharp ridge where they join the sterno-costal processes. The latter are of nearly equal size, longer than broad; their united length being less than one half of the central part of the sternum. The sixth pair is subrhomboidal, longer than broad. The axillary and inguinal pairs are large; the former subrhomboidal or lozenge-shaped, the latter subtriangular. The head is conic, the muzzle short-pointed, the vertex irregularly wrinkled. On the temples, cheeks, and round the orbits and the lower jaw appear some large polygonal scales. The occiput, angle of the mouth, and the rounded tympanum are covered with similar minute scales. The eyes are large, prominent; the iris silvery grey, the pupil round, black. The nostrils are minute, round, horizontally pierced, close together at the apex of the muzzle. The jaws are minutely toothed; the upper has at the symphysis two larger teeth, between which fits a similar single one in the lower jaw, thus hermetically closing the mouth. The neck, the throat, and the other soft parts are studded with minute tubercles, except the fore-arm, the posterior tarsal margin, and the back of the fingers and toes, which are covered with broad but very short polygonal scales. On the ulnar margin of the fore-arm are four to five large rounded flexible scales. The interdigital web is large and lax. The nails are strong, of nearly equal size, sharp, and arched. The conical tail reaches but little beyond the shell, with a longitudinal furrow behind the vent. The head, neck, throat, and the limbs are of the same greyish-green olive as the shell. The interdigital membrane is blackish, except the web connecting the fourth and fifth (nailless) toe, which is of a bright greenish-yellow colour. Of three individuals observed, differing but little in size, the largest was of the following dimensions :—

Length of the head .	. . . . . .	$0\frac{6}{8}$ inch.		
„ „ neck .	. . . . . .	$0\frac{3}{8}$ „		
„ „ shell .	. . . . . .	$2\frac{4}{8}$ inches.		
„ „ tail .	. . . . . .	$0\frac{4}{8}$ inch.		
Greatest transverse diameter of the shell		$2\frac{6}{8}$ inches.		

Two were at different times found in fishing stakes placed along the sea-shore of Pinang; a third was also taken out of the sea with a small hook baited with a shrimp. The Malays assert that this tortoise also inhabits estuaries and rivers on the peninsula, and that it grows to a considerable size. The young is very timid, withdrawing the head and extremities when touched, and thus it remained immovable while a sketch was taken.

From the description of the young of *Tetraonyx Lessonii*, Dum. and Bibr., given in "Erpétologie Générale," tome 2, p. 338, and from the plates of *Emys batagur* and *Emys baska* in "Illustr. Ind. Zool.," from B. Hamilton's MSS., the present appears to differ in too many particulars to warrant the conclusion of its being the young of those or that species.* The detailed description of the young will enable future observers who may succeed in examining the adult finally to decide the question.

FAM. POTAMIDA, or RIVER TORTOISES, *Dum. and Bibr.*

Gen. GYMNOPUS, *Dum. and Bibr.*

(*Trionyx*, Geoffroy ; *Aspidonectes*, Wagler ; *Tyrse, Dogania, Chitra*, Gray.)

Shell cartilaginous in its circumference, very broad, flexible behind and externally not bony ; sternum too narrow behind completely to cover the extremities, when the animal withdraws them under the shell.

GYMNOPUS GANGETICUS, Cuvier.

SYN.—Testudo ocellatus (young), ⎫
       Testudo hurum,   ⎬ Buchan. Ham. MSS.
       Testudo (adult),   ⎭
       Trionyx gangeticus, Cuvier.
       Trionyx hurum, Gray.
       Trionyx hurum, Illust. Ind. Zool.
       Trionyx ocellatus, Illust. Ind. Zool. (young).
       Trionyx gangeticus, var. Guerin. (young).
       Gymnopus ocellatus, Dum. and Bibr. (young), Hardwicke
         (young) apud Jaquemont : " Atlas," pl. ix.
       Gymnopus Duvaucellii, Dum. and Bibr.
       Tyrse gangetica, Gray, Catal.

Young.—Testudo ocellatus, B. Ham. MSS. Head, above pale olive, with one large yellow spot between the eyes and a similar behind each eye ; neck, limbs, and posterior margin of the shell dark olive, with paler round spots ; shell olive, with black irregular lines, and four or five central ocelli, black in the centre, edged with red, round which a black leg ; sternum pale whitish-olive.

Testudo hurum, B. Ham. MSS. is the transition state of the former, being about changing the livery. Head yellow olive, with

-* MM. Duméril and Bibron describe them as two distinct species ; Mr. Gray is of opinion that they are identical.

irregular dark lines; shell light olive, vermiculated with blackish or dark olive. The four ocelli are present, but are altered in colours and shape : the centre, instead of being black, is like the rest of the surface, light olive, vermiculated with black ; the red ring is changed to black, and the outer black one to light olive. The shape is changed from round to irregular oval.

Adult.—Testudo chim. B. Ham. MSS. Dark olive-green, vermiculated, and spotted with light olive-brown. Beneath greenish-white.

HAB.—*Malayan Peninsula, Pinang (rivers and sea-coast).*
   Rivers and Bay of Bengal.

It is of fierce habits, desperately defending itself by biting, emitting when excited a low, hoarse, cackling sound. At Pinang the present species appears to be far less numerous than the two following. The largest individual was of the following dimensions :

Length of the head	.	.	.	.	o	foot	4	inches.
„	„	neck	.	.	.	o	„	$4\frac{4}{8}$	„
„	„	shell	.	.	.	1	„	11	„
„	„	tail	.	.	.	o	„	5	„

GYMNOPUS CARTILAGINEA, Boddaert.

SYN.—*Young :*
   Testudo cartilaginea, Boddaert.
   Testudo Boddaertii, Schneider.
   Testudo rostrata, Thunberg ?
   Testudo rostrata, apud Schoepff. and Daudin ?
   Trionyx stellatus, Geoffroy.
   Trionyx stellatus, apud Merrem.
   Aspidonectes javanicus, Wagler.
   Adult :
   Trionyx javanicus, Geoffroy.
   Trionyx javanicus, apud Schweigger and Gray.
   Gymnopus javanicus, Duméril and Bibron.
   Tyrse javanica, Gray, Catal.

Very Young.—Above olive-green ; the head and upper part of the neck with numerous small white spots, becoming larger and more distant on the cheeks and chin ; on the vertex, two round black spots; on the occiput two diverging black lines ; the shell with several large black white-ringed spots, between which numerous smaller indistinct white spots ; margin pale white ; several longitudinal ridges, composed of close minute tubercles. Beneath greenish-white.

Older.—Above uniformly olive-green ; the longitudinal ridges of the shell consisting of tubercles, more distant and proportionally smaller than in the very young.

HAB.—*Malayan Peninsula, Pinang.*
  Java, Dekhan, " India," " China."

This species is numerous in rivers and ponds. The largest individual observed was of the following dimensions :—

Length of the head . . . . $2\frac{1}{3}$ inches.
  „   „ neck . . . . $2\frac{2}{8}$ „
  „   „ shell . . . . $6\frac{3}{4}$ „
  „   „ tail . . . . $0\frac{6}{8}$ inch.

GYMNOPUS INDICUS, Gray.

SYN.—Testudo chitra, Buchan, Ham. MSS.
  Trionyx indicus, Gray.
  Trionyx ægyptiacus, var. indica, Gray : " Ill. Ind. Zool."
  Gymnopus lineatus, Duméril and Bibron.
  Chitra indica, Gray, Catal.

Shell remarkably depressed, smooth.* Above greenish olive, vermiculated and spotted with brown or rust colour; beneath greenish white.

HAB.—*Pinang, Malayan Peninsula (estuaries, sea-coast).*
  Rivers in India, Philippine Islands.

At Pinang this species is frequently taken in the fishing stakes. The Chinese inhabitants greatly relish this as well as the preceding species of *Gymnopus,* as articles of food. Individuals weighing 240 lbs. occur in the Ganges, and others of gigantic dimensions are not uncommon at Pinang. It is very powerful, and of ferocious habits. The largest individual measured :—

Length of the head . . . . 0 feet 6 inches.
  „   „ neck . . . . 0 „ 5 „
  „   „ shell . . . . 3 „ 1 inch.
  „   „ tail . . . . 0 „ 4 inches.

FAM. THALASSIDÆ, or TURTLES, *Dum. and Bibr.*

Gen. CHELONIA, *Brogniart.*

Body covered with horny plates ; fins with one or two nails.

Sub-Gen. CHELONIA LIBRÆ (*Chelonées franches*), *Dum. and Bibr.*

Discal shields 13, not imbricate ; muzzle short, rounded ; upper jaw slightly notched in front, toothed on the sides ; lower jaw

---

* In the living adult no longitudinal central depression is apparent, nor the outline of the costæ, as represented in the figure in " Ilustrations of Indian Zoology."

formed of three pieces, and with the edges deeply toothed; the first finger of each fin nailed.

CHELONIA VIRGATA, Schweigger.

SYN.—Turtle of the Red Sea, Bruce.
Chelonia virgata, apud Cuvier, Guérin, Duméril and Bibron, Gray, Catal.
Chelonia midas, var. D. Gray.
Chelonia fasciata, Cuvier apud Schlegel.
" Pinyú " of the Malays of Pinang.

Young.—Head, shell and fins greenish-black; margin of the shell and fins and sternum white.

Adult.—Head and fins chestnut, scales edged with yellow; shell greenish-yellow with chestnut rays and spots; sternum gamboge, or greenish-yellow.

HAB.—*Malayan Seas.*
Teneriffe, Rio Janeiro, Cape of Good Hope, New York, Indian Ocean, Red Sea.

This species is at all seasons plentifully taken in fishing stakes in the Straits of Malacca, and is the "Green Turtle" of the European inhabitants of our Malayan settlements and of the seaports of India. In size it equals *Chelonia midas*, Schweigger, which it rivals in flavour. About December and January is the season when the female deposits her eggs in the sandy beach of some sequestered island, and then the fishermen watch during the moonlight nights to "turn turtles." The eggs are of a spherical shape, about one inch in diameter, covered by a soft hemitransparent membrane of a pale yellow colour. The expert eye of the fisherman baffles the pains with which the turtle conceals her eggs, and prodigious numbers are disinterred. They are very rich, flavoured like marrow, and will keep for weeks although exposed to the air.

MM. Duméril and Bibron have pointed out the differences between the adult of the present species and *Chelonia midas*, Schweigger, principally consisting in colours, and in the form of the vertebral and costal shields, to which may be added the comparatively greater length of the fronto-nasal shields in *Chelonia virgata*, in which the breadth is one-third of the length, whereas in *Chelonia midas* it is one-half, and these proportions appear to be constant in all ages of the two species. The very young of both greatly resemble each other in colours and shape. Six living young of the present species were all of the following dimensions :

Length of the head	. . . . .	$0\frac{7}{9}$ inch.
„ „ neck	. . . . .	$0\frac{4}{8}$ „

Length of the shell . . . . . 2 inches.
„ „ tail . . . . . o⅔ inch.

The following slight differences are the result of a comparison between the living young of *Chelonia virgata* and the representation of *Chelonia midas* given by Schoepff. tab. xvii. fig. 2.

Chelonia virgata.	*Chelonia midas.*
1. Shell cordiform ; the length exceeds the breadth by one-eighth.	1. Shell ovate ; the length exceeds the breadth by more than two-eighths.
2. 2nd vertebral shield much broader than 1st, and is altogether the largest of the series.	2. 1st and 2nd vertebral of equal dimensions.
3. 2nd costal shield larger than the 3rd.	3. 2nd and 3rd costal equal.
4. Sincipital plate broader than long.	4. Sincipital plate longer than broad.
5. Breadth of fronto-nasal shields one-third of their length.	5. Breadth of fronto-nasals one-half of their length.
6. Each fin with a single nail.	6. Each fin with two nails.

Sub-Gen. CHELONIÆ IMBRICATÆ (*Chélonées imbriquées*), *Dum. and Bibr.*

Discal shields thirteen, imbricate ; muzzle long, compressed ; jaws with the edge straight, not toothed, at the extremity slightly recurved : each fin with two nails.

CHELONIA IMBRICATA, Linné.

SYN.—La Tortue Caret, Dutertre.
Scaled Tortoise, Grew.
Caret, Labat, Fermin, Lacép., Bosc, Cuvier.
Testudo marina americana, Seba.
Hawksbill Turtle, Brown, Catesby.

Testudo imbricata, Linné, apud ⎰ Gmelin.
⎰ Pennant.
⎰ Donnd.
⎰ Schoepff.
⎰ Latreille.
⎰ Schneider.
⎰ Shaw.
⎰ Daudin.

Testudo caretta, Knorr.
La Tuilée, Daubenton.
Caretta imbricata, Merrem apud Gray : Catal.
Chelonia multiscutala, Kuhl ?

Chelonia imbricata, Schweig-
ger, apud . . . . . . {
Prince Maxim.
Gray.
Duméril and Bibron.
Prince Musignano.
Bell.
}

Chélonée faux caret, Lesson.
Chelonia caretta, Temminck and Schlegel.
" Kúra-kúra " of the Malays of Pinang.

Head brown, scales edged or rayed with yellow; shell yellow, marbled or rayed with rich brown; sternum yellowish-white. In the young the areola of the sternal shields black.

HAB.—*Malayan Seas.*
Atlantic and Indian Oceans.

The largest individual observed was of the following dimensions :—

Length of the head	.	.	.	.	o foot	$4\frac{4}{8}$	inches.
,,	,,	neck	.	. .	o ,,	$3\frac{4}{8}$	,,
,,	,,	shell	.	. .	1 ,,	7	,,
,,	,,	tail	.	. .	o ,,	$2\frac{2}{8}$	,,

Sub-Gen. CAOUANÆ (*Caouanes*), *Dum. and Bibr.*

Discal shields fifteen, not imbricate; jaws at the extremity slightly recurved.

CHELONIA OLIVACEA, Eschscholtz : Atlas.

SYN.—Chelonia caouana, var. B. Gray.
Chelonia Dussumierii, Dum. and Bibr.
Caouana olivacea, Gray : Catal.

Young.—Above, blackish olive, lighter than in the adult; shell and fins edged with pale yellow; sternum pale greenish-yellow, washed with chestnut; areolæ blackish.
Adult.—Head brown; shell blackish-green; some of the marginal scales of the fins yellow; sternum yellow, washed with chestnut; twenty-seven marginal shields; fins with one nail.

HAB.—*Malayan Seas.*
Bay of Bengal, Chinese Seas.

This species is at Pinang of rare occurrence. A single young individual observed was of the following dimensions :—

Length of the head	.	. . . . . .	$1\frac{7}{8}$	inches.
,,	,,	neck	1	inch.
,,	,,	shell	6	inches.
,,	,,	tail	$0\frac{7}{8}$	inch.

The shell is broad sub-cordiform (its length exceeding its breadth by half an inch), three-keeled, the vertebral keel strongest, dentated behind; the marginal shields 27, obliquely placed. The 1st and 4th pairs of costals, and the 4th vertebral shield each divided in two pieces.

In a not quite full-grown specimen in the Museum of the Asiatic Society the length of the shell is 2 ft. 1$\frac{4}{8}$ in.; its greatest breadth is 2 ft. 0$\frac{4}{8}$ in., the length exceeding the breadth by one inch. The vertebral shields are still slightly keeled. The 1st and 4th pairs of costals, the 2nd left costal, and the 4th vertebral are divided. The central part of the margin is slightly curved upwards. The edges of the jaws are not toothed, but they are transparent, with fine white vertical lines, which give them a fringed appearance.

The flesh of this turtle, though relished by the Chinese settlers, is unpalatable to Europeans.

SAURIA.

Fam. CROCODILIDÆ, *Bonaparte* (ASPIDIOTES, *Dum. and Bibr.*)

Sub-Gen. Crocodilus, apud Cuvier.

Muzzle oblong, depressed ; teeth unequal, the fourth of the lower jaw fitting into lateral notches, and not into hollows of the upper jaw. Skull behind the eyes with two large holes, perceptible through the integuments. Hind-feet with an external dentated crest, and the toes palmated.

Crocodilus vulgaris, Cuvier (var. B.), Dum. and Bibr.

Syn.—Crocodilus palustris, Lesson.
Crocodilus vulgaris, var. E. Gray.
Crocodilus biporcatus raninus, Müller, tab. 3, fig. 7.
Crocodilus palustris, apud Gray : Catal.
" Buáya " of the Malays.

Muzzle a little widened, thick, transversely very slightly curved ; head covered with angular rugosities ; lateral margins of the skull not raised. Above greenish-olive, speckled with black ; beneath yellowish or greenish white.

Hab.—*Malayan Peninsula and Islands.*
Java, Sumatra, Tenasserim, Bengal, Coromandel, Malabar.

It inhabits not only rivers and estuaries, but also the sea-coasts, and may in calm weather be seen floating at a distance of two to three miles from the shore. Although numerous at Pinang and the opposite coast, it appears to be less so than *Crocodilus biporcatus*. Fishermen while working the nets are not seldom attacked by crocodiles, and would, but for their presence of mind, oftener than they do, forfeit their lives. When seized they force their fingers into the eyes of the crocodile, which immediately lets go its victim, who is farther rescued by his comrades. From 1842 to 1845 amputations from accidents of this description were unfortunately of no rare occurrence in the General Hospital at Pinang.

Individuals 15 ft. in length are not uncommon ; some attaining to 20 ft. and upwards are reported to occur. In rivers a single one will often appropriate to himself a limited district, which, if it happens to be in the vicinity of a village, will soon be perceived in the loss of the grazing cattle. Instances of Malays, who, to avenge the loss of a relative, have watched the crocodile, and by diving from below plunged a *kris* into its heart, are on record. The eggs are white, the shell hard, of a cylindrical form, upwards of 3 in. in length, and about 1½ in. in diameter.

CROCODILUS POROSUS, Schneider.

SYN.—Crocodili Ceylonici ex ovo prodiens, Seba.

Cr. biporcatus, Cuvier apud	⎧ Tideman, Oppel, Liboschitz. ⎪ Merren. ⎪ Bory de St. Vincent. ⎪ Fitzinger. ⎨ Lesson. ⎪ Guérin. ⎪ Wagler. ⎪ Gray. ⎩ Horsfield, *l.c.*

Crocodilus biporcatus raninus, Müller, tab. 3, fig. 8.
Crocodilus porosus, Schn. apud Gray : Catal.
" Buáya " of the Malays.

Upper jaw surmounted by two rugged ridges, each commencing from the anterior angle of the eye ; nuchal plates, either none or two very small. Above, yellowish-green with large black oval spots ; keels of the dorsal scales green ; beneath greenish-white.

HAB.—*Malayan Peninsula, Pinang, Singapore.*
India, Tenasserim, Sumatra, Java, Timor, Seychelle Islands.

This, in the Malayan countries exceeding numerous species, is of the same habits and attains to the same size as the preceding.

FAM. GECKONIDÆ, *Bonaparte* (ASCALABOTES, *Dum. and Bibr.*).

Gen. PLATYDACTYLUS, *Cuvier.*

Toes more or less dilated throughout their length, beneath with transverse imbricate plates, either entire or divided by a central longitudinal groove.

PLATYDACTYLUS LUGUBRIS, Dum. and Bibr.

SYN.—Amydosaurus lugubris, Gray.

Thumbs nailless ; transverse plates beneath all the toes ; back finely granular. Above, whitish, with black spots.

HAB.—*Pinang.*
Otaheite.

A single male was captured in my house in the valley of Pinang. The integuments correspond to the description given by MM. Duméril and Bibron, to which may be added the following characters :—The skin is somewhat loose, forming a slight longitudinal fold on each side of the body and on the anterior margin of the thigh. The anus is covered by a transversal fold, reaching across from the one thigh to the other. There are no femoral pores. The tail is tapering, much depressed, convex on the upper surface, flat beneath, sharp at the sides. Near the root, about ⅔ of an inch distant from the anus, the skin forms an annular fold, completely encircling that part of the tail. The colour slightly differs from that of the Otaheite individuals. The upper parts and the lower surface of the tail from the annular fold are of a buff or pale dust colour, so closely and minutely dotted with reddish-brown that the parts have a pale greyish-brown appearance. On the loins and between the shoulders are a few distant blackish spots ; besides, in the latter place, appear two short lateral lines, and an indistinct band proceeds from the nostril across the eye to the shoulder. The throat, inner side of the limbs, abdomen, and the lower surface of the root of the tail to the annular fold are buff-coloured. The pupil is black, veitical, dentilated, the iris silvery, dotted with reddish brown.

Length of the head	. . . .	0¼	inch.
„ „ trunk	. . . .	1⅔	„
„ „ tail	. . . .	1¾	„
Entire length	. . . .	3⅛	inches.

PLATYDACTYLUS GECKO, Linné.

Syn.—Salamandra indica, Bontius.
Gekko ceilonicus, Seba.
Lacerta cauda tereti mediocri, Linné mus. Adolph.
Lacerta gecko, Linné.
Gekko teres,   } Laurenti.
Gekko verticillatus, }
Salamandre, ou Gecko de Linneus, Knorr.
Stellio Gecko, Schneider.
Common Gecko, Shaw.
Gecko guttatus, Daudin apud Gray.
Lacerta guttata, Hermann.
Gecko verus, Merrem apud   { Gray : "Zool. Journ."
                        { Gray, Catal.
Gecko annulatus, Kuhl.
Gecko à gouttelettes, Cuvier.
Platydactylus guttatus, Cuv. apud Guérin, Dum. and Bibr.
" Toké " of the Malays.*

Above, ash-coloured, with numerous pale orange spots ; beneath yellowish-white. Between the scales of the back twelve longitudinal rows of large distant tubercles, and six similar on the tail; the latter with minute scales beneath.

Hab.—*Malayan Peninsula.*
Philippine Islands, Java, Tenasserim, Burmah, Bengal, Coromandel Coast.

On the Malayan Peninsula this species appears to be less numerous than in the Tenasserim Provinces, where its shrill cry, " To-ke," is nightly heard in houses. The male has two tubercular scales on each side of the root of the tail. The largest individual observed was of the following dimensions :—

Length of the head . . . . $1\frac{7}{8}$ inches.
"   "   trunk . . . . . . $4\frac{2}{8}$ "
"   "   tail . . . . . . $4\frac{5}{8}$ "

Entire length . . . . . . $10\frac{6}{8}$ "

PLATYDACTYLUS STENTOR, N.S.

Syn.—" Toké " of the Malays.

Above, light bluish-grey, with numerous irregular blackish spots forming on the vertex an angle like an inverted V., and on the neck short oblique lateral bands. Beneath, pearl-coloured. On

* The Malays denominate the family of Geckotidæ: *Gékko, Kéko, Gágo, Goké,* evidently Onomatopœias, in imitation of the cry of these lizards.

the back and sides ten longitudinal rows of large distant lenticular scales, and six similar on the tail ; the latter with scutella beneath.

HAB.—*Pinang.*

In form and size this species closely resembles the preceding, from which it, however, differs in the following particulars :—The oval nostrils are bordered in front by three scales—viz., the first upper labial, a smaller rectangular, and a larger pentagonal scale, both of which latter are situated between the nostril and the rostral. Above, the nostrils are surrounded by two smaller irregular triangular, and behind by a narrow crescent-shaped scale. Of labial scales there are fourteen above, twelve below. There are about seventy-two teeth in each jaw. The eye is very large ; pupil, black, dentilated ; iris, silvery bluish-grey. The ear is very large, obliquely oval, without dentilations. The cheeks are much swollen. The scales of the back are small, rounded, hexagonal, becoming more rectangular on the sides. The rows of lenticular scales along the vertebræ are smaller than the rest, but not so close as in *P. guttatus.* Behind the mental scale is a pair of large elongated scales, and five pentagonal larger appear on each side behind the lower labials. The gular scales are small, polygonal ; the abdominal are rounded, hexagonal, not imbricate, and below the root of the tail become somewhat larger. The rest of the lower surface of the tail is covered with scutella. Above, the covering of the tail is like that of *P. guttatus.* On each side of the posterior margin of the cloaca are two very large tubercular scales, and towards the centre two rather large post-anal pores, covered by a loose fold of the skin. Fourteen femoral pores are placed on a slightly angular line. This species is also closely allied to *Platydactylus monarchus*, Schlegel, from which it, however, readily may be distinguished by the regular rows of lenticular dorsal scales, by its far greater size, and by its loud note. It is not numerous at Pinang. The only individual obtained, from the villa on the Pentland Hills, was a male of the following dimensions :—

Length of the head	$2\frac{2}{8}$ inches.
,, ,, trunk	$5\frac{4}{8}$,,
,, ,, tail	$8\frac{2}{8}$,,
Entire length	16 ,,

PLATYDACTYLUS MONARCHUS, Schlegel, MS.

SYN.—Platydactylus monarchus, Schl. apud Dum. and Bibr.
Gecko monarchus, Gray : Catal.

On the back, sides, and limbs numerous conical tubercles irregularly scattered among the smaller flat polygonal scales : on the upper surface of the tail six to thirteen transversal series of small spines ; beneath scutella, sometimes mixed with scuta. Chin with two larger oblong scales.

New-born.—Above, brown, with the dorsal and caudal tubercles (no spines) white ; the posterior part of the tail indistinctly white-ringed ; beneath, uniformly paler brown.

Adult.—Above, buff or ash-coloured, or reddish-brown, with eight to twelve pairs of irregularly rounded, distant, dark brown spots along the spine ; the head, limbs, and sides with numerous more or less distinct, irregular, dark brown spots ; in some younger individuals the tail with whitish rings. Beneath, yellowish·white.

HAB.—*Malayan Peninsula, Pinang, Singapore.*
Philippine Islands, Amboyna, Borneo.

The Malayan Geckonidæ have the power of somewhat changing the ground colour ; none, however, in a greater degree than the present species. In the valley and on the hills of Pinang it is very numerous, swarming at night in rooms, on the walls, and under the ceiling, occasionally giving out a sound resembling the monosyllable " Tok," repeated six or eight times with increased celerity. The aim of these lizards is by no means unerring ; they frequently miss an insect, and fall from the ceiling. Among themselves they are pugnacious ; when two or more covet an insect, the successful one has to defend its prize, or give it up to the stronger. The new-born (with umbilical aperture) and adult are of the following dimensions :—

			New-born.	*Adult.*
Length of the head	.	.	$0\frac{3}{8}$	$1\frac{2}{8}$ inches.
,,	,, trunk	.	$0\frac{5}{8}$	$2\frac{2}{8}$,,
,,	,, tail	.	$1\frac{1}{8}$	$3\frac{1}{8}$,;
	Entire length	.	$2\frac{1}{8}$	$6\frac{5}{8}$,,

Sub-Gen. PTYCHOZOON, Kuhl.

Toes webbed to the last compressed joint; thumbs nailless; sides of the head, body, limbs, and tail with broad, scaly membranes, those of the tail anteriorly scalloped. Male with femoral pores. On the sides scattered tubercles.

PTYCHOZOON HOMALOCEPHALUM, Creveld.

SYN.—Lacerta homalocephala, Creveld.
Gecko homalocephalus, Tilesius.

Ptychozoon homalocephalum, apud $\left\{\begin{array}{l} \text{Fitzinger.} \\ \text{Wagler.} \\ \text{Wiegmann.} \end{array}\right.$

Pteropleura Horsfieldii, Gray.
Platydactylus homalocephalus, Cuv. apud Dum. and Bibr.
Ptychozoon homalocephala, Kuhl. apud Gray : Catal.

Head.—The ground colour yellowish-green olive. Between the eyes and muzzle a double figure, in whitish outline, representing in front a broad arrowhead, posteriorly united by a narrow stalk to a rectangular transversal band, situated in front of the eyes. On the vertex another, larger figure, traced in whitish outline, rectangular in front, spreading like a four-rayed star over the occiput. A dark brown band proceeds from behind the eye, across the ear, to the shoulders, where it is lost in the general dark brown colour of the sides of the body. The superior margins of these two lateral bands are white, proceeding backwards in zig-zag line, approaching each other over the shoulders, where they join the anterior black transversal line. The lips white. The membranes of the cheeks pale flesh-colour, with dark blue spots, and with the interstices between the scales pale lilac. The pupil vertical, dentilated ; the iris rich golden brown.

Back.—Of the same ground colour as the head, becoming dark reddish-brown on the sides, relieved by four to six distant transversal black dotted lines, on the upper part, of the form of the letter M, sending oblique, forwards pointed, lines on the sides. The upper part of the lateral membrane reddish-brown ; the interstices of the small rectangular scales purple.

Tail and limbs.—Same ground-colour as that of the head and back, with broad, distant, indistinctly whitish, transversal bands. On each elbow a whitish ring. Membranes of the tail, limbs, and toes are yellowish-grey, with numerous minute spots of brown, purple, blue, and red, which impart a purple, changing appearance to the general colour. The number of the indentations of the caudal membranes varies individually ; the posterior part is entire, with waving surfaces.

Lower parts.—Brownish-white, with a few pale brown spots on the throat, inner side of the limbs, in the palms and soles. The tail and its membranes brownish.

HAB.—*Pinang Hills.*
Singapore, Java, Ramree Island (Arracan).

As correctly observed by MM. Duméril and Bibron, the scales of the female, corresponding to those with the femoral pores of the male, have a slight yet distinct central depression. The female has a large tubercular scale on each side of the root of the tail, as well as the male. In colour and size the two sexes resemble each other. Two individuals were at different times captured in the villa occupied by Sir William Norris on the Great Hill of Pinang. When the lizard is at rest, the membranes of the cheeks and the body are kept in close contact with these parts ; in leaping, those of the body are somewhat stretched out, and all the membranes together then act as a parachute. Also, this lizard has in some degree the power of changing the ground colour from a darker to a lighter shade. The apex of the tongue is rounded, with a small notch in the centre. A female while in my possession refused insects and water. She deposited a single egg, of a spherical form, about half an inch in diameter, soft, and of a yellowish-white colour, which the following day she devoured. A male ate the integuments he had been changing. The female was of the following dimensions :—

Length of the head .	. . . . . .	1	inch.
„ „	trunk.	$2\frac{6}{8}$	inches.
„ „	tail	$3\frac{5}{8}$	„
	Entire length	$7\frac{3}{8}$	„

In the Museum of the Asiatic Society is preserved a specimen of *Leptophis ornatus* (Merrem) in the act of devouring one of the present species. The serpent was captured in the island of Ramree, on the coast of Arracan.

Gen. HEMIDACTYLUS, *Cuvier*.

End of the toes widened into an oval disk, with a double series of transverse imbricate plates beneath. From the middle of the disk rise the slender second and third nailed phalanx. A series of scuta beneath the tail.

HEMIDACTYLUS PERONII, Dum. and Bibr.

SYN.—Hemidactylus leiurus, Gray.
    Peripia Peronii, Gray : Catal.

Under the chin a large triangular figure, composed of six elongated, towards the sides decreasing, scales ; thumbs nailless ; male with femoral pores ; tail much depressed, very broad at the root, tapering towards the point (sometimes with a small membrane on each side of the point), with a series of scuta beneath ; pupil vertical, shaped like two rhombs placed with the angles towards each other.*

Above, ash-coloured, labial scales whitish, each with a brown spot ; beneath, whitish. Iris silvery grey, spotted with brown.

HAB.—*Pinang*.
    Isle of France.

---

* Such is its appearance in the living animal, when the eye is exposed to the influence of light. MM. Duméril and Bibron note the pupil being "elliptical," which probably originates in their describing from preserved specimens, although my own, in spirits of wine, have retained the original form of the pupil.

Of two individuals captured at different times in my house in the valley of Pinang, the larger was of the following dimensions:—

Length of the head	$0\frac{6}{8}$	inch.
„ „ trunk	$1\frac{5}{8}$	inches.
„ „ tail	$2\frac{3}{8}$	„
Entire length.	$4\frac{6}{8}$	„

HEMIDACTYLUS COCTÆI, Dum. and Bibr.

Thumbs well developed, nailed;* back with minute granular scales; in some individuals with a few larger ones on the sides; tail broad at the root, tapering, a little depressed, with from four to fifteen indistinct rings and six series of minute spines; beneath with scuta; chin with four larger scales; the central pair elongate pentagonal; male with twelve femoral pores; pupil as in *Hemidactylus Peronii.*

Above, ash-coloured, whitish beneath.

HAB.—*Pinang.*
Bengal, Bombay.

Of two males observed in houses in the valley of Pinang, the larger was of the following dimensions:—

Length of the head	$1\frac{2}{8}$	inches.
„ „ trunk	$2\frac{4}{8}$	„
„ „ tail	$3\frac{2}{8}$	„
Entire length.	7	„

HEMIDACTYLUS FRENATUS, Schlegel, MS.

SYN.—Hemidactylus frenatus, Schlegel, apud Dum. and Bibr.
Hemidactylus lateralis, } Gray: B.M.
Hemidactylus quinquelineatus, }

Back with some larger granular scales; tail rounded, tapering above, with six series of small spines, scuta beneath; chin with four or six larger scales; ears very small; pupil as in the preceding species; thumbs very small, femoral pores twenty-six to twenty-eight, disposed on a slightly angular line.

Young and Adult.—Buff or ash-coloured, with or without brown spots; some with one or two brown lateral bands, commencing one above the other from the muzzle, interrupted or continued to the tail; the latter in some with indistinct brown rings. Beneath, whitish or buff.

* Mr. Gray gives the present species as a syn. of *Boltalia sublævis*, Gray (Catalogue, p. 158). As the latter species is characterised as having the thumbs "clawless," it cannot be identical with *H. coctæi.*

HAB.—*Malayan Peninsula, Pinang, Singapore.*
Amboyna, Timor, Java, Marianne Islands, Ceylon, Bengal, Assam,* South Africa, Madagascar.

In the Malayan valleys and hills this small species is very numerous. It is of fierce habits, like several other *Geckonidæ,* destroying its own species. Its normal colour appears to be greyish, which it, however, has in its power to change. The largest individuals observed were of the following dimensions :—

Length of the head . . . . 0$\frac{5}{8}$ inch.

„ „ trunk. . . . . . . 2 inches.

„ „ tail . . . . 2 „

Entire length. . . . . . 4$\frac{5}{8}$ „

HEMIDACTYLUS PLATYURUS, Schneider.

SYN.—Stellio platyurus, Schneider.
Lacerta Schneideriana, Shaw.
Gecko platyurus, Merrem.
Hemidactylus platyurus, Wiegmann.

Hemidactylus marginatus, Cuvier, apud $\left\{ \begin{array}{l} \text{Wagler.} \\ \text{Wiegmann.} \\ \text{Gray.} \end{array} \right.$

Platyurus Schneiderianus, Gray : Catal.

Sides of the body and posterior margin of the thighs with a loose membrane ; tail tapering, depressed, with sharp, fringed margins, with scuta beneath ; toes webbed half their length ; chin with four pentagonal broad scales, placed in pairs, behind each other : six femoral pores placed on a continued line.

Young and Adult.—Above, ash-coloured, in some with a greyish-brown lateral band from the muzzle continued to the tail ; the latter with indistinct brownish transversal bands ; others irregularly spotted and marbled with blackish-brown ; pupil and iris as in the preceding species. Whitish beneath.

HAB.—*Pinang.*
Philippine Islands, Borneo, Java, Bengal, Assam.*

The individuals were observed in houses in the valley of Pinang. In a male the posterior half of the tail happens to be divided so as to appear double ; one of the pieces, the continuation of the normal tail, is depressed, slightly fringed, and beneath with the row of scuta continued, the other is cylindrical, somewhat shorter, and above and below covered with minute scales. The largest individual was of the following dimensions :—

* Specimens in the Museum of the Asiatic Society.

Length of the head . . . . o⅝ inch.

„   „   trunk. . . . . . . 2 inches.

„   „   tail . . . . 2⅛ „

Entire length. . . . . 4⅝ „

Gen. GYMNODACTYLUS, *Spix.*

Toes not widened into a disk, nor with dentilated margins ; all five with non-retractile nails ; fifth hind toe versatile or capable of turning from the others under a right angle.

GYMNODACTYLUS PULCHELLUS, Gray.

SYN.—Cyrtodactylus pulchellus, Gray.
Gonyodactylus pulchellus, Wagler.
Gymnodactylus pulchellus, Duméril and Bibron.

Head, back, and limbs with numerous three-sided tubercles among the smaller flat scales ; sides of the body with a longitudinal fold of the skin ; the anterior upper part of the cylindrical tail with distant rings of rounded, pointed tubercles ; beneath, a row of scuta. Chin with six scales, the centre pair elongated pentagonal. Males with thirty-six femoral pores on two not connected lines, between which, in front of the anus, a short, narrow, longitudinal furrow. Both sexes with three or four tubercles obliquely situated on each side of the root of the tail.

Young and Adult.—Above a rich brownish ochre ; the nape of the neck and back with six broad transversal bands (the two anterior horse-shoe shaped), of a rich velvety mulberry, or snuff-colour with sulphur or chrome-yellow margins. The tail with eight or nine complete rings of similar colour, without the margins. Beneath, throat and belly whitish-yellow, or pale brownish, each scale minutely dotted with brown. Pupil vertical, dentilated ; iris golden, finely vermiculated with Vandyke brown.

HAB.—*Pinang Hills.*
Singapore.

In the male the two rows of femoral pores commence as two short, parallel, longitudinal lines, separated from each other by a narrow, short furrow, on the sides of which (vertically) the first five femoral (preanal) pores are placed. In front of the anus the short vertical portions turn right and left under a nearly right angle, continuing the entire length of the thigh, each supporting thirteen more femoral pores. The interval between the anus and the latter is partly occupied by a flat, slightly raised, triangular space, covered by rather large imbricate rounded scales. In the female the two lines of larger scales carrying the femoral pores of the males are present, each scale having a small, shallow, round depression. The short, longitudinal furrow of the male is either wanting or barely distinguishable ; but the triangular space with larger scales, in front of the anus, is present. The species appears to be rather numerous on the hills at Pinang, where the individuals obtained were captured in houses at an elevation of 2,200 feet. The largest male was of the following dimensions :—

Length of the head . . . . $1\frac{4}{8}$ inches.

,, ,, trunk . . . . 3 ,,

,, ,, tail . . . . $5\frac{4}{8}$,,

Entire length . . . . . 10 ,,

Its habits offer nothing peculiar ; it bites fiercely in defence. In captivity it refuses insects. The integuments, when about being renewed, are piecemeal torn off by the teeth and devoured. A single egg deposited was of a spherical form, about half an inch in diameter, of a whitish-yellow colour. MM. Duméril and Bibron assign Bengal as the habitat of this species. The specimen originally described by Mr. Gray, some in the Museum of the Asiatic Society, and a number in my own collection, are all from the hills of Prince of Wales Island (Pulo Pinang), but no authenticated record exists of this species ever having been observed in Bengal. Another, widely different, species of *Gymnodactylus* inhabits Bengal, as yet not published, and only known from three specimens, preserved in spirits, in the Museum of the Asiatic Society, where they are marked *Gymnodactylus lunatus*, Blyth. One of these came from Midnapore, the others from Chyebassa. The species somewhat approaches to *G. fasciatus*, Dum. and Bibr. (*Cubina fasciata*, Gray). The Museum possesses another nondescript species from Almorah, *Gymnodactylus nebulosus*, Blyth MSS., allied to *G. marmoratus*, Gray.

The plate of *Cyrtodactylus pulchellus* in Gray's illustrations of Indian zoology is not taken from life, and gives a most inadequate idea of the physiognomy and beauty of the living animal This should be observed, as MM. Duméril and Bibron praise the figure, which evidently has served as the original of their own description, and of copies introduced in illustrative works upon that order of animals.

FAM. VARANIDÆ, *Bonaparte* (PLATYNOTES, *Dum. and Bibr.*).

Gen. VARANUS, *Merrem.*

Scales set side by side, surrounded by an annular series of very minute tubercles ; tail above more or less trenchant ; on the throat a fold in front of the chest.

VARANI AQUATICI, Dum. and Bibr.

VARANUS NEBULOSUS, Duméril and Bibron.

SYN.—Tupinambis nebulosus, Cuvier MSS.
Monitor nebulosus, Gray.
Monitor nebulatus, Schlegel.
Uranus nebulosus, apud Gray: Catal.

Muzzle very elongated; nostrils obliquely cleft, situated half-way between the muzzle and the anterior angle of the eye; lips each with fifty scales; teeth compressed, with sharp but not den-tilated edges.

Young.—Above: ground-colour deep chocolate brown; the head largely marbled with greenish-yellow; neck with indistinct obliquely converging gamboge lines; back, sides, and limbs with gamboge spots, consisting of one to five scales (those of the upper margins of the fingers forming continued lines); sides of the anterior half of the tail similarly coloured; the double row of scales covering the back of the tail gamboge; the posterior half deep chocolate, with two distant (the second subterminal) indis-tinct gamboge-coloured rings.

Beneath: ground-colour pale chocolate; chin, throat, chest, and fore-limbs transversely undulated with greenish-yellow; abdo-men with short, interrupted, transversal yellow bands, consisting of from four to twelve scales; hind-limbs with larger similar spots; anterior half of the tail indistinctly marbled with yellowish-green; posterior half like the upper surface; pupil round; iris narrow, golden.

Adult.—Above, brownish-olive with yellow dots; anterior half of the tail yellow, with minute square brown spots; posterior half, brown and yellow-ringed; margin of the toes yellow. Beneath, marbled and barred with brown and yellow.

HAB.—*Pinang.*
Java, Siam, Bengal.

The only individual observed was a young male, captured in the hills at Pinang, of the following dimensions:—

Length of the head	$1\frac{5}{8}$	inches.
,, ,, trunk	$5\frac{2}{8}$	,,
,, ,, tail	$9\frac{1}{8}$	,,
Entire length	16	,,

VARANUS FLAVESCENS, Gray.

SYN.—Monitor flavescens, Gray.
Monitor Hardwickii, Gray MSS.

Varanus Russellii, Schlegel MSS.
Monitor exanthematicus, var. indica, Schlegel.
Varanus Picquotii, Dum. and Bibr.
Empagusia flavescens, Gray : Catal.

Muzzle obtuse; nostrils oval, oblique, nearer the muzzle than the orbit; a series of supraorbital scales larger than the rest; scales of the back distant, bluntly keeled; of the tail and outside of the hind limbs, closer, sharply keeled; toes very short, nails yellow.

Above : ground-colour light green-olive, with numerous distant, interrupted, transversal yellow bands; temples, cheeks, and lips yellow. Beneath, yellow; the throat with transversal pale brownish bands.

HAB.—*Pinang.*
Bengal, Nipal.

A single male observed was of the following dimensions :—

Length of the head	. . . . .	0 foot	3	inches.
„ „ trunk	. . . .	1 „	$0\frac{5}{8}$	„
„ „ tail	. . . . .	1 „	$6\frac{1}{8}$	„
Entire length	. . .	2 feet	$9\frac{6}{8}$	„

VARANUS SALVATOR, Laurenti.

SYN.—Lacertus indicus, Lochner?
Lacerta mexicana, Seba.
Lacertus americanus amphibius, Tupinambis dictus, Seba.
Stellio salvator, Laurenti.
Monitor lizard, Shaw.
Lacerta monitor? Hermann.
Tupinambis bivittatus, Kuhl apud Boie.
Monitor elegans, Gray.
Monitor à deux rubans, Cuvier.
Hydrosaurus bivittatus, Wagler.
Monitor vittatus, Lesson.
Varanus bivittatus, Duméril and Bibron.
Hydrosaurus salvator, Gray : Catal.
" Beyáwak " of the Malays of the Peninsula.

Head very elongated; nostrils oval, nearly transversal, close to the muzzle; a series of supraorbital scales, larger than the rest; teeth with dentilated edges; toes very long. Above, ground-colour dark brown or black; a band on the side of the neck from the shoulder to the eye, five to seven distant transversal series of separate rings, between which numerous spots or interrupted transversal lines, all yellow or yellowish-white; the outside of the limbs and the tail spotted, the latter indistinctly banded with yellow. Beneath, yellow, the throat with indistinct transversal black bands and minute spots; the sides of the body and limbs in some individuals with large blackish dentilations.

HAB.—*Malayan Peninsula, Pinang.*
Philippine and Molucca Islands, Amboina, Java, Bengal.

This species is very numerous both in hilly and marshy localities. It is commonly during the day observed in the branches of trees overhanging rivers, preying upon birds and their eggs, and smaller lizards, and when disturbed it throws itself from a considerable height into the water. When attacked on level ground it attempts its escape by running, if possible towards the water. Its quickness, however, is not so great as to prevent a man from overtaking it, when it will courageously defend itself with teeth and claws and by strokes of the tail. The lowest castes of Hindoos capture these lizards commonly by digging them out of their burrows on the banks of rivers for the sake of their flesh, which by these people is greatly relished. Some individuals attain to nearly seven feet in length, but the majority are smaller. A female examined was of the following dimensions:—

Length of the head	. . . .	0 foot $4\frac{4}{8}$ inches.
„ „ trunk	. . . .	1 „ $3\frac{4}{8}$ „
„ „ tail	. . . .	2 feet $8\frac{4}{8}$ „
Entire length	. . .	4 feet $4\frac{4}{8}$ „

FAM. IGUANIDÆ, Gray (EUNOTES, *Duméril and Bibron*).

SUB.-FAM. ACRODONTINÆ (ACRODONTES, *Dum. and Bibr.*).

Gen. CALOTES, *Cuvier.*

Head quadrangular pyramidal, more or less elongated, with small angular scales of nearly equal diameter; occipital scale minute; tongue thick, fungous, rounded, with the apex slightly notched; in the upper jaw five incisors and two canines; nostrils lateral, pierced through a plate situated close to the muzzle; no transversal fold on the throat, sometimes with a large longitudinal fold on both sides; a gular pouch varying in size; a crest from the nape of the neck to the tail; scales of the sides of the trunk homogeneous, imbricated in oblique series; no femoral pores.

Sub.-Gen. BRONCHOCELA, *Kaup.*

Scales of the trunk in oblique series, inclined backwards, their points directed downwards; posterior part of the sides of the head not swollen.

BRONCHOCELA CRISTATELLA, Kuhl.

SYN.—Lacerta mexicana strumosa, &c., Seba, 89, 1.
Agama cristatella, Kuhl.
Agama gutturosa, Merrem.
Bronchocela cristatella, Kaup apud Dum. and Bibr.
Agama moluccana, Lesson apud Schinz.
Calotes gutturosa, Guérin.
Calotes cristatellus, Schinz.
Calotes gutturosus, Wiegmann.
" Grúning " of the Malays of the Peninsula.

Cervical crest (six to ten scales) abruptly decreasing on the anterior part of the back; scales of the side of the trunk keeled, scarcely half the size of those of abdomen ; behind the posterior angle of the orbit three to five flattened scales, pointing outwards, forming a minute longitudinal crest.

Normal colours.—Beautiful grass green, lighter beneath, entirely or partially changeable to light grey, greyish-olive, greenish-brown, or blackish ; sometimes with orange spots, or with indistinct black network ; large isolated round spots on the head or back, or the lips, eyelids, or margins round tympanum momentarily black ; sometimes with transversal distant brown bands, particularly on the tail.* Scales of the outside of the limbs and feet edged with brown. Pupil circular ; iris brown, with a narrow golden ring.

HAB.—*Malayan Peninsula, Pinang, Singapore.*
Amboyna, Island of Buru, Java, Sumatra.

This species is very numerous in the Malayan countries, both in the valleys and on the hills. It moves and leaps with great quickness among the branches of trees. The most striking feature is the great power of suddenly changing its colours. The Malayan denomination of this species is " Gruning," which in Marsden's Dictionary is translated "a species of lizard which changes its colour as it is affected by fear or anger ; the chameleon." No chameleon, however, appears to inhabit the Malayan countries, but the present lizard passes under that name among the European inhabitants. One of the largest males was of the following dimensions :—

Length of the head	o foot	$1\frac{3}{8}$	inches.
,, ,, trunk	o ,,	$3\frac{6}{8}$	,,
,, ,, tail	1 ,,	$2\frac{6}{8}$	,,
Entire length . . .	1 ,,	$7\frac{7}{8}$	,,

* During life there is no trace of blue, or even bluish-green, about this lizard, but after death it sometimes acquires this colour from the effects of spirits of wine, to which circumstance must be attributed the denomination of " Blue Calotes," Gray, in Griffith's edition of Cuvier, vol. ix. p. 55.

Those of the intestinal canal :—

Small intestines	$3\frac{4}{9}$	inches.
Large	$1\frac{4}{9}$	inch
Cæcum	$0\frac{4}{9}$	„

The stomach is cylindrical, simply a continuation of œsophagus without fundus, but separated from the small intestines by a valve. In several dissected it contained nothing but mucus. The length of œsophagus and the stomach together was $1\frac{6}{8}$ inch. The anterior part of the small intestines is widened till about a quarter of an inch from the pyloric valve, where ductus coledochus enters. Cæcum is very widened, more so than any other part of the canal, of a crescent shape.

Gen. LOPHYRUS, *Duméril.*

Head triangular, more or less elongated, shelving in front; orbital edge arched or angular ; nostrils lateral, circular, or oval ; tongue papillary, rounded, and very slightly notched at the point ; in the upper jaw five incisors and two canines ; tympanum superficial ; skin of the throat lax, forming in some a scarcely perceptible, in others a highly developed pouch, and an angular cross fold in front of the chest ; neck, trunk, and tail compressed, with a crest, generally most elevated on the nape of the neck ; scales of the trunk rhombic, sub-imbricate, unequal (with scattered larger scales); femoral pores none.

LOPHYRUS ARMATUS, Gray.

SYN.—Agama armata, Gray.
Calotes tropidogaster, Cuvier.*
Acanthosaura armata, Gray.

Orbital edge slightly angular, with a long spine at its posterior extremity ; no spinous tubercles on the occiput ; on each side of the nape of the neck, immediately above the ear, another long spine, surrounded with five or six shorter ones at its base, from whence proceed obliquely over the temple and cheek a curved series of eighteen larger polygonal keeled scales ; tympanum thick, circular ; on the neck a crest of eight to twelve long spines, surrounded with numerous smaller ones at the base ; at a short interval the dorsal crest, the anterior five to six spines of which are very long, the rest rapidly decreasing towards the tail ; gular pouch very small, not toothed, with scales of equal size ; tail subtriangular, with a toothed crest above.

Above : head chestnut ; trunk and limbs blackish-green, with a black transversal band in the interval between the cervical and

---

* By mistake, Calotes lepidogaster ("Règne Anim." 1829, t. ii. p. 39).

dorsal crests, continued over the shoulders, with numerous pale yellowish-white, black-edged, rounded spots, assuming the shape of transversal bands on the limbs and the tail ; the larger single scales on the sides, limbs, and tail, clear sky-blue ; from the orbit over the lip five to six radiating black lines. Beneath, yellowish white. Pupil circular, iris brown, with a narrow golden ring.

HAB.—*Pinang, Singpaore.*
Cochin China.

At Pinang this species appears to be very local, and not numerous ; two individuals examined were obtained from spice plantations in the valley. They were very active and fierce, possessed in a slight degree the power of changing the ground-colour to a lighter hue, and in captivity refused food and water. In a female were found thirteen eggs of a yellowish-white colour, of an oval shape, $\frac{6}{8}$ inch in length. The stomach contained fragments of leaves and twigs, and a quantity of earth and lime. The latter probably originated from the lime-water with which the spice-trees are copiously sprinkled, to secure them against the attacks of insects. The dimensions of the lizard were :—

Length of the head . . . . $1\frac{1}{8}$ inches.
„ „ trunk . . . . . . $3\frac{5}{8}$ „
„ „ tail . . . . 6 „

Entire length . . . . . $10\frac{6}{8}$ „

Of the intestinal canal :—

Small intestines . . . . $7\frac{4}{8}$ inches.
Large . . . . $1\frac{6}{8}$ „
Cæcum . . . . $0\frac{4}{8}$ „

The stomach capacious, with thick parietes. The first portion of duodenum is much widened till within half an inch from pylorus, where ductus coledochus enters. Cæcum is of a crescent shape, much widened, as well as the large intestine.

Gen. DILOPHYRUS, *Gray.*

Head four-sided. Forehead rather concave, face-ridge high. Eyebrows rounded. Occiput with three or four larger tubercles on each side.

Parotids unarmed. Nape and back with a crest of high compressed scales, with series of smaller scales at their base. The throat rather lax,* with a cross fold behind,† extending up the front of the shoulders. Scales of the back small, rhombic, equal ;

---

* Add : *with a compressed pouch, minutely toothed in front.*
† *Questionable.*

of the belly rather larger, smooth. Tail compressed, keeled and toothed above, with two series of elongated keeled scales beneath. Femoral and preanal scales none.

DILOPHYRUS GRANDIS, Gray.

HAB.—*Pinang Hills.*
Rangoon.

As the only published characters of this species leave its identity with the Malayan somewhat doubtful, they are here preposed.

" *Olive-green ; sides white spotted, beneath whitish ; tail black-banded ; head with lines of rather larger scales ; crest very high, formed of broad compressed close-set scales, with three or four series of scales on each side of the base, interrupted over the shoulders.*"
—GRAY : " Catalogue of the Specimens of Lizards," &c. p. 239.

Form.—The head is elongated, four-sided pyramidal, its greatest height and breadth being equal, and less than one-half of the length. The muzzle is narrow, rounded, depressed. The upper surface of the head is very sloping, with a narrow furrow between the arched orbital parietes ; the forehead depressed or concave. The scales are polygonal, keeled ; those of the margin of the orbits and forehead larger, imbricate, forming a sharp ridge ; four similar scales form a short ridge in the centre of the forehead, close to the muzzle. Behind the orbit, over tympanum, and on each side of the nape of the neck, are similar short, oblique ridges, each composed of five larger pointed tubercular scales. The rostral shield is very broad, narrow, triangular ; the mental is much smaller, pointed, triangular, with two large polygonal scales on each side. The upper jaw is covered with twenty-six, the lower with twenty-four elongated, narrow, rectangular scales. Dentition :—

$$\text{Incis. } \frac{6}{4}; \text{ Canin. } \frac{1-1}{1-1}; \text{ Mol. } \frac{14.14}{14.14} = \frac{36}{34}$$

The incisors and anterior molars are very small ; the latter gradually increasing in size, flat, sharply edged, bluntly tricuspidate. The tongue is thick, flattened, very slightly notched in front, the anterior half spongy, the posterior with large backward-pointed papillæ. The nostrils are nearly circular, pierced in a large oval scale, in front of which three scales intervene between the rostral. The eyes are large, sunk in the orbits ; the pupil circular, black ; the iris blue, with golden spots and a narrow ring. The eyelids are covered with very minute polygonal tubercular scales. Each tarsus with a double row of scales, the inner one of small, polygonal, tubercular ; the outer one of rhombic, flat, with the angles overlapping, so as to give the free margin a toothed appearance. The tympanum is large circular. The skin of the throat is very lax, forming a compressed pouch, the anterior margin of which is slightly toothed, owing to the series of scales overlapping each other. But there is during life no trace of any "cross fold behind, extending up the front of the shoulders. The scales of the neck and back are very minute, rhombic, or sub-rectangular, smooth, increasing in size, and becoming imbricate on the sides, abdomen, limbs, and throat. On the neck is a high-arched, toothed crest, composed of twenty-six large ensiform scales, the thirteen anterior gradually increasing in length, the rest decreasing. The base of the crest is supported by two parallel, slightly arched series of rectangular scales, much larger than those of the rest of the body, but those of the upper series double the size of those of the inferior. The dorsal crest commences at a short interval a little behind the shoulders. In shape and component parts it resembles the former, but is double the extent, consisting of forty-five scales, all of which, however, are inferior in height to those of the cervical crest, which, as well as the somewhat lower, sloping level, renders the dorsal crest less conspicuous than the former. The skin is somewhat lax on the sides of the body, leaving the ribs visible. The tail is very much compressed, attenuated, elongated. Its sides are covered with rather large, smooth, imbricate, rhombic scales. The anterior third of the upper margin is toothed, composed of a single row of large, gradually decreasing, sharply keeled scales. The other two-thirds are covered by two rows of keeled scales, thus giving the posterior part of the tail a bidentated appearance. The lower surface of the tail is covered by two series of large, gradually decreasing, imbricate, keeled scales, giving it a bidentated appearance. The limbs are slender; the anterior little more than half the length of the posterior, and the toes very short. The posterior fourth toe is excessively long. The palms and soles are covered with minute, pointed, rough scales; the toes above and beneath with sharply keeled, imbricate, rhombic scales. The claws are large, trenchant, curved.

Colours.—The ground-colour of the head, neck, throat, gular pouch, and the chest is impure gamboge, the scales edged with brown; the eyelids dark brown, the tarsi buff. A dark blue triangular streak proceeds from the anterior angle of the orbit to the nostril; another is placed parallel with the upper labial scales, which, as well as the lower, are of a pale blue, as also the tympanum. From the labial scales and tympanum on each side across the throat, the pouch, and the sides of the neck, proceed seven oblique, undulating, dark blue bands. The tympanum is enclosed by two oblique, broad, purple-brown bands, which join each other under an angle at the anterior extremity of the cervical crest, where a third broad, longitudinal, purple-brown band commences, proceeding over the side of the neck, then expanding, covers the back and the upper half of the sides of the body, where its lower margin describes two large curves. The lower part of the sides are of a deep lilac, changing on the abdomen to bluish-white. On the sides of the body and on the abdomen appear several oblique series of lozenge-shaped spots: a few on the brown portion of the sides of a deep Indian red, the rest bright gamboge. The cervical and dorsal crests are mulberry-brown; the former with the upper half of each of the first thirteen scales light green; the latter with the upper half of the first ten scales pale yellow. The scales at the base of the crest partake of the general colour, but many of them have a pale yellow spot. The tail is coloured above and beneath with alternate broad rings of impure white, the scales edged with brown and purple-brown, changing to black on the posterior half. The legs, feet, and toes are dark purple-brown with indistinct transversal yellowish bands. Dimensions:—

Length of the head	. . . .	0 foot	2	inches.
„ „ trunk	. . . .	0 „	$4\frac{4}{9}$	„
„ „ tail	. . . .	1 „	4	„

Entire length . . . 1 „ $10\frac{4}{8}$ „

Length of cervical crest .	$1\frac{7}{8}$ in.	height of 13th scale	$0\frac{6}{8}$ in.
„ dorsal crest .	3 „	„ 15th „	$0\frac{4}{8}$ „
„ humerus . .	1 „	of femur . . .	$1\frac{1}{8}$ „
„ fore-arm . .	$1\frac{1}{8}$ „	of tibia	2 „
„ hand and 4th toe	1 „	of foot and 4th toe	$2\frac{7}{8}$ „

Entire length $3\frac{1}{8}$ „   6 „

The only individual examined was captured on a botanical excursion by Sir William Norris, on the Pinang Hills, on the bank of a mountain stream, at an elevation of about 2,000 feet. It appeared slow in its movements, of general sluggish habits, showed no power of changing colours, and in confinement it refused insects, vegetable food, as well as water. After having been preserved in rectified spirits of wine for upwards of three years, the specimen has retained the original brown and white colours and the Indian red spot; but the yellow, light green, and light blue have changed to whitish, and the dark blue marks to blackish. Although the colours in this state do not agree with those given by Mr. Gray, apparently, though not stated, taken from a preserved specimen, the peculiar distribution of the markings correspond, and induce me to believe in the identity of the animals.

Gen. DRACO, *Linné apud Duméril and Bibron.*

Head triangular, obtuse in front, slightly depressed, covered with small scales of unequal diameter. Three or four incisors and two canines in the upper jaw. Tongue spongy, thick, rounded, entire.* Tympanum hidden † in some, visible in others. In the centre of the throat an elongated vertical pouch; on each side a smaller horizontal. In general a small cervical crest.‡ Trunk depressed, with a lateral membrane, supported by the spurious ribs. No femoral pores. Tail very long, thin, angular, slightly depressed at the root.

A. *Tympanum visible, metallic iridescent.*

DRACO VOLANS, Linné.

SYN.—Draco volans, apud Gmel., Latr., Gray.
Draco præpos, Linné apud Gmelin.
Draco major, Laurenti.
Draco minor, Laurenti.
Le Dragon, Deubenton, Lacépède, Bonnat.
Flying Draco, Shaw.
Draco viridis, Daudin apud Merr., Kuhl, Wolf, Waglr.
Draco fuscus, Daudin apud Merr., Kuhl.
Draco bourouniensis, Lesson?
Draco Daudinii, Duméril and Bibron.
"Chíchak terbang" or "Kubin" of the Malays.

Scales of the back rhomboidal, imbricate, indistinctly keeled; of the throat granular, of equal size; the adult male with a small cervical crest; tongue minutely notched in front; gular pouch of the male very long, narrow, nearly double the length of the head; of the female, shorter, broad, triangular.

Adult male and female.—Head metallic brown or green, with a black spot between the eyes. Back and inner half of the wing membrane varied with metallic, iridescent dark brown, and rose colour, in some disposed in alternate transversal bands, with numerous black spots and short, irregular waved or zigzag lines. Limbs and tail in some with rose-coloured transversal bands. Sides of the neck and lips also rose-coloured with black spots. Cheeks and eyelids silvery-white or sky-blue, the latter with short radiating black lines. Throat and gular pouch bright yellow, the former dotted with black; lateral pouches yellow or silvery rose, dotted with black. Outer half of the wing membrane black with indistinct transversal bands, composed of large, sometimes confluent, spots of silvery rose or whitish colour; the margins appearing as minutely fringed with silver. Beneath, either whitish-yellow

---

* In the following species the tongue is minutely yet distinctly *notched*.
† i.e., *Dracunculus, Weigmann.*
‡ The *female* of *Draco fimbriatus,* Kuhl (i.e., *Draco abbreviatus,* Gray), *D. volans,* and *D. maculatus,* differs from the male in having no cervical crest, and in having a smaller, less elongated gular pouch.

or pale sky-blue with metallic lustre; the membrane largely, the abdomen in some minutely, spotted with black or brown. Iris hazel, with a golden narrow ring. *Young* of the same more vivid colours, with a series of double black spots along the spine of the back, and some scattered on the sides.

HAB.—*Malayan Peninsula, Pinang.*
Philippine Islands, Borneo, Java.

The transcendent beauty of the individually varying colours baffles description. Such as are current of this and other species appear to have been taken from preserved specimens. As the lizard lies in the shade along the trunk of a tree, its colours, at a distance, appear like a mixture of brown and grey, and render it scarcely distinguishable from the bark. Thus it remains, with no signs of life except the restless eyes, watching passing insects, which, suddenly expanding the wings, it seizes with a sometimes considerable, unerring leap. It is but on close inspection, exposed to the light or in the sun, that the matchless brilliancy of its colours is visible. But the lizard itself appears to possess no power of changing them. This species is numerous on trees, in valleys and hills. The female, apparently less numerous than the male, carries three to four eggs of an oval cylindrical shape, $\frac{3}{8}$ of an inch in length, and of a yellowish-white colour. Of a number examined none exceeded the following dimensions:—

Length of the head . . . . $0\frac{4}{8}$ inch.
    ,,   ,,   trunk . . . . . . $2\frac{4}{8}$ inches.
    ,,   ,,   tail . . . . $4\frac{4}{8}$,,

$7\frac{4}{8}$,,

B. *Tympanum hidden by scales.*

Gen. DRACUNCULUS, *Wiegmann.*

DRACO MACULATUS, Gray.

SYN.—Dracunculus maculatus, Gray.*
HAB.—*Pinang.*
Tenasserim.

Form.—This species closely resembles *Draco lineatus,* Daudin (*Dracunculus lineatus,* Wiegman), from which it differs in the following particulars. The adult *male* carries a very elongated,

---

* "Grey, black-spotted; wings black-spotted; throat grey; pouch of the male elongate; scales of the back rather unequal, rhombic, keeled; of the sides rather smaller; sides with a series of large-keeled scales; ears rather sunk, with unequal flat scales; tail slender, with a central keel above, and five more small ones on the sides, base dilated, with five nearly equidistant equal keels above.—*Catalogue of the Specimens of Lizards,* &c., p. 236.

pointed gular pouch, double the length of the head, and a slightly elevated cervical crest, consisting of six to eight pointed tubercular scales, and continued along the anterior half of the back in the shape of a ridge composed of a raised fold of the skin. The *female* has neither cervical crest nor dorsal ridge, and her gular pouch is much reduced, its length being about one-half of the length of the head. Both sexes have the following characters in common:—From each side of the neck commences a series of spinous scales, sometimes close together on one side, distant on the other, which, increasing in size and becoming more distant, continue along the side of the body, where they deviate outwards, marking the origin of the wings, and again converge towards the root of the tail, where they terminate. The scales of the back are generally smooth, consisting of smaller polygonal, mixed with some larger rhombic, indistinctly keeled, imbricate scales. In some individuals the latter are disposed so as to form a series on each side of the dorsal spine. The supraorbital margin has from three to four large pointed tubercles, of which but the one situated at the posterior angle appears to be constant. The scales of the neck and throat are small granular, from which those covering the tympanum differ by being larger, flattened, and polygonal. The tubercles of the throat and neck, and many of the scales of the back, wing membranes, and the limbs, have each a minute rounded cavity at the point, discernible by a lens. The pouches, chest and abdomen are covered with rhombic, imbricate, keeled scales without apical cavities. Each jaw has sixteen labial scales. The tail is long, very broad at the base, particularly in the male, suddenly tapering, rounded above, and covered with strongly keeled, imbricate, rhombic scales. The first large ones of the lowest series of the root form a more or less conspicuous toothed crest. The lower surface is flattened, with scales like the upper. The apex of the tongue is notched. Dentition:—

$$\text{Incis. } \frac{4}{2} \; ; \; \text{Canin. } \frac{1-1}{1-1} ; \; \text{Mol. } \frac{15.15}{15.15}$$

Colours.—This species bears so close a resemblance to *Draco volans*, that it is scarcely possible to point out any difference. The upper parts of the body are metallic greenish-brown, varied with golden rose-colour or isabella, indistinctly dotted and lined with black. The wings are golden isabella with transversal black bands, formed by series of black rounded spots, either separate or confluent on the inner half, but blending into one another on the outer half. In some individuals numerous undulating golden rose-coloured or buff lines longitudinally intersect the bands. The margins are finely fringed with silver. The limbs and tail are indistinctly ringed with black or brown. A black spot on the vertex, between the eyes, appears to be constant also in this species. The gular pouch and the throat are bright yellow, the latter in some dotted with pale brown. The chest and abdomen whitish-yellow in some, bluish-white in others. The under surface of the wings is of the latter colour, in some with single large rounded black spots near the margins, independent of the upper markings; which may be distinguished through the hemitransparent membrane.

Of this species but four, of which two males were received from Sir Wm. Norris. They were all from the Hills of Pinang ; * none exceeded the following dimensions :—

Length of the head		. . . .	$0\frac{5}{8}$ inch.
,,	,,	trunk	3 inches.
,,	,,	tail	$5\frac{2}{8}$,,
			$8\frac{7}{8}$,,

The intestinal canal of a female measured :—

Small intestines	3 inches.
Large ,, ...	$0\frac{7}{8}$,,
Cæcum ,, ...	$0\frac{2}{8}$,,

The capacious stomach contained remains of insects, particularly of the gigantic black ant, inhabiting the Malayan hill forests. The first portion of duodenum is much widened till within a quarter of an inch from pylorus, where ductus coledochus enters. Cæcum is of a short crescent shape, much widened, as well as the large intestine. In the abdominal cavity appeared five eggs, of an oval form, yellowish-white colour, each half an inch in length.

Gen. LEIOLEPIS, *Cuvier apud Duméril and Bibron.*

Head sub-pyramidal, quadrangular, with minute polygonal tubercular scales. Tympanic membrane a little sunk. Tongue scaly on the anterior, papillary on the posterior half, apex bifid. Chest with a transversal fold in front. Two canines in each jaw. Trunk sub-cylindrical with granular scales above ; beneath, with larger, smooth, imbricate, rectangular scales. Femoral pores. Tail conical, very long ; the root broad and depressed, the rest excessively slender.

To these characters it will be necessary to add : *Skin of the sides of the trunk excessively lax, capable of being expanded into a large wing-like membrane by means of the six anterior very long spurious ribs.*

---

* The Museum of the Asiatic Society possesses two females, obtained by the late Dr. Spry in the Tenasserim Provinces.

LEIOLEPIS BELLII, Gray.

SYN.—Uromastix Bellii, Gray.
  Uromastix belliana, " Ill. Ind. Zool."*
  Leiolepis guttatus, Cuvier apud { Guérin. Duméril and Bibron.
  Cynosaurus punctatus, Schlegel.
  Leiolepis Bellii, Gray : Catal.

Ground-colour above, blackish-grey; the back and sides with seven parallel lines of pale sulphur colour, edged with black, the second from below, the fourth and sixth composed of more or less confluent spots, the other three of distant round spots. The expanded membrane black with seven or eight broad distant, transversal bars of a brilliant orange. The tail above with numerous small pale yellow spots. The fore-legs with orange-coloured rounded spots, some of which tipped with azure; the hind-legs minutely spotted with yellow. The throat pale azure; abdomen pale orange marble with broad bluish-black veins; the tail beneath pale yellowish-white. The lower eyelid is pure white; pupil circular, iris hazel with a narrow golden ring.

HAB.—*Malayan Peninsula, Pinang.*
  Cochin-China.

The head is covered with small elongated polygonal keeled scales; the upper jaw with twenty-six, the lower with eighteen to twenty. The mental shield is elongated, polygonal; the upper part of the sides is joined to the first lower labial scale; the centre part is on each side in contact with the first series of thirteen to fifteen elongated polygonal scales, which follow the track of the labial, between which there is a narrow intervening space covered with smooth polygonal scales, larger than those of the rest of the throat. The back and wing membranes are covered with minute granular scales; the abdomen with larger smooth rhombic scales. Those of the tail, above and beneath, are verticillated, rectangular, sub-imbricate, and strongly keeled. The tongue is thick, fungous, not scaly, as incorrectly represented, with the tip much flattened, free and slightly extensile, divided in two laterally compressed sharp points. The molar teeth are tricuspidate, increasing in size, the anterior being the smallest. In the adult they are much worn and incrustated with brown tartar, like the teeth of *Semnopitheci* and *Ruminantia.* Dentition :—

* In the supposition that this incorrectly drawn and coloured figure has been taken from the living animal, MM. Duméril and Bibron have been led to publish an erroneous description and figure. The last description of this species of Mr. Gray appears to be founded on the same authority. It runs thus: " Olive with black-edged white spots, and a black-edged white streak on each side ; beneath, whitish."—*Catal.* &c., p. 263.

$$\text{Incis.} \; \frac{4}{\text{I—I}} \; ; \; \text{Canin.} \; \frac{\text{I—I}}{\text{I—I}} \; ; \; \text{Mol.} \; \frac{12.12}{11.11}$$

The nails are long, slightly arched, of a pale yellowish horn-colour.

The wing membrane in a state of repose appears like a longitudinal loose fold, extending along each side from the axilla to the inguinal region. Expanded, the external margin becomes arched, the trunk and the membranes forming a greatly flattened oval disk (strongly contrasting with the bulky appearance of the parts in a state of repose), resembling the hood of *Naja*. The transversal diameter of the disk across axilla and the inguinal region is $1\frac{1}{8}$ inch; across the centre $2\frac{2}{8}$ inches. Like the mechanism of the genus *Draco*, the membranes are expanded by means of the very long six anterior pairs of spurious ribs, which the lizard has the power of moving forward under a right angle with the vertebral column. The six posterior ones are excessively short, and, though equally movable, do not appear materially to assist in expanding the membranes. The latter are used as a parachute in leaping from branch to branch, after which they immediately resume their state of repose. Sudden fear or anger will also cause a momentary expansion. The femoral pores are situated on a series of rather large rhombic scales on each thigh. In a number of twelve adult individuals, the pores varied from thirteen to nineteen on each thigh. In the specimens in the Paris Museum, described by MM. Duméril and Bibron, there are from twenty to twenty-four on each thigh.

This species appears to be numerous, but local. Twelve were at one time obtained from a spice plantation in province Wellesley, some of which were in the act of changing the integuments. They were very active and swift, more so than their rather heavy make would induce one to believe, and they would bite and scratch when handled, although among themselves in a spacious cage they appeared peaceable, and patiently submitted to being trodden or run over by a neighbour, about ascending the perch. The Malay who brought the lizards asserted they were frugivorous, and might be fed with soft fruit and boiled rice, which was perfectly true. In one immediately examined, the stomach and intestines contained rounded seeds of various kinds, from the smallest size to that of a large pea, and vegetable fibres.*

The rest refused insects and different kinds of fruit, but during the several months' confinement each would daily eat a little boiled rice, and occasionally take water. Of these none exceeded the following dimensions :—

---

* The latter, however, as well as sand and fragments of stone, also occur in carnivorous and insectivorous lizards, as well as serpents, which swallow these substances to stimulate digestion.

Length of the head . . . . o foot $1\frac{1}{8}$ inches.

,, ,, trunk . . . . o ,, $4\frac{2}{8}$,,

,, ,, tail . . . . . 1 ,, o ,,

Entire length . . . 1 ,, $5\frac{3}{8}$,,

Length of the intestinal canal :—

Small intestines . . . . $5\frac{6}{8}$ inches.

Large ,, ... 3 ,,

Cæcum . . . . $0\frac{2}{8}$,,

The stomach is of a lengthened pyriform shape, one inch in length ; duodenum, narrow, receives ductus coleductus at $\frac{3}{8}$ in. distance from pylorus. Cæcum is very short, nearly circular. The large intestine is sacculated, terminating in a short simple rectum.

There seems to be reason to believe that *Leiolepis revesii*,* Gray, inhabiting " China " and Arracan, is also found on the Malayan Peninsula.

FAM. SCINCIDÆ, *Gray* (LEPIDOSAURES, *Duméril and Bibron*),

SUB-FAM. SAUROPHTHALMINÆ, *Cocteau.*

Gen. GONGYLUS, *Wagler apud Duméril and Bibron.*

Nostrils lateral, pierced either through the nasal or between the nasal and rostral shield ; tongue notched, squamous ; teeth conical,

* Syn. *Uromastix revesii*, Gray. " *Olive with a series of bright red spots on each side.*" (Griffith, " Animal Kingdom," ix. p. 62.) Such was the only account of this species at the time of the publication of " Erpétologie Générale," where it is not introduced. Mr. Gray's latest description runs thus : " *Olive with longitudinal series of pale whitish spots ; when alive, blackish, with orange spots on the back, and a series of bright red spots on the sides. China.*" (" Catalogue," &c., p. 263.)

The Museum of the Asiatic Society possesses an adult male and a young specimen sent from Arracan by Capt. Phayre. The form resembles in every particular that of *Leiolepis guttatus*, from which the present species principally differs by its colours, larger, heavier make and size. Each jaw is covered by twenty scales. From the mental scale proceeds a series of ten larger scales on each side below the labial. On the throat appear two or three strong transversal folds, of which the anterior commences from the posterior margin of the tympanum. The tail is covered with keeled verticillate scales, as in *L. guttatus*, but not with " rings of smooth scales," as Mr. Gray's generic character states. Dentition :—

Incis. $\frac{4}{1-1}$; Canin. $\frac{1-1}{1-1}$; Mol. $\frac{10.10}{10.10}$; Femoral pores 20.

Length of the head . . . . o foot $1\frac{4}{8}$ inches.

,, ,, trunk . . . . o ,, $6\frac{1}{2}$,,

,, ,, tail . . . . 1 ,, o ,,

Entire length . . . . 1 ,, $7\frac{5}{8}$,,

often slightly compressed, and as it were wedge-shaped, simple ; palate toothed or not, with a posterior notch or a longitudinal groove ; auricular apertures ; four feet, each with five unequal, slightly compressed, not dentilated, nailed toes ; sides rounded ; tail conical or slightly compressed, pointed.

Sub-Gen. EUMECES, *Wiegmann*.

Nostrils pierced through the nasal shield, near the posterior margin ; two supernasal shields ; palate not toothed, with a rather shallow triangular notch behind ; scales smooth.

EUMECES PUNCTATUS, Linné, var.

SYN.—Lacerta punctata, Linné.
    Stellio punctatus, Laurenti.
    La Double raie, Daub. apud Lacép. Bonnat.
    Lacerta interpunctata, Gmelin apud $\begin{cases} \text{Donnd.} \\ \text{Shaw.} \\ \text{Latreille.} \end{cases}$
    Scincus bilineatus, Daudin.
    Scincus punctatus, Schneider apud Merrem.
    Seps scincoïdes, Cuv. apud Griffith, A.K.
    Lygosoma punctata, Gray apud Griff. A.K.
    Riopa punctata, Gray.
    Tiliqua Cuvierii, Cocteau.
    Tiliqua Duvaucellii, Cocteau.
    Eumeces punctatus, Wiegmann apud Dum. and Bibr.
    Riopa Hardwickii, Gray : Catal. (young).

Trunk individually varying in length ; limbs very small, giving the lizard a blindworm-like appearance; tail very thick at the root, fusiform, tapering to a very sharp point, its length varying from one to two-thirds of the entire length of the animal. On the anterior margin of the ear a small tubercle. Above, metallic chestnut, or greenish-bronze, in some with six more or less distinct dotted black lines along the back, or with two rows of scales nearest each side of a lighter shade than the ground colour, thus forming two lighter longitudinal bands. From the nostril to the middle of the side of the tail a black or brown band, with numerous small white spots on the sides. Limbs outside dotted with white. Beneath, sulphur-coloured, in some the throat and tail minutely dotted with black. Iris dark brown, with a narrow circular golden ring.

HAB.—*Malayan Peninsula, Pinang, Singapore.*
    Malabar and Coromandel Coast, Bengal.

The variety described above is numerous in the Malayan

countries, both on hills and in valleys. Of several the largest individual was of the following dimensions :—

Length of the head	. . . .	$0\frac{3}{8}$ inch.
,, ,,	trunk	. . . . . .	$2\frac{1}{8}$ inches.
,, ,,	tail	. . . .	$1\frac{7}{8}$,,
Entire length	. . . .	$4\frac{3}{8}$,,

Sub-Gen. EUPREPIS, *Wagler.*

Nostrils pierced through the posterior part of the nasal shield ; two super-nasals ; palate with a more or less deep triangular incision ; pterygoid teeth ; scales keeled.

EUPREPIS RUFESCENS, Shaw.

SYN.—Lacerta maritima maxima, &c., Seba ii. tab. 105, fig. 3.
Lacerta rufescens, Shaw, iii. p. 1. p. 285.
Scincus rufescens, Merrem apud { Cuvier.
{ Gray in Griffith, A.K.
Scincus multifasciatus, Kuhl.
Mabouya multifasciata, Fitzinger.
Euprepis multifasciatus, Wagler.
Tiliqua fufescens, Gray.
Eumeces rufescens, Wiegmann.
Tiliqua carinata, Gray.
Tiliqua affinis, Gray (Young).
Euprepis Sebæ, Duméril et Bibron.

Body strong ; limbs proportionate ; tail rounded, slightly compressed, little exceeding half the entire length. Scales of the back and sides : in the young with five to seven keels ; in the adult the dorsal scales with three to five keels, the rest smooth. The anterior margin of the ear with three or four minute lobules. Lower eyelid with a series of four or five larger, square scales. Pterygoid teeth minute, few, hid in the palatal membrane, forming a short line on each side of the triangular incision of the palate.

HAB.—Sandwich Islands, Philippines, Timor, Celebes, Borneo, Java, Coromandel, Bengal.

Var. D., Duméril and Bibron.

Above : ground colour shining bronze with five to seven zigzag, or dotted black lines, in some continued on the tail ; sides with many of the scales black, with a square white spot in the middle, in some arranged so as to produce numerous distant transversal bands. The margins of some or all the shields of the head black. Beneath, sulphur-coloured. Iris black, with a golden circular ring.

HAB.—*Malayan Peninsula, Pinang, Singapore.*

Var. E., Duméril and Bibron.

Above, uniformly shining bronze; sides in some sprinkled with blood-red; rest like the preceding.

HAB.—*Same localities.*

Var. F., Duméril and Bibron.

Above, uniformly shining bronze; the anterior half of the sides with a blood-red stripe, which in specimens preserved in spirits of wine changes to whitish, or disappears; the posterior part of the sides of the body and the anterior of the tail in some with square sky-blue spots in the middle of some of the scales; rest like the preceding.

HAB.—*Same localities.*

These three varieties are exceedingly numerous in the hills and valleys of the Malayan countries. They may be seen basking in the sun in bamboo hedges or on trees, and they fearlessly enter houses in pursuit of insects, in which they display great agility. The female deposits six to twelve yellow-white, oval cylindrical eggs, half an inch in length. Nearly all have on the lower two-thirds of the tail a series of large scuta. In one individual observed the last two-thirds of the back of the tail was covered with a single series of very broad scales, of which each of the anterior had fifteen to sixteen keels. In another the tail had been lost near the root, and reproduced by a pyramidal, soft, naked process, $\frac{2}{3}$ inch long, with circular folds like those of the body of *Ichthyophis*. Var. E. appears to exceed the others in size: the largest was of the following dimensions :—

Length of the head	. . . . . .	$0\frac{5}{8}$	inch.
,, ,, trunk	. . . . . .	$3\frac{4}{8}$	inches.
,, ,, tail	. . . . . .	$4\frac{4}{8}$	,,
Entire length	. . . . .	$8\frac{3}{8}$	,,

EUPREPIS ERNESTII, Duméril and Bibron.

SYN.—Scincus Ernestii, Boie, MSS.
Psammite de Van Ernest, Cocteau.
Dasia olivacea, Gray : Catal.

Form like *E. rufescens*. Triangular incision of the palate very small, with a few minute pterygoid teeth on each side. Ears obliquely oval, small, appearing more so, being half-covered by two of the temporal scales; no lobules on the anterior margin. Scales of the back with minute, longitudinally waved lines, and from three to eight indistinct keels. The outer half of the toes and the nails sharply compressed. A series of scuta beneath the tail.

Very young.—Head light green-bronze, shields edged with black, and a black line, edged with silver, from the muzzle to the ear. Back, sides, root of the tail, and outside of the limbs shining black, with numerous transversal silvery lines. Feet and toes rose or flesh coloured. Tail brilliant scarlet.* Throat, abdomen, and inside of the limbs silvery-white.

Adult.—Ground colour, greyish-brown bronze. Frontal and supraorbital shields black-edged; fronto-parietals, inter-parietals and parietals black, each with a whitish elongated mark, united, forming a symmetrical figure. From the nostril to the eye a black streak. Neck and body with a number (twelve to fourteen) of distant, transversal, waved bands, composed of black scales, each with a rectangular white spot in the middle. Outside of limbs with four or five similar bands. In some a buff-coloured lateral band on the posterior part of the back, and the anterior half of the side of the tail. Beneath, iridescent light bluish-green; scales with whitish edges. Iris black with a golden narrow circle.

HAB.—*Malayan Peninsula, Pinang.*
Java.

In habits this species resembles *uprepis Erufescens*, but appears to be far less numerous. In a female were found eleven eggs, in shape, size, and colours resembling those of *E. rufescens*. The young above described was of the following dimensions :—

Length of the head	. . . . .	$0\frac{3}{8}$	inch.	
,, ,, trunk	. . . . .	1	,,	
,, ,, tail	. . . . .	$1\frac{6}{8}$	,,	

Entire length . . . . . $3\frac{1}{8}$ inches.

Of the two adult individuals the larger measured :—

Length of the head	. . . . .	$0\frac{6}{8}$	inch.	
,, ,, trunk	. . . . .	$3\frac{2}{4}$	inches.	
,, ,, tail	. . . . .	$4\frac{4}{8}$	,,	

Entire length . . . . . $8\frac{4}{8}$,,

Sub-Gen. LYGOSOMA, *Gray apud Dum. and Bibr.*

Nostrils pierced through the nasal shield; no supranasals

---

* The very young of *Eumeces lessonii*, Dum. and Bibr. (*Scincus cyanurus,* Lesson), is distinguished by a similar distribution of colours.

palate toothless, with a small triangular incision, situated far back, scales smooth.

LYGOSOMA CHALCIDES, Linné.

SYN.—Scincus pedibus brevissimis, &c., Gronov. p. ii. No. 43.
Lacerta chalcides, Linné.
Angvis quadrupes, Linné apud Hermann.
Le Chalcide, Daubenton.
Der Vierfuss, Müller.
Lézard vert à ecailles lisses, Vosmaer.

Lacerta serpens, Bloch apud {
Hermann.
Gmelin.
Leske.
Donnd.
Shaw.
}

Angvis quadrupède, Lacépède.
Chalcida serpens, Mayer.
Lacerta serpens, Donnd apud Shaw.
Scincus brachypus, Schneid. apud Merrem.
Chalcides serpens, Latreille.
Seps pentadactylus, Daudin.
Seps (Angvis quadrupedes, Lin.), Cuv. apud Griffith, A.K.
Mabouya serpens, Fitzinger?

Lygosoma serpens, Gray apud { Wagler.
Griffith, A.K.
}
Lygosoma aurata, Gray apud Griffith, A.K.
Tiliqua de Vosmaer, Cocteau.
Lygosoma brachypoda, Duméril and Bibron.
Podophis chalcides, Gray : Catal.

Blindworm-like; limbs excessively small; tail strong, conical, about two-fifths of the entire length. A single large lozenge-shaped fronto-parietal shield. Ear minute, circular. Lower eyelid scaly, with a few larger scales. Preanal scales larger than the rest.

Ground colour : iridescent, lighter or darker copper or bronze, in some with indistinct dark-brown zigzag lines, produced by the scales being laterally edged or dotted with that colour. Beneath, pale or whitish-yellow. The tail in some minutely dotted with brown. Iris black, with a minute golden ring. The supraorbital scales being somewhat transparent, the black colour of the eye gives them a blackish appearance.

HAB.—*Pinang.*
Singapore, Java.

But two individuals were observed on the Great Hill of Pinang—one by Sir W. Norris, the other by myself. The latter made its appearance through a hole in the soft moist mould beneath a group of *Polycopodium Horsfieldii.* Above ground its movements were very quick, serpent-like, apparently little assisted by the tiny limbs. The head of the larger measured $\frac{2}{3}$ inch, the trunk $2\frac{7}{8}$ inches in length. One had but four toes on the anterior feet. In both the tail was reproduced, which is also the case in a third, from Singapore, preserved in the Museum of the Asiatic Society.

OPHIDIA.

(*Innocuous Serpents.*)

FAM. TYPHLOPIDÆ, GRAY.

BURROWING.

Gen. PILIDION, *Duméril and Bibron.*

Head covered with shields, cylindrical, very short, as if truncated, convex above, declivous in front ; muzzle rounded; rostral shield like a large rounded cap covering the head and muzzle ; an anterior frontal, a frontal, a pair of supraorbital, ocular, nasal, and fronto-nasal shields; neither parietals, interparietals, nor preorbitals; nostrils hemispherical, under the muzzle, between the nasal and fronto-nasal shields ; eyes excessively small, hidden by the ocular shields.

PILIDION LINEATUM, Boie.

SYN.—Acontias lineatus, Reinwardt, MS.
　　　Typhlops lineatus, H. Boie.
　　　Typhlina, Wagler.
　　　Typhlops lineatus, Gray in Griffith, A.K.
　　　Typhlops lineatus, Schlegel.
　　　Pilidion lineatum, Duméril and Bibron.
　　　Typhlinalis lineatum, Gray : Catal.

Ground-colour pale gamboge or orange, uniform on the head, the apical third of the tail, and the abdomen ; interrupted on the back and sides by twelve longitudinal serrated brown lines, produced by a minute triangular spot on each side of the scales.

HAB.—*Pinang Hills.*
　　　Java, Sumatra, Singapore.

A single individual, captured by Sir William Norris, differs from the description given by MM. Duméril and Bibron in the comparatively greater dimensions of the tail. It is strongly arched ; its length equals twice the breadth of the head ; it is covered with sixteen transversal series of scales, and it is considerably thicker than the rest of the uniformly cylindrical body. The anterior frontal shield is very broad, larger than the frontal. It was of the following dimensions :—

Length of the head . . . . 0 foot $0\frac{2}{8}$ inch.
„ „ trunk . . . . 1 „ $0\frac{7}{8}$ „
„ „ tail . . . . . 0 „ $0\frac{4}{8}$ „

1 „ $1\frac{5}{8}$ „

Circumference of the trunk, $\frac{5}{8}$ in. ; of the tail, $\frac{6}{8}$ in.

Gen. TYPHLOPS, *Schneider.*

Head covered with shields, depressed ; muzzle rounded, covered above and beneath by the rostral shield ; an anterior frontal, a frontal, a pair of supraorbitals, one or two pairs of parietals and interparietals ; a pair of nasals, fronto-nasals, preorbitals, and oculars ; nostrils lateral, hemispherical, opening in the suture between the nasal and fronto-nasal ; eyes lateral, more or less distinct ; pupil round.

TYPHLOPS NIGRO-ALBUS, Duméril and Bibron.

SYN.—Argyrophis bicolor, Gray : Catal.

Shining black above ; on the head some transversal and radiating whitish-yellow lines ; scales of the back edged with white ; beneath, whitish-yellow.

HAB.—*Pinang Hills, Singapore.*
Sumatra.

This species is closely allied to *T. Diardi*, Schlegel,* an inhabitant of Assam and the Khassia Hills. Of two individuals observed, the larger was of the following dimensions :—

Length of the head . . . . . 0 foot $0\frac{4}{8}$ inch.
„ „ trunk . . . . . 1 „ 0 „
„ „ tail . . . . . 0 „ $0\frac{3}{8}$ „

1 „ $0\frac{7}{8}$ „

Circumference of the trunk, $\frac{7}{8}$ inch ; of the tail, $1\frac{1}{8}$ inch.

TYPHLOPS BRAMINUS, Daudin.

SYN.—L'Orvet lombric, Lacépède.
Anguis. Rondoo Talooloo Pam. Russell, i. pl. 43.
Punctulated Slow-worm, Shaw.
Eryx braminus, Daudin.

* Syn. *T. Diardii*, apud Dum. and Bibr. ; *Argyrophis Horsfieldii*, Gray, Catal.

Typhlops rondoo talooloo, Cuvier.
Tortrix Russellii, Merrem.

Typhlops braminus, apud $\left\{\begin{array}{l}\text{Cuvier.} \\ \text{Fitzinger.} \\ \text{Gray in Griffith, A.K.}\end{array}\right.$

Typhlops Russellii, Schlegel.
Typhlops braminus, Cuvier apud Duméril and Bibron.
Argyrophis bramicus, Gray : Catal.

Shining copper-coloured or brown, of various shades above, paler beneath. Some individuals of a uniformly bluish white. All the scales with a dark-brown spot at the anterior part. The shields of the head have a whitish line close to their margins. In the young the latter is crenulated, and the sides of the head, lips, throat, the anal region, and the point of the tail are yellowish or whitish, and the body is semitransparent.

HAB.—*Pinang, Singapore, Malayan Peninsula.*
Canton Province, Philippines, Guam (Marian Isles), Java, Tenasserim, Bengal, Assam, Coromandel, Ceylon, Malabar.

In the Malayan countries this species is numerous in hills and valleys. The eyes are black, the pupil round, which is also the case in *T. nigro-albus.* The largest of a great number examined was of the following dimensions :—

Length of the head . . . . $0\frac{3}{8}$ inch.
„ „ trunk . . . . $7\frac{2}{8}$ inches.
„ „ tail . . . . $0\frac{1}{8}$ inch.
_____
$7\frac{6}{8}$ inches.

Circumference of the neck, $\frac{4}{8}$ inch ; of the tail, $\frac{3}{8}$ inch.

The preceding species of this family are all of similar habits. They mostly live under ground, but appear occasionally in shady places, particularly after showers of rain, in Bengal, in the rainy season. They are very agile, and appear to make use of the horny point of the tail as a propeller. When taken, they frequently press it against the hand in their attempts to escape. Reposing on the ground, *Typhlops braminus* may easily be mistaken for an earthworm, until its serpentine movements, the darting of the white furcated tongue, while the head and neck are raised, make it known. In confinement they refuse food and water. In all dissected, the stomach contained some earth ; in a few, remains of insects (Myriapoda, ants). A young female had a string of six cylindrical soft eggs, of a yellowish-white colour, each about $\frac{2}{8}$ of an inch in length, $\frac{1}{16}$ in diameter.

Fam. BOIDÆ, Bonaparte.

BURROWING.

Gen. CYLINDROPHIS, *Wagler.*

Scales smooth, imbricate, hexagonal; those of the abdomen broader than the rest; nostrils subvertical, opening in the lower part of the anterior frontal shield; neither nasals, frenals, nor preorbitals; a single postorbital; frontals large, reaching the minute eye, and the large second and third labials; supraorbitals, occipitals, and vertical distinct; tail very short.

CYLINDROPHIS RUFUS, Laurenti.

Syn.—Anguis rufa, Laurenti apud $\left\{ \begin{array}{l} \text{Gmelin.} \\ \text{Schneider.} \\ \text{Shaw.} \end{array} \right.$

Anguis striatus, Gmelin.
Anguis scytale, Linné apud Russell, ii. pl. 27.
Shilay Pamboo, Russell, ii. pl. 28 (young).
Anguis corallina, Shaw.
Eryx rufa, Daudin.

Tortrix rufa, Merrem apud $\left\{ \begin{array}{l} \text{Gray.} \\ \text{Schinz.} \\ \text{Schlegel.} \\ \text{Filippi.} \end{array} \right.$

Scytale Scheuchzeri, Merrem.
Ilysia rufa, Lichtenstein apud Fitzinger.
Cylindrophis resplendens, Wagler.
Cylindrophis rufa, Gray apud Duméril and Bibron.

Iridescent blackish-brown above; beneath, with alternate black and yellowish-white transversal bands or interrupted bars. Iris black, pupil vertically contracted by the light; tongue whitish. Central series of abdominal scales, 206; subcaudal, six.

Hab.—*Singapore.*
Java, Tranquebar, Bengal (?).

A single individual, turned up with the earth in a garden at Singapore belonging to Dr. Montgomerie, differs from the description given by MM. Duméril and Bibron in the following particulars. The head is uniformly black, without the two scarlet frontal spots; the apex of the tail whitish; the posterior part of the body is more robust than the anterior; the length of the head forms more than $\frac{1}{38}$ of the entire length of the animal; there are six pairs of labial shields on each jaw, and the scales of the trunk are disposed in twenty longitudinal series. It unites characters assigned by MM. Duméril and Bibron as distinguishing *Cylindrophis rufus* from *C. melanotus,* Wagler, and it would therefore appear that Dr. Schlegel is justified in considering the latter from Celebes (*Tortrix melanota,* Boie, MS.) as a variety of *rufa.* In the present individual there is no external appearance of the very rudimentary anal hooks. It was slow in its movements; attempted to escape, but not to bite.

Length of the head . . . . . 0 foot 0⅘ inch.
    ,,   ,, trunk . . . . . 1 ,, 6⅔ inches.
    ,,   ,, tail . . . . . 0 ,, 0⅝ inch.
                               1 ,, 7⅛ inches.

Gen. XENOPELTIS, *Reinwardt.*

Head rather narrower than the trunk, depressed, obsoletely angular; eyes small, round; nostrils large, apical; frenal shield very large; preorbital none;* postorbitals three;† interparietal very large, equalling the vertical; trunk thick, short, with imbricate, smooth, hexagonal scales, disposed in longitudinal series, increasing in size towards the narrow abdominal scuta; tail thick, short, awl-shaped, beneath with scutella.

XENOPELTIS UNICOLOR, Reinwardt.

SYN.—Xenopeltis concolor, Reinwardt.
    Xenopeltis leucocephala, Reinwardt (young).
    Guérin : Iconog. pl. xxi. fig. 3.
    Tortrix xenopeltis, Schlegel.

Adult.—Blackish or reddish-brown above, with strong metallic blue, purple, and green lustre; lips and throat buff; the lowest lateral series of scales, scuta, and scutella pale reddish-brown, with broad whitish margins. Iris black; pupil lanceolate, with the apex downwards, vertically contracted by the light; tongue buff.

Young.—Head yellowish-white, with a brown spot on the crown and labial shields; the scales of the sides edged with white, producing longitudinal zig-zag lines; the two lowest series of scales and scuta yellowish-white; scutella of the same colour, with a brown transversal line.

Scuta, 175 to 179; scutella, 26 to 27.

HAB.—*Pinang, Singapore, Malayan Peninsula,* Celebes, Java, Sumatra.

Of three young individuals, one was found by Sir William Norris on the Great Hill at Pinang, a second by Dr. Montgomerie at Singapore, and a third was obtained in province Wellesley, where

---

* The single preorbital is very large, the frenal small, subrectangular; the nostrils open between the latter and the nasal shield.
† Three individuals examined presented two postorbitals.

also a single adult male was killed. As this serpent in general appearance bears a strong resemblance to *Lycodon aulicus*, Linné, (syn. *L. hebe*, apud Schlegel), so it also does in its fierce habits and mode of attack. The scales are smooth, rhombic-hexagonal, disposed in fifteen longitudinal series. Labial shields $\frac{8-8}{8-8}$. The stomach of a young individual examined contained the remains of a rat. The adult attains to a much larger size than supposed; a male was of the following dimensions :—

Length of the head . . . . o feet $1\frac{4}{5}$ inch.

„ „ trunk . . . . 3 „ $2\frac{3}{8}$ inches.

„ „ tail . . . . o „ 4 „

_____

3 „ $7\frac{7}{8}$ „

Circumference of the neck $2\frac{6}{8}$, of the trunk $4\frac{2}{8}$, of the root of the tail 2 inches.

TERRESTRIAL.

Gen. PYTHON, *Daudin*.

Entire shields under the abdomen and tail, the latter cylindrical, sometimes with scutella; anus with scales and a hook on each side.

PYTHON RETICULATUS, Schneider.

Syn.—Seba i. tab. lxii. fig. 2; ii. tab. lxxix. fig. 1, and tab. lxxx. fig. 1.

Ular sawa, Wurmb.

La jaune et bleue, Lacépède.

L'oularsawa, Bonnaterre.

Boa reticulata, Schneider apud Daudin.

Boa rhombeata, Schneider (?).

Boa amethystina, Schneider.

Boa constrictor, var. ε, Latreille.

Boa phrygia, Shaw.

Coluber javanicus, Shaw.

Boa constrictor, var. 5, Daudin.

Python amethystinus, Daudin.

Python des îles de la Sonde, Cuvier, R.A.

Python Schneiderii, Merrem apud { F. Boie. / Guérin. / Schlegel.

Coluber javanensis, Fleming.

Python javanicus,* Kuhl apud { Fitzinger. / Gray in Griffith, A.K. / Eichwald.

* *Pytho javanicus*, figured and described in Abel's "Narrative," &c., is *Python molurus*, Linné.

Constrictor (P. Schneiderii, Kuhl), Wagler.
Python reticulatus, Gray apud Duméril and Bibron.
" Ular sawa " of the Malays.

Ground-colour above, light yellowish-brown, chestnut, or olive-green, assuming a greyish hue on the sides ; all the colours strongly iridescent, particularly reflecting metallic blue or green. The head is divided from the muzzle to the nape of the neck by a black line, continued along the back to the point of the tail, and describing a series of large lozenges, sometimes linked to each other by a small black ring, sometimes broken up into large irregular patches. A black oblique line proceeds from behind the eye towards the angle of the mouth, continuing on the sides as a series of more or less regular lozenges, which are joined to the lateral angles of those of the back by a large, black, triangular spot, with a white arched mark in the centre. The scales nearest the black margins of the lozenges are of a lighter colour than the rest, sometimes whitish. Between and within the lateral lozenges appear numerous black spots, or interrupted lines. The lips (the lower in some present a black line) and abdominal scuta are gamboge or pale yellow, as well as the lowest two or three series of scales, but the latter with irregular black spots. The caudal scutella and scuta, when present, are yellow marbled with black. The iris is silvery flesh-coloured or yellowish-brown, sometimes with a black bar ; the pupil vertically contracted by the light. The tongue is black above, bluish-white beneath. In the young the colours are brighter than in the adult.

Scuta, 297 to 330; scutella, 82 to 102.

HAB.—*Malayan Peninsula and Islands.*
Chusan ? * Amboina, Java, Banka, Sumatra, Bengal.†

The two fossets of the rostral shield are pyriform, with the apex diverging, and those of the nearest three or four upper labials are of similar shape. The inferior fossets are square, occupying the lower margin of the shield, varying from seven to nine on each side. The foremost of these is situated on the shield corresponding to that of the upper jaw, which borders the orbit.

This species is very numerous in the Malayan hills and valleys,

---

* Skins are of frequent occurrence at Chusan, and the natives assert that the serpent is found there and on the neighbouring continent. Serpents from 14 to 16 feet in length, "rock-snakes," were observed by several officers during our occupation of the island.

† MM. Duméril and Bibron state that this species has been sent from Bengal by M. A. Duvaucel. The natives are not acquainted with it, and the specimens in the Museum of the Asiatic Society are from Pinang. The living animal is occasionally brought from the Straits of Malacca to Calcutta, and such is probably the history of the specimen sent from Bengal by M. Duvaucel. *Python molurus*, Linné (*Pedda poda* and *bora* of Russell), is very numerous in Bengal.

feeding upon quadrupeds and birds. It often takes up its abode in outhouses, preying at night, and is thus useful in destroying vermin, although plunder is occasionally committed in poultry-yards. Dr. Montgomerie has seen in Georgetown, Pinang, a young one which the inhabitants suffered to retain unmolested possession of the rice stores in order to secure them against the ravages of rats. Individuals of 16 ft. in length are of no rare occurrence. In 1844 one was killed at the foot of Pinang, which a gentleman informed me measured more than 30 ft. During the expedition to China, in 1840, one was shot from the poop of one of H.M. transports, then riding in Singapore roads, between three and four miles from the shore. It was about 9 ft. long, and had the upper part of the head infested with *Ixodes ophiophilus*, Müller. The Chinese attribute great medicinal qualities to the heart and the gall-bladder, and use the skin to cover the bodies of some of their musical instruments. *Python molurus*, Linné (*Pedda poda*, Russell, i. pl. 22, 23, 24, and *bora*, pl. 39), is said also to occur, but rarely, in the Malayan Peninsula, but I never had an opportunity of seeing it.

AQUATIC.

Gen. ACROCHORDUS, *apud Schlegel.*

(*Acrochordus*, Hornstedt, 1787; *Chersydrus*, Cuvier, 1817.)

Acrochordus, Hornstedt.—Nostrils vertical, eyes encircled by a ring of minute scales; trunk compressed, attenuated towards both extremities; tail tapering, compressed; all the scales small, trifid, strongly keeled.

ACROCHORDUS JAVANICUS, Hornstedt.

SYN.—Acrochordus javanicus, apud Shaw.
    Acrochordus javensis, Lacép. apud Cuvier.
    Acrochordus javanicus, apud Schlegel.
    " 'Ular károng, or sápi, or lembu " of the Malays.*

Young.—Above, dull greyish-brown; sides and lower parts pale yellow or dirty ochre; back with three longitudinal, undulating, frequently interrupted black bands; sides and abdomen with rows of rounded spots, marbled and dotted with black.

Adult.—Of similar but less distinct colours. Iris brown, pupil elliptic, vertically contracted by the light; tongue whitish.

HAB.—*Pinang, Singapore.*
    Java.

---

* *'Ular* signifies a serpent, *károng* a sac, *sápi* and *lembu* a cow or ox. These expressive vernacular names refer to the loose skin and the bulk of the animal.

A female captured on the Great Hill at Pinang, at a distance from water, was of the following dimensions :—

Length of the head . . . . o feet $1\frac{4}{8}$ inch.

    ,,   ,,   trunk . . . . 4 ,, 7 inches.

    ,,   ,,   tail . . . . . . o ,, 9   ,,

                            5 ,, $5\frac{4}{8}$,,

Greatest circumference, 1 foot.

Notwithstanding the sharply compressed abdomen, the serpent moved without difficulty, but sluggishly, on the ground, and preferred quiet. When touched she attempted to bite, but the pupil being contracted by the glare, she missed her aim. Shortly after being brought, while the rest of the body remained motionless the posterior ribs were observed moving, and the serpent successively, in the course of about twenty-five minutes, brought forth twenty-seven young ones. Each birth was followed by some sanguinolent serum. With two exceptions the fœtus appeared with the head foremost. They were very active, bit fiercely, and their teeth were fully developed. Shortly after birth the integuments came off in large pieces, which is also the case with the fœtus of several species of *Homalopsis*. The present ones were placed in water, which, however, appeared to distress them, as they all attempted to escape on dry ground. Nearly all were of the following dimensions :—

Length of the head . . . . o foot $0\frac{6}{8}$ inch.

    ,,   ,,   trunk . . . . 1 ,, $1\frac{2}{8}$,,

    ,,   ,,   tail . . . . . o ,, 3 inches.

                            1 ,, 5   ,,

The Malays of Pinang assert that this species is of very rare occurrence. During a residence of twenty years at Singapore, Dr. Montgomerie observed it but in a solitary instance. The physiognomy of this species bears a striking resemblance to that of a thorough-bred bull-dog, which, in a somewhat less degree also may be said of the following.

*Sub-Gen. Chersydrus,** Cuvier.—Head and body uniformly covered with small scales.

ACROCHORDUS GRANULATUS, Schneider.

SYN.—Hydrus granulatus, Schneider.

        Angvis granulatus, Schneider.

        Acrochordus fasciatus, Shaw.

* This sub-gen. was founded upon the erroneous supposition that *Acrochordu fasciatus*, Shaw, possessed venomous organs.

Acrochordus dubius, Shaw.
Pelamis granulatus, Daudin.
Chersydrus (A. fasciatus, Shaw), Cuvier.
Acrochordus fasciatus, apud Raffles.
Chersydrus granulatus, Merrem apud Wagler.
Acrochordus fasciatus, apud Schlegel.
" 'Ular limpa "* or " 'Ular laut " of the Malays.

Young.—Blackish-brown or liver-coloured; the head with a few scattered yellowish-white spots, the rest of the body with numerous rings of the latter colour, some interrupted on the back, others on the abdomen.

Adult.—The dark colours fade to a dull greyish-black, uniform on the back, and the sides and abdomen present alternate dark and whitish vertical bands. Iris black, pupil vertically contracted ; tongue whitish.

HAB.—*Rivers and sea-coast of the Malayan Peninsula and Islands.* Bay of Manilla, New Guinea, Timor, Java, Sumatra, Coromandel.

This species appears not to exceed about 3 ft. in length. The body is less bulky and the skin less loose than in *A. javanicus ;* but the form is more compressed, particularly the sword or oar-. like tail, and, like that of the pelagic venomous serpent, appears exclusively calculated to aquatic habits. The scales also resemble those of the latter, and are generally smaller than in *A. javanicus.* Those of the back, the largest, are rounded rhombic, each with a minute tubercle in the centre. The skin in the interstices is finely wrinkled. On the abdomen the scales are mucronate, with a sharp, reclining central point. In both species the medial line is raised by two or three quincunx rows of scales with their points overlapping each other. The orbit is surrounded by a ring of scales a little larger than the rest. The nostrils, pierced high up on the muzzle, are almost vertical, slightly more so than they are in *A. javanicus.* In both they are tubular, larger in the present species, sinuous, and provided with a deeply seated membranous fold, which can hermetically close the passage. The mouth is secured in a similar manner by a central arched notch and two lateral protuberances, which correspond to a protuberance and two lateral cavities in the lower jaw. This contrivance also occurs in *Hydrus,* and to a certain extent in *Homalopsis.* With the exception of the dentition and the absence of venomous organs, in anatomical details both species of *Acrochordus* closely resemble *Hydrus.* As observed by M. Schlegel, the most striking feature is the great development of the lung, which occupies nearly three-fourths of the extent of the abdominal cavity. A somewhat

---

* *Limpa*—*i.e.,* liver, liver-coloured.

similar arrangement also occurs in *Homalopsis.* All the maxillary teeth (inter-maxillary none) are strong, pointed, inwardly reclining and disposed in double or treble rows. The three anterior teeth are the shortest ; the upper jaw has on each side upwards of twenty teeth, the lower three or four less. The palatal teeth number twelve on each side, the pterygoid nine, and are shorter than the rest. *Acrochordus granulatus* is of no rare occurrence in the sea of the Malayan coasts, although, according to Raffles, it is rarely seen on the coasts of Sumatra. At Pinang they are found among the fishes taken in the stakes some three or four miles distant from the coast. M. Schlegel is mistaken in stating that this species never inhabits the sea,* and in censuring M. Eschscholtz for his stating that the fishermen often take it in the Bay of Manilla. A female of the following dimensions had six eggs :—.

Length of the head	.	.	.	.	o feet	$0\frac{6}{8}$ inch.
„	„	trunk	.	.	. 2 „	$7\frac{2}{8}$ inches.
„	„	tail	.	.	. o „	$3\frac{6}{8}$ „

$$2 \text{ „ } 11\frac{6}{8} \text{ „}$$

Greatest circumference, 4 inches.

The egg is cylindrical, soft, coriaceous, whitish, about $1\frac{1}{2}$ inch in length. In each egg was coiled up a living young one of the following dimensions :—

Length of the head	.	.	.	$0\frac{3}{8}$ inch.
„	„	trunk	.	9 inches.
„	„	tail	.	$1\frac{4}{8}$ inch.

$$10\frac{7}{8} \text{ inches.}$$

Greatest circumference, 1 inch. In food and general habits this species resembles the pelagic venomous serpents ; in its element it is active, but on dry land, blinded by the daylight, it is sluggish and of uncertain movements.

Fam. COLUBRIDÆ, Bonaparte.

TERRESTRIAL.

Gen. Calamaria, *H. Boie.*

Body diminutive, elongated, obtuse at both extremities, throughout of equal diameter, cylindrical ; eyes very small, with round pupil ; frontals one pair, laterally extending to the labials ; frenals none ; nostrils lateral, opening in a small shield between the frontal, rostral, and anterior labial ; one preorbital, one post-

* " Essai," &c., p. 492.

orbital, four mental shields; dorsal scales rhombic, polished, smooth; tail very short.

CALAMARIA LUMBRICOIDEA, Schlegel, var.

SYN.—Calamaria lumbricoidea, Boie, MS.
Calamaria virgulata, Boie, MS. (Young).

Strongly iridescent, brownish-black, lighter on the head, scales with whitish edges; cheeks, lips, and throat citrine; the lowest row of scales and abdominal surface yellowish-white; subcaudal scutella faintly marked with brown; eyes and tongue black.
Scuta, 169; scutella, 26.

HAB.—*Pinang, Singapore.*
Celebes, Java.

This variety differs in nothing but colours from the species described by M. Schlegel. Of three individuals observed, two were taken by Sir W. Norris and W. T. Lewis, Esq., in the hills of Pinang, the third by Dr. Montgomerie at Singapore. The largest was of the following dimensions :—

Length of the head . . . . $3\frac{3}{8}$ inches.
   ,,   ,,   trunk . . . . . . $11\frac{6}{8}$,,
   ,,   ,,   tail . . . . $1\frac{3}{8}$ inch.

                 1 ft. $1\frac{1}{4}$,,
Circumference, $\frac{6}{8}$ inch.

The livery bears a remarkable resemblance to that of *Calamaria alba*, Linné (*C. brachyorrhos*, Schlegel), from which it, however, differs in the absence of the anterior frontal shields, and in having thirteen instead of seventeen longitudinal series of scales.

CALAMARIA LINNEI, H. Boie, var. Schlegel.

SYN.—Calamaria reticulata, Boie, MS.?
Changulia albiventer, Gray: "Ill. Ind. Zool." pl. lxxxvi. figs. 6–9.*
Calamaria Linnei, var. Schlegel.

Adult.—Head brown, minutely dotted with black, lips and cheeks pale gamboge; trunk reddish-brown, on each side with two vermillion longitudinal bands with black serrated edges; beneath, carmine, with a black serrated line on each side ; subcaudal scutella with a central black zig-zag line; all the colours strongly iridescent; eyes black, tongue vermilion.

---

* Referred by M. Schlegel to *C. lumbricoidea,* but the characteristic distribution of the colours is that of the present var. The figure, however, is not good, and not coloured from life.

Young.—Like the adult, but with a broad black nuchal band edged with white, a vermilion band at the root of the tail, and in some a similar near the point.

Scuta, 166; scutella, 17.

Hab.—*Pinang.*
    Java.

The present variety corresponds in all particulars to the description of *C. Linnei* by M. Schlegel, who, however, does not mention that the two or three anterior teeth on each side of the lower jaw are longer than the rest. Of six individuals from the hills of Pinang, the largest individual measured :—

Length of the head . . . . 0$\frac{2}{8}$ inch.
    „   „   trunk . . . . . . 10$\frac{1}{8}$ inches.
    „   „   tail . . . . 0$\frac{5}{8}$ inch.
                                    ―――――
                                    11   inches.

Circumference of the neck $\frac{3}{8}$, of the trunk $\frac{4}{8}$ inch.

CALAMARIA LONGICEPS, N.S.

Strongly iridescent soot-coloured, a shade lighter beneath; the scuta and scutella edged with whitish. Eyes and tongue black.

Scuta, 131; scutella, 26.

Hab.—*Pinang.*

The head is elongated, narrow, conical, the muzzle rounded, projecting over the lower jaw. The anterior frontals are much smaller than the frontals, which on the sides occupy the place of the absent frenal shield, and thus reach the second upper labial; the nasal is very small, rectangular, perforated by the rather large nostril near the lower anterior angle. The eye is comparatively large, between an obliquely placed rectangular preorbital and a similar postorbital shield; the supraorbitals are narrow, rectangular; the vertical, moderate, pentagonal, arched, and somewhat narrower at the anterior margin. The occipitals, the largest, are elongated, bordered below by the large fifth upper labial, and behind by a single pair of post-occipitals. Each jaw has five pairs of labials. Of the two pairs of mentals, the anterior is the longer, and is enclosed by the rostral and three anterior labials, the posterior pair by the fourth labial. The teeth are minute, sharp, reclining, all of equal size. The trunk is cylindrical, narrowed towards both extremities, covered with fifteen longitudinal series of smooth rhombic imbricate scales. The abdomen is arched, the short tail tapering to a blunt point. This species approaches to *Calamaria alba*, Linné (*C. brachyorrhos*, Schlegel), but differs by its elongated shape of the shields of the head and its larger

eyes. A single individual, captured by W. T. Lewis, Esq., on
the Great Hill of Pinang, was of the following dimensions :—

Length of the head	$0\frac{3}{8}$	inch.
„ „ trunk	5	inches.
„ „ tail	$0\frac{6}{8}$	inch.

$6\frac{1}{8}$ inches.

Circumference of the trunk $\frac{9}{16}$, of the neck $\frac{3}{8}$, at the root of the
tail $\frac{3}{8}$ inch.

CALAMARIA SAGITTARIA.

Syn.—Calamaria sagittaria, Cantor: Spicil.

Head yellow or white, marbled with black, forming a streak
above the citrine lips ; neck white, with a black arrow-shaped
mark ; back partly ash, partly rust-coloured, with a medial series
of distant minute black spots ; sides bluish-black or grey, with a
narrow black line above ; beneath citrine, the throat marbled with
black, and with a minute black spot near the lateral angle of each
scutum. Iris golden, tongue carmine.
Scuta, 216 to 227 ; scutella, 57 to 70.

Hab.—*Malayan Peninsula.*
Bengal, Assam.

But for the diminutive size and the reduced shields of the head
and throat, this species might be taken for a *Coronella.* The head
is but little distinct, depressed, ovate, covered by the normal
number of shields. The anterior frontals are very small, pentagonal ; the frenal short, rectangular. The nostrils are rather
large, piercing the middle of the nasal. The eyes are large,
prominent, with one preorbital, two postorbitals ; the upper jaw,
but slightly longer than the lower, has on each side six labials, the
lower seven, enclosing two pairs of small mentals. The temples are
covered by three shields. The trunk, with seventeen longitudinal
series of smooth rhomboidal imbricate scales, is slightly thicker
towards the middle than at the extremities ; the back throughout
depressed, forming an angle with the sides, and the abdomen is flat,
which makes a vertical section of the body square. The tail is very
slender, tapering to a sharp point, and exceeds one-fifth of the
entire length. The teeth are very minute, of equal size. A single
specimen from the Malayan Peninsula was of the following
dimensions :—

Length of the head	$0\frac{2}{6}$	inch.
„ „ trunk	$9\frac{3}{11}$	inches.
„ „ tail	$2\frac{2}{3}$	„

$11\frac{7}{8}$ „

Circumference of the trunk $\frac{4}{8}$, of the neck and root of the tail $\frac{3}{8}$ inch.

In Bengal this species is of no uncommon occurrence, particularly during the rainy season, when the water compels the serpents to leave the shady recesses which most of them occupy to avoid the heat of the day. The present species appears to be closely allied to the African *C. arctiventris*, Schlegel.

Of the preceding four species, the three first appear at Pinang exclusively to inhabit the hills, but the variety of *C. lumbricoidea* occurs at Singapore in valleys. They are nowhere to be met in numbers. They are of gentle, peaceable habits, never attempting to bite, and scarcely to escape. They are sluggish, move but slowly and to a short distance, even when compelled by danger, and soon resume the motionless position which they appear to affect. The remarkable abstinence of most of their congeners they possess but in a very limited degree. In captivity they refuse food, and soon expire; besides, they are so delicate that slight pressure in examining them is sufficient to kill them. Their bodies are very smooth, and brilliantly reflect rainbow-colours, which continue in preserved specimens long after the gay livery has faded. They feed upon slugs, earthworms, and insects. The stomach of a *C. sagittaria* contained remains of an *Iulus* and some sand. In general appearance and habits these species of *Calamaria* strongly resemble the Malayan *Elaps* (*vide infra*).

Gen. CORONELLA, *Laurenti*.

Head above covered with large plates, of which one between the eyes; sides of the head and occiput with imbricate scales; trunk narrowed near the head, thicker towards the middle; tail conical, elongated, tapering to a sharp point.

CORONELLA BALIODEIRA, Schlegel.

SYN.—Patza tutta, Russell, i. pl. 29?
    Coluber pictus, Daudin?
    Coluber Plinii, Merrem?
    Coronella baliodeira, Boie MS.

Above lighter or darker olive-brown, yellowish on the head, the scales minutely dotted with dark brown; the anterior part of the trunk with a number of distant transversal ocellated lines, composed of single transversal series of white scales edged with black, labial shields yellow edged with black; beneath, pearl-coloured or yellowish-white; iris golden, lower half blackish; tongue black.

Scuta, 122 to 132; scutella, 65 to 72.

HAB.—*Pinang*.
    Java.

Of two individuals from the hills of Pinang, the larger was of the following dimensions :—

Length of the head	. . . .	$0\frac{5}{8}$	inch.
„ „ trunk	. . . . . .	$8\frac{5}{8}$	inches.
„ „ tail	. . . .	$3\frac{6}{8}$	„

1 ft. 1 inch.

Circumference of the neck $\frac{4}{8}$, of the trunk $\frac{7}{8}$, of the root of the tail $\frac{5}{8}$ inch.

Both agree with the description of M. Schlegel, except in having two small preorbitals instead of one. Russell's No. 29, from Casemcotta, which, according to M. Schlegel, is *Coluber pictus*, Daudin, *C. Plinii*, Merrem, is probably intended to represent the present species. It is of fierce habits.

Gen. XENODON, *H. Boie*.

Head scarcely distinct, muzzle obtuse, nostrils rounded, between three shields ; eyes encircled behind only by three shields ; trunk short, robust ; tail rather short, slowly tapering ; four very large mentals, the last upper maxillary tooth the longest.

XENODON PURPURASCENS, Schlegel.

SYN.—Coronella albocincta, Cântor, var.

Above, olive-brown, with black spots and numerous pale red transversal zig-zag bands, each with a submarginal black line. The first occupies the space between the eyes, continuing obliquely backward over the cheeks and lips ; the second, arrow-shaped, diverging over the neck ; labial shields yellow with brown margins. Beneath, strongly iridescent pale carmine ; every other scutum entirely or partially black near the lateral angles. Iris circular, golden, lower half dotted with black ; tongue black.

Scuta, 179 to 183 ; scutella, 36 to 65.

HAB.—*Pinang*.
Java, Tenasserim, (var.) Chirra-Punji, Assam, Darjeeling, Midnapore (Bengal).

A solitary individual observed on the summit of the Great Hill of Pinang defended itself vigorously. The dimensions were :—

Length of the head	. . . .	0 foot	1	inch.	
„ „ trunk	. . . .	1 „	$8\frac{2}{8}$	inches.	
„ „ tail	. . . . .	0 „	$3\frac{5}{8}$	„	

2 feet 1 inch.

Circumference of the neck $1\frac{4}{8}$, of the trunk 2, of the root of the tail $1\frac{1}{4}$ inches. It differs from the description of M. Schlegel in having twenty-one longitudinal series of scales instead of nineteen, and on the right side three preorbitals. Labials on each side $\frac{8}{10}$. The variety described as *Coronella albocincta* inhabits Assam, Chirra-Punji, Darjeeling, and Midnapore (Bengal). It differs from those of the southern localities in having the head not distinct from the trunk, and its shields are shorter. The eyes are smaller, and, owing to the much swollen cheeks, appear sunk, which, with the remarkably shelving profile, contribute to render the physiognomy singularly scowling. The largest specimen in the Museum of the Asiatic Society measures in length 2 feet $5\frac{3}{8}$ inches, of which the head $\frac{8}{8}$, the trunk 2 feet $1\frac{5}{8}$, and the tail 3 inches. In all, the livery is individually varying, but the arrow-shaped mark, double in some, appears to be constant. Labials on each side $\frac{7}{8}$.

Gen. LYCODON, *H. Boie.*

Head not very distinct, oblong, depressed ; supraorbital shield triangular, narrowed in front ; preorbital, one ; postorbitals, two; frenal, one ; eyes sunk, far removed from the muzzle ; pupil vertical ; trunk elongated, somewhat compressed, with smooth, rhomboidal, imbricate scales ; tail short, tapering ; anterior maxillary teeth longer than the rest.

LYCODON AULICUS, Linné.

SYN.—Coluber aulicus, Linné (not apud Daudin).
  Russell, * i. pl. 16, Gajoo Tutta.
  Coluber striatus, Shaw ?
  Coluber malignus, Daudin.
  Lycodon hebe, Boie apud Wagler, Schlegel (*excl. synon. Col. hebe, Daud.*)

Lighter or darker chestnut with numerous white transversal bands (in some spotted with black) on the sides, forming a forked network, composed of brown scales edged with white ; on each side of the hind-head a white triangular spot (confluent in some) with brown spots ; lips similarly coloured ; beneath, pearl-coloured; eyes black ; tongue whitish.

Scuta, 208 to 257 ; scutella, 57 to 91.

HAB.—*Pinang.*
  Bengal, Coromandel.

Var. A.

SYN.—Lycodon hebe, var. Schlegel.

---

* Russell, i. pl. 26, Karetta, upon which is founded *Coluber galathea,* Daudin, appears to represent the present species, or one of its varieties.

With a number of large, square, white spots, with black edges and central spots.

HAB.—*Pinang.*
　　Bengal.

Var. B.

SYN.—Russell, ii. pl. 37.
　　Lycodon capucinus, Boie.
　　Lycodon hebe, var. javan., Schlegel.
　　Lycodon atropurpureus, Cantor.

Chestnut or deep purple marbled with white veins, edged with black, with or without a white collar.

HAB.—*Pinang, Malayan Peninsula.*
　　Tenasserim Provinces, Java.

Var. C.

SYN.—Lycodon hebe, var. timorensis, Schlegel.

Chestnut, with a white collar and indistinct traces of white network.

HAB.—*Pinang, Malayan Peninsula.*
　　Pulo Samao, Timor.

Var. D.

SYN.—Russell, ii. pl. 39.
　　Lycodon subfuscus, Cantor.

Uniformly light brown above, the lips white edged with brown.

HAB.—*Malayan Peninsula.*
　　Bengal.

This species occurs in the Malayan countries, both in the hills and valleys, but it is apparently not so numerous as it is in Bengal. It is of fierce habits, and defends itself vigorously. In one examined the stomach contained a young *Euprepis rufescens*, Shaw.

The largest individual observed, var. B., was of the following dimensions :—

Length of the head	. . . .	o foot	o$\frac{6}{8}$	inch.	
„　　„　　trunk	. . . .	1　„	8$\frac{7}{8}$	inches.	
„　　„　　tail	. . . .	o　„	4$\frac{1}{8}$	„	

2 feet 1$\frac{6}{8}$ inch.

Circumference of the neck 1 inch, of the trunk 1$\frac{4}{8}$, of the root of the tail $\frac{7}{8}$ inch.

Ophites.—Wagler, differing from *Lycodon* in the absence of the preorbital shield; frenal elongated; eyes small; scales rhombic, with truncated points; some of the posterior dorsal scales keeled.

LYCODON PLATURINUS, Shaw.

SYN.—Seba, Thes. i. 83, 3.
Russell, ii. pl. 41.
Coluber platurinus, Shaw.
Coluber platyrhinus, Merrem.
Lycodon subcinctus, H. Boie.
Ophites, Wagler.
Lycodon subcinctus, apud Schlegel.

Shining blackish-brown with steel-blue reflections, and a varying number of broad, distant bands ; the lips, throat, and a collar all white, spotted with black ; beneath, pale blackish-brown, the anterior part of the abdomen, the sharp lateral angle, and the broad posterior margins of the scuta and scutella whitish ; eyes black ; tongue flesh-coloured.

Scuta, 221 ; scutella, 74.

HAB.—*Pinang.*
Java, Bengal.*

On both sides of each jaw the anterior four or five teeth increase in size, and are longer than the rest. The fifth upper maxillary tooth is removed from the preceding, which, in addition to the general shape of the head and the lax integuments, imparts to this serpent a striking resemblance to the venomous genus *Bungarus.* In fierceness it resembles the preceding species. The only individual observed was captured near the summit of the Great Hill of Pinang, where it had seized a large *Euprepis rufescens,* Shaw. It was of the following dimensions :—

Length of the head	. . . .	0 feet	1	inch.
„	„	trunk	. . . .	2	„	$8\frac{4}{5}$	inches.
„	„	tail .	. . . .	0	„	$7\frac{4}{8}$	„

$$3 \quad „ \quad 5 \quad „$$

Circumference of the neck $1\frac{5}{8}$, of the trunk $2\frac{4}{8}$ inches.

LYCODON EFFRÆNIS, N.S.

Shining bluish-black above, with a few minute white spots, not affecting the ground colour ; the throat, lips, and a band bordering the sides of the head from the muzzle to the hind head, buff-coloured, finely marbled with black ; beneath, strongly iridescent, pale bluish-black, the scuta with whitish edges ; the body encircled

* According to M. Schlegel, who observes that a specimen has been forwarded from Bengal by M. Duvaucel. No specimen exists in the Museum of the Asiatic Society, nor are the natives acquainted with the species.

by a number (eleven) of broad distant buff rings, above with indentated margins ; eyes black, pupil elliptical ; tongue whitish. Scuta, 228 ; scutella, 72.

HAB.—*Pinang.*

The head is elongated, ovate, depressed, broader than the neck, the muzzle rounded, slightly projecting ; the anterior frontals are orbicular pentagonal, much smaller than the frontals, which are bent over the sides, substituting the absent frenal, so as to meet the second upper labial ; the nasal is small, rectangular, obliquely wedged in between the rostral, the two pairs of frontals, and the anterior upper labial ; the nostril large, piercing the middle of the shield ; the vertical is elongated pentagonal, broader in front, so as to render the posterior part of the moderate supraorbitals broader than the anterior ; the occipitals are the largest, elongated, on each side surrounded by three scales, somewhat longer than the rest covering the temples, and behind by two small postoccipitals. The eyes are proportionally large and prominent, surrounded by one preorbital and two smaller postorbitals, the lower of which touches the narrow projecting fifth upper labial, which with the fourth borders the lower part of the orbit ; the jaws are covered by eight pairs of upper, nine of lower labials. The gape is moderate ; the particulars of the dentition noted in *L. platurinus* exist in the present species. The two anterior of the three pairs of small elongated mental shields are bordered by the six anterior pairs of labials ; behind by a number of small scales. The trunk is slender, decreasing towards both extremities, with seventeen longitudinal series of smooth, rhomboidal, slightly imbricate scales. The back is depressed, forming an angle with the compressed somewhat bulging sides. The latter are joined to the flat narrow abdomen under a right angle on the sides of the scuta, so that the vertical section of the body is quadrangular. A single individual found by Sir Wm. Norris on the Great Hill of Pinang was of the following dimensions :—

Length of the head .	. . . . . .	$0\frac{4}{x}$ inch.
„ „	trunk.	. . . . . .	$9\frac{8}{8}$ inches.
„ „	tail	. . . .	$2\frac{2}{8}$ „

$$\text{1 ft. } 0\frac{4}{8} \text{ inch.}$$

Circumference of the neck $\frac{4}{8}$, of the trunk $\frac{6}{8}$, of the root of the tail $\frac{2}{8}$ inch.

In fierceness the present species resembles its congeners, but, unlike them, it raises vertically the anterior part of the body, and bites after a few oscillating movements from side to side. *Lycodon platurinus* and *aulicus*, like many other harmless and some venomous serpents, the pupils of which are vertically closed by the light, prepare to attack horizontally coiled on the ground, with the head bent close to the body, and drawn as far backwards as possible, when, suddenly uncoiling the anterior part of the body, they dart obliquely upwards, but as they are blinded, not always in the direction apparently aimed at, and they frequently miss the aim.

Gen. COLUBER, *Linné.*

Abdomen with scuta ; scutella under the tail.

COLUBER FASCIOLOTUS, Shaw.

SYN.—Russell i. pl. xxi. Nooni Paragoodoo.
Coluber hebe, Daudin (syn. apud Boie, Wagler, Schlegel).

" Cineritious grey with an obscure cast of reddish-brown, particularly about the head and neck. The back variegated by black and white or black and yellowish, narrow bands ; and on the sides are two or three rows of short, separate oblique lines, formed by the yellow or white edges of the lateral scales ; but in general these bands are not visible on the tail. The scuta (192) and scutella (62) are of a dusky pearl colour." (Russell, i. p. 26.)

HAB.—*Malayan Peninsula.*
Coromandel Coast.

A young individual, killed in Province Wellesley, corresponds to the description of Russell, copied by Shaw and Daudin. It has two small postorbitals, one elongated preorbital, one minute irregularly hexagonal frenal, and on each side eight upper, nine lower labial shields. The trunk is covered by twenty-one longitudinal series of smooth imbricate scales, which are rhombic on the sides, rhomboidal above, all with rounded points. The teeth are of uniform size, and, as Russell correctly describes them, very small, reflex, sharp, numerous. The dentition, therefore, sufficiently indicates that the species cannot be placed in the gen. *Lycodon*, to which it has been referred by MM. H. Boie, Wagler, and Schlegel. The young one is of the following dimensions :—

Length of the head .	. . . . . .	$0\frac{4}{8}$ inch.
„	„	trunk	$8\frac{1}{8}$ inches.
„	„	tail . , ...	$2\frac{1}{8}$ „
			$10\frac{6}{8}$ „

Greatest circumference of the trunk, $\frac{5}{8}$ inch.
Scuta, 281 ; scutella, 73.

COLUBER RADIATUS, Schlegel.

SYN.—Russell, ii. pl. xlii.
Coluber quadrifasciatus, Cantor (var.).

Head and back light yellowish-bay, paler on the sides ; the hind head with a transversal black line, branching off along the exterior margins of the occipitals ; a black oblique streak behind the eyes, and another beneath them dividing both jaws. On each side of the back a broad longitudinal black band, relieved at intervals by a short network, produced by three or four scales of each series being edged with pale brown, and the skin between them white. The bands, in some commencing at a distance from the head, are continued or interrupted, terminating on the posterior part of the back. Below them is on each side a parallel black line ; lips, throat, and lower surface yellow ; iris bright gamboge, with a concentric black ring ; tongue bluish-black.

Young.—Above, of clearer colours ; beneath, pearl-coloured. Scuta, 222 to 248 ; scutella, 82 to 94.

HAB.—*Pinang, Singapore, Malayan Peninsula.* Java, Sumatra, Cochin China, Tenasserim, Assam.

This species is numerous in marshes and paddy-fields, and often becomes a tenant of outhouses, where during the day it remains concealed, till nightfall favours its pursuit after rats. It is, however, equally diurnal, preying upon smaller birds, lizards, and frogs. Assam produces a local variety distinguished by eighteen instead of seventeen longitudinal series of scales, of which the three upper ones are all lineated, whereas normally such is the case on those of the posterior part of the body. It makes a vigorous defence, and in darting at an enemy is capable of raising nearly the anterior two-thirds of the body from the ground. In a female were found twenty-three whitish, soft, cylindrical eggs, of which the largest measured $1\frac{1}{8}$ inch in length. The largest individual observed was of the following dimensions :—

Length of the head	. . . .	0 feet	$1\frac{4}{8}$ inch.
„ „ trunk	. . . .	4 „	$3\frac{4}{8}$ inches.
„ „ tail	. . . . .	0 „	$10\frac{4}{8}$ „
		5 „	$3\frac{4}{8}$ „

Greatest circumference, $3\frac{6}{8}$ inches.

Habits and general appearance link the present species to *Col. dhumnades,* Cantor,* and *Col. mucosus,* Linné (*Col. Blumenbachii,* Merrem), but the latter, as well as its variety with uniformly smooth scales (*Col. dhumna,* Cantor : Spicil.), utter when irritated a peculiar *diminuendo* sound, not unlike that produced by a gently struck tuning-fork.

---

* *Chusan.*—It is covered by fourteen to sixteen long it. series of rhomboidal scales, of which those of the two uppermost series commence at a short distance from the head, exhibiting the central raised line.

COLUBER KORROS, Reinwardt.

SYN.—Coluber karros, Reinwardt apud Wagler, Schlegel.

Brownish-green above, the scales of the posterior part of the trunk and of the tail with black points and edges, producing a regular network ; beneath, yellowish-white or pearl-coloured ; the lateral part of the scuta light bluish-grey ; iris bright yellow with a bluish-grey or blackish concentric ring; tongue black.

Young.—Above, with some indistinct transversal bands, produced by two lateral white spots on some of the scales ; the posterior part of the trunk with dark longitudinal lines.

Scuta, 162 to 190; scutella, 79 to 136.

HAB.—*Pinang, Singapore, Malayan Peninsula.*
Java, Sumatra, Arracan, Tenasserim.

It is numerous in the Malayan valleys. The largest individual measured—

Length of the head	.	.	.	.	o feet	$1\frac{2}{8}$ inch.
„	„	trunk	.	. . .	2 „	$6\frac{2}{8}$ inches.
„	„	tail	.	. . .	1 foot	$4\frac{2}{8}$ „

3 feet $11\frac{6}{8}$ „

Greatest circumference of the trunk, 3 inches.

Its habits are similar to those of the last-mentioned species, from which it is easily distinguished by its fifteen longitudinal series of smooth rhomboidal scales with rounded points.

COLUBER HEXAHONOTUS, N.S.

Head and back dark brown, changing to pale brownish-buff on the sides ; trunk with numerous close transversal black bands, each with a few white spots on the lower parts, becoming indistinct towards the posterior extremity of the trunk, from whence the colour is uniformly dark brown ; labial shields yellow, edged with black ; beneath, yellowish-white, scutella edged with brown. Iris gamboge, with a black concentric ring; pupil round ; tongue black ; central series of dorsal scales hexagonal.

Scuta, 191 ; scutella, 148.

HAB.—*Pinang.*

The head is distinct, elongated, with the muzzle broad, truncated, covered above with the normal number of shields, in form resembling those of *Col. korros.* The eyes are large, prominent, with two preorbitals, of which the superior is the larger, the inferior is wedged in between the third, fourth, and fifth upper labials. In addition to two postorbitals there is an elongated crescent-shaped infraorbital resting on the sixth and seventh upper labials. The latter are eight on each side, of which the fifth, broad hexagonal, borders the orbit ; the following are elongated, gradually increasing in size. The lower labials, nine on each side, lie on the chin in contact with two pairs of elongated shields. The nostrils are rather large, orbicular, opening near the margin of the anterior frontals. The frenal is small, obliquely situated between the surrounding shields. The temples are covered by two pairs of elongated shields. The gape is wide, the teeth minute, of equal length. The trunk is slender, much compressed, with seventeen longitudinal series of smooth, rhombic, subimbricate scales, of which the central series is hexagonal. The abdomen narrow, arched. The tail is very slender, elongated, tapering to a sharp point.

A solitary individual, discovered by Sir William Norris on the Great Hill of Pinang, was of the following dimensions :—

Length of the head	. . . . . .	$0\frac{5}{8}$	inch.
„ „	trunk	10	inches.
„ „	tail	$4\frac{5}{8}$	„
		1 ft. $3\frac{2}{8}$	„

Circumference of the neck $\frac{5}{8}$, of the trunk 1, of the root of the tail $\frac{3}{8}$ inch. In fierceness it resembles the preceding species.

ARBOREAL.

Gen. DIPSAS, *Laurenti.*

Head large, broad, depressed, cordate, covered with shields; neck narrow ; trunk much narrower than the head, compressed, very long, beneath covered with scuta; tail cylindrical, imbricate.

DIPSAS DENDROPHILA, Reinwardt.

SYN.—Scheuchzer, 662, fig. 11 (Col. variabilis apud Merrem).
Dipsas dendrophila apud Wagler.
Dipsas dendrophila, Wagler apud Horsfield: "Life of Raffles."
Dipsas dendrophila, apud Schlegel.

Head, back, and sides intense black with steel-blue, lilac, and green reflections ; beneath, pale black, iridescent ; body and tail with numerous bright yellow transversal bands, widened below, sometimes joined on the back or abdomen, occasionally reduced to irregular spots ; throat and lips bright yellow, labials with black edges. Pupil elliptical, vertical ; iris and tongue black.

Scuta, 218 to 225; scutella, 100 to 112.

HAB.—*Pinang, Singapore, Malayan Peninsula.*
Java, Celebes.

It inhabits the Malayan hills and valleys, but apparently in no great numbers. The largest individual measured :—

Length of the head . . . . 0 feet 1$\frac{4}{8}$ inch.
„ „ trunk . . . . 3 „ 3$\frac{7}{8}$ inches.
„ „ tail . . . . . 1 foot 0 „
_____
4 feet 5$\frac{3}{8}$ „
Greatest circumference of the trunk, 4 inches.

DIPSAS MULTIMACULATA, Schlegel.

SYN.—Scheuchzer, 657, fig. 2.
Russell, ii. pl. xxiii.
Dipsas multimaculata, Schlegel.

Ground colour : above, light greenish-grey, minutely spotted and marbled with brown ; on the head an angular backwards diverging black mark with whitish edges ; a black oblique line from behind the eyes to the hind head, where it joins a lozenge-shaped black spot with whitish edges ; along the back and tail a series of large, irregularly oval, black spots with whitish edges, arranged in close quincunx series ; the sides with numerous, similarly coloured, oblique or arched, often interrupted bands ; labials greenish-white, black-edged ; beneath, greenish-white, tinged with rose-colour, minutely spotted with brown, and with a double or treble lateral series of irregular black spots. Iris pale greenish-golden, minutely dotted with black ; pupil elliptical, vertical ; tongue whitish.
Scuta, 202 to 235; scutella, 80 to 106.

HAB.—*Pinang, Malayan Peninsula.*
Celebes, Java, Tenasserim, Bengal.

On the hills of Pinang this species appears to be more numerous than the former. The largest individual measured—

Length of the head . . . . 0 foot 0$\frac{5}{8}$ inch.
„ „ trunk . . . . 1 „ 10$\frac{4}{8}$ inches.
„ „ tail . . . . 0 „ 5$\frac{6}{8}$ „
_____
2 feet 4$\frac{7}{8}$ „
Greatest circumference, 1$\frac{2}{8}$ inch.

The central hexagonal scales are elongated, narrow on the anterior part of the trunk, which is covered by nineteen longitudinal series of smooth, lanceolate, imbricate scales ; from thence commence seventeen series of broader scales.

DIPSAS CYNODON, Cuvier.

SYN.—Dipsas cynodon, apud Boie, Guérin, Schlegel.

Young.—Ground colour yellowish-brown, head with a dark black-edged arrow-shaped mark, and a black oblique streak from the eye to the nape of the neck; labials pearl-coloured, edged with black ; back with numerous black transversal marks, shaped like two letters Y placed horizontally towards each other or in quincunx, becoming indistinct towards the tail. Beneath, pearl-coloured with a black spot near the lateral part of the scuta ; scutella edged and minutely dotted with brown.
Scuta, 225 ; scutella, 92.

Adult.—Head and back uniformly greyish-brown, tinged with lilac, with a number of distant large, transversal, purple bands (the scales edged with black), lozenge-shaped, with triangular lateral appendages, becoming indistinct towards the tail, which is alternately brownish-buff and purple, with black-edged scales. Beneath, pale yellow, scutella minutely dotted and edged with brown. Iris pale golden, minutely dotted with purple ; pupil elliptical, vertical ; tongue whitish.
Scuta, 275 ; scutella, 158.

HAB.—*Pinang, Malayan Peninsula.*
Java, Tenasserim.

A young one was captured on the Great Hill of Pinang by W. T. Lewis, Esq. An adult killed in Province Wellesley was of the following dimensions :—

Length of the head	. . .	o feet	$1\frac{4}{9}$ inch.
„ „ trunk	. . .	4 „	$0\frac{3}{8}$ „
„ „ tail	. . . .	1 foot	4 inches.

$$5 \text{ feet } 5\frac{7}{8} \text{ „}$$

Circumference of the neck $1\frac{8}{8}$, of the trunk $2\frac{4}{4}$ inches.

The young had twenty-one, the adult twenty-three longitudinal series of smooth, lanceolate, imbricate scales. The long maxillary and palatal teeth are disproportionally less developed in the young than in the adult

DIPSAS BOA, H. Boie.

SYN.—Amblycephalus boa, H. Boie : Isis.
Dipsas boa, apud Schlegel.

Ground colour : above, rose-coloured washed with brown, varying in intensity and shade from light bay to umber, prevailing so
as to make the ground colour appear as minute spots, and with
numerous irregular black spots, confluent on the head ; cheeks
and lips carnation, with a vertical black streak from the middle of
the orbit. Beneath, carnation, dotted with umber, sometimes
assuming the shape of large irregular spots. Iris, silvery rose-
coloured, lower half dotted with black ; pupil elliptical, vertically
contracted by the light ; tongue whitish.

Scuta abdominalia, 164 ; scuta subcaudalia, 112 ; or 170 +
109.

HAB.—*Pinang.*
Java.

The head is depressed, elongated, conical, with the muzzle
truncated ; the rostral shield is very large, vertically placed ; the
cheeks compressed, but the lips very tumid below the eyes. Of
the nine crown shields the occipitals are distinguished by their
reduced size and frequent subdivision in two linear interoccipitals,
bordered by two large polygonal postoccipitals, enclosing a
smaller third, linear. Behind the latter appears on each side a
small hard tubercle, covered like the rest of the hind-head with
minute polygonal scales. Each temple is protected by five to six
large shields, and as many smaller resting upon the labials. The
nasal is large, pyramidal, with the rounded nostril in the centre,
and the apex wedged in between the three frenals, placed obliquely
or vertically one above the other. The eye is large, prominent,
encircled by a supraorbital and seven smaller shields, so that none
of the upper labials reach the orbit. The lips are arched, and
outwardly appear to reach to the hind-head ; but the commissure,
or the angle of the mouth, is situated immediately below the eye,
which greatly reduces the opening of the mouth. Of the nine
pairs of upper labials, the anterior six are narrow, but very deep
and bulging ; the posterior three are broader, elongated ; the inferior labials, eleven pairs, are, as well as the rostral, greatly reduced
by the three pairs of very large mentals. The front view of the
head grotesquely resembles that of a mastiff. All the teeth are
strong, but the front tooth on each side of the lower jaw is longer
than the rest ; the palatal rows are very close together and converging. The trunk is much compressed, covered by thirteen
longitudinal series of scales, of which the dorsal row is composed
of very large hexagonal ones, each with a strong keel ; the rest
are smooth, rhombic, imbricate. The abdomen is very narrow,
and the sides of the scuta are bent upwards. The tail is elongated,
slender, tapering, and much less compressed than the trunk. Of
two individuals from the hills of Pinang, the larger, a male, was of
the following dimensions :—

Length of the head . . . . o foot 1 inch.

„ „ trunk . . . . 1 „ 11 inches.

„ „ tail . . . . . o „ 11$\frac{1}{8}$ „

2 feet 11$\frac{1}{8}$ „

Circumference of the neck 1 inch, of the trunk 1$\frac{5}{8}$, of the root of the tail $\frac{7}{8}$ inch. In a female were observed four cylindrical whitish eggs, each $\frac{6}{8}$ inch in length. The stomach contained a few remains of insects.

This species is closely allied to *Dipsas carinata*, Schlegel (*Amblycephalus*, Kuhl; *Pareas*, Wagler), in which also the dorsal series of scales are keeled. M. Schlegel's short description and figure appear to have been taken from an immature specimen.

The preceding four species are very fierce ; their mode of attack is that of *Lycodon aulicus.* Kuhl has observed vibrating movements in the tail of *Dipsas multimaculata*, which, however, are also exhibited by *Dipsas trigonata*, Schneider (*Col. catenularies*, Daudin), *D. cynodon*, Cuvier ; and among the venomous serpents by *Vipera Russelli*, Shaw, and several Asiatic species of *Trigonocephalus*, when they are irritated and preparing to bite.

Gen. HERPETODRYAS, *H. Boie.*

Head trigonal, very long, depressed, smooth, rather sharp ; trunk and tail very elongated ; scales, particularly those of the tail, large ; those of the back partially carinate ; in other respects resembling *Coluber.*

HERPETODRYAS OXYCEPHALUS, Reinwardt.

SYN.—Coluber oxycephalus, Reinwardt.

Gonyosoma viride, Wagler.

Herpetodryas oxycephalus, apud Schlegel.

Head, above, shining dark green with a blackish straight line from the nostrils to the angle of the mouth ; lips and throat pale yellowish-green ; trunk sea-green, changing to light yellowish-green on the lower part of the sides—all the scales with black edges ; the anterior half of the tail, separated from the trunk by a transversal orange band, ochre, gradually changing to greyish-brown on the posterior half, all the scales edged with black. Abdominal scuta light yellowish-green with pale yellow edges ; subcaudal scutella grey with black margins. Eyes moderate, little prominent ; iris pale sea-green with a narrow pale yellow inner ring and a transversal black band ; pupil circular, black. Tongue ultramarine, divided in the middle by a black longitudinal line. The exposed part of the larnyx black.

Scuta, 268; scutella, 149.

Hab.—*Pinang.*
Java, Celebes.

The shields of the head are elongated, most so the linear frenal. The teeth are numerous; in each row the anterior six or eight are longer than the rest, which gradually decrease. The scales of the trunk, in twenty-five longitudinal series, are rhombic with rounded points, imbricate, and all smooth except those covering the spinous processes, which are faintly lineated.

Of two individuals from the hills of Pinang, the larger, taken by Sir William Norris, was of the following dimensions :—

Length of the head.	. . .	o foot $1\frac{4}{8}$ inch.
„ „ trunk	. . .	3 feet 4 inches.
„ „ tail	. . . .	1 foot 1 inch.

4 feet $6\frac{4}{8}$ inches.

Circumference of the neck 2, of the trunk 3, of the root of the tail $1\frac{4}{8}$ inch. The ferocious habits of this serpent have been accurately described by M. Reinwardt. It has in a remarkable degree the power of laterally compressing the neck and the anterior part of the body, when the greyish-blue skin becomes visible between the separated scales. In such state of excitement it raises nearly the anterior third vertically from the ground, continues fixed during several seconds with vibrating tongue, and bites. It then throws itself down, to rise to a renewed attack. A similar mode of attack characterizes the following species—viz. *Dryinus*, *nasutus*, Lacépède (Russell i. pl. xii. and xvi.) ; *D. prasinus*, Reinwardt (*Dryiophis prasina*, apud Schlegel) ; *Deptophis pictus*, Gmelin ; and *Leptophis caudalineatus*.

Gen. DRYINUS,* *Merrem*, 1820.

Upper jaw much longer than the lower ; muzzle attenuated, more or less acute at the apex, which in some species is mucronate and moveable.

DRYINUS PRASINUS, Rienwardt.

Syn.—Seba, ii. tab. liii. fig 4.
Coluber nasutus,† Shaw apud Russell, ii. pl. xxiv.
Dryinus nasutus, Bell (not Merrem, 1820).

---

* In H. Boie's genera, published in "Isis," 1827, *Dryiophis* (Dahlman), is substituted for this genus. Wagler in 1830 separated some species under the denomination of *Tragops*, and M. Schlegel in his "Essay" has exclusively retained *Dryiophis*, although Prof. Thos. Bell already in 1825 had published his article on *Leptophina* (comprising *Dryinus*, Merrem, and *Leptophis*, Bell).

† The specific name was previously applied by Lacépède in 1790 to the other Asiatic species.

Dryiophis prasinus, Reinwardt.
Tragops, Wagler.
Dryinus nasutus, Bell apud Horsfield: "Life of Raffles."
Passerita, Gray.
Dryiphis prasina, apud Schlegel.
"Ular daun" of the Malays.

Leek-green above, with some irregular white and black oblique lines, paler on the cheeks and upper lips; tail cinnamon; under lips and throat white, scuta and scutella light green or mother-of-pearl, on each side with a white or pale yellow longitudinal line, below which in some a second green line. Pupil black, elongated, pyriform, with the apex turned forwards, horizontally contracted by the light. Iris pale burnished golden, bright on the pupillary margin, the upper half of which forms a little behind its middle a small pointed lobe. Tongue bluish-white.
Scuta, 186 to 228; scutella, 140 to 203.

HAB.—*Malayan Peninsula and Islands.*
  Celebes, Java, Cochin-China, Siam, Burmah, Tenasserim, Arracan, Bengal, Assam.

Var. A.

SYN.—Dryiophis xanthozonius, Kuhl?

Head less elongated and the rostral shield unusually small; upper lips in some white; besides the yellow and green lateral line a central green; scuta and scutella in some with brown edges.
HAB.—*Same localities.*

Var. B.

Head above, light brownish-grey, tinged with sky-blue and rose-colour cheeks and lips pale rose; trunk light brownish ash, changing to pale rust colour on the tail; whitish-grey on the sides; beneath, buff, with a white longitudinal line on each side. Iris burnished silver, tongue white.

HAB.—*Pinang Hills.*

Var. C.

Upper parts saffron yellow, paler on the sides; beneath, sulphur-coloured, with a lateral white line. Pupil deep burnished golden; tongue white.

HAB.—*Pinang Hills.*

This species is exceedingly numerous in the Malayan forests, both in the hills and valleys, preying upon small birds, arboreal lizards, frogs, and in early age upon insects. It may readily be distinguished from *Dryinus nasutus*, Lacép. (Merrem, not Bell; Russell, i. pl. xii. xiii.), by two, sometimes three frenals on each side. The trunk is covered by fifteen longitudinal series of smooth rhomboidal scales with rounded points, imbricate so as to appear linear; those of the tale are all broad rhombic. The anterior upper maxillary teeth gradually increase towards the sixth, which is the longest, and enclosed in a pointed fold of gingiva. The following teeth, commencing at a short interval, are short, but the last is very long, with a furrow on the convex edge. The inferior maxillary teeth also increase in length towards the sixth, the longest, and are protected by a broad triangular scabbard, containing several additional loose teeth; the rest are uniformly small, commencing at a short interval from the sixth. The palatal are uniformly very short. The largest individual of a great number measured—

Length of the head	. . . .	o feet 2	inches.
„ „	trunk	. . . .	4 „ $3\frac{5}{8}$	„
„ „	tail .	. . . .	2 „ $6\frac{4}{8}$	„

$$7 \text{ „ } 0\frac{1}{8} \text{ inch.}$$

Circumference of the neck $1\frac{1}{8}$, of the trunk $2\frac{2}{8}$, of the root of the tail 1 inch.

The varieties, of which B and C were from the hills of Pinang, are not numerous, and of a comparatively small size. The very young ones are as gentle as those of a more advanced age are ferocious. Their power of expanding the anterior part of the body and their mode of attack have been noted under *Herpetodryas oxycephalus*.

Gen. LEPTOPHIS, *Bell*, 1825.

Rostrum obtuse, and the upper jaw projects but very slightly beyond the lower.

LEPTOPHIS PICTUS, Gmelin.

SYN.—Coluber pictus, Gmelin.
Coluber decorus, Shaw.
Russell, ii. pl. xxvi., Cumberi muken.
Bungarus filum, Oppel.
Dipsas Schokari, Kuhl (not Forskal).
Dendrophis chairecacos, H. Boie.
Dendrophis, Wagler.
Dendrophis picta, Schlegel.

Head and body above, bronze with strong golden reflections; skin between the scales of the anterior part of the body alternately ultramarine and black. Lips, throat, the two lowest lateral rows of scales, and the abdominal surface silvery mother-of-pearl. From the muzzle to the root of the tail a black line, bordering above the silvery sides, which below are circumscribed by a second black line, commencing a little behind the head. Iris bright golden with a transversal black line; pupil black, circular; tongue scarlet. Scuta, 167 to 187; scutella, 109 to 149.

HAB.—*Malayan Peninsula and Islands.*
> Manilla, New Ireland, Waigiou, Amboina, New Guinea, Pulo Samao, Java, Sumatra, Cochin-China, Tennasserim, Burmah, Bengal, Assam, Coromandel.

Var. A.*

SYN.—Coluber filiformis, Linné, young.
Fil, Double Raie, Lacépède, young.
Russell, ii. pl. xxv., Mancas, Rooka, Maniar.
Coluber bilineatus, Shaw.
Leptophis mancas, Bell.
Dendrophis maniar, Boie.
Ahœtula Bellii, Gray: " Ill. Ind. Zool."
Chrysopelea Boii, Smith.
Dendrophis picta, var. Schlegel.
Dendrophis Boii, apud Cantor.

Above, dull brownish-black, with a light brown dorsal line; the two lowest series of scales pale greenish-white, forming a lateral band, bordered above by a black line, commencing from the muzzle, more or less distinct, in some irregularly broken up on the anterior part of the body. A second faint black line below. Iris golden, in some dotted with black; tongue black.

HAB.—*Malayan Peninsula.*
> Bengal, Assam, Ceylon.

The species occurs numerously in the Malayan hills and valleys, but the contrary appears to be the case with the plain variety, which in Bengal is equally common. The following must be added to the description of M. Schlegel:—The frenal shield is small, rectangular; superior labials nine, inferior ten or eleven: one preorbital, two, in some three small postorbitals. The trunk is covered by fifteen longitudinal series of smooth imbricate scales; the central dorsal series is wedge-shaped, in some almost hexagonal; the next six are linear; but the lowest, as well as all the scales of the tail, are broad rhombic with rounded points. In a female were found seven coriaceous, whitish eggs of an elon-

---

* The variety, *Col. polychrous*, Reinwardt, appears to inhabit neither the Malayan Peninsula nor Bengal.

gated cylindrical shape, each $1\frac{3}{8}$ inch in length. In habits and mode of attack this species resembles *Dryinus prasinus*, but it is not exclusively arboreal. Probably no instance affords a more striking difference in colours between species and variety than the present: the former with dazzling brilliant livery, the latter in its plain dull colours. Both attain to similar size: the largest male examined was of the following dimensions :—

Length of the head	. . . . .	0 feet	$1\frac{1}{8}$ inch.
„ „ trunk	. . . . .	2 „	6 inches.
„ „ tail	. . . . .	1 foot	1 inch.

3 feet $8\frac{1}{8}$ inches.

Circumference of the neck $1\frac{3}{8}$, of the trunk 2, of the root of the tail 1 inch. This serpent appears to possess uncommonly acute hearing, and turns its head in the direction of the sound.

LEPTOPHIS CAUDALINEATUS, N.S.

SYN.—Ahætula caudolineata, Gray: "Illust. Ind. Zool."
Dendrophis ornata, var. Schlegel.

Head, trunk, and tail, above, light brownish-bronze, the scales with black edges; on the posterior half of the trunk four parallel black lines, terminating at the root of the tail, from whence commences a single central black line; sides metallic mother-of-pearl, from a short distance behind the head bordered by two parallel black lines, of which the lower, the broader, covers the lower half of the last series of scales and the lateral part of the scuta; both the lines continue to the apex of the tail. Lips, throat and abdominal surface pale metallic citrine; the tail beneath with a black central line. Iris golden, dotted with brown; pupil round; tongue bluish-white, the forked part black.

Young.—Upper parts of the body Indian red, with metallic reflections.

Scuta, 183 to 188; scutella, 105 to 110.

HAB.—*Pinang, Singapore.*

The head large, less depressed than in the preceding species, the muzzle broad, blunt; cheeks tumid: all the shields of the crown are short and broad, except the vertical, which is laterally arched, and very narrow behind. There is a single elongated postoccipital, and the rest of the hind head is covered with broad hexagonal shields. Each temple is covered by two pairs of large shields, in front of which a pair of very minute ones, bordering upon the equally small postorbitals. The eye is large, prominent; the preorbital and the linear frenal proportionally small; the nostrils large, opening in the middle of the nasal; the rostral broad, slightly arched beneath. The labials, nine on each side of both jaws, resemble those of the preceding species. The mouth is large; the maxillary teeth strong, distant. In the lower jaw the anterior ones gradually increase in length till the fourth, which appears like a canine; the rest, as well as the palatal teeth, are all smaller, of uniform length. The chin is covered by the second pair of labials and two pairs of mentals, of which the posterior pair is elongated. The trunk is strong, less compressed than in the preceding species, with thirteen series of smooth imbricate scales, of which the two lowest series are large rhombic with rounded points, the next four elongated rhomboidal (linear), and the odd central dorsal rhomboidal, not larger than the rest. The tail is covered with broad hexagonal, not imbricate, scales. The abdomen is narrow, flattened; the centre part of the scuta with strongly arched margins; the sides turned upwards and forming a continued sharp lateral ridge. The tail is slender, tapering; its vertical section nearly square.

Of this species but two individuals were observed: a young one at Singapore, an adult on the Great Hill of Pinang. The latter measured—

Length of the head	. . . .	o feet $1\frac{2}{8}$ inch.		
„ „	trunk	. . .	3 „	$5\frac{6}{8}$ inches.
„ „	tail	. . . .	1 foot 2	„

4 feet 9 „

Circumference of the neck 2, of the trunk $3\frac{6}{8}$, of the root of the tail $1\frac{1}{8}$ inch.

In its mixed arboreal and terrestrial habits and in fierceness it resembles *L. pictus;* but its power of compressing and expanding the fore-part of the body is somewhat limited.

This species appears somewhat to approach to *Leptophis formosus* (*Dendrophis formosa,* Schlegel), but besides other distinguishing characters, it differs from that and all other Asiatic species in having but thirteen series of scales. The indifferent figure of *Ahætula caudolineata* in "Illustrations of Indian Zoology," which appears to be all which has been published concerning this species, has led M. Schlegel to suppose it was intended to represent a variety of *Leptophis pictus,* although the black outline of the head is correct.

LEPTOPHIS ORNATUS, Shaw.

SYN.—Scheuchzer, t. 606.
Seba, i. t. xciv., fig. 7; h. t. vii., fig. 1; t. lxi., fig. 2.
Russell, ii. pl. 2, Kalla Jin.
Coluber ornatus, Shaw.
Coluber ibiboboca, Daudin.

Coluber ornatus, Merrem apud Horsfield: "Life of Raffles."
Chrysopelea paradisi, H. Boie.
Dendrophis ornata, Schlegel.

HAB.—Bengal, Ceylon.

Var.

SYN.—Ular Chindi, Raffles.
Dendrophis chrysochloros, Reinwardt (young).

Head above, intense velvety black, with three or four distant transversal bands, and numerous irregular spots of gamboge or sulphur colour; all the scales with an oval gamboge spot; from the hind head to the point of the tail a number of large rounded vermilion spots; lips, throat, and abdominal surface greenish-gamboge, scuta and scutella with black margins. Iris and tongue black.

Scuta, 198 to 236; scutella, 113 to 147.

Young.—Head, trunk, and tail above, greenish-olive, with a series of transversal black bands, in pairs; the intervals between the bands vermilion; the sides with numerous distant, irregular, small black spots; lateral part of the scuta and scutella white, the ridge and the anterior margin black; the centre part pale greenish-yellow; scutella partially edged with black, and with a central light blue line. Tongue vermilion, the forked part black.

HAB.—*Pinang, Malayan Peninsula.*
Java, Sumatra, Tenasserim, Arracan.

The variety in which the black colour prevails appears to be confined to the more southern countries, while that with yellow ground colour preponderating—the one described and figured by Russell—occurs in Bengal. The latter has the tongue alternately vermilion and black. Individuals without the frenal shield are not uncommon, and such was the one described by H. Boie as a distinct species (*Chrysopelea paradisi*). It inhabits the Malayan hills and valleys, but is there apparently less numerous than in Bengal. The largest male observed was of the following dimensions:—

Length of the head	0 feet	$1\frac{1}{8}$	inch.
" " trunk	2 "	$7\frac{6}{8}$	inches.
" " tail	0 "	$11\frac{4}{8}$	"
	3 "	$8\frac{3}{8}$	"

Circumference of the neck $1\frac{1}{8}$, of the trunk $1\frac{7}{8}$, of the root of the tail $\frac{7}{8}$ inch.

The trunk is covered by seventeen longitudinal series of

smooth, imbricate, rhomboidal scales with rounded points. It is but seldom seen in trees; it is more frequently found on the ground in the grass, watching for its prey—lizards (*Geckonidæ**) and frogs. The female has six to eight white elongated cylindrical eggs, about 1⅝ inch in length. It differs from the other species in its being deprived of the power of compressing and expanding the anterior part of the body, and in its gentleness. The young ones never attempt to bite, the adult but seldom, and without raising vertically the anterior part of the body. In the latter the four anterior teeth of the lower jaw are a little longer than the rest, which are uniformly small.

AQUATIC.

Gen. TROPIDONOTUS, *Kuhl.*

Head oblong ovate, rather indistinct, depressed; nostrils between the sutures of two shields; eyes moderate, with circular pupil, scales of the back lanceolate ovate, keeled, imbricate; trunk elongated, cylindrical; tail moderately long, tapering.

TROPIDONOTUS UMBRATUS, Daudin, var.

SYN.—Tropidonotus trianguligerus, Schlegel.

Above, shining brownish, or yellowish-green olive; lips gamboge, with a black oblique line between the sixth and seventh labials, a second from the orbit to the angle of the mouth, a third from the under lip to the upper part of the neck; trunk and tail with numerous black spots, in some very minute, irregular—in others larger, approaching to quincunx order; the sides with numbers of large square or triangular scarlet spots, separated from each other by broader or narrower black vertical bands. Scuta and scutella gamboge, with black margins, the latter with a black central line. Iris black, with a narrow golden circle; tongue black.

Scuta, 121 to 130; scutella, 76 to 84.

HAB.—*Malayan Peninsula and Islands.*
Java, Bengal.

The vertical and supraorbital shields are of an elongated narrow form; the anterior frontals triangular, longer than broad; the nostrils small, placed high on the sides; the frenal is elongated pentagonal, with the largest margin touching the preorbital. Of the three postorbitals the lowest is the longest, wedged in between the fifth, sixth, and seventh upper labials, of

---

* Vide *Ptychozoon homalocephalum*, supra.

which the fifth is the only one which reaches the orbit; the eye is moderate, prominent; the upper labials are nine, the lower eleven on each side. The mouth is very large, the teeth small, crowded, except the two last of the upper jaw, which are longer than the rest. The trunk is slightly compressed, covered by nineteen longitudinal series of scales, of which the two lowest are broad rhombic, the rest elongated rhomboidal with rounded points; those of the back lineated. The abdomen is broad, arched. This variety differs in nothing but colours from *Tropidonotus umbratus,* * Daudin, and, to judge by the description of M. Schlegel, it appears to be identical with *T. trianguligerus.* In the Malayan valleys the variety is very numerous; in Bengal it is less so, but there the species abounds in and near fresh water, where it preys upon fishes and frogs. The variety attains to a size similar to that of the species, both of which are equally fierce. The largest individual was of the following dimensions :—

Length of the head . . . . o foot $1\frac{2}{8}$ inch.
,, ,, trunk . . . . 1 ,, $9\frac{5}{8}$ inches.
,, ,, tail . . . . . o ,, $9\frac{3}{8}$,,

2 feet $8\frac{2}{8}$

Circumference of the neck 2, of the trunk $2\frac{5}{8}$, of the root of the tail $1\frac{5}{8}$ inch.

TROPIDONOTUS STOLATUS, Linné.

SYN.—Seba, ii. tab. ix. fig. 1, 2.
Coluber stolatus, Linné.
Le Chayque, Daubenton, Lacépède.
Russell, i. pl. x. xi. xix.
La vipère chaque, Latreille.
Coluber stolatus, Lin. apud Shaw, Daudin.
Coluber tæniolatus, Daudin.
Natrix stolatus, Merrem.
Tropidonotus stolatus, Gray, Schlegel.

Head shining brownish-olive, with several black spots in the sutures of the shields; lips gamboge, with several black oblique streaks; head and trunk brownish-olive, with numerous distant black transversal bands, becoming indistinct towards the tail, and intersected by two parallel bands of a pale ochre or buff, the scales of which on the anterior part of the body edged with black. Beneath, gamboge or mother-of-pearl; in some the scuta with a

---

* SYN.—Russell, ii. pl. iii., *Dooblee*, young ; pl. v., *Dora*, adult; *Col. umbratus*, Daudin ; *Col. dora*, Daud. ; *Col. brunneus*, Hermann ; *Col. autratus*, Herrm. ; *Col. lugubris*, Merrem ; *Tropidonotus umbratus*, Schlegel ; *Tropidonotus dora*, apud Cantor.

small lateral black spot, or edged with black. Iris black, with a narrow golden ring; tongue black.

Scuta, 143 to 156; scutella, 69 to 79.

HAB.—*Pinang, Malayan Peninsula.*

Philippines, Tenasserim, Bengal, Assam, Nipal, Coromandel, Ceylon, Bombay.

This species, so exceedingly numerous in Bengal, is but rarely seen in the Malayan valleys. It is of very gentle habits, and feeds upon young frogs and toads. The largest male observed was of the following dimensions :—

Length of the head	. . . .	0 foot	$0\frac{7}{8}$	inch.
,, ,, trunk	. . . .	1 ,,	$4\frac{2}{5}$	inches.
,, ,, tail	. . . . .	0 ,,	$5\frac{1}{8}$	,,
		1 ,,	$10\frac{2}{3}$	,,

Circumference of the neck $\frac{7}{8}$, of the trunk $1\frac{3}{8}$, of the root of the tail $\frac{6}{8}$ inch.

The female has six small cylindrical white eggs, each about half an inch in length.

TROPIDONOTUS SCHISTOSUS, Daudin.

SYN.—Russell, ii. pl. iv., Chittee.
Coluber schistosus, Daudin.
Tropidonotus schistosus, Schlegel.
Tropidonotus moestus, Cantor.

Above, blackish-olive, some with an indistinct blackish line from behind the eye along the side; the lips, the two lowest series of scales on each side, and the abdominal surface whitish-yellow. Iris black, with a narrow golden ring; tongue small, flesh-coloured.

Scuta, 138; scutella, 77.

Var.

SYN.—Tropidonotus surgens, Cantor.

Above, bright greenish-olive, with a black serrated lateral line. Scuta, 148; scutella, 23.

HAB.—*Malayan Peninsula.*

Philippines, Tenasserim, Bengal, Madagascar.

The shields of the head are short; there is but a single anterior frontal, of a triangular shape, truncated in front; the frontals are small pentagonal; the nasals nearly squal to the latter; the small semicircular nostrils almost vertical, and appearing linear, as they are provided with a valvule as in *Homalopsis ;* from the lower part of the nostril a minute arched groove descends to the inferior margin of the shield; the frenal is small; the preorbital in length nearly equals the three postorbitals. The scales of the trunk are disposed in seventeen longitudinal series, of which the two lowest on each side are hexagonal, each scale with a minute round protuberance near the apex ; the scales of the next two series present a raised line terminating in a protuberance, but the remaining scales are elongated rhomboidal, with truncated, slightly notched points, keeled, imbricate. These marks become indistinct when the integuments are about to be changed, which probably caused them to escape the notice of Russell. This species is not numerous in Bengal, and apparently less so on the Malayan Peninsula. The largest individual measured—

Length of the head . . . . o feet 1 inch.
   ,,   ,,   trunk . . . . 2 ,, o$\frac{4}{8}$,,
   ,,   ,,   tail . . . . . o ,, 2$\frac{4}{8}$ inches.

                              2 ,, 4   ,,

Circumference of the neck 1$\frac{6}{8}$, of the trunk 2$\frac{4}{8}$, of the tail 1$\frac{6}{8}$ inch.

The length of the tail is very variable ; in some it is contained 3$\frac{1}{2}$, in other six times in the entire length. This species is very fierce, and prepares to attack by raising the head three or four inches vertically from the ground, and it has the power of flattening and laterally expanding the skin of the anterior part of the body, like *Naja*, but in a much slighter degree. It bites, uttering a faint hissing sound. Frogs and fishes form its food.

TROPIDONOTUS CERASOGASTER.

SYN.—Psammophis cerasogaster, Cantor.

Above, yellowish-brown with pale golden reflections ; lighter on the sides, the scales of which in some partially edged with yellow; cheeks, lips, throat, and abdominal surface cherry-coloured, with a bright yellow lateral line from the muzzle to the point of the tail. Iris and tongue cherry-coloured.

Scuta, 144 to 149 ; scutella, 60 to 69.

HAB.—*Malayan Peninsula.*
     Bengal, Assam.

The head is elongated, depressed ; sides angular, compressed ; muzzle truncated ; rostral broad, hexagonal, nearly vertical, arched below; the anterior frontals the smallest, next to them the frontals; the rest of the crown shields are narrow, elongated ; each occipital bordered by two pairs of elongated temporals, below which three smaller. Nasals rectangular, placed at a right angle with the anterior frontals; nostrils moderate, lateral; the frenal smaller than the nasal; preorbital longer than either; the eye moderate, prominent. Besides three postorbitals, there is a minute infra-orbital wedged in between the fifth and sixth upper labials, of which but a small portion of the sixth touches the orbit below. The lips are straight, turned up near their commissure, covered with eight or nine pairs of upper, ten lower shields. The mouth is large; the teeth small, crowded, of equal length. The trunk is cylindrical, compressed, covered with nineteen longitudinal series of imbricate, elongated rhomboidal scales, with rounded, slightly notched points, keeled, except the two lowest series on each side, which are larger than the rest, rhombic, smooth. The abdomen is broad, arched; the tail robust at the root, cylindrical, tapering to a sharp point. A solitary individual from Province Wellesley was of the following dimensions :—

Length of the head	. . . .	o foot	$0\frac{7}{8}$	inch.
„ „ trunk	. . . .	1 „	$5\frac{7}{8}$	inches.
„ „ tail	. . . .	o „	$6\frac{1}{8}$	„

$$2 \text{ feet } 0\frac{7}{8} \text{ inch.}$$

Circumference of the neck $\frac{7}{8}$, of the trunk $1\frac{4}{8}$, of the root of the tail $\frac{7}{8}$ inch.

In Bengal this species is not numerous. It is very fierce, attacks in a vertical attitude, but without expanding the anterior part of the body. Its food is that of the preceding. The elongated angular head makes this species resemble a *Psammophis*.

TROPIDONOTUS JUNCEUS, N.S.

Head above, shining light brown, lips and throat gamboge; from the angle of the mouth an oblique gamboge band, both joining under a sharp angle on the neck; trunk and tail dull greyish-olive, with a series of distant rounded whitish spots on each side; each scutum and scutellum with a small black spot on the sides, which, as well as their anterior margins, are minutely dotted with brown. Iris black with a golden ring; tongue small, greyish.

Scuta, 157; scutella, 88.

HAB.—*Pinang*.

The head is elongated ovate, with the sides angular, compressed; the muzzle truncated; the rostral shield moderate, square, deeply arched beneath, vertically fixed; the anterior frontals small, tetragonal; the frontals larger; angularly bent over the side, where they border the small square frenal; the other crown shields are rather small, the occipitals on each side bordered by small elongated shields, like the rest of the temples; the eyes large, prominent; preorbital, one; postorbitals, three; nasal rectangular; nostrils lateral, large, rounded; upper labials, nine, of which the fourth, fifth, and sixth border the orbit; lower labials, eleven; mentals, two pairs, elongated. The lips are slightly arched, the mouth wide; the teeth small, crowded; the last upper maxillary tooth longer than the rest. The trunk is very slender, cylindrical, with the centre of the back raised, forming a sharp ridge, the sides bulging near the abdomen, which is arched. The scales are imbricate, very elongated rhomboidal, with the apex notched, except the two lowest series on each side, which are broad rhombic; they are all sharply keeled, and disposed on the anterior part of the trunk in nineteen, on the middle part in seventeen longitudinal series. The tail elongated, cylindrical, very slender, tapering to a fine point. A single individual observed on the Great Hill of Pinang by W. T. Lewis, Esq., was of the following dimensions :—

Length of the head	. . . .	o foot $o\frac{6}{8}$ inch.	
„ „ trunk	. . . .	I „ 7	inches.
„ „ tail	. . . .	o „ $7\frac{3}{8}$	„

$$2 \text{ feet } 3\frac{1}{8} \quad \text{„}$$

Circumference of the neck $\frac{7}{8}$, of the trunk $1\frac{1}{8}$, of the root of the tail $\frac{3}{4}$ inch.

Like most of the Asiatic species of this genus, the present is of fierce habits. It twice unprovokedly bit a woodcutter who happened to pass it. The bite of course was productive of no consequences except a slight momentary pain. The very slender make and the elongated tail are characters which approach this species to the arboreal *Colubridæ*.

Gen. HOMALOPSIS, *apud Schlegel.*

(*Erpeton*, Lacépède, 1803; *Rhinopirus*, Merrem, 1820; *Pseuderyx*, Fitzinger, 1826; *Homalopsis*, Kuhl, 1827; *Cerberus*, Cuvier, 1829; *Hypsirhina*, Wagler, 1830; *Hydrops*, Wagler, 1830; *Helicops*, Wagler, 1830; *Potamophis*, Cantor, 1836.)

Homalopsis, Kuhl.—Nostrils opening vertically in the centre of the small nasals, with a valvule; crown shields small; dorsal scales imbricate, keeled; chin with many small shields, throat scaly; labials narrow; abdomen with scuta; tail short, tapering to a sharp point; beneath with scutella.

HOMALOPSIS RHINCHOPS, Schneider.

Syn.—Seba, ii. t. xv. fig. 3.
   Hydrus rhinchops, Schneider.
   Russell, i. pl. 17, Karoo Bokadam.

Russell, ii. pl. 40 (young).
Boa moluroides, Schneider.
Elaps boæformis, Schneider.
Enhydrus rhynchops, Latreille.
Hydrus cinereus, Shaw
Hurria Schneideriana, Daudin.
Coluber Schneiderianus, Daudin.
Coluber cerberus, Daudin.
Python rhynchops, Merrem.
Python elapiformis, Merrem.
Python molurus, Merrem.
Coluber obtusatus, Reinwardt.
Cerberus (Homalopsis obtusatus), Cuvier.
Homalopsis Schneiderii, Schlegel.
Cerberus cinereus, Cantor.

Young.—Ash-coloured above, the head with black irregular
spots and a short black line behind the eyes ; trunk and tail with
numerous distant black transversal bands ; lips and throat white
dotted with black ; the three or four lowest series of lateral scales
white ; beneath, white, with a black undulating band, frequently
interrupted.

Adult.—Ash, lead-coloured, or blackish-grey, with the black
marks indistinct or invisible. Iris black ; pupil elliptical, vertically
contracted by the light ; tongue very small, pale greyish.

Scuta, 143 to 156 ; scutella, 49 to 72.

HAB.—*Malayan Peninsula and Islands.*

New Guinea, Amboina, Timor, Sarapua, Java, Sumatra,
Tenasserim, Bengal, Coromandel.

The shields of the upper part of the head, which appear to be
of a constant form, are the nasals, the frontals, which enclose the
small pair of triangular anterior frontals (sometimes soldered
together), and the supraorbitals. The rest are broken up in small,
irregular, smooth pieces, differing in outline in each individual.
The small eye, placed in a partly vertical, partly lateral position,
is surrounded by a preorbital, a postorbital, and two or three
infraorbitals. The frenal is comparatively large, irregular tetragonal.
The anterior seven upper labials are narrow, very high ; the
posterior five or six each divided in two. A similar arrangement
is observed in the inferior thirteen or fourteen of which the
posterior six or seven are very small. On the chin there is a pair
of elongated shields immediately behind the two pairs of labials.
The posterior upper maxillary tooth is longer than the rest, and
furrowed. The three anterior teeth in the lower jaw are longer
than the rest. The trunk is covered with imbricate, finely lineated
and keeled scales, of a rhomboidal form, with rounded points,
disposed on the anterior part in twenty-five, on the posterior part

in seventeen longitudinal series. The tail is robust, tapering, and prehensile. In the Malayan countries this species occurs in numbers in rivers, estuaries, and occasionally along the sea-coasts. It feeds upon fishes. Single individuals measuring between three and four feet in length are of very rare occurrence. Of a great number the largest was of the following dimensions :—

Length of the head	. . . .	0 feet	$1\frac{2}{8}$	inch.
„　„　trunk	. . . .	2 „	3	inches.
„　„　tail	. . . . .	0 „	7	„
		2 „	$11\frac{2}{8}$	„

Circumference of the neck $1\frac{7}{8}$, of the trunk $3\frac{3}{8}$, of the root of the tail $1\frac{6}{8}$ inch. It is of peaceful habits; the female brings forth eight living young, each of which measures from seven to seven and a half inches in length.

HOMALOPSIS BUCCATA, Linné.

SYN.—Scheuchzer, pl. 660, fig. 1 (young).
　　Seba, ii. tab. xii. fig. 1 ; t. xiii. fig. 1 ; t. xxi. fig. 3 (young).
　　Coluber buccatus, Linné.
　　Coluber monilis, Linné
　　Coluber subalbidus, Boddaert apud Gmelin.
　　Le Demicollier, Lacépède.
　　Vipernköpfige Natter, Merrem.
　　Coluber buccatus, apud Shaw.
　　Russell, ii. pl. xxxiii. (young).
　　Coluber viperinus, Shaw.
　　Coluber buccatus, Daudin.
　　Coluber horridus, Daudin.
　　Echidna semifasciata, Merrem.
　　Homalopsis buccata, Schlegel.

Young.—Ground colour, white or buff, becoming brownish on the crown shields, hind-head, and lips ; on the muzzle an angular mark, with the apex between the frontals, vandyke-brown or chestnut ; an oblique streak proceeds from the eye over the cheek, joining a broad cervical band, which, sending a narrow straight line to the occipitals, gives the upper part of the head a heart-shaped outline ; the back and tail with numerous broad transversal brown bands, between which the ground colour appears in the shape of white, often interrupted, narrower bands, and of a white spot in the centre and on each side of the brown bands. The latter reach but as far as the lowest four or five series of scales on the sides, which, as well as the throat and abdomen, are white ; on each side of every third or fourth scutum a brown spot ; scutella black or white, closely spotted with black.

Adult.—The livery of the young indistinct : the ground colour of the upper parts pale greyish-brown or olive ; the bands of a darker shade of the same colour, edged with black ; sides and beneath impure buff, the brown marks pale. Pupil black, elliptical, vertically closed by the light ; tongue small, whitish. Scuta, 155 to 167 ; scutella, 73 to 89.

HAB.—*Pinang, Malayan Peninsula.*
    Java.

From the small, nearly vertically opening nostrils proceeds a furrow downwards to the lower margin of the nasal. The anterior frontal is either entire and of a large rhombic shape, or consisting of two triangular shields ; the frenal is elongated, rectangular ; the small eye is situated more laterally than in the preceding species, and surrounded by two postorbitals, one preorbital, and two infraorbitals. The seven anterior upper labials are very high, the posterior five are double ; of sixteen or seventeen lower labials the nine anterior are the highest. The last tooth in the upper jaw is furrowed, and as well as the three or four anterior palatal and inferior maxillary teeth, longer than the rest. The folds of gingiva enveloping the teeth are very ample, and contain, in addition to the fixed, numerous, five to six deep, accessory teeth. The chin is covered by four pairs of elongated scales, decreasing in length from the centre towards the labials. The scales of the trunk are rhombic, imbricate, slightly keeled and finely lineated, disposed on the anterior part in thirty-nine, on the posterior in twenty-five longitudinal series. The tail is robust, tapering, and somewhat prehensile. The largest individual observed was of the following dimensions :—

Length of the head	. . . .	0 foot	$1\frac{1}{8}$	inch.	
„ „ trunk	. . . .	1 „	11	inches.	
„ „ tail	. . . .	0 „	7	„	
		2 feet	$7\frac{1}{8}$	„	

Circumference of the neck 2, of the trunk $3\frac{4}{9}$, of the root of the tail $1\frac{6}{8}$ inch.

In the valleys of Pinang and on the opposite continent this species is numerous in streamlets, tanks, and in the irrigated fields, where it feeds on fishes. The young ones are very gentle, and the old but seldom bite. In their movements they are sluggish, and on dry land very awkward. The female brings forth six or eight living young at a time, each between seven and eight inches in length.

Hypsirhina, Wagler.—Resembling *Homalopsis* in the form and situation of the nostrils, the integuments and general appearance of the head, trunk, and tail; but the dorsal scales are smooth, and the labials are square, equal (frenal, one).

HOMALOPSIS SIEBOLDI, Schlegel.

SYN.—Seba, ii. tab. xlvi. fig. 2.?

Young.—Ground colour white, which on the upper part of the head appears in the shape of two lines diverging from the muzzle over the eyes to the sides of the head. From each side of the vertical shield a line diverging towards the hind-head, where it branches in two, sending a portion transversely to the throat, and another to the upper part of the neck, joining under an angle that of the opposite side. On the trunk and tail the ground colour shows itself as numerous narrow, transversal bands, which on the centre are frequently interrupted and placed in quincunx series; on the sides the bands are bipartite. The intervals between the ground colour are chestnut with dark brown edges. The lips and the abdominal surface white with numerous pale brown irregular spots. Iris greyish with a transversal black bar; pupil elliptical, tongue white.*

Scuta, 155 ; scutella, 48.

HAB.—*Malayan Peninsula.*
Bengal.

The description is taken from a solitary young individual which was killed in Province Wellesley. It measured—

Length of the head	.	.	.	.	.	$0\frac{4}{8}$ inch.
„ „ trunk	.	.	.	.	.	$5\frac{7}{8}$ inches.
„ „ tail	.	.	.	.	.	$1\frac{5}{8}$ „

8   ..

Circumference of the neck $\frac{5}{8}$, of the trunk $\frac{7}{8}$, of the root of the tail $\frac{4}{8}$ inch.

In livery and in general appearance this species resembles *H. buccata*, from which it differs in the following particulars:—Both the upper and the lower rostral shield are very small; the anterior frontals are much broader than long, each like a small transversely placed cone, surrounded by the nasal (with a slit towards the lower margin), the tetragonal frenal, and behind by the frontal.

---

* *Adult.*—A preserved specimen in the Museum of the Asiatic Society differs from the young in having the head above of a uniform colour, while the rest of the peculiar design is retained. The ground colour is yellowish-white; the brown of the young is faded to a dull lead grey. Scuta, 156 ; scutella, 55. Dimensions: head, $\frac{3}{4}$ inch; trunk, 1 foot $8\frac{3}{4}$ inches; tail, $3\frac{3}{8}$ inches = 2 feet 1 inch. Circumference of the neck $1\frac{7}{8}$, of the trunk $2\frac{3}{8}$, of the root of the tail $1\frac{3}{8}$ inch. The locality from whence this specimen was obtained is not known ; Bengal is given by M. Schlegel.

The vertical in extent nearly equals each of the short occipitals. The eye is rather large, prominent, surrounded by a single elongated, arched preorbital and two postorbitals, of which the inferior is the larger, bordering the fifth and sixth upper labials. Of the latter there are eight on each side : the fourth borders the eye below ; the two posterior are broken up in small pieces. Of the eleven or twelve pairs of lower labials, the four nearest the angle of the mouth are the smallest. The chin is covered by three pairs of oval shields, of which the anterior is the largest, and by some minute scales. The mouth is small, the teeth minute, uniform, except the last upper maxillary tooth, which is the longest, with a furrow on the convex margin. The back is slightly angular in the centre, much depressed ; the sides bulging ; the abdomen narrow. The anterior part of the trunk is covered with twenty-nine, the posterior with nineteen series of small, smooth, imbricate scales, all rhombic with rounded points. The tail is tapering and compressed.

HOMALOPSIS ENHYDRIS, Schneider.

SYN.—Russell, i. pl. xxx. Mutta Pam, Ally Pam.
Hydrus enhydris, Schneider.
Enhydris cærulea, Latreille.
Hydrus atrocæruleus, Shaw.
Coluber pythonissa, Daudin.
Homalopsis aer,* Boie.
Hypsirhina, Wagler.
Potamophis Lushingtonii, Cantor.
Homalopsis aer, Schlegel.
Homalopsis olivaceus, Cantor.

Iridescent dark greenish or brownish olive above ; the scales edged with black ; in some two parallel light greyish lines from between the eyes to the tip of the tail ; the lower half of the sides pale greenish or brownish grey ; lips and throat white, edged and dotted with black. Abdominal surface white or buff, with a greenish or brownish line on each side, and a black central line dividing the scuta and scutella. Iris greyish or pale olive ; pupil circular ; tongue whitish.

Young.—With lighter and more strongly iridescent colours than the adult.

Scuta, 148 to 167 ; scutella, 53 to 71.

HAB.—*Malayan Peninsula and Islands.*
Java, Tenasserim, Bengal, Coromandel.

---

* This specific name is singularly ill chosen, as the denomination *Ular ayer* (water-serpent) is applied by the Malays to all fresh-water serpents. The word *ayer* applied to a single species is as eligible as would be *aqua, eau,* or *wasser.*

The head is small, ovate, scarcely distinct; the nostrils are hemispherical, with a slit towards the external margin of the shield; the single anterior frontal is small, rhomboidal, much broader than long; the eye is rather large, prominent, lateral and surrounded by two rather broad postorbitals, one or two narrow preorbitals, and beneath by the fourth upper labial; the frenal is small, rhombic. The external margins of the occipitals are bordered by three elongated shields, and each temple by five similar. The eight upper labials are larger than the ten lower. The chin is covered by two central pairs of elongated shields, between which and the labials is, on each side, a single very elongated shield. The mouth is small, the teeth minute, numerous and equal, except the last tooth of the upper jaw, which is longer than the rest and furrowed. The trunk is very robust, broadly depressed; the sides obliquely compressed, and the abdomen very narrow, flattened. The scales are broad rhomboidal with rounded points, slightly imbricate, and disposed on the anterior part in twenty-five, in the middle in twenty-one, and near the tail in nineteen longitudinal series. The tail is very slender, somewhat compressed, tapering and prehensile. The largest individual was of the following dimensions :—

Length of the head	0 foot	1	inch.
„ „ trunk	1 „	$5\frac{6}{8}$	inches
„ „ tail	0 „	$5\frac{2}{8}$	„
	2 feet	0	„

Circumference of the neck $1\frac{2}{8}$, of the trunk $2\frac{6}{8}$, of the root of the tail $\frac{7}{8}$ inch.

Numbers of this species may be seen in rivers, as well as in irrigated fields and estuaries, preying upon fishes, which, however, it refuses in a state of captivity. It is of timid and peaceful habits. A large female, after having been confined upwards of six months in a glass vessel filled with water, brought forth eleven young ones in the manner noted above under *Acrochordus javanicus.* During the process she lay motionless on the bottom of the vessel; the anterior part of the abdomen was retracted towards the vertebral column, while the muscles of the posterior part were in activity. Shortly after the parturition she expired under a few spasmodic movements, and also two of the young ones died in the course of about two hours, after having, like the rest, shed the integuments. In length they varied from 6 to $6\frac{2}{8}$ inches. The living nine presented a singular appearance : they remained a little way below the surface of the water, coiling themselves round the body of an adult male, which was also kept in the vessel, occasionally lifting their heads above the surface to breathe, at the same time resisting the efforts of the senior to free himself. Fishes and aquatic insects were refused, in consequence of which the young ones expired from inanition in the course of less than two months.

HOMALPOPSIS PLUMBEA, Boie.

SYN.—Hypsirhina, Wagler.
Hypsirhina Hardwickii, Gray: " Illust. Ind. Zool."
Homalopsis plumbea, Schlegel.

Iridescent dark brownish or greyish olive above, uniformly or with small irregular black spots; the two or three lowest series of scales yellowish, each scale spotted or edged with brown; lips and throat yellow; scuta and scutella yellowish-white, the former in some partially edged with black, the latter with a black central zig-zag line; iris grey; pupil elliptical, vertically contracted by the light; tongue whitish.

Scuta, 125 to 126; scutella, 36 to 44.

HAB.—*Pinang*.
Java.

The head is broad, ovate, depressed; the muzzle blunt, the nostrils small, triangular, with a slit towards the lower margin of the nasal; the single anterior frontal broad triangular; the rest of the crown shields are of normal form. The eye is small, placed in a half-lateral half-vertical position, enclosed by two post-orbitals, one elongated preorbital, and beneath by the fourth upper labial; the frenal is very small, tetragonal; the upper labials eight, rather high; lower labials ten; on both jaws the shields increase in size towards the angle of the mouth. The chin is covered with two pairs of elongated shields and a few gulars. The mouth is small; the posterior upper maxillary tooth longer than the rest, furrowed, and the anterior lower maxillary teeth also exceed the following. In addition to the fixed teeth there are several accessory series. The trunk is nearly cylindrical, slightly depressed, covered with small rhombic scales, smooth, and not imbricate, disposed on the anterior part in nineteen, on the posterior part in seventeen longitudinal series. The tail is short, conic, tapering, and slightly prehensile. Two individuals, taken at different times from rivulets in the valley of Pinang, in habits resembled *H. rhinchops*. The larger was of the following dimensions :—

Length of the head	0 foot	$1\frac{1}{8}$	inch.
,, ,, trunk	1 ,,	5	inches.
,, ,, tail	0 ,,	$2\frac{6}{8}$	,,
	1 ,,	$8\frac{7}{8}$	,,

Circumference of the neck 1⅝, of the trunk 2⅘, of the root of the tail 1⅛ inch.

HOMALOPSIS LEUCOBALIA, Schlegel, var.

Young. — Above, light brownish-olive, or greenish-grey with single irregular distant brown spots; lips and throat whitish-yellow; the lowest three or four lateral series of scales, and the abdominal surface greenish-white or pearl-coloured.

Adult.—Uniformly blackish-olive above, otherwise like the young. Iris dark brown; pupil elliptical, vertically contracted by the light. Tongue whitish.

Scuta, 130 to 148; scutella, 26 to 37.

HAB.—*Pinang, Malayan Peninsula.*

The head is very broad, depressed, and the muzzle blunt; the rostral broad, hexagonal, very slightly arched beneath; the superior margin borders the single small elongated anterior frontal, which is of a narrow hexagonal form, broader behind, where it is wedged in between the two broad frontals. The nasals are rather large; nostrals small, crescent-shaped; the vertical very broad, short, hexagonal; occipitals large, elongated with a pair of very broad shields on each side, below which the temples are covered by three smaller shields. The eye is very small, in a half-vertical position, with two postorbitals, one preorbital, which extends to the large oval nasal; frenal none, or when present, excessively minute. Of the five large upper labials, the anterior is the smallest and borders the nasal; the second the preorbital, the third the orbit, and the lower postorbital, the fourth and fifth the temporals. The lower rostral is very small, triangular. The seven or eight inferior labials are much smaller than the upper. The two pairs of mentals are very short. The mouth is small; the teeth are very strong, short, and of nearly equal size, except the furrowed last upper maxillary tooth, and the anterior teeth of the lower jaw, which are longer than the rest. The trunk is robust, back slightly raised in the centre, the sides sloping, their lower half compressed, the abdomen broad, arched. The scales are smooth, rhombic, with rounded points, slightly imbricate; those of the sides have the points bent inwards and firmly adhering to the skin, so as to appear hexagonal. On the anterior part of the trunk they are disposed in twenty-seven, on the posterior in twenty-five longitudinal series. The tail is short, robust, tapering, and somewhat prehensile. In the male the sides are compressed, very high in the middle, and the lower surface is flattened, very broad, more so than is the posterior part of the abdomen. In the female it is shorter, the sides less high, and the lower surface less broad. The largest male of a considerable number was of the following dimensions :—

Length of the head . . .	0 foot	$0\frac{7}{8}$ inch.	
" " trunk . . .	1	$10\frac{2}{8}$ inches.	
" " tail . . .	0	$2\frac{6}{8}$ "	
	2 feet	$1\frac{7}{8}$ inch.	

Circumference of the neck $1\frac{7}{8}$, of the trunk $2\frac{4}{8}$, of the root of the tail, $1\frac{4}{8}$ inch. With the exception of its colours, the present offers no difference from *H. leucokalia*, from the rivers of Timor. At Pinang it is numerous not only in fresh water and estuaries, but in the sea at some distance from the shore, where it sometimes occurs in fishing nets. It is of sluggish, not fierce habits, and feeds upon fishes and crustacea, aquatic and pelagic. In a young female the oviduct enclosed four white cylindrical eggs, which when they were observed contained but yolk; each measured about an inch in length.

HOMALOPSIS HYDRINA, N.S.

Adult.—Ash-coloured above, with a few scattered black spots on the neck; the back and tail with numerous transversal black bands: the lips, sides, and abdomen uniformly pearl-coloured. Iris ashy; pupil elliptical, vertically contracted by the light; tongue small, whitish.

Scuta, 161; scutella, 34.

Young.—Resembling the adult, but the ash colour of a much lighter shade.

Scuta, 153; scutella, 35.

HAB.—*Sea off Pinang, and the Malayan Peninsula.*

The head is moderately distinct, elongated, depressed, oval, with rounded blunt muzzle; the rostral shield moderate, hexagonal; its lower margin with a central minute tubercle, on each side of which a triangular impression. The upper margin of the minute triangular lower rostral presents a central cavity, and two lateral elevations fitting into the margin of the upper rostral. A similar contrivance in the pelagic serpents enables them hermetically to close the mouth. As in *H. leucobalia*, the single small anterior frontal is elongated hexagonal, broader behind, and enclosed by the rostral, the nasals, and the frontals. Although the nasals are placed laterally, the small arched linear nostrils open vertically, and send a slit to the posterior margin of the shield; the frontals are hexagonal, smaller than the latter; the vertical is the longest of the crown-shields, very narrow, hexagonal, pointed at both extremities, but broader behind; the supraorbitals are small, narrow; the occipitals are broken up in minor shields—viz., two postoccipitals, in size equal to the occipitals, and a minute conical interoccipital, enclosed by the four shields, with the broader extremity wedged in between the occipitals. Each temple is covered with two pairs of large shields, of which the lower borders the fifth, sixth, and seventh upper labials. The eye is very minute, prominent, almost vertically placed, surrounded by two post-orbitals, of which the lower is broad pentagonal, meeting beneath the elongated single oblique preorbital. Thus none of the upper labials border the orbit. The frenal is moderate, pentagonal. Of the seven upper labials the anterior three pairs are much smaller than the rest, which suddenly become very large and deep, so as to make the margin of the lip very bulging in a downward direction. The lower ten or eleven labials are smaller than the upper, except the sixth, which is the largest. The chin with two pairs of shields, of which the anterior is very elongated; the throat with numerous minute scales; the mouth is small, the dentitiom resembles that of *Homalopsis leucobalia*, var.; the trunk would be orbicular but for the narrow flattened abdomen, the scuta of which are angulated, forming on each side a sharp ridge ; the scales are very small, smooth, on the neck disposed in thirty-three, successively in thirty-seven, but near the root of the tail in twenty-nine longitudinal series. Those of the back are rhomboidal with rounded points ; those of the sides lanceolate with the point bent inwards, so as to appear truncated, each scale leaving a small square interval, in which appears the naked skin. The tail is short, much compressed, tapering, and slightly prehensile. In the male the sides are very high, and the lower surface very broad, as noted under *H. leucobalia*, var. On the broadest part there are as many as twenty-one longitudinal series of scales. In the female this organ is shorter, the sides less high, and the abdomen less broad.

Of three individuals observed, two were captured in fishing stakes placed in the sea off the shores of Keddah, a third was washed on shore by the waves on the coast adjoining my house at Pinang. The largest male was of the following dimensions :—

Length of the head	.	.	.	.	0 foot	$0\frac{5}{8}$	inch.
,,	,,	trunk	.	.	.	1 ,,	$4\frac{4}{8}$ inches.
,,	,,	tail	.	.	.	0 ,,	$2\frac{2}{8}$,,
						1 ,,	$7\frac{3}{8}$,,

Circumference of the neck, $\frac{6}{8}$; of the trunk, $1\frac{6}{8}$; of the root of the tail, $\frac{7}{8}$; of the middle of the tail, 1 ; two-eighths from the apex, $\frac{3}{8}$ inch.

It moved actively and without difficulty on the sand, and did not offer to bite. In one examined the stomach contained remains of two small pelagic fishes. In general appearance and colours the present is more closely allied to the pelagic serpents than any other known species. Whether it exclusively inhabits the sea, or, like *Homalopsis rhinchops, enhydrus,* and *leucobalia,* as an occasional visitor, must be a matter of future investigation.

VENOMOUS SERPENTS.

FAM. VIPERIDAE, BONAPARTE.

SUB-FAM. BUNGARINÆ, BONAPARTE.

TERRESTRIAL.

Gen. ELAPS, *Schneider.*

Head more or less indistinct, neck not dilatable; mouth and eyes small, trunk elongated, throughout of nearly equal circumference, very smooth; tail short, tapering, beneath with scutella.

ELAPS MELANURUS, Shaw.

SYN.—Russell, i. pl. 8 (young).
Coluber melanurus, Shaw (young).
Vipera trimaculata, Daudin (young).
Elaps trimaculatus, Merrem apud $\left\{\begin{array}{l}\text{Wagler}\\\text{Schlegel}\end{array}\right\}$ (young).

Strong iridescent light bay above; from the muzzle a longitudinal black band, joining on the neck a broader transversal black band with whitish edges; a short oblique black line behind the eye, and a similar from the nostril to the middle of the upper lip; on each side of the anterior part of the back a series of distant black dots; a broad black transversal band with whitish edges at the root of the tail; a second similar at a short distance from the apex; lips, throat, and the anterior part of the abdomen iridescent yellowish-white, changing to yellow or orange on the posterior part; the tail beneath bluish-white, with large irregular black spots. Iris black; pupil circular; tongue black.

Scuta, 205 to 247; scutella, 24 to 32.

HAB.—*Malayan Peninsula.*
Tenasserim, Nerva (Coromandel).

In general appearance this species nearest approaches *Elaps intestinalis,* Laurenti, but the eye is comparatively larger, while the nearly equilateral, hexagonal, vertical shield is smaller in the present. The eye is surrounded by two postorbitals, one preorbital, and beneath by the third and fourth upper labials. Of the latter, seven pairs cover the jaws. The trunk is throughout covered by thirteen series of smooth, subimbricate, rhombic scales. The one described by Russell, hitherto the only describer from nature, was a young animal. A similar, upwards of a foot in length, was killed in Province Wellesley. But the late Mr.

VOL. II. P

Griffith in one of his botanical excursions captured an individual of the following dimensions :—

Length of the head	. . .	0 foot	$0\frac{5}{8}$ inch.
,, ,, trunk	. . .	1 ,,	$10\frac{2}{8}$ inches.
,, ,, tail	. . .	0 ,,	$1\frac{4}{8}$ inch.

$$2 \text{ feet } 0\frac{3}{8} \text{ ,,}$$

Circumference of the trunk, 1 inch.

ELAPS INTESTINALIS,* Laurenti, var.

SYN.—Maticora lineata, Gray : " Ill. Ind. Zool."
Elaps furcatus, Schneider, var. apud Schlegel, Cantor.

Young and Adult.—Head above, light chestnut ; lips and throat yellowish-white, upper lips spotted with black ; from the hind-head to the tip of the tail a vermilion line, on each side of which a narrow, serrated, black line. On the nearest two longitudinal series of scales the ground colour appears as a reddish light grey longitudinal line, beneath bordered by an equally broad black line, under which a narrow buff-coloured line, bordered by a black serrated line, the teeth of which are directed downwards, wedged in between the lateral margins of the scuta and scutella. Scuta alternately pale citrine and iridescent black, the latter colour occupying three to four scuta together, while the former rarely appears on more than two. Tail above with two or three distinct black transversal bands ; beneath vermilion, with a continuation of the superior transversal bands. Iris black, pupil circular ; tongue black.

Scuta, 223 to 238 ; scutella, 24 to 26.

HAB.—*Pinang, Singapore, Malayan Peninsula.*
Sumatra.

Excepting the colours, this variety otherwise perfectly agrees with *E. intestinalis.* The neck is covered by fifteen, the rest of the trunk by thirteen longitudinal series of smooth, not imbricate rhombic scales. It is of no uncommon occurrence in the hills of Pinang, at Malacca, and at Singapore. The largest individual was of the following dimensions :—

* SYN.—Seba ii. pl. 2, fig. 7.—*Aspis intestinalis,* Laurenti ; *Coluber intestinalis,* Gmelin ; Russell, ii. pl. 19 ; *Elaps furcatus,* Schneider ; *Coluber intestinalis,* Shaw ; *Vipera furcata,* Daudin ; *Elaps furcatus,* Schneider apud Wagler, Schlegel.
HAB.—Java, Malwah (Central India).
A collection of reptiles, which Mr. J. W. Grant obtained from Saugor, Malwah, contained a single specimen.

Length of the head . . . o foot o⅜ inch.

,, ,, trunk . . . 1 ,, 10 inches.

,, ,, tail . . . o ,, 1⅘ ,,

Circumference of the trunk, 1⅔ inch. ———
1 ,, 11⅞ ,,

ELAPS NIGROMACULATUS, Cantor.

SYN.—Calliophis gracilis, Gray : " Ill. Ind. Zool." young.
" Probablement˙ nouvelle espèce d'Elaps," Schlegel :
" Essay," p. 451.
Elaps nigromaculatus, Cantor : Spicil.

Head above, yellowish-brown, each shield with a pale black
spot in the middle ; lips and throat yellowish-white, spotted with
pale black. Ground colour of the trunk and tail reddish light
grey, longitudinally divided by a central black line, with small
round, black, white-edged spots about an inch apart ; on each side
two parallel black lines, the lower of which bordering the two
lowest series of scales of the sides, which are white, edged with
black, so as to appear longitudinally intersected by two black lines.
All the lateral black and white lines are on each side intersected
by a series of large rounded (the anterior pair elongated) black
spots with white edges, placed in pairs, opposite each other, but
in quincunx order with the smaller black spots of the dorsal line.
Beneath, alternately yellowish-white or pale citrine, and iridescent
black, both colours nearly equally divided. Tail at the root and
near the apex with a broad transversal black band edged with
white, both continued on the vermilion lower surface, and there,
between them, a third similar band. Iris black, pupil round ;
tongue, bluish-grey.

Young.—Marked like the adult, but the ground colour of the
back and tail inclines to light reddish-brown.

Scuta, 238 to 311 ; scutella, 21 to 28.

HAB.—*Pinang, Singapore.*

In general appearance this species very closely resembles *Elaps
intestinalis*, from which it is distinguished by the following characters.* The two pairs of frontal shields are remarkably dispro-
portionate, the frontals (proper) being much the larger : next to
the occipitals, they are the largest of the crown-shields. The
nearly equilateral, hexagonal vertical, and the supraorbitals are
remarkably small ; more so than in any other species of this genus.
The occipitals are very narrow elongated ; their external margin
bordered by two pairs of shields, of which the anterior, the larger,

* The (magnified ?) representation of the head of *Calliophis gracilis*, fig. 2,
" Ill. Ind. Zool.," is in every particular incorrect.

covers the temples, and is beneath bounded by the fifth and sixth upper labials. The eye is sunk, excessively minute, surrounded by two small postorbitals; beneath by the third and fourth upper labials, and by a single narrow triangular preorbital. The latter is placed obliquely, so that the downwards-pointed apex meets the linear posterior part of the nasal, or, as it is considered by some, the frenal. The nostrils are comparatively large. The upper labials number six on each side : the two posterior are the largest. The chin is covered by two pairs of elongated narrow shields, externally bordered by the third and fourth, the largest of the six inferior labials. The gular scales are more numerous than those of *E. intestinalis*. The neck is covered by fifteen, the trunk by thirteen longitudinal series of smooth rhombic scales with rounded points. This species is of no uncommon occurrence in the hills of Pinang. The largest individual was of the following dimensions :—

Length of the head	o feet	$0\frac{4}{9}$ inch.
„ „ trunk	2 „	$1\frac{3}{9}$ „
„ „ tail	o „	$1\frac{3}{9}$ „
	2 „	$3\frac{2}{9}$ inches.

Circumference of the trunk, 1 inch.

ELAPS BIVIRGATUS,* Kuhl, var.

SYN.—Elaps flaviceps, Cantor, Spicil.
Elaps flaviceps, apud J. Reinhardt : Beskrivelse, &c.

Head, lips, and throat vermilion ; trunk above, brilliant iridescent, intense black, most of the scales partially edged with azure, not, however, sufficiently to produce regular network ; the two lowest series of scales on each side azure, forming a continued lateral band, longitudinally divided by a white zig-zag line, produced by the scales being partially edged with white. Beneath, vermilion ; each scutum with two lateral, square, black spots, forming a continued black band bordering the azure. Tail above with a narrow black dorsal line ; sides and scutella vermilion. Iris and tongue black.

Scuta, 248 to 277 ; scutella, 38 to 45.

HAB.—*Pinang, Malayan Peninsula.*

In colours the young ones resemble the adult. The neck is covered by fifteen, the trunk by thirteen longitudinal series of smooth rhomboidal scales. The anterior part of larynx, instead of adhering to the upper part of the membranous sheath enclosing

---

* SYN.—"Erpétologie de Jav." pl. xliv. ; *Elaps bivirgatus*, apud Schlegel.
HAB.—Java, Sumatra.

the tongue, presents the peculiarity of being free, and projecting in the mouth like a small tube.

Of four individuals observed, three were from the hills of Pinang. The largest was of the following dimensions :—

Length of the head	. . . . .	o	feet	$0\frac{5}{8}$	inch.
„ „ trunk	. . . . .	2	„	$7\frac{6}{8}$	inches.
„ „ tail	. . . . .	o	„	$3\frac{2}{8}$	„
		2	„	$11\frac{5}{8}$	„

Circumference of the trunk, $1\frac{4}{8}$ inch.

Elaps intestinalis, var., *E. nigromaculatus* and *bivirgatus*, var., appear at Pinang exclusively to inhabit the hills at a considerable elevation, but on the Malayan Peninsula and at Singapore they occur in the valleys. Although not numerous, they cannot be said to be of rare occurrence. They are strictly terrestrial, and have their hiding-places under the roots of trees and in the crevices of rocks. They are sluggish, awkwardly dragging their long slender bodies, and they are generally observed lying motionless, with the body thrown in many irregular folds, but not coiled. Although they are diurnal, their sight, from the minuteness of the pupil, appears to be as defective as their sense of hearing, and they may be closely approached without apparently their being aware of danger. If touched with a stick, they make a few strenuous efforts to slide away, but they soon stop, and if further pursued, they make some irregular spasmodic-like movements, but they have not been observed to bite. An adult *Elaps bivirgatus*, var., was on a single occasion seen to raise the head vertically about two inches from the ground. In captivity they refuse food and water, and die in a short time from inanition. Of a number examined, only one of the latter species had in the stomach the remains of a small serpent, the genus of which could not be determined. M. Schlegel has observed *Calamariæ* in the stomach of *Elaps intestinalis*. In the peculiar distribution of colours, in diminutive size, and in habits, they resemble the genus *Calamaria*. It is solely the smallness of the mouth which renders the preceding species of *Elaps* harmless to man, as from the following it will be perceived that their venom is as virulent as that of other venomous serpents. From the diminutive size of the venomous glands, the quantity of fluid secreted is small : scarcely more than a drop from each. It is a pellucid, colourless fluid, slightly reddening litmus paper.

After several unsuccessful attempts to make an adult *Elaps nigro-maculatus* spontaneously bite a fowl, the jaws were forcibly closed over a protracted fold of the skin on the inner side of the left thigh of the bird. On account of the small gape, some difficulty was experienced in making the jaws close over the fold of the skin, and as it appeared doubtful if the fangs had penetrated, the serpent was in a quarter of an hour compelled again to wound the fowl in the skin below the right eye. Twenty minutes after the first wound the fowl became purged, and manifested symptoms of pain in the left thigh, which was continually drawn up towards the body, although the wounds inflicted there and below the eye were, from the smallness of the fangs, barely visible. Twenty-eight minutes after the first wound the bird commenced drooping, occasionally attempting to raise itself, and in ten minutes more soporism occurred, interrupted by spasms of the neck, flow of saliva, and pecking the earth with the beak, while the pupil was spasmodically contracted and alternately dilated. The latter symptoms continued during thirty minutes, when death occurred in an hour after the first wound had been inflicted. Fowls wounded by *Elaps furcatus*, var., and *Elaps bivirgatus*, var., expired under similar symptoms, from within an hour and twenty minutes to upwards of three hours. The serpents, which all had forcibly to be made to inflict the wounds, shortly afterwards expired, apparently from the violence to which they had been subjected.

Gen. BUNGARUS, *Daudin.*

Body elongated, slightly cylindrical; tail short; head oval, trunk and tail with a dorsal series of large hexagonal scales; the tail beneath with scuta, in the middle sometimes with scutella; behind the fangs some simple maxillary teeth.

BUNGARUS FLAVICEPS, J. Reinhardt.

Young.—Head and neck blood-red, with a pointed elongated black mark between the occipitals, and a short black dorsal line on the neck; the trunk black with steel-blue reflections, at the anterior part of each dorsal hexagonal scale a short longitudinal white streak; near the tail blood-red; each scale of the two lowest lateral series white with a black spot, placed so as to produce a continued lateral white zig-zag line; the posterior part of the sides blood-red. Lips and throat blood-red; abdomen black, posterior part as well as the tail blood-red, with a few black spots. Iris and tongue black.

Scuta abdominalia, 209; scuta sub-caudalia, 16; scutella, 38.

HAB.—*Pinang.*
Java.

M. J. Reinhardt has described the adult from an unique specimen in the Royal Museum, Copenhagen. Spirits of wine changed the brilliant blood-red to a pale yellow colour. The diagnosis must therefore be altered accordingly. The adult appears to differ from the young in having none of the black marks of the head and tail and no lateral white line.

A single young individual, found by Sir William Norris on the Great Hill of Pinang, was of the following dimensions:—

Length of the head	. . . .	0 foot	$0\frac{5}{9}$	inch.
„ „ trunk	. . . .	1 „	$4\frac{4}{8}$	inches.
„ „ tail	. . . .	0 „	3	„
		1 „	$8\frac{1}{8}$	„

Circumference of the neck 1, of the trunk $1\frac{2}{8}$, of the root of the tail $\frac{5}{8}$ inch.

The centre of the back forms a ridge, from whence the sides slope; the abdomen is broad, slightly arched, so that the vertical section of the body becomes broad triangular. The neck is covered by fifteen, the trunk by thirteen longitudinal series of smooth, imbricate, rhomboidal scales. As observed by M. J. Reinhardt, the correspondence of colours, and their distribution, between this species and *Elaps bivirgatus*, is very striking. Besides, the number of series of scales is another character approximating this species to the genus *Elaps*.

BUNGARUS CANDIDUS, Linné.

SYN.—Seba, ii. t. lxvi. figs. 3 and 4.
   Coluber candidus, Linné.
   Russell, i. pl. i. Paragoodoo.
   Russell, ii. pl. xxxi. Sew Walaley.
   Pseudoboa cœrulea, Schneider.
   Boa lineata, Shaw.
   Bungarus cœruleus, Daudin.
   Bungarus semifasciatus, Kuhl.
   Aspidoclonion semifasciatum, Wagler.
   Bungarus semifasciatus, Schlegel.

Above, black with steel-blue reflections, interrupted by numerous narrow transversal white bands, produced by the white edges of the scales. On each side the bands are bifurcated, and the two or three lowest series of scales white with black spots. Lips and throat white; abdominal surface yellowish-white. Iris black; tongue white.

Scuta, 201 to 221; scuta sub-caudalia, 38 to 56.

HAB.—*Malayan Peninsula.*
   Java, Tenasserim, Bengal, Assam, Coromandel, Ceylon, Malabar.

A single young individual, killed by Capt. Congaiton near Keddah, was of the following dimensions:—

Length of the head	. . . . .	o feet 1	inch.
„ „ trunk	. . . . .	2 „ $3\frac{6}{8}$	inches
„ „ tail	. . . . .	o „ $4\frac{5}{8}$	„

$$2 \text{ „ } 9\frac{3}{8} \text{ „}$$

Circumference of the neck $1\frac{6}{8}$, of the trunk 2, of the root of the tail $1\frac{1}{8}$ inch.

Assam produces also a constant variety (*B. lividus,* Cantor) of a uniform blue-black above; beneath, yellowish-white; in some the scuta blackish with white edges. In the very young the head is white with a black line between the occipital shields. It farther differs in having the hexagonal scales smaller, less distinct from the rest, and the tail more robust than the normal individuals

BUNGARUS FASCIATUS, Schneider.

SYN.—Scheuchzer, pl. dclv., fig. 8.
  Seba, ii. pl. lviii. fig. 2.
  Russell, i. pl. iii. Bungarum Pamah.
  Pseudoboa fasciata, Schneider.
  Boa fasciata, Shaw.
  Bungarus annularis, Daudin.
  Aspidoclonion, Wagler.
  Bungarus annularis, Schlegel.

Ground colour bright gamboge; the anterior half of the head and the cheeks black, with steel-blue reflections; from the vertical shield a black longitudinal band, expanding over the neck and sides, and with the former forming a broad-arrow mark; lips and throat gamboge, upper lips edged with black; the rest of the body completely surrounded by a number of broad alternate gamboge and shining black rings. Iris black; tongue flesh-coloured.

Scuta, 200 to 233; scuta abdominalia, 32 to 36.

HAB.—*Pinang Malayan Peninsula.*
  Java, Tenasserim, Bengal, Coromandel.

The neck is covered by seventeen, the trunk by fifteen longitudinal series of smooth scales, which, with the exception of the dorsal hexagonal series, are imbricate, rhombic. As noted under *Elaps bivirgatus,* var., the larynx is not attached to the scabbard of the tongue. Of three young individuals from the valley of Pinang and Province Wellesley, the largest was of the following dimensions :—

Length of the head	. . . . .	o feet $1\frac{2}{8}$	inch.
„ „ trunk	. . . . .	3 „ 5	inches.
„ „ tail	. . . . .	o „ $4\frac{4}{8}$	„

$$3 \text{ „ } 10\frac{6}{8} \text{ „}$$

Circumference of the neck 2, of the trunk 3⅔, of the root of the tail 2, of the apex 1⅜ inch.

In the Malayan countries the species of *Bungarus* are not numerous; but *B. candidus* and *fasciatus* are of no uncommon occurrence in Bengal and on the Coromandel Coast, where, however, it should be observed, a class of the natives ("serpent-charmers") earn a livelihood by capturing and exhibiting serpents, but this craft is unknown among the Malays. The preceding three species, like the rest of the venomous serpents, are very ferocious when attacked, but unprovokedly they are not known to attack man; on the contrary, when met in the jungle they attempt to escape. When trod upon or struck, their rage is instantly excited; in self-defence they will even turn from their retreat, and then their habitual sluggishness is roused to furious activity. Preparing to attack, the head is by a short curve of the neck brought closely to the body, and drawn far backwards, when suddenly darting the anterior part of the body obliquely upwards, they bite. The height of the place where the wound is inflicted of course depends on the length of the serpent, which is capable of darting nearly the anterior half of the body. Notwithstanding the circular pupil, they appear to shun the light, hiding the head under the folds of the body, and they are singularly uncertain in their movements, often suddenly jerking the head or tail without any apparent object. Like all serpents of tropical Asia, they seldom expose themselves to the sun; when during the day they leave their hiding-places, they select the shade. The genus *Bungarus* is terrestrial, feeding on rats, mice, serpents (*Col. mucosus*, Lin.), and toads. Like other venomous serpents, when the venom has been inflicted on their prey, they disengage it from the fangs, sheathe and place them as horizontally as possible, in order that they may offer no resistance to the introduction into the mouth of the lifeless prey, which is now seized head foremost. The innocuous serpents bite or strangle their prey, which when life is extinct is either swallowed at once, or if it happens to have been killed in a position likely to render the deglutition difficult, is often disengaged from between the teeth and seized a second time by the head. In captivity these serpents refuse food, but greedily lap up and swallow water.

A fowl, four minutes after it had been bitten on the inner side of the thigh by a *Bungarus fasciatus*, fell on the wounded side, and was shortly after seized with slight purging. The eyes were half closed, the pupils alternately dilated and contracted, immobile. In seventeen minutes slight spasms occurred, under which the bird expired forty-three minutes after it had been wounded.

Another fowl, wounded in the same place as the former by the same serpent, but after an interval of seven hours, expired under similar symptoms, only more violent spasms, in the course of twenty-eight minutes.

Venom taken from another serpent, the fangs of which had been extracted, was inoculated by a lancet incision in the right thigh; four minutes after, the fowl was seized with trembling, fell, and remained lying on the wounded side, with the eyes closed, but it gradually recovered, and rose, apparently recovered, thirty minutes after the inoculation of the venom.

Other fowls were killed by different serpents of this species, in twenty to thirty-one minutes.

Fowls bitten by *Bungarus candidus* expired under similar symptoms within thirty to forty-five minutes; dogs from within one hour ten minutes to two hours, under symptoms noted in Russell's experiments (Russell, i. p. 53).

Sub-Fam. NAJINÆ, Bonaparte.

Hamadryas, *Cantor*.

Head broad, subovate, depressed, with a pair of very large postoccipital shields, and a short blunt muzzle; cheeks tumid; eyes large, prominent, pupil circular; nostrils wide, between two shields; behind the fangs a few maxillary teeth; neck dilatable; trunk thick, cylindrical; tail short, with scuta and scutella.

Hamadryas ophiophagus, Cantor.

Syn.—Hamadryas hannah, Cantor.
　　Naja elaps, Schlegel (young).
　　Naja bungarus, Schlegel (young).
　　Naja vittata, Elliot.
　　Hamadryas ophiophagus, apud Elliot.

Olive green above; the shields of the head, the scales of the neck, posterior part of the body and of the tail edged with black; the trunk with a number of distant, oblique, alternate black and white bands, converging towards the head; the throat and anterior part of abdomen impure gamboge, the rest of the scuta and scutella bluish-grey marbled with black, or pale yellowish-green with a narrow submarginal brown line. Iris golden, spotted with black; tongue bluish-black.

Scuta, 215 to 256; scuta subcaudalia, 13 to 32; scutella subcaudalia, 63 to 96.

Hab.—*Pinang, Singapore, Malayan Peninsula.*
　　Java, Sumatra,* Bengal, Assam,† Coromandel.

---

* Sir Stamford Raffles' specimen in the Museum of the Zoological Society, London.
† Specimen in the collection of H. Walker, Esq., surgeon, G. G.

Of two individuals, from the summit of the Great Hill of Pinang and from Province Wellesley, the larger was of the following dimensions :—

Length of the head . . . . . o feet 3 inches.
,, ,, trunk . . . . 8 ,, 1 inch.
,, ,, tail . . . . . 2 ,, 4 inches.
_____
10 ,, 8 ,,

Circumference of the neck $5\frac{2}{8}$, of the trunk $8\frac{5}{8}$, of the tail $4\frac{1}{8}$ inches.

The neck is covered by twenty-one, the trunk by seventeen longitudinal series of smooth imbricate scales : those of the two lowest series are large rhombic, of the sides irregular rhomboidal, appearing linear, all with rounded apex. The Malayan individuals are of a lighter colour, more inclining to yellow, than those observed in Bengal.

Gen. NAJA, *Laurenti.*

Head covered with shields ; muzzle truncated ; the anterior part of the trunk, between the sixth and twelfth abdominal scutum, considerably dilatable in the shape of a disk, with a large white transparent spot above, edged with black and somewhat resembling a pair of spectacles.

NAJA LUTESCENS,* Laurenti, var. (D. Daudin).

SYN.—Seba, ii. t. xcvii. fig. 4.
Naja peruviana, Lacépède.
Russell, i. pl. vi. fig. 4 ; Sankoo Nagoo.
Latreille, iv. pl. 27.
Vipera naja, var. D. Daudin.
Aspis, Wagler.
Naja tripudians, var. Gray : " Illus. Ind. Zool."
Naja tripudians, Merrem, var. Schlegel.
" 'Ular mata-ári " of the Malays.

Head shining, dark brown above; on the sides and lips brownish-white ; ground colour of the trunk buff, the anterior half of each scale pale greyish-brown ; beneath buff. Iris black, with a

* *Coluber naja,* Linné ; *Naja lutescens,* Laurenti (the *Cobra di Capello*), has probably the widest range of the Asiatic venomous serpents. The species, or its varieties, inhabits the countries between the Sutlej and Cape Comorin, and Ceylon. According to Mr. Hodgson's observations, it does not occur in the valley of Nepal, but it ranges through Hindustan down to Cape Romania, the southern extremity of the Malayan Peninsula, and from thence to Chusan, 30° N.E. 122° E. It is also found in the Philippines, Ternate, Borneo, Java, Sumatra.

narrow light-grey margin towards the orbit; tongue light flesh-coloured.

Young.—Much lighter brown than the adult, and strongly iridescent.

Scuta, 189 to 193; scutella, 49 to 54.

HAB.—*Pinang, Singapore, Malayan Peninsula.*
Bengal, Coromandel.

It is numerous in the Malayan hills and valleys, but apparently of uncommon occurrence in Bengal.

Var. NIGRA.

SYN.—Naja tripudians, var. nigra, Gray: " Illus. Ind. Zool."
Naja tripudians, var. Schlegel.

Upper parts intense black with strong purple or blue reflections; temples, lips, and throat pale orange, largely spotted with black; the lateral part of the anterior eight or ten, and of the fourteenth, fifteenth, and seventeenth scuta, pale orange, black in the centre, and with a broad black margin; the scales and interstitial skin on each side of the anterior eighteen or twenty scuta white or buff. appearing on the lower surface of the hood as two short parallel bands. The rest of the abdominal surface paler black than above, strongly iridescent, in certain lights pale silvery. Iris black, with the orbital margin pale grey; tongue light flesh-coloured.

Scuta, 184 to 187; scutella, 49 to 52.

HAB.—*Pinang, Singapore.*

At Pinang the preceding variety prevails, at Singapore the present. Both are local, and they appear respectively to congregate on single spots of limited extent. Another black variety (*Naja atra*, Cantor), which inhabits Chusan, differs from the present in having a number of distant transversal double lines of a yellow colour. Beneath, it is slate or pearl coloured.

The food of *Naja lutescens* consists of rats, small birds (it occasionally ascends trees), lizards, and fishes, in search of which latter it frequently takes the water, and even the sea, along the coasts. The largest individual of the two Malayan varieties was of the following dimensions :—

Length of the head	.	.	.	o feet	$1\frac{7}{8}$ inch.
,, ,,	trunk	.	.	. 4 ,,	1 ,,
,, ,,	tail	.	.	. o ,,	9 inches.
				4 ,,	$11\frac{7}{8}$,,

Circumference of the neck $2\frac{7}{8}$, of the trunk $4\frac{5}{8}$, of the root of the tail $2\frac{3}{8}$ inches.

The following memorandum relative to the venom of *Naja*

lutescens, Laurenti, has kindly been communicated by J. W. Laidlay, Esq., joint-secretary, Asiatic Society :—

" The venom was carefully obtained, so as to avoid any admixture of saliva, by compressing the venomous glands. It issued from the lower aperture of the fangs in viscid drops of a syrupy consistency, and was received as it fell from the fangs in platina capsules. The serpents operated upon were an adult *Cobra di Capello* (*Naja lutescens*), Laurenti, and one of its varieties (*Naja kaouthia,* apud Belanger), and were supplied by the kindness of J. W. Grant, Esq., C.S.

" In every instance the venom readily changed the blue of litmus to red, and restored the bright yellow to turmeric paper that had been reddened by the application of caustic alkali; an unequivocal proof of acidity. When left to spontaneous evaporation, it dried into a varnish resembling mucilage or the glair of an egg, cracking in all directions ; and on being heated it deposited an abundant coagulum, apparently albuminous. In either instance when redissolved it retained its acid property.

" What the nature of this acid may be it was impossible to determine from the small quantity operated upon ; nor am I prepared to say that the poison *itself* is an acid, although if it be not so, it is certainly associated with one. Most probably, from the rapid and spontaneous disappearance of its properties by keeping, the poison itself consists of some exceedingly unstable compound, which would be wholly disorganized under any attempt at isolation by chemical means."

SUB-FAM. VIPERINÆ, BONAPARTE.

Gen. TRIGONOCEPHALUS, *Oppel.*

Head broad, triangular, scaly, with a pit before the eyes ; trunk robust, cylindrical ; tail short, tapering to a point, with scutella beneath.

TRIGONOCEPHALUS GRAMINEUS, Shaw.

SYN.—Russell, i. pl. ix. Bodroo Pam ; ii. pl. xx.
Coluber gramineus, Shaw.
Vipera viridis, Daudin.
Trimeresurus viridis, Lacépède.
Cophias viridis, Merrem.
Coluber gramineus, apud Raffles : Tr. Linn Soc. xiii.
Bodroo Pam, Russell apud Davy : Ceylon, &c.
Bothrops, Wagler.
Trigonocephalus viridis, Schlegel.
Trigonocephalus erythrurus, Cantor (young).
" Ular daun " of the Malays.

Grass-green above, lighter on the sides, frequently interrupted by zig-zag lines, produced by the black interstitial skin; the tail in some bright cinnamon-red; from the sides of the neck along the lowest series of scales a pale yellow line. Lips, throat, and abdominal surface greenish-yellow; scutella in some spotted with cinnamon-colour. Iris golden, dotted with brown, but leaving a narrow margin bordering the elliptical black pupil, which is vertically contracted by the light. Tongue pale bluish, with black apex. Scuta, 165 to 170; scutella, 58 to 71.

HAB.—*Pinang, Singapore, Malayan Peninsula.*
New Holland,[*] Timor, Pulo Samao, Celebes, Eastern Java, Banka, Sumatra, Tenasserim, Bengal, Chirra Púnji, Nipal,[†] Coromandel, Ceylon.

Var.

SYN.—Coluber gramineus, var. apud Raffles, *l.c.*

Differs from the preceding by its Indian or brick-red line on each side.

HAB.—*Pinang, Singapore, Malayan Peninsula.*
Sumatra, Tenasserim.

In the Malayan hills and valleys the variety is by far the more numerous; it is indeed the most common of the venomous serpents. In Bengal I never observed but a single young one (*T. erythrurus*), captured in the Sunderbuns. It is generally observed on trees, hanging down from the branches or concealed under the dense foliage; it preys on small birds and tree-frogs *Polypedates leucomystax*, Gravenhorst; but occasionally it descends to the ground in search of frogs and toads. The neck is covered by twenty-seven, the trunk by twenty-three or twenty-five ovate imbricate keeled scales. The tail is prehensile.

Of the number examined none exceeded the following dimensions :—

Length of the head . . . 0 feet $1\frac{4}{8}$ inch.
„ „ trunk . . . 2 „ 0 „
„ „ tail . . . . 0 „ $5\frac{6}{8}$ inches.
————
2 „ $7\frac{2}{8}$ „

Circumference of the neck $1\frac{4}{8}$, of the trunk $2\frac{2}{8}$, of the root of the tail 1 inch.

---

[*] Lacépède, on the authority of M. Baudin.
[†] Specimen in Mr. Hodgson's collection.

TRIGONOCEPHALUS SUMATRANUS, Raffles,* var.

SYN.—" 'Ular kápak" of the Malays of the Peninsula.

Young.—Grass-green above, lighter on the sides and lips ; from the pit beneath the eye, over the cheek, a cinnamon-red line with the upper margin buff ; on each side of the back a series of distant spots, half cinnamon, half buff-coloured, each of the two or three scales composing the spots being of these two colours ; on the tail the spots are confluent, forming transversal lines. Beneath light yellowish-green. The largest individual in this garb measured 1 foot 3⅝ inches in length.

Adult.—Ground colour above, light yellow or pale greenish-yellow, largely mixed with intense dull black, so as to make the general appearance black, through which the ground colour appears on the head as irregular spots, and a continued line, beneath which a black line proceeds from the eye to the occiput ; on the trunk and tail as narrow, distant, transversal bands, continued or broken up into spots. Labials, gulars, the lowest two or three lateral series of scales, and scuta, gamboge with black margins ; scutella largely spotted with black. Iris golden dotted with black, and with a black transversal bar ; pupil elliptical, vertically contracted by the light ; tongue bluish-grey.

Scuta, 141 to 147 ; scutella, 42 to 52.

HAB.—*Pinang, Singapore, Malayan Peninsula.*

Unfortunately, in the Malayan countries this variety is not of so rare occurrence as the species appears to be in Sumatra. Both are equally dreaded. The natives of Sumatra denominate it "Púchuk," a young, green shoot of a tree, a name expressive both of its colour and arboreal habits. The Malays of the Peninsula, who only know the black variety, call it, from its broad cordate head, the " hatchet-shaped " serpent ; " Kápak," or " Kápah," signifying an axe. At Pinang it generally occupies the lower parts of the hills or the valleys, either on the ground or on trees ; but Dr. Montgomerie in one instance observed it at on elevation of 2,200 feet. It preys upon rats, small birds, tree-frogs, and toads. The neck is covered by twenty-seven, the trunk by twenty-three to twenty-five longitudinal series of ovate, imbricate keeled scales. The labials and the gular scales are sharply keeled, but the keels of the former become obliterated with age. The tail is prehensile.

Of nine examined, the largest individual was of the following dimensions :—

* SYN.—Seba, ii. t. lxviii. fig. 4 ; *Coluber sumatranus*, Raffles, Ular Poochook ; *Cophias Wagleri*, H. Boie ; *Tropidolæmus*, Wagler ; *Trigonocephalus Wagleri*, Schlegel.
HAB.—Sumatra.

Length of the head . . . . . 0 foot 2 inches.
,, ,, trunk . . . . 1 ,, $6\frac{4}{3}$,,
,, ,, tail . . . . . 0 ,, $6\frac{1}{8}$,,

2 feet $2\frac{5}{8}$,,

Circumference of the neck $2\frac{6}{8}$, of the trunk $4\frac{4}{8}$, of the root of the tail $1\frac{6}{8}$ inch.

TRIGONOCEPHALUS PUNICEUS, Reinwardt.

SYN.—Seba, ii. tab. lxiv. fig. 1.
Klein : " Tentamen," p. 10, No. 25.*
Vipera acontia, Laurenti.
Coluber acontia, Gmelin.
Vipera acontias, Daudin.
Echidna acontia, Merrem.
Trigonocephalus puniceus, Reinwardt.
Atropos, Wagler.
Trigonocephalus purpureomaculatus, Gray : " Ill. Ind. Zool."
Trigonocephalus puniceus, Schlegel.

Dull reddish-brown or olive tinged with purple ; in some an indistinct black line from the eye to the sides of the neck ; the scales dotted or finely marbled with black, their keels pale ochre ; the posterior part of the trunk and tail with irregular dark brown spots ; the interstitial skin reddish-brown, lighter or darker than the scales ; lips, throat, the three or four lowest series of scales, and beneath, pale greenish-yellow ; scuta and scutella with brown margins, the latter largely spotted with brown. Iris greenish-golden marbled with black ; pupil elliptical, vertically contracted by the light ; tongue light brownish-grey.

Scuta, 162 to 171 ; scutella, 65 to 70.

HAB.—*Pinang, Malayan Peninsula.*
Singapore, Java.

The Malayan individuals differ slightly from the Javanese in having very few dark spots and no reddish line above the black one on the sides of the head. The oval gular scales have a tubercular appearance. The integuments of the head and body are remarkably lax, like those of *Acrochordus javanicus.* The neck is covered by thirty-one, the trunk by twenty-seven longitudinal series of ovate or conical scales ; they are not imbricate, but are frequently surrounded by the naked skin. The tail is prehensile, but less so than in the preceding species. The Malayan individuals appear to be less numerous than the Javanese.

* As several serpents have by Klein been indicated under the name of *Acontias,* the specific name of Reinwardt has been substituted.

The four observed were all found on the ground in valleys. The largest, which had been feeding on a rat, was of the following dimensions :—

Length of the head	. . . .	0 feet	$1\frac{3}{8}$ inch.
„ „ trunk	. . . .	2 „	$5\frac{3}{4}$ inches.
„ „ tail .	. . . .	0 „	$5\frac{1}{8}$ „
		3 „	$0\frac{3}{8}$

Circumference of the neck 2, of the trunk $3\frac{4}{3}$, of the root of the tail $1\frac{2}{3}$ inch.

In general sluggish, but when roused, ferocious habits, the preceding three species resemble the genus *Bungarus ;* their mode of attack is also similar : like *Vipera Russellii* (Shaw),[*] when it prepares to dart they vibrate the prehensile tail and utter a faint hissing sound. As the pupil is vertically contracted by the light, they frequently miss their aim, and like *Bungarus, Naja, Vipera Russellii,* and *Hydrus,* in the extreme of fury they will fix the fangs in their own bodies. Although they are averse to motion, they are not of quite so stationary habits as represented by M. Schlegel (Essay, "Partie Déscriptive," p. 520). In the jungle I have noticed them moving between the branches of trees or on the ground, either in search of prey, or after heavy rains have flooded their hiding-places. In Bengal most terrestrial serpents keep the latter during the hot season, but the rains send them abroad in search of dry localities. Although the present genus has venomous organs as highly developed as *Crotalus* or *Vipera,* the effects produced by wounds, of two species at least, appear to be less dangerous than might *à priori* be supposed. According to Russell's experiments with the venom of *Trigonocephalus gramineus,* chickens expired within eight to thirty-three minutes, pigeons in fourteen to eighteen minutes. A pig recovered in six or seven hours, a dog in two to three hours, after having been wounded (Russell, i. p. 60). Mr. Hodgson has seen a man who was wounded by this species, the only venomous known to inhabit Nepal, fearfully suffering from pain and swelling, but he never heard of a fatal case (" Transactions Zoological Society, London," vol. ii. p. 309).

A male *Trigonocephalus puniceus* successively wounded two fowls, one in the chest, the other in the left thigh. In both cases the fangs of both sides acted, but neither of the birds experienced any other effect except a slight pain, which lasted a few minutes after they had been wounded. It should, however, be observed that the serpent at the time had gorged itself with food, in which state it was observed close to the General Hospital, in the valley

[*] Syn.—Russell, i. pl. vii. ; *Katuka Rekula Poda,* ii. pl. xxxii. ; *Coluber Russellii,* Shaw ; *Vipera elegans,* Daudin.

of Pinang. Another individual was subsequently caused to wound a fowl on the inside of the thigh. The bird immediately drew up the wounded leg, fell down, and was purged three minutes after being wounded. In three minutes more slight spasms of the head and neck appeared at short intervals, but they ceased in five minutes, when the fowl made at first some unsuccessful attempts to rise. Twenty-one minutes after having been wounded the bird rose, shook the wings, and had perfectly recovered. The same serpent subsequently was made to wound another fowl on the inside of the left thigh. The bird drew up the wounded leg and was slightly purged, but showed no other inconvenience from the wound.

The following experiment is communicated by Dr. Montgomerie. An adult *Trigonocephalus sumatranus*, var., was made to bite a fowl in the fleshy part of the thigh. The bird limped about for a short time, and a minute after it was wounded commenced purging. At the end of two minutes it fell, breathing laboriously, and was strongly convulsed. At the end of six minutes a few drops of water exuded from the eyes; in fifteen seconds more it was quite dead : six minutes and a quarter after it had been wounded. Both fangs had acted; the wound was livid, and similar lines were observed in the course of the absorbents. On another occasion, after some unsuccessful attempts to make another individual bite a fowl, a terrier accidentally was wounded in the fleshy part of the fore-arm. The serpent fixed the fangs for an instant in the flesh; the dog, pitifully screaming, jumped, and shook it off. A ligature was immediately applied above the elbow, and the dog secured in a cage. It continued for some time whining from pain, probably aggravated by the tight ligature, which was removed at the close of half an hour, and the dog let free. In a short time it had regained the free use of the limb and was apparently well ; but on the third day following a perfectly circular slough, including the bitten spot, of about ¾ of an inch in diameter, was thrown off; the sore readily healed up, and the dog suffered no further inconvenience.

PELAGIC.

FAM. HYDRIDÆ, BONAPARTE.

Gen. LATICAUDA, *Laurenti.*

Tail compressed, with two surfaces, gradually increasing in height, and with three furrows (sutures) on each side.

LATICAUDA SCUTATA, Laurenti.

SYN.—Coluber laticaudatus, Linné, Mus. A. fig. 1754.
Laticauda imbricata Laurenti ? 1768.

Le serpent large-queue, Daubenton, 1784.
Coluber laticaudatus, apud Thunberg, 1787.
Coluber laticaudatus, apud Gmelin and E. W. Gray, 1789.
La queue plate, Lacépède, 1801.
Hydrus colubrinus, Schneider, 1801.
Platurus fasciatus, Latreille, 1802.
Hydrus colubrinus, apud Shaw, 1802.
Platurus fasciatus, Daudin, 1803.
Aipysurus lævis, Lacépède, 1804 (var. ?).
Platurus semifasciatus, Reinwardt, MS.
Platurus fasciatus, apud Wagler, 1830.
Hydrophis colubrina, Temminck and Schlegel, " Fauna Japonica," tab. x.
Hydrophis colubrina, Schlegel, 1837.

New-born.—Ground colour gamboge, greenish above, with numerous distant broad rings of a blue reflecting black colour encircling the body ; the first and second black mark of the head and neck are beneath joined by a short longitudinal line, commencing on the lower labial shields ; another shorter black line borders above the gamboge upper labials ; the scales between the rings, the scuta and scutella, with blackish margins.

Older.—Of paler colours, lead-grey on the back ; the rings impure, light blue on the sides and abdomen. The scales and scuta without blackish margins. Iris black, pupil circular ; tongue grey.

Scuta, 227 to 246; scutella, 32 to 41.

HAB.—*Sea of the Malayan Peninsula and Islands.*

Bay of Bengal (Ramree, Pondicherry, Nicobars), Sea of Timor, Molucca and Liewkiew Islands, Celebes, New Guinea, Tongataboo, China Sea.

This species is readily identified by the abdominal scuta and the scutellated very broad tail. The anterior frontals are separated by a small elongated pentagonal or rhombic shield, bordered behind by the vertical, which is proportionally the largest shield, either equalling or exceeding each of the occipitals. The eyes are comparatively large and prominent, surrounded by two postorbitals, one preorbital, and beneath by the third and fourth of the seven large upper labials. The lower jaw is covered in front by the rostral and the two first labials ; the succeeding seven are elongated linear, and placed horizontally so as to be hid by the upper labials, when the mouth is closed. The chin is covered by two pairs of pentagonal shields, between which and the labials appear two or three series of elongated scales. The neck is covered by twenty-five, the anterior part of the trunk by twenty-three, increasing to twenty-five, and again decreasing to nineteen longitudinal series of large smooth scales. The nostrils are small, opening laterally. The tail, though much compressed, presents a broad flat surface beneath, till near the apex, where it becomes two-edged. The largest individual examined was of the following dimensions :—

Length of the head	. . . .	o feet	1	inch.
„ „ trunk	. . . .	3 „	2	inches.
„ „ tail	. . . . .	o „	$5\frac{3}{8}$	„

$$3 \text{ „ } 8\frac{3}{8} \text{ „}$$

Circumference of the neck $1\frac{7}{8}$, greatest do. of the trunk 4 inches.

Gen. HYDRUS, *Schneider.*

Body slender in front, gradually thickening, covered with scales ; tail compressed, two-edged.

HYDRUS STRIATUS, Lacépède.

SYN.*—Leioselasma striata, Lacépède, 1804.
Hydrophis striata, Temminck and Schlegel: " Fauna Japon." pl. vii.
Hydrophis striata, Schlegel : Essay, 1837.
Hydrophis striata, Schlegel apud Cantor, " Tr. Zool. Soc. Lon." vol. ii.

Adult ?—Crown shields light chestnut; lips and throat pale yellow ; ground colour above, pale greenish-yellow, sides and abdomen buff with numerous distant black transversal bands, becoming indistinct towards the tail and on the sides, where the scales are partially edged or spotted with black. The interstitial skin of the back and sides black, of the abdomen buff. Iris dark grey, with a buff orbital margin ; pupil black, minute ; tongue buff.

Central abdominal series of larger scales, 347 + 41.

HAB.—*Sea of Pinang and Malayan Peninsula.*
Sea of Liewkiew Islands, Timor, Sumatra, Bay of Bengal.

* DOUBTFUL SYNONYMY.—Russell, ii. pl. ix, *Chittul,* 1801, agrees with this species in the following characters : the eyes high, small, orbicular ; the trunk round till near the anus, where it becomes compressed ; the scales smooth, imbricate, orbicular on the sides ; the central abdominal series much larger than in any of the other species (Russell). The difference of colours is unimportant, as it is liable to variations, not only individually, but according to age. Besides, all the species acquire a light bluish appearance about the period when the integuments are to be changed. Russell's description was copied by Daudin, who merely supplied the denomination of *Hydrophis cyanocinctus* (*Hydrus Brugmansii,* Boie, 1827), upon which Wagler founded his genus *Enhydris,* 1830. According to M. Schlegel, all these are synonymes of *Hydrus nigrocinctus,* Daudin. The only means of deciding the synonymy of this and most of the other species appears to be a close examination of such original specimens, described by Russell and Shaw, which may at present exist in the collection of the British Museum.

The eyes are lateral, sunk, excessively small, of a diameter equalling the large, almost vertically opening nostrils. The single preorbital shield is beneath wedged in between the second and third upper labial. The latter, as well as the fourth and fifth, border the orbit beneath. Of the two postorbitals the lower is wedged in between the fifth upper labial and the large shield resting upon the sixth upper labial. Above the latter and the seventh the cheeks are covered by three very large shields. The seven upper labials are large and very high. ˙ Of the nine inferior labials the two anterior are the largest, and placed vertically; the succeeding seven are smaller, and placed nearly horizontally, so as to become partially hid when the jaws are closed. The chin is covered by the first pair of labials and two pairs of elongated mentals, between which and the inferior labials intervene on each side the second labial, three very large shields and three smaller. The neck is covered by thirty-seven, the anterior part of the trunk by thirty-three, and the thickest by forty longitudinal series of rhombic scales. In the individuals examined by M. Schlegel, all of less length than my own, the series varied from thirty-one, twenty-nine, to twenty-seven. The scales are rhombic with rounded apex, each scale with a small central tubercle, or an elevated (keeled) line, which, however, with age becomes indistinct or obliterated. The central larger abdominal scales are hexagonal, with or without a small tubercle on each side. The anus is covered by three or four excessively large scales. The larger individual of two was of the following dimensions :—

Length of the head	. . . .	0	feet	$1\frac{5}{8}$	inch.
„ „ trunk	. . . .	5	„	$6\frac{3}{8}$	inches.
„ „ tail	. . . . .	0	„	$4\frac{6}{8}$	„
		6	„	$0\frac{6}{8}$	inch.

Circumference of the neck $3\frac{3}{8}$, greatest do. of the trunk $4\frac{2}{8}$ inches.

HYDRUS NIGROCINCTUS, Daudin.

SYN.*—Russell, ii. pl. vi. Kerril Pattee, 1801.
  Hydrophis nigrocinctus, Daudin, 1803.
  Hydrophis melanurus, Wagler, 1828.
  Polyodontes annulatus, Lesson, 1833.
  Hydrophis nigrocincta, Schlegel, 1837.
  Hydrophis nigrocincta, Schlegel apud Cantor, *l.c.*

New-born.—Ground colour buff or bluish-white; upper lips and muzzle black, and a transversal band across the hind-head, from whence proceeds a triangular or cross mark towards the vertex;

* DOUBTFUL SYN.—Russell, ii. pl. xiii. *Kaddell Nagam,* 1801 (*Enhydris gracilis,* Merrem, 1820); *Hydrus spiralis,* Shaw, 1802.

gular and inferior labial shields edged and spotted with black; trunk and tail with numerous black transversal bands, either encircling the body or interrupted on the abdominal ridge, where appear a few indistinct black spots; apex of the tail black. Entire length, $8\frac{4}{8}$ inches.

Older.—Greyish-green olive above, yellowish on the sides, buff beneath; the bands less intense black, often placed obliquely so as to join each other on the back. Iris grey; pupil circular, black; tongue buff. Central abdominal series of larger scales, $281 + 41$; $284 + 43$; $289 + 39$.

HAB.—*Sea of Malayan Peninsula, Pinang, Singapore.*
Estuaries of the Ganges, Bay of Bengal.

This species greatly resembles *H. striatus*, from which it differs in the more compressed general form; the eye, though small, is of a larger diameter than the nostril, and it is surrounded by a single postorbital shield, which beneath is wedged in between the fourth and fifth upper labial, and the preorbital between the second and third. The orbit is bordered beneath almost entirely by the fourth upper labial. The sixth upper labial is the largest, in some individuals covering the cheek and bordering above the occipital. Of the seven or eight inferior labials, the four anterior are very large; above the third there is one or two small triangular shields; the other three or four posterior labials are very small, elongated. There is no horizontal series of labials as in *H. striatus,* and the two elongated pairs of mentals immediately border the labials. The neck is covered by thirty-three, the thickest part of the trunk by fifty-three longitudinal series of scales. Those examined by M. Schlegel, the length of which exceeds those come under my own observation, had twenty-seven, twenty-nine, to thirty-one series of scales. Those of the anterior part of the back are rhomboidal, those of the posterior part rhombic with rounded apex, and slightly imbricate; those of the sides hexagonal; all have either a sharply raised keel or a central tubercle, both of which frequently become obliterated. The central series of abdominal scales are a little larger than the rest, frequently divided in two hexagonal, and with a small tubercle on each side, which often becomes indistinct or obliterated. The anus is covered by three or four very large, or by a series of small scales. The largest of six individuals was of the following dimensions :—

Length of the head	.	.	.	.	0 feet	$0\frac{6}{8}$ inch.
,,	,,	trunk	.	.	2 ,,	$0\frac{2}{8}$,,
,,	,,	tail	.	.	0 ,,	$2\frac{6}{8}$ inches.

$$2 \text{ ,, } 3\frac{6}{8} \text{ ,,}$$

Circumference of the neck $\frac{6}{8}$, greatest do. of the trunk 2 inches.

Var. ?

Crown shields olive green with a blackish band from the eyes over the anterior part of the upper lip ; the posterior part and the lower lip pale yellow; ground colour of the trunk greenish lead-grey above, pale yellow on the sides, beneath buff, with numerous black transversal bands. Iris amber-coloured, with the orbital margin dark grey. Central abdominal series of scales, 235 + 38.

It differs from the preceding in the following particulars :—The head is proportionally shorter, broader, triangular, the muzzle more pointed, and the upper surface from the vertical shield very declivous. The eyes are much larger than the nostrils, with a single pre- and post-orbital, but bordered beneath by the third and fourth upper labial. The latter, six in number, present nothing abnormal. The lower labials are also six, proportionally larger than in the preceding. The mouth is smaller. The make of the trunk is more robust ; the neck is covered by fifteen, the thickest part of the body by twenty-one longitudinal series of proportionally much broader hexagonal scales, tuberculated on the anterior part of the trunk, on the rest keeled, forming series of sharp, continued ridges. The central abdominal series is at first somewhat larger than the rest, angular, with a small more or less distinct tubercle on each side. A single individual, captured in a fishing stake off Pinang, was of the following dimensions :—

Length of the head	.	.	.	.	o foot $0\frac{6}{8}$ inch.	
„	„	trunk	.	.	. . 1 „	$6\frac{2}{8}$ inches.
„	„	tail	.	.	. . o „	$2\frac{4}{8}$ „

$$1 \text{ „ } 9\frac{4}{8} \text{ „}$$

Circumference of the neck $1\frac{3}{8}$, greatest do. of the trunk $2\frac{1}{8}$ inches.

HYDRUS GRACILIS, Shaw.

Syn.*—Russell, i. pl. xliv. Tatta Pam, 1796 (very young).
    Hydrus fasciatus, apud Shaw (Russell, i. xliv., excluding the other syn.), 1802.
    Angvis mamillaris, Daudin, 1803.
    Hydrus, apud Wagler, 1830.
    Russell, ii. pl. vii. Shootur Sun, 1801.
    Hydrus chloris, Daudin, 1803.
    Hydrophis, apud Wagler, 1830.
    Russell, ii. pl. viii. Kalla Shootur Sun, 1801.
    Hydrophis obscurus, Daudin, 1803.
    Hydrophis, apud Wagler, 1830.

* Doubtful Syn.—*Angvis laticauda*, Linné, Mus. A. F. 1754 ; *Vosmaer, Monogr.*, fig. 2, 1774 ; *Hydrus fasciatus*, Schneider, 1801.

Hydrus fasciatus, apud Guérin: "Iconog. Rept." pl. xxv. 1, 1829.

Pelamis chloris, Merrem apud Horsfield: "Life of Raffles," 1830.

Microcephalus gracilis, Lesson, 1833.

Hydrophis gracilis, Schlegel (syn. Angvis xiphura, Hermann, Typhlops, Merr. Tent. p. 158), 1837.

Hydrophis gracilis, Schlegel apud Cantor, *l.c.*, pl. lvi. (young).

New-born.— Head shining, intense black ; ground colour of the trunk and tail bright gamboge, on the back and sides interrupted by numerous black rings, which above are widened into lozenge shape, narrowed on the sides.   Throat and anterior half of abdomen intense black, continued as a more or less distinct line to the black apex of the tail.   On the sides the yellow ground colour appears in the shape of oval spots, gradually increasing in depth towards the tail.   Entire length, 1 foot 3 inches.

Adult ?—Head and back uniformly dark olive or brown, becoming greyish on the posterior half, and very indistinct or obliterated on the sides.   In some a pale yellow spot on each side of the hind-head, and a third on the frontal shields.   The lateral oval spots pale sulphur-coloured on the anterior half, pale greenish-yellow on the posterior.   The black of the lower surface very pale but distinct.   Iris black ; tongue buff.

Central abdominal series of larger scales, 454 + 60.

HAB.—*Sea of Malayan Peninsula and Islands.*
Bay of Bengal, Malabar, Sumatra, Borneo.

In form and number the shields of the head resemble those of *Hydrus nigrocinctus,* so as to afford no distinguishing character. Yet it may be readily distinguished from that and other species by the excessive slenderness of the anterior, cylindrical part of the trunk, which from thence becomes much compressed, gradually increasing in bulk and vertical diameter till towards the tail, where the diameter again decreases.   The scales of the cylindrical anterior part of the trunk are rhomboidal with rounded points and slightly imbricate ; the rest are hexagonal.   The central abdominal series continued beneath the tail consists of hexagonal scales, a little larger than the rest, and frequently longitudinally divided. In the very young all the scales are smooth ; with age the central abdominal ones acquire a small tubercle on each side, and those of the compressed sides and of the back each a central tubercle. In the largest individuals the central abdominal scales have three longitudinally placed minute tubercles on each side, and the rest of the hexagonal scales three or four similar central tubercles.   In the new-born the neck is covered by thirty-two, the bulkiest part of the body by forty-nine longitudinal series; these parts are covered by twenty-six and forty-four series in the largest individual, which is of the following dimensions:—

Length of the head	.	.	.	.	o feet	o⅝ inch.
„	„	trunk	.	.	. 3 „	2⅝ inches.
„	„	tail	.	.	. o „	4 „

$$3 \text{ „ } 7\tfrac{2}{8} \text{ „}$$

Circumference of the neck 1⅔, of greatest do. of the trunk 3⅝ inches.

HYDRUS SCHISTOSUS, Daudin.

SYN.*—Russell, ii. pl. x. Hooglí Pattee, 1801.
Russell ii. pl. xi. Valakadyen, 1801.
Hydrophis schistosus, Daudin, 1803.
Hydrus Valakadyen, H. Boie, 1827.
Disteira Russelli, Fitzinger, 1827.
Hydrophis, apud Wagler, 1830.
Leioselasma schistosa, Fitzinger, 1827.
Hydrus, apud Wagler, 1830.
Hydrophis schistosa, Schlegel, 1837.
Hydrophis schistosa, Schlegel, apud Cantor, *l.c.*

New-born.—Head above, blackish or dark brown; back and sides with numerous transversal blackish bands, broad above, narrow on the sides; lips, throat, sides, and abdomen buff; tail blackish, with a few transversal buff bands above. Entire length, 10⅝ inches.

Adult ?—Head above and back either uniformly pale greenish-grey, or with darker transversal bands, becoming more or less indistinct on the sides; lips, throat, sides brownish-white or buff; tail uniformly blackish, or greyish olive-green. Iris pale amber or greenish-yellow, with a grey orbital margin; pupil black; tongue buff.

Central abdominal series : 239 + 47; 242 + 42; 312 + 58.

HAB.—*Sea of Malayan Peninsula and Islands.*
Bay of Bengal, Malabar, Sumatra.

The head is elongated conical, the muzzle sloping, and the rostral shield beneath terminating in a vertically projecting point, which fits into a corresponding cavity in the lower jaw. The anterior elongated triangular frontal shields are next to the occipitals the largest; the large oval nostrils send a slit towards the external margin of the shield. The eyes are lateral, moderate,

* DOUBTFUL SYN.—*Hydrus major*, Shaw, 1802; *Disteira doliata*, Lacépède, 1804.

surrounded by a preorbital, a postorbital, frequently cut in two smaller, and beneath by the fourth upper labial shield. Behind the latter the lip is covered by three or four horizontally placed small shields, above which appear three large vertically placed shields, of which the last borders the sides of the occipital pair. The lower rostral is remarkably elongated, linear, and hid in a furrow between the first pair of inferior labials. Of the latter the anterior five on each side are much elongated, followed by five or six smaller. The chin is covered with numerous minute scales, and, like the rest of the body, with very lax skin. In the young ones the neck is covered by forty-seven, the bulkiest part of the body by fifty-seven longitudinal series of smooth, somewhat tubercular scales. Older individuals have these parts covered by forty-eight and sixty series of hexagonal scales, either with a short keel dividing the anterior half, or a central tubercle. The central slightly raised abdominal series commences very far back, from one to three inches behind the chin. The anterior scales are wedge-shaped hexagonal, the posterior are broader but slightly larger than the rest, with a small elongated tubercle on each side. The largest individual of a great number was of the following dimensions :—

Length of the head . . . . o feet 1 inch.

,, ,, trunk . . . . 3 ,, $1\frac{4}{8}$,,

,, ,, tail . . . . . o ,, $4\frac{4}{8}$ inches.

3 ,, 7 ,,

Circumference of the neck $2\frac{3}{8}$, greatest do. of the trunk 5 inches.

HYDRUS PELAMIDOIDES, Schlegel.

SYN.*—Pelamis carinata, Cuvier, MS.
Hydrophis (Disteira doliata, Lacép.), Wagler, 1830.
Lapemis Hardwickii, Gray : " Ill. Ind. Zool.," 1832.
Hydrophis pelamidoides, Schlegel, 1837.
Hydrophis pelamidoides, Temminck and Schlegel : "Fauna Japon.," tab. ix.
Hydrophis pelamidoides, Schlegel apud Cantor, *l.c.*

Young.—Sulphur-coloured, paler on the sides and abdomen ; the head largely spotted with blackish, through which the ground colour appears in the form of a rectangle, the two sides of which pass from the hind-head to the orbit, the anterior across the frontals, the posterior over the hind-head ; two yellow spots between the nostrils ; lips yellow, cheeks and throat blackish ; on the back a number of transversal blackish bands to the middle of

* DOUBTFUL SYN.—Russell, ii. pl. xii. Shiddil, 1801 ; *Hydrus curtus,* Shaw, 1802.

the sides, broader than the intervening yellow lines; tail black. Entire length, 10⅓ inches.

Adult?—Head uniformly reddish-brown above; ground colour greenish-yellow, lighter on the sides and beneath, with broad lozenge-shaped transversal bands of a blackish olive, continued on the anterior half of the tail; posterior half blackish. Iris dark olive; pupil black; tongue buff.

HAB.—*Sea of Malayan Peninsula and Islands.*

> Bay of Bengal, Sea of Celebes, Molucca Islands, China Sea.

The head is much depressed, not broader than the neck; the muzzle broad, rounded; the rostral shield is large, rectangular pentagonal, broader that high, the lower margin with a central point and a notch on each side. The eyes are moderate, lateral, not prominent, surrounded by a preorbital, a postorbital, and beneath by the third and fourth upper labials. The frenal shield, observed by M. Schlegel, was not present in four individuals examined in the Straits of Malacca; its existence therefore appears not to be constant; in all *Hydri* the shields of the head are liable to considerable individual variations of form. Of the eight upper labials the posterior three are very small, which is also the case with the posterior five of the nine inferior labials. The two pairs of elongated mentals are outside bordered by the three first inferior labials; inside, by several small scales. In the young the neck is covered by thirty-seven, the thickest part of the trunk by forty longitudinal series of hexagonal, smooth, comparatively small scales. In the older individual these parts are covered by thirty-two and thirty-seven large hexagonal scales, each with a central tubercle. The lower series of the sides are slightly larger than the rest, and vertically elongated, so as to require a rectangular appearance. The central abdominal series is much smaller than the rest. Each scale is either rhombic, and, as represented in the excellent plates of "Fauna Japonica," hemmed in between four[*] of the two lowest lateral series, or they are absent, and their place is occupied by a pair of the former, which are soldered together. In the young individuals the central series frequently consists of alternate broad triangular and very minute rectangular scales, both kinds smaller than the rest. The largest individual of four was of the following dimensions :—

Length of the head	. . . . .	0 foot	1	inch.
„ „ trunk	. . . . .	1 „	8	inches.
„ „ tail	. . . . .	0 „	2⅛	„
		1 „	11⅛	„

---

[*] A somewhat similar disposition is observed in the central dorsal series of the however differently shaped scales of *Xenodermus javanicus,* Reinhardt.

Circumference of the neck 2⅛, greatest circumference of the trunk 4 inches.

HYDRUS BICOLOR, Schneider.

SYN.—Seba, ii. tab. lxxvii. fig. 1.
Angvis platura,* Linné, 1766.
Vosmaer : " Monogr." fig. 1, 1774.
Angvis platuros, apud Gmelin, 1788.
Russell, i. pl. xli. Nalla Wahlagillee Pam. 1799.
Lacépède, v. tab. xv. fig. 2, 1801.
Hydrus bicolor, Schneider, 1801.
Hydrophis platurus, Latreille, 1802.
Hydrus bicolor, apud Shaw, 1803.
Pelamis bicolor, Daudin, 1802.
Pelamys (Angvis platura, Lin.), Wagler, 1830.
Pelamis bicolor, apud Horsfield : " Life of Raffles," 1830.
Pelamis bicolor, apud Oken, 1836.
Hydrophis pelamis, Schlegel, 1837.
Hydrophis pelamis, Temminck and Schlegel : " Fauna Japonica," p. 60.

Head and back black (inky), forming a straight line on the sides till towards the posterior part, where it becomes largely undulating, so as to appear as broad bands ; lips, throat, and sides sulphur-coloured, turning into yellowish-white or buff on the abdomen † and tail ; posterior parts of the sides with some more or less distinct rounded black spots ; tail largely banded or spotted with black. Iris pale yellow with a broad black orbital margin ; pupil black ; tongue buff.

HAB.—*Sea of Malayan Peninsula.*
Bay of Bengal, Malabar, Sea of Sumatra, Java, Celebes, Molucca Islands, China Sea (to 27° N. lat.), Otaheite, Bay of Port Jackson (33° 55′ S. lat., 151° 25′ E. long.).

The head is very elongated, depressed ; viewed from above, it presents a striking resemblance to *Herpetodryas oxycephalus*, Reinwardt. The eye is larger than in any other species of *Hydrus*, surrounded by two, three, or even four postorbitals, one large preorbital, and beneath, by the fourth upper labial shield. A frenal shield has been observed in some individuals, but it was absent in that examined in the Straits of Malacca, nor does it exist in the specimens in the Museum of the Asiatic Society.

---

* In consequence of the specific name of Linné having been applied by Latreille to a genus (Platurus), that of Schneider, the next different in succession, has been substituted.

† In the individual figured by Russell the bright yellow colour formed a narrow lateral line, below which the sides and abdomen were of a dusky greenish-yellow.

The neck is covered by forty-four, the thickest part of the trunk by fifty-two longitudinal series of small scales. Those of the upper parts are smooth, hexagonal; those of the sides approach the orbicular form, and have in the centre one, two, or three longitudinally placed minute tubercles. Similar tubercles are observed on each side of the scales, forming the central abdominal series, which is composed either of entire hexagonal scales, a little larger than the rest, or they are longitudinally divided into pairs of smaller pentagonal scales, which have the appearance of being divided by an abdominal suture. A single individual, taken in a fishing stake off the coast of Province Wellesley, was of the following dimensions :—

Length of the head . . . . . . o feet $1\frac{5}{8}$ inch.
„ „ trunk . . . . . 2 „ $1\frac{7}{8}$ „
„ „ tail . . . . . o „ $3\frac{6}{8}$ inches.

2 „ $7\frac{2}{8}$ „

Circumference of the neck $2\frac{1}{8}$, greatest circumference of the trunk $3\frac{2}{3}$ inches.

The preceding, comprising all the hitherto known species of Pelagic serpents, were observed chiefly at Pinang among the abundant supply of fishes daily carried to the markets. Of their general habits some account appears in the "Transactions of the Zoological Society, London," vol. ii. p. 303. One of them, *Hydrus schistosus*, is incredibly numerous in the Bay of Bengal, at Pinang and Singapore, far more so than any known terrestrial serpent. The fishing-nets are hardly ever worked but one or more are among the contents. The other six species are of rare occurrence at Pinang and Singapore, as will be perceived from the disproportionally small number of each examined during four years—viz., of *Laticauda scutata*, 3 ; *Hydrus striatus*, 2 ; *nigrocinctus*, 6 ; *gracilis*, 7 ; *pelamidoides*, 4 ; *pelamis*, 1. Of these, *Laticauda scutata* is excessively numerous in Timor, *Hydrus pelamis* in New Guinea, the Molucca Islands, and Otaheite, where the natives use it as an article of food. The remaining species, as far as is known, have been observed nowhere in such overwhelming numbers. Large individuals of every species are very seldom seen ; it is the young individuals which frequent the coasts, and it appears to be questionable if even the largest observed are animals arrived at their full size. The large individuals are very ferocious, the young ones are less so. Fortunately for the fishermen, the light blinds these serpents, which when out of their proper element become very sluggish and soon expire. This accounts for the safety of the class of men whose daily calling brings them in immediate contact with animals the wound of which is fatal. The fishermen in the Straits of Malacca are aware of their danger, and therefore take care to avoid or destroy these reptiles while landing the fishes. The Malays denominate them *Ular laut—i.e.*, serpents of the sea, among which, however, the innocuous *Acrochordus granulatus*, Schneider, is also comprised as an inhabitant of the coasts.

BATRACHIA.

FAM. CÆCILIDÆ, BONAPARTE.

Gen. ICHTHYOPHIS, *Fitzinger*, 1826 (EPICRIUM, *Wagler*, 1828).

Head depressed, elongated; muzzle obtuse; maxillary and palatine teeth slender, pointed, and couched backwards; tongue entire, with velvety surface; eyes distinct, below and a little in front of which a fosset with a minutely tentaculated border; body subfusiform with numerous close circular folds.

ICHTHYOPHIS GLUTINOSUS, Linné, var. ?

Of a uniform sooty brown, paler on the lower surface. Circular folds two hundred and fifty-four, of which eight are caudal.

HAB.—*Singapore.*

The transversal diameter, taken at the occiput, is nearly equal to that of the root of the tail, and but little less than the uniform diameter of the trunk, which is between the twenty-fourth and twenty-fifth part of the entire length. Compared with a specimen of *Ichthyophis glutinosus*, Linné, the present is of a more robust make, the head is shorter, the muzzle blunter, and the transversal distance between the nostrils greater. The apex of the tongue and the arches formed by the teeth are broader, more rounded. The palatal and upper maxillary teeth are blunter and appear less recurved. Those of the lower jaw, the largest, present an appearance as if each was composed of two distinct parts: a lower, which is vertical, broadly triangular, the posterior margin of which supports the upper part, which is curved backwards and with rounded apex. The circular folds of the skin are fewer, more distant, and, with the exception of the three or four anterior ones, complete. They are disposed in a manner similar to that of *Ichthyophis glutinosus.* The crowded imbricate scales appear to be of a somewhat rectangular form, less rounded than in *I. glutinosus*; in both their surface presents a minute network. The fosset of the upper lip is situated in the centre of a small tubercle. The circumference of the fosset is provided with a very short, minute, membranous tube, which, however, after the animal for some years has been preserved in spirits of wine, can scarcely any longer be distinguished.

Length of the head . . . . $0\frac{3}{8}$ inch.
 ,, ,, trunk . . . . . . $10\frac{1}{8}$ inches.
 ,, ,, tail . . . . $0\frac{2}{3}$ inch.

            $10\frac{6}{8}$ inches.

Circumference of the neck 1, of the trunk $1\frac{2}{8}$, of the root of the tail $\frac{6}{8}$ inch.

A single individual was observed by Dr. Montgomerie at Singapore in 1843, in whose garden it was turned up with the earth, from about two feet below the surface, and from whom I received the specimen shortly after it had been killed. Although, as stated, it differs in colours and in other characters from the description given by MM. Duméril and Bibron of *Ichthyophis glutinosus* (*Epicrium glutinosum*, Wagler apud D. and B.), as well as from a specimen $10\frac{2}{8}$ inches in length from Assam, the data appear to me insufficient with certainty to determine whether the present is a distinct species or a variety of *Ichthyophis glutinosus*, Linné.

FAM. RANIDÆ, BONAPARTE.

Gen. RANA, *Linné*.

Skin smooth, hinder extremities very long, formed for leaping; toes palmated; teeth in the upper jaw and in the palate.

RANA LESCHENAULTI, Dum. and Bibr.

A line of minute conical tubercles along the sides of the body and across the throat. Above, uniformly chocolate-coloured; beneath and on the inner side of the extremities white, more or less vermiculated with pale brown. Iris narrow golden, rhomboidal, the two lower sides not joining each other, but leaving a small open space between them. Web of the toes orange with purple spots.

HAB.—*Malayan Peninsula.*
  Pondicherry, Bengal.

The marbled appearance of the upper parts, described by MM. Duméril and Bibron, does not exist during life, but is acquired when the frog is immersed in alcohol. The species is apparently not numerous. Of two the larger was of the following dimensions :—

Length of the head . . . . $0\frac{7}{8}$ inch.
 ,, ,, trunk . . . . $1\frac{6}{8}$,,
 ,, ,, anterior extremity . . $1\frac{4}{8}$,,
 ,, ,, posterior . . . . . $3\frac{6}{8}$ inches.

Rana bengalensis, Gray, " Illustr. Ind. Zool.," is perhaps intended to represent this species.

RANA TIGRINA, Daudin.

SYN.—Rana tigrina, Daudin : "Hist. Nat. Gren." &c., p. 64, pl. xx.
Rana mugiens, Daudin, *l.c.* pl. xxiii.
Rana mugiens, Latreille : "Hist. Rept. F." ii. p. 153, fig. 2.
La grenouille taureau, Cuvier, R. A., l. Ed.
Rana tigrina, Merrem.
Rana limnocharis, Boie, MS.
Rana cancrivora, Boie, MS.
Rana cancrivora, Gravenhorst.
Rana picta, Gravenhorst.
Rana brama, Lesson.
Rana rugulosa, Wiegmann.
Rana vittigera, Wiegmann.
Rana cancrivora, Tschudi.
Rana tigrina, apud Duméril and Bibron.
"Kodók, Kátak, Lancha" of the Malays.

Body and limbs above, golden greyish-olive or brown ; in some with large rounded black spots, and with a yellow line from the muzzle down the back, and a similar broad band from the side of the muzzle to the loins. Beneath and on the inner side of the limbs, white or yellow, with or without black spots. Iris burnished golden, the lower half sometimes black ; pupil elliptical, rhombic.

HAB.—*Malayan Peninsula and Islands.*
Coromandel, Bengal, Assam, Tenasserim, Java, Sumatra, Timor, Philippines, Canton Province.

The species is excessively numerous in valleys and hills after heavy falls of rain, but adult individuals are of comparatively rare occurrence. At night the deep short baying sound denotes its presence. The largest individual measured—

Length of the head . . . . $1\frac{4}{8}$ inch.
     „   „   trunk. . . . . . . $3\frac{4}{8}$ inches.
     „   „   anterior extremities . . $2\frac{4}{8}$ „
     „   „   posterior . . . . . $7\frac{4}{8}$ „

Gen. MEGALOPHRYS, *Kuhl.*

Head very large, broader than the trunk, depressed ; rostral angle and upper eyelid elongated to a point. Tympanic membrane hidden. Nostrils lateral, below the rostral angle. Mouth enormous ; tongue circular, slightly notched behind. Posterior extremity with a short interdigital membrane.

MEGALOPHRYS MONTANA, Wagler, var.

Above, pale greyish-brown, with a small black triangular tubercle on each shoulder, and a similar in the centre of the sacrum. From the sides of the muzzle a black band edged with white, continued round the orbit and then downwards, obliquely over the dark brown cheeks. Outside of the limbs indistinctly marked with black. On the elbows, knees and heels a large round black spot. Posterior margin of the limbs rose-coloured. Fingers and toes yellowish-white with transverse black bands. Palms and soles black. Throat and chest sooty with a large white blotch on each side of the latter. Abdomen and inner side of the limbs sooty, vermiculated and spotted with white. Iris rich golden brown, with minute black network. Pupil vertically rhomboidal.

HAB.—*Pinang.*

Wagler's short description of *M. montana* is drawn up from a preserved specimen, which apparently is also the case with that communicated in " Erpétologie Générale." From the latter the present animal differs both in colours and in the following particulars. The muzzle forms a pointed lobe resembling the upper eyelids, but smaller. The nostrils are transversely oval, protected by a membranous valve fixed to their lower margin. The upper eyelids are perfectly smooth. The nearly vertical cheeks are above bordered by an angular ridge terminating near the shoulder ; behind by a short curved ridge, which at the angle of the mouth forms a small pointed lobe. The back is smooth without transversal folds, but bordered on each side by a sharp whitish ridge commencing at the upper eyelid, converging towards the cloacal orifice. On the shoulder, near the triangular tubercle, the ridge is enclosed between two short black lines.

Two males were at different times captured on the Pentland Hills, at an elevation of about 1,800 feet. One was found in a dark room, where it was observed remaining motionless during several successive days. Its forms and colours caused it at first to be mistaken for a withered leaf. The second was taken on a tree. The iris is vertically contracted by exposure to the light. The male has no vocal sacs. The larger was of the following dimensions :—

Length of the head . . . . $0\frac{7}{8}$ inch.
  „   „   trunk . . . . $1\frac{7}{8}$ „
  „   „   anterior extremities . . 2 inches.
  „   „   posterior . . . . . $3\frac{2}{8}$ „

FAM. HYLIDÆ.

Gen. LIMNODYTES,* *Duméril and Bibron.*

Tongue long, narrowed in front, widened, forked, free behind; teeth on the vomer forming two groups, between the internal openings of the nostrils; tympanum distinct; Eustachian tubes middling; four fingers free; toes completely or partially webbed; subdigital disks slightly dilated; process of the first os cuneiforme blunt, very minute; males with vocal sacs; sacral transversal processes not dilated.

LIMNODYTES ERYTHRÆUS, Schlegel.

SYN.—Hyla erythræa, Schlegel.
     Hylarana erythræa Tschudi.
     Limnodytes erythræus, Duméril and Bibron.

Back and sides brown or reddish-olive; a longitudinal silvery-white band from the eye to the loin; a second similar from the nostrils, parallel with the former. Beneath, silvery-white. The inner side of the extremities spotted and lineated with brown. Iris golden brown; pupil vertically rhomboidal.

HAB.—*Malayan Peninsula.*
     Java, Arracan.

Of three individuals observed, the largest was of the following dimensions:—

Length of the head.	$0\frac{7}{8}$ inch.
„ „ trunk	$1\frac{6}{8}$ „
„ „ anterior extremities . .	$1\frac{6}{8}$ „
„ „ posterior	$4\frac{2}{8}$ inches.

Gen. POLYPEDATES, *Tschudi apud Duméril and Bibron.*

Terminal joints of the fingers and toes widened into a large disk; fingers slightly webbed at their base; Eustachian tubes large; in other particulars resembling *Limnodytes.*

POLYPEDATES LEUCOMYSTAX, Gravenhorst.

SYN.—Hyla maculata, Gray: "Illust. Ind. Zool."
     Hyla leucomystax, Gravenhorst.
     Polypedates leucomystax, Tschudi apud Dum. and Bibr.

Upper parts changeable; buff, ashy-grey, chocolate-brown, tinged with rose or lilac, minutely or largely spotted with black.

---

* This denomination has with propriety been substituted for the inadmissible *Hyla-Rana,* Tschudi.

Upper lips white. A blackish band occupying the sides of the head, from the muzzle to tympanum. Beneath, whitish or grey, uniformly or minutely dotted with black. Posterior surface of the thighs blackish or vermiculated with white. Iris silvery or buff ; pupil horizontally rhomboidal.

HAB.—*Pinang, Singapore, Malayan Peninsula.*
Malabar and Coromandel Coast, Bengal.

This species has the power of changing its colours as above described. Although it inhabits Singapore and the sultry plains of Bengal, it appears not to occur in the valleys at Pinang, but to affect the hills at an elevation of more than 2,000 feet, with a mean annual temperature of about 71°.

Length of the head . . . . $0\frac{6}{8}$ inch.
„ „ trunk . . . . $1\frac{6}{8}$ „
„ „ anterior extremities . . $1\frac{6}{8}$ „
„ „ posterior . . . . . $4\frac{4}{8}$ inches.

FAM. BUFONIDÆ, FITZINGER.

Gen. BUFO, *Laurenti.*

Body inflated ; skin warty ; parotids porous ; toes united by a rudimentary membrane ; no teeth.

BUFO MELANOSTICTUS, Schneider.

SYN.—Bufo scaber, Daudin.
Bufo bengalensis, Daudin.
Bufo scaber, Latreille.
Bufo scaber, Daudin : " Hist. Rep."
Bufo bengalensis, Daudin : " Hist. Rept."
Le Crapaud de Bengale, Lesson.
Bufo dubia, Shaw apud Gray : " Illustr. Ind. Zool."
Bufo carinatus, Gray : " Illustr. Ind. Zool."
Bufo melanostictus, apud Gravenhorst.
Bufo scaber, Tschudi.
" Kákong," " Kátak púru," of the Malays of the Peninsula.

Above, earthy brown, grey or buff, in some marbled with black ; lips, parotids, crests of the head, points of the tubercles, and last joints of fingers and toes, sooty or black. Beneath, buff, in some vermiculated with black. Iris golden brown ; pupil transversely rhombic.

HAB.—*Malayan Peninsula and Islands.*
Java, Tenasserim, Bengal, Coromandel.

R. 2

In the Malayan countries this species swarms in valleys and hills. It has in a slight degree the power of changing its colours, and it utters a chirping, plaintive sound. The largest individuals examined measured—

Length of the head .	. . . . . .	1	inch.
,,	,,	trunk.	3	inches.
,,	,,	anterior extremities . .	$2\frac{2}{8}$	,,
,,	,,	posterior extremities. .	$4\frac{2}{8}$	,,

Gen. HYLÆDACTYLUS, *Tschudi.*

Tongue an oval disk, thick, free only at the lateral margins. Palatal teeth. Eustachian tubes very minute. No parotids. Four free fingers with the terminal joint widened, truncated. Five toes united at the base by a very small membrane, the terminal joint not widened : sole with two soft tubercles between tarsus and metatarsus. Sacral transversal processes forming triangular palettes.

HYLÆDACTYLUS BIVITTATUS, N.S.

Upper parts and outside of extremities brownish-olive with distant small black spots. Head from the muzzle to the middle of the orbit whitish. A broad whitish band edged with black from the posterior angle of the eye, along each side to the loins. A shorter, oblique, similar band from the posterior angle of the eye. Beneath whitish, vermiculated with brown. The throat of the males black. Iris golden brown ; pupil transversally rhombic.

HAB.—*Malayan Peninsula.*

From *H. baleatus*, Tschudi, the present species differs both in colours and in the following particulars :—The profile from the nose to the coccyx forms a considerable arch, the highest part of which is the centre of the back. The male is provided with a vocal sac, the large openings of which are situated on each side of the tongue, and their presence is easily detected by the laxity of the (black) skin of the throat, which forms a broad transversal fold. Between the small openings of the Eustachian tubes the palate presents a considerable transversal fold of the skin, the free margin of which is fringed, which gives it the appearance of a row of teeth. A similar fold has been observed by MM. Duméril and Bibron in the genera *Plectropus*, Dum. and Bibr., and in *Uperodon*, Dum. and Bibr. In front of this fold is another smaller, between the orbital protuberances. Behind each of the large internal openings of the nostrils is an arched bony ridge, which in *H. baleatus* supports a few teeth. In the only individual of the present species examined the free margin of the ridge is cutting, but without teeth. Over the symphysis of the lower jaw there is a small pointed process, fitting into a corresponding cavity in the margin of the upper jaw. In this species, no less than in *Uperodon marmoratum*, Dum. and Bibr., nearly the whole of the thigh is hidden by the skin of the body, so that the posterior extremities are free but from a little above the knees. This character does not appear to exist in *Hylædactylus baleatus*, as it is not mentioned in the description of that species by MM. Duméril and Bibron. On the anterior part of the back appear some indistinct rounded elevations; the rest of the upper parts is smooth. The skin of the throat and abdomen presents numerous transversal wrinkles, and is covered with minute tubercles. The toes are more slender than the fingers, and their last joint, although flattened, is not so broad as that of the fingers, which is of a somewhat triangular form, truncated in front. In *H. baleatus* the fingers are longer than the toes. In the present species, however, the longest finger, the third, is nearly one-fourth shorter than the fourth toe.

The only individual which I had an opportunity of examining, after its death, was a male taken in a field near Malacca. It was of the following dimensions :—

Length of the head	$0\frac{3}{8}$ inch.
„ „ trunk	$2\frac{6}{8}$ inches.
In a straight line from the muzzle to coccyx, following the arch of the back	$3\frac{1}{8}$ „
Length of the anterior extremities . .	$1\frac{6}{8}$ inch.
„ „ posterior extremites, following the posterior margin . . .	$2\frac{7}{8}$ inches.

I have to acknowledge my sense of obligation to the Hon. Sir William Norris, late Recorder of H.M. Court of Judicature in the Straits of Malacca; to W. T. Lewis, Esq., Asst. Res. Councillor, Prince of Wales Island; to W. Montgomerie, Esq., M.D., late Senior Surgeon, Straits of Malacca; and to Capt. Congalton, H.C., steamer *Hooghly*, for their assistance, to me so much more acceptable as the limited leisure left me by the superintendence of six hospitals in Prince of Wales Island, and a seventh in Province Wellesley, was latterly curtailed by additional extra professional duties imposed upon me by the present local head authority in the Straits.

F ORT W ILLIAM, *June 1st,* 1847.

LATITUDINAL DISTRIBUTION OF REPTILES

Inhabiting the Malayan Peninsula and Islands and other localities.

[*Sp.* prefixed to localities signifies that they are inhabited by *species* of which varieties occur in Malayan countries.]

CHELONIA.

1. Geoemyda spinosa, Gray. Pinang, Sumatra.
2. Emys crassicollis, Bell, MS. Pinang, Malayan Peninsula, Sumatra, Java.
3. Emys platynota, Gray. Pinang, Malayan Peninsula, Sumatra.
4. Emys trivittata, Dum. and Bibr. Pinang, Malayan Peninsula, Bengal, Assam.
5. Cistudo amboinensis (Daud.). Singapore, Malayan Peninsula, Java, Amboina, Philippines, Tenasserim Provinces.
6. Tetraonyx affinis, Cantor. Pinang.
7. Gymnopus gangeticus (Cuvier). Pinang, Malayan Peninsula, rivers and Bay of Bengal.
8. Gymnopus cartilagineus (Boddaert). Pinang, Malayan Peninsula, Java, Dukhun, " India," " China."
9. Gymnopus indicus (Gray). Pinang, Malayan Peninsula, rivers of India, Philippines.
10. Chelonia virgata, Schweigger. Malayan seas, Teneriffe, Rio Janeiro, Cape of Good Hope, New York, Indian Ocean, Red Sea.
11. Chelonia imbricata (Linné). Malayan seas, Atlantic and Indian Ocean.
12. Chelonia olivacea, Eschscholtz. Malayan seas, Bay of Bengal, China Sea.

SAURIA.

1. Crocodilus vulgaris, Cuvier. Var. B. Dum. and Bibr. Malayan Peninsula and Islands, Java, Sumatra, Tenasserim, Bengal, Coromandel, Malabar.
2. Crocodilus porosus, Schneider. Pinang, Singapore, Malayan Peninsula, Seychelle Islands, Timor, Java, Sumatra, Tenasserim, Bengal.
3. Platydactylus lugubris, Dum. and Bibr. Pinang, Otaheite.
4. Platydactylus gecko (Linné). Malayan Peninsula, Philippines, Java, Tenasserim, Burmah, Bengal, Coromandel.
5. Platydactylus stentor, Cantor. Pinang.
6. Platydactylus monarchus, Schlegel. Pinang, Singapore, Malayan Peninsula, Philippines, Amboina, Borneo.

7. Ptychozoon homalocephalum (Creveld). Pinang, Singapore, Ramree Island (Arracan).
8. Hemidactylus Peronii, Dum. and Bibr. Pinang, Isle of France.
9. Hemidactylus Coctæi, Dum. and Bibr. Pinang, Bengal, Bombay.
10. Hemidactylus frenatus, Schlegel, MS. Pinang, Singapore, Malayan Peninsula, Amboina, Timor, Java, Marian Isles, Ceylon, Bengal, Assam, South Africa, Madagascar.
11. Hemidactylus platyurus (Schneider). Pinang, Philippines, Borneo, Java, Bengal, Assam.
12. Gymnodactylus pulchellus (Gray). Pinang, Singapore.
13. Varanus nebulosus, Dum. and Bibr. Pinang, Java, Siam, Bengal.
14. Varanus flavescens (Gray). Pinang, Bengal, Nipal.
15. Varanus salvator (Laurenti). Pinang, Malayan Peninsula, Philippines, Moluccas, Amboina, Java, Bengal, Assam.
16. Bronchocela cristatella (Kuhl). Pinang, Singapore, Malayan Peninsula, Amboina, Island of Buru, Java, Sumatra.
17. Lophyrus armatus (Gray). Pinang, Singapore, Cochin China.
18. Dilophyrus grandis, Gray. Pinang, Rangoon.
19. Draco volans (Linné). Pinang, Singapore, Malayan Peninsula, Philippines, Borneo, Java.
20. Draco maculatus (Gray). Pinang, Tenasserim.
21. Leiolepis Bellii (Gray). Pinang, Malayan Peninsula, Cochin China.
22. Eumeces punctatus (Linné), var. Pinang, Singapore, Malayan Peninsula ; *sp*. Coromandel, Malabar, Bengal.
23. Euprepis rufescens (Shaw).

Var. D. Dum. and Bibr. ⎫
Var. E. Dum. and Bibr. ⎬ Pinang, Singapore, Malayan
Var. F. Dum. and Bibr. ⎭ Peninsula.

Sp. Sandwich Islands, Philippines, Timor, Celebes, Borneo, Java, Coromandel, Bengal.
24. Euprepis Ernestii, Dum. and Bibr. Pinang, Malayan Peninsula, Java.
25. Lygosoma chalcides (Linné). Pinang, Singapore, Java.

OPHIDIA.

INNOCUOUS.

1. Philidion lineatum (Boie). Pinang, Singapore, Java.
2. Typhlops nigro-albus, Dum. and Bibr. Pinang, Singapore, Sumatra.
3. Typhlops braminus (Daudin). Pinang, Singapore, Malayan Peninsula, Canton Province, Philippines, Guam (Marian Isles), Java, Tenasserim, Bengal, Assam, Coromandel, Ceylon, Malabar.

4. Cylindrophis rufus (Laurenti). Singapore, Java, Tranquebar, Bengal?
5. Xenopeltis unicolor, Reinwardt. Pinang, Singapore, Malayan Peninsula, Celebes, Java, Sumatra.
6. Python reticulatus (Schneider). Malayan Peninsula and Islands, Chusan? Amboina, Java, Banka, Sumatra, Bengal?
7. Acrochordus javanicus, Hornstedt. Pinang, Singapore, Java.
8. Acrochordus granulatus (Schneider). Rivers and sea of the Malayan Peninsula and Islands, Bay of Manilla, New Guinea, Timor, Java, Sumatra, Coromandel.
9. Calamaria lumbricoidea, Schlegel, var. Pinang, Singapore; *sp*. Celebes, Java.
10. Calamaria Linnei, Boie, var. Schlegel. Pinang, Java.
11. Calamaria longiceps, Cantor. Pinang.
12. Calamaria sagittaria, Cantor. Malayan Peninsula, Bengal, Assam.
13. Coronella baliodeira, Schlegel. Pinang, Java.
14. Xenodon purpurascens, Schlegel. Pinang, Java, Tenasserim.
    Var. Chirra Punji, Assam, Darjeeling, Midnapore (Bengal).
15. Lycodon aulicus (Linné). Pinang, Bengal, Coromandel.
    Var. A. Pinang, Bengal.
    Var. B. Pinang, Malayan Peninsula, Java, Tenasserim.
    Var. C. Pinang, Malayan Peninsula, Pulo Samao, Timor.
    Var. D. Malayan Peninsula, Bengal.
16. Lycodon platurinus (Shaw). Pinang, Java, Bengal?
17. Lycodon effrænis, Cantor. Pinang.
18. Coluber fasciolatus, Shaw. Malayan Peninsula, Coromandel.
19. Coluber radiatus, Schlegel. Pinang, Singapore, Malayan Peninsula, Java, Sumatra, Cochin China, Tenasserim, Assam.
20. Coluber korros, Reinwart. Pinang, Singapore, Malayan Peninsula, Java, Sumatra, Arracan, Tenasserim.
21. Coluber hexagonotus, Cantor. Pinang.
22. Dipsas dendrophila, Reinwardt. Pinang, Singapore, Malayan Peninsula, Celebes, Java.
23. Dipsas multimaculata, Schlegel. Pinang, Malayan Peninsula, Celebes, Java, Tenasserim, Bengal.
24. Dipsas cynodon, Cuvier. Pinang, Malayan Peninsula, Java, Tenasserim.
25. Dipsas boa, Boie. Pinang, Java.
26. Herpetodryas oxycephalus (Reinwardt). Pinang, Celebes, Java.

27. Dryinus prasinus (Reinwardt). Malayan Peninsula and Islands, Celebes, Java, Cochin China, Siam, Burmah, Tenasserim, Arracan, Bengal, Assam.
    Var. A. Same localities.
    Var. B. Pinang.
    Var. C. Pinang.
28. Leptophis pictus (Gmelin). Malayan Peninsula and Islands, Manilla, New Ireland, Waigiou, Amboina, New Guinea, Pulo, Samao, Java, Sumatra, Cochin China, Tenasserim, Burmah, Bengal, Assam, Coromandel.
    Var. A. Malayan Peninsula, Bengal, Assam, Ceylon.
29. Leptophis caudalineatus, Cantor. Pinang, Singapore.
30. Leptophis ornatus (Shaw). *Sp.* Bengal, Ceylon.
    Var. Pinang, Malayan Peninsula, Java, Sumatra, Tenasserim, Arracan.
31. Tropidonotus umbratus (Daudin). *Sp.* Bengal, Assam, Coromandel, Ceylon.
    Var. Malayan Peninsula and Islands, Java, Bengal.
32. Tropidonotus stolatus (Linné). Pinang, Malayan Peninsula, Philippines, Tenasserim, Bengal, Assam, Nipal, Coromandel, Ceylon, Bombay.
33. Tropidonotus schistosus (Daudin). Malayan Peninsula, Philippines, Tenasserim, Bengal, Madagascar.
    Var. Same localities.
34. Tropidonotus cerasogaster (Cantor). Malayan Peninsula, Bengal, Assam.
35. Tropidonotus junceus, Cantor. Pinang.
36. Homalopsis rhinchops (Schneider). Malayan Peninsula and Islands, New Guinea, Amboina, Timor, Sarapua, Java, Sumatra, Tenasserim, Bengal, Coromandel.
37. Homalopsis buccata (Linné). Pinang, Malayan Peninsula, Java.
38. Homalopsis Sieboldi, Schlegel. Malayan Peninsula, Bengal.
39. Homalopsis enhydris (Schneider). Malayan Peninsula and Islands, Java, Tenasserim, Bengal, Coromandel.
40. Homalopsis plumbea, Boie. Pinang, Java.
41. Homalopsis leucobalia, Schlegel, var. Pinang, Malayan Peninsula ; *sp.* Timor.
42. Homalopsis hydrina, Cantor. Sea off Pinang and the Malayan Peninsula.

VENOMOUS.

43. I. Elaps melanurus (Shaw). Malayan Peninsula, Tenasserim, Nerva (Coromandel).
44. II. Elaps intestinalis (Laurenti), var. Pinang, Singapore, Malayan Peninsula ; *sp.* Java, Malwah (Central India).
45. III. Elaps nigromaculatus, Cantor. Pinang, Singapore.

46. IV. Elaps bivirgatus, Kuhl, var. Pinang, Malayan Peninsula; *sp.* Java, Sumatra.
47. V. Bungarus flaviceps, J. Reinhardt. Pinang, Java.
48. VI. Bungarus candidus (Linné). Malayan Peninsula, Java, Tenasserim, Bengal, Assam, Coromandel, Ceylon, Malabar.
49. VII. Bungarus fasciatus (Schneider). Pinang, Malayan Peninsula, Java, Tenasserim, Bengal, Coromandel.
50. VIII. Hamadryas ophiophagus, Cantor. Pinang, Singapore, Malayan Peninsula, Java, Sumatra, Bengal, Assam, Coromandel.
51. IX. Naja lutescens, Laurenti. *Sp.* countries between the Sutlej and Cape Comorin, Ceylon, Hindoostan to Cape Romania, Sumatra, Java, Ternate, Borneo, Philippines, Chusan.
    Var. D (Daudin). Pinang, Singapore, Malayan Peninsula, Bengal, Coromandel.
    Var. nigra. Pinang, Singapore.
52. X. Trigonocephalus gramineus (Shaw). Pinang, Singapore, Malayan Peninsula, New Holland, Timor, Pulo Samao, Celebes, Eastern Java, Banka, Sumatra, Tenasserim, Bengal, Chirra Punji, Nipal, Coromandel, Ceylon.
    Var. Pinang, Singapore, Malayan Peninsula, Sumatra, Tenasserim.
53. XI. Trigonocephalus sumatranus (Raffles), var. Pinang, Singapore, Malayan Peninsula ; *sp.* Sumatra.
54. XII. Trigonocephalus puniceus, Reinwardt. Pinang, Singapore, Malayan Peninsula, Java.
55. XIII. Laticauda scutata, Laurenti. Sea off the Malayan Peninsula and islands, Bay of Bengal, sea off Timor, Celebes, Molucca, and Liewkiew Islands, New Guinea, Tongataboo, China Sea.
56. XIV. Hydrus striatus (Lacépède). Sea of Pinang, Malayan Peninsula, sea off Liewkiew Islands, Timor, Sumatra, Bay of Bengal.
57. XV. Hydrus nigrocinctus (Daudin). Sea off Pinang, Singapore, Malayan Peninsula, Bay of Bengal, estuaries of the Ganges.
    Var. ? Sea off Pinang.
58. XVI. Hydrus gracilis, Shaw. Sea off Malayan Peninsula and islands, Bay of Bengal, Malabar, Sumatra, Borneo.
59. XVII. Hydrus schistosus (Daudin). Sea off Malayan Peninsula and islands, Bay of Bengal, Malabar, Sumatra.
60. XVIII. Hydrus pelamidoides (Schlegel). Sea off Malayan Peninsula and islands, Bay of Bengal, sea off Celebes, Molucca Islands, China Sea.

61. XIX. Hydrus bicolor (Schneider). Sea off Malayan Peninsula, Bay of Bengal, sea off Sumatra, Java, Célebes, Moluccas, China Sea (to 27° N.L.), Otaheite, Bay of Port Jackson
(33° 55′ S.L., 151° 25′ E.L.).

BATRACHIA.

1. Ichthyophis glutinosus (Linné), var.? Singapore; *sp.* Java,
Ceylon, Assam.
2. Rana Leschenaulti, Dum. and Bibr. Malayan Peninsula, Bengal, Pondicherry.
3. Rana tigrina, Daudin. Malayan Peninsula and islands, Coromandel, Bengal, Assam, Tenasserim, Java, Sumatra,
Timor, Philippines, Canton Province.
4. Megalophrys montana, Wagler, var. Pinang; *sp.* Java.
5. Limnodytes erythræus (Schlegel). Malayan Peninsula, Java,
Tenasserim, Arracan.
6. Polypedates leucomystax (Gravenhorst). Pinang, Singapore,
Malayan Peninsula, Bengal, Coromandel, Malabar.
7. Bufo melanostictus, Schneider. Malayan Peninsula and
islands, Java, Tenasserim, Bengal, Coromandel.
8. Hylædactylus bivittatus, Cantor. Malayan Peninsula.

ALTITUDINAL DISTRIBUTION OF REPTILES

INHABITING THE MALAYAN PENINSULA AND ISLANDS, AND OTHER
LOCALITIES.

[The extra-Malayan localities have necessarily been confined to
such of which the elevation has been specified by authors ; the
Malayan are given from personal observation.]

PRINCE OF WALES ISLAND (PULO PINANG), 5° 25′ N.L.
100° 19′ E.— *Valley.*—Mean annual temperature, 80°·3 Fahr.
Average monthly range of the thermometer, 11° ; greatest daily
range, 13°. Annual quantity of rain, 65·5 inches (145 days).
Hills.—Granite. Highest elevation (Western Hill) 2,500 feet.
Mean annual temperature 71°. Average monthly range of the
thermometer 10° ; greatest daily range 9°. Annual quantity of
rain 116·6 inches (174 days). Vegetation, even for a tropical, distinguished by luxuriance, beauty and variety. Characteristic
features, Filices. (Alsophila contaminans, Wal. ; Schizæa dicho-
toma ; Neuroplatyceros (Acrostichum) biforme, Desvontaine.
Polypodium Horsfieldii, Bennett.)
Pandanaceæ. (Freycinetia.)

Taccaceæ. (Tacca cristata, Jack.)
Palmaceæ. (Areca catechu, Willd.; Arenga saccharifera, Labill.; Nipa fruticans; Euoplus tigillaria, Jack; "Pinang Lawyer;"* Calamus.)
Scitamineæ. (Hedychium sumatranum, Jack; Amomum biflorum, Jack.)
Orchidaceæ.
Taxaceæ. (Dacrydium; Podocarpus.)
Gnetaceæ. (Gnetum gnemon; Gnetum brunonianum.)
Artocarpeæ. (Phytocrene palmata, Wal.; Phytocrene bracteata,† Wal.)
Nepenthaceæ. (Nepenthes distillatoria; Nepenthes ampullaria, Jack.)
Gesneraceæ. (Didymocarpus crinitus, Jack.)
Euphorbiaceæ.
Corylaceæ. (Quercus racemosa, Jack; Lithocarpus javensis, Blume.)
Begoniaceæ. (Begonia orbiculata, Jack.)
Sterculiaceæ. (Sterculia coccinea, Roxburgh; Durio Zibethinus, Lin.)
Dipteraceæ. (Dipterocarpus.)
Aurantiaceæ. (Murraya paniculata, Loar.)
Anacardiaceæ. (Stagmaria verniciflua, Jack.)
Connaraceæ. (Eurycoma longifolia, Jack.)
Garcinieæ.
Melastomaceæ. (Melastoma bracteata, Jack; M. exigua, Jack; M. glauca, Jack; Sonerila moluccana, Rob.)
Myrtaceæ.

SINGAPORE ISLAND, 1° 24′ N.L.; 104° E. Mean annual temperature 80°. Greatest daily range of thermometer 10°; annual number of rainy days 185. Surface gently undulating. Sandstone hills, indicating remote convulsions; highest hill (Bukit Timah) 530 feet, granite. In the valleys occur vegetable and animal forms which at Pinang have been observed at or near the summit of the hills, but not in the plains. Thus, at Singapore occur Alsophila, Schizæa, Tacca cristata, Gnetum, Nepenthes, Begonia, Eurycoma, and others, which at Pinang appear to affect a much greater elevation. Instances of reptiles in common to the plains of Singapore and the hills of Pinang are : Ptychozoon homalocephalum, Gymnodactylus pulchellus, Lygosoma chalcides, Pilidion lineatum, Typhlops nigro-albus, Calamaria lumbricoidea, var. Leptophis caudalineatus, Elaps intestinalis, E. nigromaculatus.

MALAYAN PENINSULA.—Geographically, not politically, from

---

* An undescribed dwarf palm, hitherto supposed to be confined to the hills of Pinang. Sir William Norris found it on Mount Ophir in 1847.
† This species appears to be confined to the lower parts of the hills and valleys.

12° N.L. between 98° and 104° E. computed to about 80,000 square miles, or about 4,000 square miles less than Great Britain. Zoological information has hitherto been confined almost exclusively to the plains of the western part. The productions of the chain of mountains dividing the peninsula, and terminating in Cape Romania in 1° 17′ N.L. (Point Búrus in 1° 15′ N.L.) are almost entirely unknown. The late Mr. Griffith, on a visit in the early part of 1842 to Mount Ophir (Gúnong Lédang, in about 2° 30′ N. L. on the eastern boundary of the district of Malacca, granite, and computed about 4,000 feet), made the interesting discovery, that from 1,500 feet and upwards the vegetation changes completely, and in many respects assumes a Polynesian or Australian character. Early in 1847 Lieutenant-Colonel James Low visited Keddah Peak (Gúnong Jerai), opposite to the town of Keddah, in about 6° 5′ N.L., which he observes is not granite but stratified, abounding in minerals. According to observation of the boiling point of water, the summit, a small platform on the edge of the strata, is 5,705½ feet above the sea. Towards the summit the vegetation becomes very stunted, and partakes of Australian character.* Colonel Low further observes that during the ascent he did not see a single animal, but found footprints of a rhinoceros, smaller than usual, he supposes up to the very summit. To a casual visitor of the Malayan hill forest during the day, the paucity of animals is a striking feature. The noonday light, subdued by the dense foliage of the towering stems, gives to the scene a sombre character, heightened by the unseen denizens. Their presence is manifested in the shrill vibrations of Cicadæ (one of which on the Pinang hills is noted for its resemblance to the cavalry trumpet), the call of the Tupai, the dismal tap of the gigantic woodpecker, the creaking flight of a Buceros, or the retreat of a frightened Semnopithecs.

CHELONIA.

Geoemyda spinosa, Gray. Pinang.

Emys crassicollis, Bell, MS. Ponds and rivulets Malayan Peninsula, Pinang.

Emys platynota, Gray. Malayan Peninsula, Pinang.

Emys trivittata, Dum. and Bibr. Ponds and rivers Malayan Peninsula, Pinang, Bengal.

Cistudo amboinensis (Daud.). Ponds and rivers Malayan Peninsula, Pinang, Bengal.

Tetraonyx affinis, Cantor. Sea off Pinang.

* A collection of plants from the summit of the mountain, with which Colonel Low favoured me, were examined by Capt. Munroe, H.M. 39th Regiment, the only botanist at present in Calcutta, previously to their being despatched to the Royal Gardens, Kew.

Gymnopus gangeticus (Cuvier). Rivers and sea-coast Malayan Peninsula, Bengal.

Gymnopus cartilagineus (Boddaert). Ponds and rivers Malayan Peninsula, Pinang, Java, Dukhun : " India," " China."

Gymnopus indicus (Gray). Rivers, estuaries and sea-coast Malayan Peninsula, Pinang, India, Philippine Islands.

Chelonia virgata, Schw. ⎫
Chelonia imbricata (Lin.) ⎬ Sea.
Chelonia olivacea, Eschscholtz. ⎭

SAURIA.

Crocodilus vulgaris, Cuv., var. B, Dum. and Bibr. Rivers, estuaries and sea-coast Malayan Peninsula and Islands, Java, Sumatra, Tenasserim, Bengal, Coromandel, Malabar.

Crocodilus porosus, Schneider. Rivers, estuaries and sea-coast Malayan Peninsula and Islands, Java, Sumatra, Tenasserim, Bengal, Coromandel, Malabar, Seychelle Islands, Timor.

Platydactylus lugubris, Dum. and Bibr. Pinang.

Platydactylus gecko (Linné). Malayan Peninsula, Bengal.

Platydactylus stentor, Cantor. Pinang.

Platydactylus monarchus, Schlegel. Pinang, Malayan Peninsula, Singapore.

Ptychozoon homalocephalum (Creveld). Pinang, Singapore.

Hemidactylus Peronii, Dum. and Bibr. Pinang.

Hemidactylus Coctæi, Dum. and Bibr. Pinang, Bengal.

Hemidactylus frenatus, Schlegel, MS. Pinang, Singapore, Malayan Peninsula, Bengal.

Hemidactylus platyurus (Schneider). Pinang, Bengal.

Gymnodactylus pulchellus (Gray). Pinang, Singapore.

Varanus nebulosus, Dum. and Bibr. Pinang, Bengal.

Varanus flavescens (Gray). Pinang, Bengal.

Varanus salvator (Laurenti). Pinang, Malayan Peninsula, Bengal.

Bronchocela cristatella (Kuhl). Pinang, Malayan Peninsula, Singapore.

Lophyrus armatus (Gray). Pinang, Singapore.

Dilophyrus grandis, Gray. Pinang.

Draco volans, Linné. Pinang, Malayan Peninsula.

Draco maculatus (Gray). Pinang.

Leiolepis Bellii (Gray). Pinang, Malayan Peninsula.

Eumeces punctatus (Lin.) var. Pinang, Malayan Peninsula, Singapore.

Euprepis rufescens (Shaw).
Var. D. Dum. and Bibr. ⎫
Var. E. Dum. and Bibr. ⎬ Pinang, Malayan Peninsula, Singapore.
Var. F. Dum. and Bibr. ⎭

Euprepis Ernestii, Dum. and Bibr. Pinang, Malayan Peninsula.

Lygosoma chalcides (Linné). Pinang, Singapore.

OPHIDIA.

INNOCUOUS.

Pilidion lineatum (Boie). Pinang, Singapore.
Typhlops nigro-albus, Dum. and Bibr. Pinang, Singapore.
Typhlops braminus (Daudin). Pinang, Malayan Peninsula, Singapore, Bengal, Assam.
Cylindrophis rufus (Laurenti). Singapore, Tranqubar, Bengal.
Xenopeltis unicolor, Reinwardt. Pinang, Singapore, Malayan Peninsula.
Python reticulatus (Schneider). Pinang, Malayan Peninsula, Singapore, Bengal ?
Acrochordus javanicus, Hornstedt. Pinang, Singapore, Java.
Acrochordus granulatus (Schneider). Rivers and sea-coast of Malayan Peninsula and islands, New Guinea, Timor, Java, Sumatra, Coromandel, Bay of Manilla.
Calamaria lumbricoidea, Schlegel, var. Pinang, Singapore.
Calamaria Linnei, Boie, var. Schlegel. Pinang, Java.
Calamaria longiceps, Cantor. Pinang.
Calamaria sagittaria, Cantor. Malayan Peninsula, Bengal.
Coronella baliodeira, Schlegel. Pinang.
Xenodon purpurascens, Schlegel. Pinang, Java.
Lycodon aulicus (Linné). Pinang, Malayan Peninsula, Bengal.
 Var. A. Pinang, Bengal.
 Var. B. Pinang, Malayan Peninsula.
 Var. C. Pinang, Malayan Peninsula.
 Var. D. Malayan Peninsula, Bengal.
Lycodon platurinus (Shaw). Pinang, Bengal ?
Lycodon effrænis, Cantor. Pinang.
Coluber fasciolatus, Shaw. Malayan Peninsula, Coromandel.
Coluber radiatus, Schlegel. Pinang, Singapore, Malayan Peninsula.
Coluber korros, Reinwardt. Pinang, Singapore, Malayan Peninsula.
Coluber hexagonotus, Cantor. Pinang.
Dipsas dendrophila, Reinwardt. Pinang, Malayan Peninsula, Singapore, Java.
Dipsas multimaculata, Schlegel. Pinang, Malayan Peninsula.
Dipsas cynodon, Cuvier. Pinang, Malayan Peninsula.
Dipsas boa, Boie. Pinang, Java.
Herpetodryas oxycephalus (Reinwardt). Pinang.
Dryinus prasinus (Reinwardt). Malayan Peninsula and islands.
 Var. A. Malayan Peninsula and islands.
 Var. B. Pinang.
 Var. C. Pinang.

Leptophis pictus (Gmelin). Malayan Peninsula and islands, Bengal.
 Var. A. Malayan Peninsula and islands, Bengal.
Leptophis caudalineatus, Cantor. Pinang, Singapore.
Leptophis ornatus (Shaw), var. Pinang, Malayan Peninsula.
Tropidonotus umbratus (Daud.), var. Malayan Peninsula and islands, Java, Bengal.
Tropidonotus stolatus (Linné). Pinang, Malayan Peninsula, Bengal, Nipal, Coromandel, Bombay.
Tropidonotus schistosus (Daud.). Malayan Peninsula, Bengal.
 Var. Malayan Peninsula, Bengal.
Tropidonotus cerasogaster (Cantor). Malayan Peninsula, Bengal.
Tropidonotus junceus, Cantor. Pinang.
Homalopsis. All the Malayan species inhabit fresh water, rivers, estuaries, or the sea-coast, as noted under each.

VENOMOUS.

Elaps melanurus (Shaw). Malayan Peninsula, Tenasserim, Nerva.
Elaps intestinalis (Laurenti), var. Pinang, Singapore, Malayan Peninsula.
 Sp. Java, Malwah (Central India).
Elaps nigromaculatus, Cantor. Pinang, Singapore.
Elaps bivirnatus, Kuhl., var. Pinang, Malayan Peninsula.
Bungarus flaviceps, J. Reinwardt. Pinang.
Bungarus candidus (Linné). Malayan Peninsula, Bengal, Coromandel, Malabar.
Bungarus fasciatus (Schneider). Pinang, Malayan Peninsula, Bengal, Coromandel.
Hamadryas ophiophagus, Cantor. Pinang, Singapore, Malayan Peninsula, Bengal.
Naja lutescens, Laurenti.
 Var. D (Daud.). Pinang, Malayan Peninsula, Singapore, Bengal, Coromandel.
 Var. nigra. Pinang, Singapore.
Trigonocephalus gramineus (Shaw). Pinang, Malayan Peninsula, Chirra Punji, Singapore, Bengal, Nipal.
 Var. Pinang, Malayan Peninsula, Singapore.
Trigonocephalus sumatranus (Raffles), var. Pinang, Singapore, Malayan Peninsula.
 Sp. Sumatra.
Trigonocephalus puniceus, Reinwardt. Pinang, Singapore, Malayan Peninsula.
Laticauda Hydrus. All species inhabit the sea or estuaries.

BATRACHIA.

Ichthyophis glutinosus (Linné), var. ?   Singapore.
Rana Leschenaulti, Dum. and Bibr.   Malayan Peninsula, Bengal, Pondicherry.
Rana tigrina, Daudin.   Malayan Peninsula and Islands, Bengal.
Megalophrys montana, Wagler, var.   Pinang: *sp.* Java.
Limnodytes erythræus (Schlegel).   Malayan Peninsula.
Polypedates leucomystax (Gravenhorst).   Pinang, Malayan Peninsula, Singapore, Bengal.
Bufo melanostictus, Schneider.   Malayan Peninsula and islands, Bengal.
Hylædactylus bivittatus, Cantor.   Malayan Peninsula.

XXXVIII.

SOME ACCOUNT OF THE BOTANICAL COLLECTION, BROUGHT FROM THE EASTWARD, IN 1841, BY DR. CANTOR.

By the late W. GRIFFITH, Esq., *F.L.S., Memb. Imp. Acad. Natur. Curios., Royal Ratisb. Botan. Soc., Corr. Memb. Hort. Soc., Royal Acad. Turin, Assist. Surgeon, Madras Establishment.*

["Journal of the Asiatic Society of Bengal," vol. xxiii. pp. 623-650.]

[NOTE.—The following paper has been printed for several years, and was intended to form part of an interesting communication by Dr. Cantor on the Natural History of Chusan, which was to lead off vol. xxi. of the " Asiatic Researches." This publication having been, for the present at all events, discontinued, Dr. Griffith's valuable Memoir on Chusan Botany has been reprinted. —ED.].

THIS collection consists of plants from the Straits of Malacca, from Lantao, Chusan, and a few from Pekin, the bulk of the Chinese plants being from Chusan. The Straits specimens were, I believe, given to Dr. Cantor by the Rev. Mr. White, Chaplain of Singapore.

The following lists exhibit the genera and the number of species procured from the above-mentioned localities, the names of a few species being added :—

STRAITS OF MALACCA.

ACOTYLEDONES.

No. of Species.

Lycopodineæ . . .	Lycopodium	3
	⎧ Lygodium	1
	⎪ Gleichenia	2
	⎪ Polypodium	3
Filices	⎨ Aspidium	1
	⎪ Asplenium	1
	⎪ Blechnum	1
	⎩ Pteris	1

Total . . 13

DICOTYLEDONES.

INCOMPLETÆ.

Taxineæ ?	Dacrydium ?	1
Urticeæ	Ficus	1
Amaranthaceæ . .	Amaranthus	1
Nepenthaceæ . . .	Nepenthes	2
Asarinæ	Thottea grandiflora	0
Loranthaceæ . . .	Loranthus retusus	1

Total . . 6

POLYPETALÆ.

	⎧ Excœcaria	1
Euphorbiaceæ . . ⎨	Phyllanthus	1
	⎩ Rottlera	1
Bixaceæ	Bixa	1
Dilleniaceæ . . .	Tetracera	1
Sapindaceæ . . .	Nephelium lappaceum	1
Meliaceæ	Aglaia odorata	1
Rutaceæ	Evodia triphylla	1
Ternstrœmiaceæ ?' .	Ixonanthes reticulata	1
Terebinthaceæ . .	Boueia microphylla	1
	⎧ Paritium	1
Malvaceæ . . . . ⎨	Urena	1
	⎩ Sida	1
Tiliaceæ	Grewia	1
Dipterocarpeæ . .	. . . .	1
Connaraceæ . . .	Connarus	1
Legumi- ⎧ Cassieæ . ⎧	Mezoneuron	1
nosæ ⎨	Bauhinia	4
⎩ Papiliona-		
ceæ .	Crotalaria	1

		No. of Species.
Rosaceæ	Rubus	I
Memecyleæ . . .	{ Memecylon	I
	{ Pternandra	2
Melastomaceæ . .	. . . .	3
Myrtaceæ	(Myrtus tomentosa	I
	{ Eugenia	4
	{ Melaleuca leucadendron	I
	(Tristania Whitiana	I
Lythrarieæ . . .	Lagerstroemia floribunda	I

Total . . 37

MONOPETALÆ.

Compositæ	Conyza ?	I
Rubiaceæ	(Nauclea	2
	{ Mussaenda	I
	{ Ixora	I
	(Epithinia malayana	I
Myrsineæ	{ Ardisia	I
	{ Baeobotrys	2
Styraceæ	Symplocos	I
Verbenaceæ . . .	(Clerodendrum	4
	{ Callicarpa	I
	{ Premna	I
	(Vitex	I

Total . . 17

LANTAO, CANTON.

ACOTYLEDONES.

Algæ	. . . .	I
Lycopodinæ . . .	Lycopodium cernuum	I
Filices	(Lygodium	I
	{ Gleichenia	I
	{ Niphobolus	I
	{ Cheilanthes	2
	{ Adiantum	I
	{ Pteris	2
	(Cyathea ?	I

Total . . 11

MONOCOTYLEDONES.

Cyperaceæ . . .	{ Cyperus	I
	{ Scleria	I

		No. of species.
Gramineæ	Setaria	1
	Imperata	1
	Andropogon	2
	Anthistiria	1
	Bambusa	1
Smilacineæ	Dianella	1
Orchideæ	Spiranthes	1
	Total	10

DICOTYLEDONES.

POLYPETALÆ.

Sterculiaceæ	Helicteres	1
Cucurbitaceæ	Bryonia	1
Oxalideæ	Oxalis	1
Rosaceæ	Rubus moluccanus	1
Leguminosæ	Indigofera?	2
	Lespedeza?	1
Melastomaceæ	Melastoma malabathricum	1
	————— sanguineum	1
Myrtaceæ	Myrtus tomentosa	1
	Bæckia frutescens	1
	Total	11

MONOPETALÆ.

Compositæ	Cirsium?	1
Rubiaceæ	Nauclea Adina	1
Apocyneæ	Strophanthus dichotomus	1
Scrophularineæ	Siphonostegia chinensis	1
Acanthaceæ	Acanthus ilicifolius	1
	Total	5

Among a few Indeterminatæ are two species of a radicant herbaceous genus, with opposite fleshy leaves and rubiaceous stipulæ.

CHUSAN.

ACOTYLEDONES.

Lycopodineæ	Lycopodium	1
Filices	Lygodium	1
	Pleopeltis	1
	Aspidium	3
	Pteris	2
	Total	8

MONOCOTYLEDONES.

No. of Species.

Cyperaceæ	Cyperus	1
Gramineæ	Panicum stagninum	1
Commelineæ . . .	Commelina	1
Smilacineæ . . .	{ Smilax	1
	{ Scilloidea* (without leaves) . . .	1
Orchideæ	Eulophia?	1
Alismaceæ	Sagittaria	1
Hydrocharideæ . .	Hydrocharis Morsus ranæ?*	1
Lemnaceæ	Lemna	1

Total . . 9

DICOTYLEDONES.

INCOMPLETÆ.

Taxineæ	Salisburia*	1
Coniferæ . . .	{ Juniperus	1
	{ Pinus*	1
Amaranthaceæ . .	Achyranthes	1
Polygoneæ . .	{ Polygonum*	7
	{ Rumex*	2
Elæagneæ . . .	Elæagnus	1
Cupuliferæ . .	Quercus*	1
Salicineæ . . .	Salix babylonica	1
Urticeæ	/ Humulus lupulus*	1
	Cannabis sativa	1
	Morus nigra	1
	—— alba	1
	Urticea (fragments)	1
	Urtica	1
	Ficus	1
	\ Artocarpea? (fragifera)	1

Total . . 24

POLYPETALÆ.

Euphorbiaceæ . .	{ Elæococca verrucosa*	1
	{ Stillingia sebifera	1
	{ Acalypha	1
	{ Phyllanthus	2
Ranunculaceæ . .	{ Ranunculus aquaticus?	1
	{ Clematis*	1
Nelumboneæ . . .	Nelumbium	1
Cruciferæ	Sinapis	1
Resedaceæ	Reseda*	1

		No. of Species.
Oxalideæ	Oxalis	1
Hypericineæ . . .	Hypericum*	2
Ternstrœmiaceæ . .	Camellia*	2
Aurantiaceæ . . .	Citrus	3
Meliaceæ	Aglaia	1
Ampeliddeæ . . .	Vitis	2
Celastrineæ . . .	Elæodendron	1
Rhamneæ	Zyziphus.	1
Tamariscineæ . . .	Tamarix.	1
Sempervivæ . . .	Sedum	1
Xanthoxyleæ . . .	Xanthoxylum	1
Sterculiaceæ . . .	Sterculia	1
Malvaceæ	{ Hibiscus	1
	{ Gossypium	1
Acerineæ	Acer*	1
Hamamelideæ . .	Hamamelis sinensis	1
Rosaceæ	⎧ Fragaria	1
	⎪ Agrimonia*	1
	⎪ Rubus	2
	⎨ Rosa	1
	⎪ Amygdalus	3
	⎪ Pyrus	2
	⎩ Cydonia	1
Leguminosæ . . .	Papilionaceæ	6
Melastomaceæ . .	Melastoma ? sine fl. fr.	1
Granateæ	Punica granatum	1
Myrtaceæ	Myrtus	1
Araliaceæ	Hedera helix ?*	1
Umbelliferæ . . .	{ Daucus	1
	{ Carum	1
Cucurbitaceæ . . .	{ Cucurbita	1
	{ Actinostemma (gen. nov.)	1
Begoniaceæ . . .	Begonia	1

Total . . 57

MONOPETALÆ.

Compositæ	⎧ Cichoracea	1
	⎪ Bidens	1
	⎪ Artemisia	2
	⎪ Eclipta prostrata ?	1
	⎨ Aster	1
	⎪ Chrysanthemum	1
	⎪ Pulicaria	1
	⎪ Gnaphalium	1
	⎩ Emilia	1

		No. of Species.
Rubiaceæ . . .	{ Paederia fœtida ?*	1
	{ Gardenia	1
Caprifoliaceæ . . .	Sambucus*	1
Ericineæ	Rhododendron,* efl. efr.	1
Convolvulaceæ . .	Convolvulus	2
Solaneæ	(Nicotiana tabacum	1
	Datura fastuosa ?	1
	Solanum nigrum	1
	———— dulcamara*	1
	Capsicum	1
	(Lycium	1
Scrophularineæ . .	{ Veronica Anagallis	1
	{ Bonnaya ?	1
Verbenaceæ . .	{ Verbena officinalis	1
	{ Clerodendrum	2
Pedalineæ	Sesamum orientale	1
Labiatæ	(Mentha	1
	{ Rosmarinus officinalis*	1
	(Labiata alia.	1
Boragineæ	Symphytum ?	1
Oleineæ	Olea fragrans	1
Plumbagineæ . . .	Plumbago*	1
Plantagineæ . . .	Plantago*	1
	Total . .	35

TENGCHOU (PEKIN).

Geraniaceæ. . . .	Erodium.	1
Semperviræ . . .	Sedum	1
Umbelliferæ . . .	. . . .	1
Compositæ	Artemisioides	1
Indeterminata eflor :	Statices facie	1
	Total . .	5

TOKI (PEKIN).

MONOCOTYLEDONES.

Gramineæ	Poa vel Festuca	2
Smilacinæ	Allium	3
Irideæ	Pardanthus.	1
	Total . .	6

DICOTYLEDONES.

Polygoneæ	Polygonum Fagopyrum ?	1
Urticeæ	Cannabis sativa	1

			No. of Species.
Tamariscinæ	. . .	Tamarix	1
Silenaceæ	. . . .	Dianthus	1
Rosaceæ	. . . .	{ Potentilla	1
		{ Agrimonia	1
Leguminosæ	. . .	Papilionaceæ	4
Primulaceæ	. . .	Lysimachia	1
Asclepiadeæ	. . .	Cynanchum sibiricum ?	1
Apocyneæ ?	. . .	. . . .	1
Convolvulaceæ	. .	Convolvulus	1

Total . . 14

The total number of species in a state admitting of determination is as follows :—

Straits of Malacca 81
Canton 37
Chusan 133
Tengchou } Pekin 25
Toki . . }

Total . . 276

I shall now make such remarks as I am able on the most interesting forms of these collections.

STRAITS COLLECTION.

ASARINÆ.—The specimens of Thottea consist of a flower, part of a raceme, and a full-grown leaf. A description and drawing of this plant, first met with by König in 1779, is now in the possession of the Linnean Society.

TERNSTRŒMIACEÆ ?—I refer with some doubt to this family Ixonanthes of Jack. This genus, hitherto only known from Jack's description, has been placed doubtfully among Cedrelaceæ by Dr. Lindley and M. Endlicher, with which, however, its resemblances appear to be rather technical. A more proper place is, I think, to be found between Ternstrœmiaceæ and Hypericineæ, the major part of the affinities being with the former family.

IXONANTHES.—Jack, Mal. Misc. ("Calc. Journ. Nat. Hist." iv. p. 115.)

CHAR. GEN.—Calyx 5-6-partitus. Corolla 5-6-petala, glutinosa, convoluto-clausa. Stamina 10-20 ; filamentis capillaceis ; antheris ovatis, bilocularibus. Annulus (crenulatus) inter stamina et pistillum. Ovarium 5-loculare, loculis biovulatis. Ovula pendula ex apice anguli interioris. Stylus capillaceus. Stigma discoideum.

Fructus septicidim 5-valvis. Semina cum vel absque ala, sæpe sterilia et difformia. Albumen carnosum. Embryo lateralis. Radicula supera. HABITUS.—Arbores Malayanæ, Folia alterna, exstipulata? Venatione reticulata. Corymbi cymæve axillares. Flores parvi, inconspicui.

I. reticulata, foliis obovatis vel elliptico-obovatis integris, corymbis folia subæquantibus, staminibus 10, seminibus apice alatis.
I. reticulata. Jack, Mal. Misc. ("Calc. Journ. Nat. Hist." l.c.)
HAB.—Singapore, Rev. Mr. White.
DES.*—Rami angulati, flexuosi. Folia obovata, vel majora elliptico-obovata, obtusissima, late emarginata coriacea ; venæ secondariæ arcuatim nexæ, interveniæ reticulatæ. Pedunculi axillares, solitarii, folia subæquantia vel excedentia, dichotomi. Pedicelli plerumque ternati. Flores cujusve cymæ sub-7, materie resinosa glutinosa aspersa, parvi. Sepala ovata-oblonga vel rotundata. Petala paullo majora, convoluta, apice quasi perforata. Stamina 10, in annulo glanduloso crenulato ovarii basin arcte cingente inserta. Filamenta capillacea, petalis 4-plo longiora, per os angustum corollæ longe exserta. Antheræ oblongæ, basi affixæ ; connectivo lato ; loculis angustis. Ovarium globosoconicum. Stylus capillaceus, filamentis longior. Stigma discoideum.

I. dodecandra (n. sp. ?) foliis obovata-lanceolatis crenato-serratis, corymbis felia superantibus, staminibus 13-16, seminibus perfectis paucis hilo processigeris, sterilibus difformibus processubus hili saepius tricruribus.
HAB.—Woods about Pringitt, and near Rhim, Malacca.
DES.†—Arbor majuscula. Folia alterna, exstipulata, breve petiolata, obovata-lanceolata, obtusa, emarginata, coriacea, crenatoserrata (sæpius distanter), subtus reticulata, sicca castaneo-brunea ; magnitudine varia, majora nempe 6-uncias longa, 2-lata, minora long. Three-uncialia, lat. 1-uncialia. Corymbi axillares, folia excedentes, multiflora, e cymis dichotomis sub-6-floris conflati. Bracteæ caducæ. Flores parvi, inconspicui, viridescentes, glutinosi. Calyx ultra medium 5 partitus, (potius 5-sepalus, pedicellis apice incrassatis); laciniæ corollam fere æquantes. oblongæ, acutæ. Corolla convoluto-clausa, apice quasi perforata, Petala rotundato-oblonga, concava, venosa. Annulus brevis, carnosus, crenulatus, inter stamina et pistillum. Stamina 13-16. Filamenta annulo basin versus inserta, capillacea, diu persistentia. Antheræ ovatæ, biloculares, longitudina-liter dehiscentes, deciduæ. Pollen tri-porosum. Ovarium conicum, sub-5-gonum, 5-loculare. Ovula 2 cuivis loculo, anatropa, pendula ex apice anguli interioris

---

* From a single specimen in flower.
† Chiefly from dried specimens ; of the seeds from living ones.

ope funiculorum longiusculorum.   Raphe extrorsa.   Stylus capillaceus, ovario 6-plo longior, stamina paullo superans, diu persistens. Stigma capitatum, margine reflexum.   Fructus anguste ovatus, acutus, 7-8 lineas longus, 3-4-latus, basi calyce et corolla circumdatus, lineis 5 notatus, septicidim 5-valvis, valvis osseis intus centro carinatis.   Semina sæpius abortientia, processu foraminis sursum et deorsum longe producto, infero sæpius bicruri; perfectum brunneum, oblongo-lanceolatum, compressiusculum, processu foraminis sub 3-auriculato.   Tegumentum exterius coriaceum: interius tenuissimum, albumen arcte vestiens.   Raphe semicompleta.   Chalaza subdepressa.   Albumen carnosum, copiosum. Embryo ad latus exterius albuminis.   Radicula longa, gracilis, longitudine cotyledonum foliacearum.   Plumula inconspicua.

This species appears to be allied to T. icosandra, Jack, from which it chiefly seems to differ in the number of the stamina.

ANACARDIEÆ. — Compilers appear to have overlooked Buchanan's * remarks on the opposite-leaved mangoes, the original species only being referred to by Steudel † and Endlicher. ‡ Yet besides the two species founded by Buchanan (loc. cit.), I believe without sufficient grounds, on the Manga sylvestris prima et altera of Rumph. § Buchanan's description of the Burmese Mariam is so different from that of Roxburgh, as to lead to the suspicion that under the name Mangifera oppositifolia, two species will be found.

Up to this time I have met with three species, of which the following are the distinguishing marks, independently of differences that may exist in their hermaphrodite flowers and fruit.

BOUEIA,‖ Meisner.¶   Cambessedea, Wight and Arnott.**

---

* "Mem. Wern. Soc." 5. p. 326.   † "Nomenclat. Bot." ed. 2da.
‡ "Gen. Pl." p. 1133, No. 5918.
§ Rumph, under the head Manga sylvestris, does not mention the opposition of the leaves, and though his figure, t. 27, might pass for Mangifera oppositifolia, yet the leaves are by no means represented as being generally opposite, and the aspect of the flowers again is rather that of a genuine Mango.
‖ This genus was first proposed, and its differences from Mangifera given, by Messrs. Wight and Arnott under the name Cambessedea, for which, from its being pre-occupied, Meisner has substituted Boueia. But no sign or mark is appended to indicate who were the original proposers of the genus, with whom the merit must in most cases necessarily rest. It is one thing to glance over a complete catalogue of names and ascertain which is pre-occupied, another to detect and define a new group. Botanists have admitted certain conventional signs, which have been generally adopted, and would do well to admit signs of a most conspicuous character by which the compiler may be known from the designer ; the botanist who names after examination and comparison, from him who names without having done either. Or as suggested in the excellent rules for reforming Zoologic Nomenclature, p. 8, par. 4, now that communication is so rapid, it might be courteously left to the framer of the genus to correct the error.
¶ "Endl. Gen. Pl." 1. cit.   ** "Prod. Fl. Pen. Ind. Or." p. 170, *in annot.*

B. burmannica, foliis oblongo-lanceolatis, paniculis laxifloris foliis brevioribus parce puberulis, petalis sæpissime 4 lineari-oblongis calycem subduplo excedentibus.

Mangifera oppositifolia.* Roxb. "Hort. Bengh." p. 18. "Fl. Indic." i. p. 640. ed. Carey.

Manga sylvestris, Rumph. "Hb. Amb." i. t. 27?

HAB.—Commonly cultivated by the Burmese, by whom it is called Mariam, or Mai-een.

Arbor parva, ramulis compressis angulatis. Folia anguste oblongo-lanceolata, obtuse acuminata vel cuspidata, coriacea, longitudine 5-uncialia, latitudine 1½-unciala. Stamina sæpissime 4. Drupa magnitudine ovi gallinulæ.

Buchanan describes the inflorescence of his plant as " spica simplicissima foliis multo longior," and the fruit as " drupa figura et sapore Mangiferæ indicæ." But he appears only to have been acquainted with Roxburgh's plant through the Hortus Benghalensis, a catalogue containing no characters or discriminative marks.

B. macrophylla (n. sp.), foliis oblongo-lanceolatis, paniculis amplis thyrsoideis pubescentibus foliis brevioribus, petalis sæpissime 3 calyce subtriplo longioribus.

HAB.—Malacca. Roomaniya Baitool of the Malays.

Arbor magna, corona densa. Ramuli tetragoni. Folia valde coriacea, obtuse et brevi cuspidata, long. 6-8 uncialia, latit. 2-2½ uncialia. Panicula dense thyrsoidea. Stamina sæpissime 3.

B. microphylla (n. sp.), foliis lanceolatis, paniculis parvis thyrsoideis foliis brevioribus, petalis 4, oblongo-rotundatis calyce duplo longioribus.

HAB.—Malacca. Roomaniya Paigo of the Malays.

Arbor, ramulis compressis. Folia longe et obtuse cuspidata, valde coriacea, longit. 2-3½ uncialia, latit. 1-1½ uncialia. Paniculæ parvæ, foliis aliquoties breviores. Flores minus elongati, minuti. Drupa magnitudine ovi gallinulæ.

The habit of these two species is different from that of the Burmese one, the leaves more coriaceous, and the secondary veins more distinct.

The fruit of both is eaten by the Malays. They have the characteristic acidity, but make excellent pickles.

The genus presents a remarkable analogy with Oleinæ.

MEMECYLEÆ.—Pternandra, Jack (Ewyckia, Blume), though referred by Dr. Lindley to Melastomaceæ, appears to me to belong to Memecyleæ. The genus is remarkable for its placentation, which is the only instance I am acquainted with of the co-existence of thoroughly parietal placentation with perfect dis-

---

* The opposition of the leaves being characteristic of the genus, it becomes necessary to change Roxburgh's name.

sepiments, independently of any apparent production inwards of any parts of the placental surface. Hypothetically this is explainable by assuming the ovula to be confined to that part of the carpellary leaf with which almost invariably they have no manner of connection. In other words, they may be declared to arise from the back of the carpel leaf, or from the midrib, and the space on either side between it and the inflected margins.*

Appearances, derived from the examination of Pternandra cœrulescens, are not perhaps altogether unfavourable to the supposition that there is a disturbance in the direction of the carpel leaves analogous to that which affects some, perhaps most, Boragineæ, by which the true apex of each carpellum is brought close to the base, and in which, as appears to me, suggested by the situation of the raphe, the placenta has a disposition to be dorsal; so that if a polysporous placenta be found to exist in a carpellum so constituted, it may, I am inclined to conjecture, be as dorsal as it is in Pternandra.

From the evidence afforded by this genus, it would appear that an " ovarium inferum " may have part of its cavities, or even of its placentæ, actually superior ; that is, above the line drawn when the term " ovarium inferum " is made use of, which term, nevertheless, is perhaps quite as admissible in many instances as that of ovarium adhærens.

MYRTACEÆ.—I refer without doubt to Tristania, one of Mr. White's plants. It is the fourth Indian species of the genus I have met with, the northerly limit of which, so far as yet known, appears to be Moulmein, 17° N.L. This is a fact of some interest, as Mr. Bennett † states that he is only acquainted with one species found beyond the limits of N. Holland. In connection with this I may mention Stylidium, which is perhaps the last Australian form that disappears, an instance of the genus having been found by Dr. Voigt, about Serampore, and by Lieut. Kittoe at Midnapore. This genus also occurs at Mergui and Moulmein, but has not hitherto been remarked on the Khassya Hills or in Assam. Another Australian form, Melaleuca leucadendron, forms, from its abundance in the low littoral tracts of Malacca, a very marked feature of vegetation. The northerly limit of this species is Mergui (12° N.L.), where it occurs in similar localities, but comparatively limited in size and numerical extent.

---

* Most of the instances hitherto cited as exhibiting dorsal placentation, appear to me to be untenable, and naturally explicable. But it is certain that Monocotyledonous monstrosities do occur, in which the buds arise from the inner surface of the leaves to the exclusion of the usually gemmiferous margins. Of this I met with a marked instance in a Liliaceous plant in Eastern Affghanistan.

† " Pl. Jav. Rar." Pt. 11, p. 128.

Three of the four species above alluded to may be thus distinguished :—

Tristania burmannica, ramulis glabris, foliis alternis obovato-lanceolatis glaberrimis, calyce extus pubescente intus cum ovario dense albo-tomentoso, staminum phalangis 4-6-andris.

HAB.—Hills about Moulmein. No. 76 of a small Burmese Collection sent to England in 1834.

Arbusculum. Ramuli et inflorescentia griseo-puberuli. Folia longitudine 4-uncialia, latitudine 1-1¼-uncialia. Pedunculi compressi. Cymæ confertifloræ, foliis duplo breviores, pedicelli plerumque terni. Florum odor pessimus. Petala integra, cum filamentis parce puberula.

T. merguensis, ramulis subglabris, foliis alternis spathulato-lanceolatis basi biauriculatis, calyce et ovario puberulis, staminum phalangibus 6-10 andris, capsula semisupera.

HAB.—Sea-shore of the island Madamacan, opposite Mergui, in flower in August No. 235, Herb. Mergui.

Arbor ramis pendentibus. Folia alterna vel subopposita, subsessilia, longitudine 7-7½ uncialia, latitudine 2-2¼-uncialia. Pedunculi ancipites, foliis subduplo breviores ; pedicelli minute puberuli. Florum odor pessimus, stercoraceus. Petala alba, denticulata. Phalanges petala excedentes. Capsula ⅔ supera, semi-inclusa, loculicidim et septifragim trivalvis, valvis extus transverse rugosulis. Semina arcte collateralia, plura paleacea abortiva, pauciora apice alata, fertilia. Cotyledones contortuplicatæ.

T. Whitiana, foliis alternis spathulato-obovatis parce puberulis, ramulis calyceque extus puberulis, calyce intus et ovario tomentoso-puberulis, staminum phalangibus 2-4 andris.

HAB.—Singapore. Malayan name Plowan. Rev. Mr. White.

Folia, in apice ramorum conferta, obtuse cuspidata, longitudine 4-4½, latitudine 1½-1¾ uncialia ; venæ secondariæ magis approximatæ et parallelæ. Corymbi folia excedentes, puberuli. Petala undulata.

Of these T. burmannia is closely allied to P. obovata, Bennett, in Horsf. " Pl. Jav. Rar." p. 127. t. 27.

The fourth species was met with sparingly in fruit on Mount Ophir ; in the form of its leaves it approaches to T. obovata, but the fruit is rounder. The peduncles appear much less branched than in any of the other extra-Australian species, but the degree of adhesion between the calyx and pericarpium is the same. It was observed with Bæckea frutescens, three species of Leptospermum, and one o. Leucopogon.*

---

* The Mount Ophir species of this genus, which is not uncommon at Paddam Bhattoo, differs from that found on the littoral tracts of Malacca in the narrow leaves crowded on short branches, the corolla scarcely partite to the middle,

I know so little of the Australian species of this genus and family that I am unable to state what value should be attached to the placentation in these four extra-Australian species, to the abortion and deformity of most of the seeds, the wing of the fertile one, and the embryo. The habit and especially geographic distribution would seem to point to some degree of separation. It is to be remembered, however, that Mr. Bennett in the " Pl. Jav. Rar.," a work of the highest authority, does not remark on any structural peculiarity presented by Tristania obovata, his specimens of which, excepting the absence of ripe seeds, appear to have been complete.

RUBIACEÆ.—I notice Epithinia mayana, to confirm Messrs. Wight and Arnott's statement, that it has stipulæ. The opposite statement, in the Malayan Miscellanies, I have ascertained was corrected* by Dr. Jack himself in a copy found thrown aside among some loose papers in the Botanic Gardens. There are at the Botanic Gardens some other MS. corrections which might have been advantageously inserted in the reprint of his writings, undertaken by Sir W. Hooker at the suggestion, I believe, of Dr. Wallich.†

The disposition of the placentæ and ovula in this genus is curious. The former, or perhaps rather their ovuliferous portions, are confined to the middle of the inner angle of each cell, from which they are produced outwards into the middle. Each bears on its apex two ovula, the upper one of which is erect, the under pendulous ; the raphe of both being on that side of the ovulum next the outer wall of the cell. The result, when both ovula are matured, is, that two anatropous seeds, of which one is erect and one pendulous, have the radicles of their embryos pointing exactly towards one another.

CANTON COLLECTION.

This is entirely tropical, and the only peculiar forms that appear to me to exist in it are Nauclea Adina, Strophanthus dichotomus, and Siphonostegia sinensis. For Bæckia frutescens is found on Mount Ophir, with some other Australasian or Polynesian forms, and Myrtus tomentosa is to be found in abundance in the Straits

the large hypogynous scales which nearly enclose the ovarium, and the smooth filiform style. For this the name L. ophirensis may be proposed.

Indeed it was improbable that an exclusively littoral plant should make its appearance suddenly on an isolated mountain, at an elevation of 2,000 feet any where, much more so on Mount Ophir, the productions of which from Paddam Bhatto upwards are very dissimilar from general Malacca vegetation, approaching much more to that characteristic of Polynesia and Australia.

* Instead of "Stipules none," it is, " stipules short, interpetiolar."

† Are there any other MSS. of Jack in existence? I find references in Dr. Wallich's handwriting to a MS. description of Hoya grandiflora, in an imperfect copy of Carey's edition of Roxburgh's " Flora Indica."

of Malacca. But Siphonostegia, the specimens of which present additional calycine lobes, is the only local or characteristic form, for Nauclea is not only a common Indian genus, but there is, I believe, a Khasiya form that approaches N. Adina itself, and Strophanthus exists on the N.E. frontier of Bengal, and about Malacca, where it is represented by a very fine species with large horn-like follicles. All the remaining genera, and probably almost all the species, may be met with either on the Tenasserim Coast or on the eastern frontier of Bengal.

CHUSAN COLLECTION.

The list of this collection given at the commencement is not limited to plants actually existing in the collection, but includes a few others, either contained in Dr. Cantor's sketches, or in his conspectus of his collections.* I have attached an asterisk to those forms which seem to me to be extra-tropical, from which it would appear that the great bulk (about five-sixths) is decidedly tropical.

This collection presents an unusual mixture of form, much of which is perhaps attributable to the effects of cultivation. Almost all the genera are to be met with in " India Orientalis," but I imagine scarcely any other like locality could present such a mix-ture as that of Commelina, Hydrocharis, Salisburia, Achyranthes, Pinus, Aglaia, Humulus lupulus, Pæderia, Juglans, Zingiber, Agrimonia, Nelumbium, Rhododendron, and a Palm.

The most marked northern forms appear to me to be Hydro-charis, Salisburia, Pinus, Quercus, Humulus lupulus, Agrimonia, Rhododendron, Solanum dulcamara?

Clematis, Rumex, Camellia, Hedera, Sambucus, and Plantago all admit of some degree of explanation, inasmuch as these genera may be found at similar levels, but in considerably lower latitudes, in certain parts of the Eastern frontier of Bengal; and some species of Juniperus under cultivation seem to defy a great amount of heat.

Other similarities to the Flora of our eastern frontier, Assam for instance, are indicated by the affinity of the Quercus to one from the Khasiya Hills, on which it is, so far as I know, the only European form of that genus; by one of the Polygoneæ which also occurs in the same direction, and which is remarkable for its armed habit, perfoliate leaves, and bright azure berries, and by the genus Actinostemma.

The only parts of this collection which I feel myself at all com-petent to illustrate are Hamamelideæ and Cucurbitaceæ.

---

* " Calc. Journ. Nat. Hist." No. V.

HAMAMELIDEÆ.—The species is Hamamelis sinensis, R. Br.; the specimens are in fruit, and look at first sight not unlike some Grewias.

The Asiatic plants of this family are Bucklandia populnea, two species of Hamamelis, one of Fothergilla? found by Dr. Falconer, and I believe M. Jacquemont, in Cashmir, and one of Corylopsis.*

* CORYLOPSIS.

Zuccar. in Sieb. "Fl. Japon." fasc. l. p. 45, t. 19, 20; Endl. "Gen. Plant." p. 804, No. 4,589.

CHAR. GEN.—Calyx semi-infernus, 4-5 dentatus vel partitus. Petala 4-5, spathulata vel obovata. Stamina fertilia 5, sepalis opposita; antheraium loculi secus centrum longitudinaliter dehiscentes, valvis extrorsum flexis persistentibus; sterilia 5, vel plura (sub-15) irregularia. Ovarium semi-inferum. Ovula solitaria. Semina ex-alata.

HABITUS.—Frutices Japanicæ et Himalayanæ, habitu Coryli. Gemmarum squamæ imbricatæ. Stipulæ scariosæ, caducæ, gemmarum squamas extimas formantes. Folia cordata, mucronato-serrata, pennivenia. Spicæ preciæ, terminales et axillares, basi squamis gemmarum involucrantibus, interdum subpetaloideis stipatæ, pendulæ, sericeopilosæ; fructus induratæ.

OBS.—Hamamelis, genus propinquum, differt habitu, et petalis elongatis æstivatione spiraliter involutis.

C. himalayana (n. sp.), spicis multifloris, calyce cyathiformi 5-dentato villoso, petalis obovatis quam genitalia longioribus, staminibus fertilibus subinæqualibus pistillo longioribus, sterilibus sub-15, 10 majoribus ante petala, 5 minoribus ante stamina.

Var.? A.—Folia subtus ad venas tantum piloso-tomentosa.

HAB.—Bootan mountains; banks of the river and sides of woods at Tassangsee, alt. 5,387 feet; on broken ground about Tongsa, alt. 6,527 feet; and near Pangee Minzee Peeza, alt. 7,500 feet.

Var.? B.—Folia subtus tomentoso-pilosa.

HAB.—Khasiya Hills; Moflung, alt. 5,500 feet, on the broken rocky ground covered with bushes, between the bungalow and the river.

DES.—Frutex arbusculoideus, 6-8 pedalis. Ramuli flexuosi, brunneo-rubri. Gemmæ floriferæ alternæ, ex axillis foliorum lapsorum, demum pendulæ, superiores præcociores; squamæ plures, imbricatæ, ovatæ, scariosæ, extimæ brunnescentes intus sericeæ, intimæ lutescentes utrinque sericeæ, in bracteas sericeo-hirsutas sensim minorifactæ. Folia alterna; petioli sub-semunciales, albido-pubescentes; lamina cordato-roundata, breviter cuspidata, mucronatoserrata, coriacea, subtus pubescens, basi sub 9-venia, junior plicata secus venns: venæ secondariæ marginem versus oblique currentes, inferiores latere exteriori 3-5-ties ramosæ, intermediæ dichotomæ versus apicem, summæ simplices; intervenia venulis transversis et anastomosantibus reticulatæ. Spicæ pendulæ, longit. 1-1½-unciales, multifloræ, sericeo-hirsutæ. Flores majusculi, lutei, suaviter odori, hermaphroditti.

Calyx breve obconicus 4-5 fidus, laciniis ovatis submembranceis. Petala 5, perigyna, lacinis calycinis alterna, lutea, obovata, breve unguiculata, irregularia, majoribus patentibus conduplicato-plicatis, margine involutis; æstivatio aperta.

Stamina fertilia 4-5, sepalis opposita, fauci calycis inserta; filamenta robusta, breviuscula, fere cylindrica; antheræ biloculares, longitudinaliter dehiscentes, valvis coriaceis, extrorsum flexis, doiso mutuo applicitis, persistentibus. Pollen globosum, plicis 3 medio 1-porosis. Stamina sterilia plura, irregularia, subbiseriata; extioriora sæpius dentiformia, interdum subulata, filamentorum basibus

Sedgwickia, which I some time ago, from examination of fruit-bearing specimens, referred to Hamamelideæ, turns out to be a species of Liquidambar* (Altingia of Noronha), on which genus Blume constructed his family Balsamifluæ. For this oversight and empty compliment Dr. Wallich is responsible, as he had Blume's "Flora Javæ" (in which folio work the family is defined and the genus figured) before him during the printing of my MSS.

The family Balsamifluæ (Balsamaceæ, Lindl.) appears to be generally considered allied to Plataneæ, Salicineæ, and some of their neighbours. And although the structure of Bucklandia was not detailed before 1836 it still appears to me odd that no indication of the similarity of Liquidambar with Fothergilla had been noticed.

From the great variety in structure presented by Hamamelideæ, in which family, limited as it is in genera and species, plants occur varying in habit, with hermaphrodite or polygamous flowers, with petals or without petals, with a quaternary or quinary number of parts, with definite or indefinite stamina, with simple or valvular dehiscence of anthers, I am inclined to believe that Balsamifluæ will be found to be a temporary, or at least a subordinate, group. Its present claims to distinction seem to me limited to the male inflorescence and flowers, which are, so far as I can judge from dried specimens of the Assam species, deficient in any envelope analogous to a perianth or even partial bracte. Its habit presents nothing peculiar; it is not more characteristic of the "Amental" order than that of Fothergilla or Corylopsis. Its anthers present no very great peculiarity, particularly if compared with those of Fothergilla, while its female flowers are in many essential points closely allied to those of Bucklandia, in which (and I take this to be of considerable importance) female capitula also occur, and the ovula are considerably increased in number.

sæpius opposita; interiora sæpissime per paria petalis opposita, majora, atro-viridia, apicibus subglanduliformibus sæpe recurvis. Ovarium semi-inferum, sericeo-pilosum, biloculare. Styli 2, subulati, staminibus subduplo breviores, apicibus recurvis subdilatatis intus stigmatosis. Ovula inloculis solitaria, pendula, anatropa; tegumenta bina; foramen magnum, extus spectans.

Spicæ fructus pendulæ, induratæ, bracteis orbatæ. Capsulæ scriebus circiter 4 spiraliter dispositæ (dimidium inferius calyce tubo indurato corticatum), biloculares, bivalves, valvis demum septicidim bipartitis, stylisque semi-partis recurvis apiculatis; endocarpium atrum. Semina non visa.

My specimens of the Khasiya plant are in fruit. I have not therefore been able to compare the flowers. The leaves vary much in size, those on the mere leaf-bearing branches being as large as those of the Minza Peeza specimens. These again differ from the other Bootan ones in the spikes being less precious, in the length of the styles, and in the longer and pale ferruginous hairyness of the spikes.

This is the fourth species of this genus, two having been defined and one indicated in the "Flora Japonica" (*loc. cit.*); of the three Japanese species, only one, C. Cesakii. Zucc. has been hitherto met with in the wild state.

* " Fl. Jav." p. l. t. l. 2.

The affinities of Hamamelideæ appear to be sufficiently complex, the first step to the simplification, the determination of the true nature of the female perianthium not being settled.* In addition to those already indicated, a relationship with certain Laurineæ may be suggested.

CUCURBITACEÆ, Zanoninæ.—Of the two plants of this family among the Chusan Plants, one belongs to a genus hitherto, I believe, undescribed.

ACTINOSTEMMA.

CHAR. GEN.—Flores monoici; masc. rotati. Sepala 5, acuminata. Petala 5, acuminatissima. Stamina 5, soluta, antheris unilocularibus. Fæm.; Sepala et petala maris. Ovarium 1-loculare; ovula 2-4 parietalia apicem versus loculi. Stylus 1. Stigmata 2, reniformia. Capsula echinata, semisupera, annulata, ad annulum demum circumscissa. Semina pendula, margine exarata.

HABITUS.—Herba scandens, tenera. Folia subhastata, dentata. Cirrhi laterales. Flore sinconspicui, viridescentes masculi paniculati, fæminei racemosi, pedicellis medium supra articulatis. Circumscissio capsulæ per annulum cicatricis perianthii.

A. Tenerum.

HAB.—In hedges, Sadiya, Upper Assam, also on the Khasiya Hills.—Chusan, Dr. Cantor.

DES.—Planta scandens, herbacea. Caules angulati, sulcati, parce puberuli. Folia longiuscule petiolata, juniora cordato-hastata, matura fere hastata, acuminata, grosse dentata, dentibus mucrone terminatis (basilaribus 1 vel 2 glanduliferis), subtus ad venas puberula. Cirrhi sæpe apice dichotomi. Inflorescentia axillaris, puberula. Paniculæ masculæ foliis sæpius longiores. Bracteæ minutæ, subulatæ. Flores caduci, inodori, evolutione centrifugi. Calyx profunde 5-partitus, laciniis lineari-lanceolatis, acuminatis, extus puberulis, basi obsolete saccatis. Petala alternantia, fundo calycis inserta, breviter unguiculata, e basi lanceolata acuminatissima, univenia, æstivatione subimbricata, margine, uti sepala, glanduloso-denticulata. Stamina imo fundo calycis inserta, sepalis opposita, omnino soluta ; filamenta filiformia, breviuscula; antheræ extrorsæ, sub-ovatæ, uniloculares, longitudinaliter dehiscentes, connectivo glanduloso-papilloso. Pollen lanceolatum,

---

* I have not been able to ascertain from dried specimens the nature of the envelope of the pistillum of Liquidambar. Judging from the Assam specimens, and the resemblance to the same part of Bucklandia, it is fairly assumable to be calyx. Blume, however, who has described and figured the genus in detail, represents the envelope as derived from scales, united among each other.

tri-plicatum, immersum globosum, granulosum. Rudimentum Pistilli nullum.

Racemi fæminei pauciflori, flore unico sæpius tantum evoluto. Pedicelli prope florem articulati. Calycis tubus subglobosus, verrucosus. Stamina castrata vel deficientia. Ovarium ⅔ inferum (parte libera conica verrucosula), 1-loculare; placentæ punctiformes, parietales apicem loculi versus. Ovula 2-4, sæpius 4, 2 nempe utroque latere, pendula, anatropa; tegumenta bina distincta. Stylus brevis, crassus, parce puberulus. Stigmata hippocrepiformia. Fructus siccus, pendulus (pedicello petiolo breviore, infra articulum gracili, supra incrassato), ovatus, apice stigmatis reliquiis notatus, medium versus annulo exsculptus, aculeis viridibus præsertim infra annulum echinatus, apice subglaber, tactu lævi ad annulum circumscissus. Semina* 2, vel sæpius 4, pendula, atro-brunnea, tactu saponacea, compressa, superficie rugosa, margine profunde exarata et varie denticulata. Embryonis cotyledones ovales, carnosæ; radicula, supera, breviuscula, conica; plumula conspicua.

This plant has to a considerable degree the habit of Feuillea tamnifolia (Humb. et. Kunth. " Nov. Gen. et Sp.," p. 175, t. 140), which appears to be a plant *sui generis;* it also appears to have considerable affinities with Sicyos, with which it agrees in habit.

I am, besides this plant, in possession of the two undermentioned genera of the same sub-family.†

---

* The seeds in the Chusan specimen are plano-convex, and scarcely grooved along the edges.

† GOMPHOGYNE.—Flores monoici?; masc. rotati. Sepala 5. Petala 5, lanceolata. Stamina 5, soluta, antheris unilocularibus. Faem. (tubus clavatus). Petala acuminatissima. Ovarium inferium, 1-loculare; ovula 3, pendula ex apice loculi. Fructus capsularis, apice truncato dehiscens. Semina 2, rugosa, margine incrassato.

HABITUS.—Herba scandens, carnosa, habitu Cissi, foliis pedatis. Fl. masculi longe paniculati, fæminei racemosi, racemis paucifloris nutantibus. Petala fl. masculi denticulato-fimbriata, pagina papillosa. Filamenta ima basi coalita. Pedicelli florum fæmineorum articulati. Perianthium reflexum. Fructus venosus, interveniis reticulatis. Semina utrinque rapheos completæ rugosomarginata.

OBS.—Genus affine Zanoniæ situ stylorum, forma et dehiscentia capsulæ; Actinostemmati calyce pentasepalo, petalis fæminei floris acuminatis, et ovarii unilocularis placentis punctiformibus.

G. cissiformis.
HAB.—Budrinath, Himalayan Range. Mr. Edgeworth.
DES.—" Scandens, glaberrima. Folia longe petiolata, pedata, foliolis septenis, lanceolatis, inciso-serratis, dentibus mucronulatis. Cirrhi oppositifolii, sæpius simplices. Fl. ♂. racemosi, in apice ramorum sæpius defoliatorum sicut paniculam longissimam formantes, breviter pedicellati, pentameri. Sepala et petala pubescentia, viridescentia. Stamina 5, libera. Fl. ♀ fasciculati, longe pedunculati. Calycis liciniæ 5, subulatæ persistentes. Petala 5, ovata, acuta. Styli 3, apice bifidi. Fructus subtrigono-campaniformis, apice truncatus et planus, cornutus stylis persistentibus, apice dehiscens, 1-locularis, ex abortu

The prominent points of the major part of this sub-family (Zano-ninæ) seem to me the membranous, scarcely marcescent, often elongated floral envelopes, the one-celled anthers with ordinary seminis unius dispermus. Semina crassa, oblonga, nigra, margine intrassato rugosa, amarissima."—Edgeworth MSS.

ENKYLIA.—Flores dioici?; masc. rotati. Sepala 5. Petala 5, acuminatissima, æstivatione involuta. (*a*) Stamina 5; filamentis complete monadelphis, antheris unilocularibus. Fœm. Perianthium maris. Ovarium inferum, bitriloculare; ovula in loculis solitaria. Style 2-3, basi coaliti, apice bifidi. Fructus globosus, medium supra annulatus, trilocularis. Semina solitaria, verrucosa-muriculata.

HABITUS.—Herbæ scandentes habitu Cissi, pilis articulati mollibus pilosæ. —Cirrhi lateralis. Folia pedata, foliolis quinis, mucronato-crenatis serratisve. Flores paniculati, minuti Baccæ pisiformes.

OBS.—Genus Actinostemmati affinis, discrepans habitu, filamentis monadelphis, forma stigmatum, et structura fructus. An Cyclantheræ affinis?

1. E. digyna, foliolis subtus glabris, paniculis molliter et parce pubescentibus, petalis fl. fæm. oblongo-lanceolatis acuminatis, stylis 2 basi coalitis, fructibus pubescentibus.

HAB.—Khalamkhet, Jingsha, at the foot of the Mishmee Hills; and towards Deelong, on the Mishmee Hills, alt. 2-3,000 feet.

DES.—Herba tenera, scandens, molliter pubescens. Petioli subunciales. Foliola subtus glaucescentia, lanceolata, acuminata, crenato-serrata vel dentata cum mucrone, supra ad venas parce puberula, subtus glabra. Cirrhi lateiales. Paniculæ flor. masculorum spithameæ, molliter pubescentes, ramis ascendenti-patentibus. Bracteæ subulaæ. Flores racemoso-fasciculati minutissimi: pedicellis subtus florem articulatis. Parianthium rotatum. Sepala parce piloso. Petala lineari-lanceolata, subulato-acuminata. Columna staminum brevis, vix exserta. Antheræ subreniformes, longitudinaliter dehiscentes. Paniculæ fl. fæm. breviores. Pedicelli calycesque pubescentes. Petala oblongo-lanceolata, acuminata, undulata. Stamina o. Ovarium superum, biloculare, pubescens; ovula solitaria, pendula, raphe extrorsa? Styli 2, basi coaliti, bifidi. Stigmata simplicia. Fructus (immaturus) pubescens.

2. E. trigyna, foliolis utrinque pubescentibus, paniculis (fructus) dense pubescenti-hirtis, petalis (fl. fæm.) e basi lanceolata subulato-acuminatissimis, stylis 3 basi discretis, fructibus glabris.

Zanonia cissoides, wall?

HAB.—Below Dewangiri, towards Dairang, Bootan Mountains, alt. 1-500 feet. In very shady moist woods, Myrung, Khasiya Hills, alt. 5,000 feet.

DES.—Habitus præcedentis. Caules et petioli dense pubescenti-hirti. Foliola lanceolata, ecuminata, crenato-serrata, supra parce pubescentia, subtus ad venas densius. Cirrhi laterales. Paniculæ fructus digitum vix excedentes, denae pubescenti-hirtæ, ramis patentibus. Pedicelli subtus flores articulati, dense pubescenti-hirti. Ovarium glabrum. Styli 3, subulati, bifidi. Stigmata simplicia. Baccæ pisi forma et magnitudine, apice stylorum reliquiis distantibus notatæ, medium supra annulatæ, atræ triloculares; epicarpium subchartaceum. Semina solitaria, cuneata, brunnea, muriculata, margine exarata. Embryo conformis, plumula conspicua.

OBS.—I have male specimens of a plant of this genus from Darjeeling, which differ materially from those of E. digyna, and which I think belong to a third

---

(*a*) This æstivation, it is proper to remark, occurs in, at least, one genuine Cucurbitacea. See Trichosanthes tuberosa, *Bot. Mag.* t. 2,703.

filaments, connectiva and loculi, the generally capsular, annulated, one-celled fruit with simple parietal placentation, and the pendulous* etunicate seeds. There does not appear to be any peculiarity in the situation of the cirrhi, the particular nature of which is besides unknown.†

It passes I imagine into typical Cucurbitaceæ through Zanonia, in which the placentæ are so produced inwards as to meet in the axis, and still more through Telfaria (Hook.), in which there appears to be a tendency to the triadelphous stamina, and which is represented as having horizontal and tunicated seeds.

It affords strong evidence against the hypothesis of the structure of Cucurbitaceous fruit advanced some time ago by Dr. Wight, and which goes so far as to reverse what has hitherto been found to be the constant disposition of the vegetable leaf. For the gradation is complete (through Zanonia)‡ between the entirely

species. The two, now attempted to be established, require to be examined in the living state.

In my Mallaca collection occur specimens of a remarkable plant, which appears to me to belong to this sub-family, although its habit is widely different, being rather that of Menispermeæ.

Calyx minutus irregularis, sub 5-partitus. Petala 5, acuminibus subulatis incurvis. Stamina 5, soluta. Antheræ lineares, uniloculares. Rudimentum Pistilli.

Frutex cirrhosus, ferrugineo-pubescens. Folia oblongo-ovata, integra, Menispermoidea vel Phytocrenoidea. Cirrhi latarales. Paniculæ amplae, folia excedentes. Flores minuti; perianthium utrumque extus ferrugineo-hirtum.

Affinis Natsiato (Ham.) ; affinior Cucurbitaceis, Zanoninis. An Enkylæ sp.?

* Feuillea is described (Endl. "Gen." p. 934) as having the ovula erect, which probably is an error.

† Compare with this Arnott's character of this sub-family, "Lond. Jour. Bot." 3, p. 272.

‡ The structure of the ovarium and fruit of Zanonia still appears to be unknown. While the ovula are distinctly parietal, the placentæ are produced inwards so as to meet in the axis, resembling in a remarkable degree, the very young state of the placentation of Coccinia.

The fruit may be thus described. Capsula (clavata) unilocularis, infra apicem annulata, apice plano valvis tribus demum inflexis dehiscens ; placentea 3 (trigonæ), magnæ, usque ad axin productæ. Semina cujusque placentæ (fol. corpellarium duorum) bina, pendula, etunicata, marginato-alata.

Dr. Arnott, I believe, considers the wing of the seed to be of secondary importance. But the common form of the margin of Cucurbitaceous seeds would seem either here to indicate the occurrence of no wing, or if any, of two. In either case Zanonia appears remarkable.

I subjoin a character of the genus :—

ZANONIA, Linn.—Floris dioici ; Masc. sepala 3, petala 5, stamina 5, soluta, antheris unilocularibus. Fœm. Perianthium maris. Ovarium (inferum) uniloculare, ob placentis intus productis pseudo-triloculare. Ovula 6, pendula. Styli 3, bipartiti. Fructus capsularis, vertice plano valvis tribus dehiscens ; placentæ trigonæ, maximæ, in axi concurrentes. Semina marginato-alata.

HABITUS.—Plantcæ indicæ, scandentes, carnosæ, glabræ. Folia indivisa, vel trisecta (Arn). Flores parvi, paniculati, viridescentes. Antherarum dehiscentia transversa. Fractus clavatus, subtrigonus, apicem infra annulatus.

OBS.—Genus ab aliis subfamiliæ distinctum, Alsomitra excepta? sepalorum and simply parietal placentation of Actinostemma, and the more complicated, but still parietal, placentation of typical Cucurbitaceæ.

I regret that it has not been in my power to give an accurate catalogue of the species contained in the Chinese collections. It cannot be too often insisted on, that the usual necessary means of botanical determination, and which are characteristic of scientific institutions, do not exist in India, not even in the Public Botanic Gardens. The only way, therefore, by which I could hope to attach any interest to this paper was by confining myself to the genera contained in it, which appeared to me either new to science, or imperfectly known.

XXXIX.

ON THE FLAT-HORNED TAURINE CATTLE OF SOUTH-EAST ASIA.

["Journal of the Asiatic Society of Bengal," vol. xxix. pp. 282-304.]

By ED. BLYTH, Esq.

THE species of Bovine animals (so far as known), whether recent or fossil, resolve into three primary groups :—viz.,
I. Bisontine. II. Taurine. III. Bubaline. Two of these groups being again divisible as follow :—
I. Bisontine (adapted for a frigid climate). Subdivided into—
1. Ovibos (the "Musk Ox" of the Arctic "barren grounds" of America ; but which formerly, during the glacial epoch, was far more extensively diffused, remains of this animal having been met with in the British Islands*). 2. Boötherium ; extinct (founded

aliquorum cohesione, placentis intus productis, ovulorum numero, et seminibus marginato-alatis. Z. Vightiana. Arn. verisimiliter genere excludenda.
* As also of the Caribou, or present barren-ground race or variety of the Reindeer ; though I am far from being satisfied that this barren-ground race differs in any respect from the *wild* Reindeer of Lapland, or of the "tundras" of Arctic Siberia ; while I much suspect that the large race or variety of Reindeer which is ridden by the Tungusi and other Siberian tribes (and to the backs of which the bales of goods are annually transferred, in Mantchuria, from those of two-humped camels), to be similarly identical with the Woodland Caribou of North America. The subject of the races of Reindeer will be more fully treated of in the sequel.
As the above is passing through the press, I learn, from Lord Wrottesley's Address to the British Association at Oxford (June 27th, 1860), that Dr. H. Falconer, "aided by Col. Wood, of Glamorganshire, has recently extracted

on two specific races, one of which is the Ovibos Pallantis of De Blainville, and the other is the Bos bombifrons of Harlan). 3. Bison (the well-known broad-fronted and shaggy Bisons of Europe and N. America, and formerly of N. Asia). 4. Pöephagus (the Yak of high Central Asia). To this Bisontine division pertain the only indigenous bovine quadrupeds of America.

II. Taurine (with the exception of the humped cattle suited to a temperate climate and restricted to mountainous countries within or near the tropics). Subdivided into—1. Zebus (the Zebu or humped cattle of the hotter regions of Asia and Africa). 2. Taurus (the humpless cattle with cylindrical horns). 3. Gavæus (the humpless cattle with flattened horns, peculiar to S.E. Asia).

III. Bubaline (the flat-horned, thinly clad, and thick-hided wallowing* cattle of Asia and Africa). Comprising only— 1. Bubalus (the Buffaloes, including the Anoa of Celebes).

According to the views so very ably expounded by Mr. C. Darwin, all the species of one genus have a common origin in the depths of time, and we may ascend in the generalization to any extent, needing only unlimited lapse of time for the ever accumulating development of small variations in any particular direction, under the unconscious guidance of the law of Natural Selection. Species, as he maintains, are only strongly marked varieties, and varieties he designates as incipient species; and most assuredly the dividing line between what are variously accepted as species or as varieties cannot oftentimes be traced; nevertheless, it is admitted by Mr. Darwin that the mass of what are generally considered as species have acquired a high degree of persistency, and arguments *pro* and *con* are abundantly supplied by the Bovines, as by endless other groups; on the one hand, we have the multitudinous races of cylindrical-horned domestic cattle, whether humped or humpless, which surely no naturalist would go the length of supposing to be so many separate and distinct creations; and, on the other hand, we have the phenomenon of three wild species, or most strongly characterized races (more strongly characterized apart than are any of the domestic races of humped or humpless Taurines respectively), yet exhibiting many peculiarities in common, inhabiting to a great extent the very same region, but maintaining their distinctive characters wherever found, and never (so far as known) hybridizing one with another,

from a single cave in the Gower peninsula of South Wales, a vast quantity of the antlers of a Reindeer (perhaps of two species of Reindeer), both allied to the living one. These fossils are most of them shed horns; and there have been already no fewer than 1,100 of them dug out of the mud filling one cave." —*Athenæum*, June 30, 1860, p. 890.

It is remarkable that Ursus arctos of the major continent should, in America, be restricted in its range to the Arctic barren-grounds.

* The true bisons wallow during the summer.

though at least two of them have interbred in a state of domestication (and one of them even in the wild state) with the ordinary tame humped cattle of the tropical regions of the major continent.* All three are domesticable, as will be shown; and as regards the reputed indomitable nature of one of them, the gigantic Gaour (G. gaurus), we have only to reflect on the fact, how very readily the tamest and one of the most thoroughly and completely domesticated of all tame creatures, the humped Ox (Bos or Zebus gibbosus) relapses into a condition of feral wildness, unsurpassed even by the Gaour itself, and assuredly beyond that of the renowned Chillingham cattle of Northumberland, if not also of the feral humpless cattle of S. America and elsewhere.†

The humped cattle are unknown in an aboriginally wild state; and I am strongly of opinion that they will prove to be of African rather than of Asiatic origin, however ancient their introduction into India; for no fossil or semi-fossil remains of this very distinct type have as yet been discovered in any part of Asia, where the only established fossil Taurine is the Bos namadicus of the Nerbudda deposits, which is barely (if at all satisfactorily) distinguishable from the European B. primogenius (or true Urus of Cæsar).‡ It need hardly be remarked that the humped type of

---

* The Bos sylhetanus, F. Cuv., is founded upon a hybrid Gayál (G. frontalis) of this kind; and the B. leucoprymnos, Quoy and Gaymard, upon a hybrid Banteng (G. sondaicus). Sir T. Stamford Raffles remarks, in his "History of Java," that "the degenerate domestic cows [of that island, humped] are sometimes driven into the forest to couple with the wild Banteng, for the sake of improving the breed." Baron Cuvier supposed that the true gayál was a hybrid between the humped cattle and the buffalo; but he seems to have known only the hybrid animal from the description and figures sent by M. Duvaucel and published by his brother in the "Mamm. Lithog."

† How readily European cattle resume the wild habit, is shown by the following passage in Mr. S. Sydney's excellent work, "The Three Colonies of Australia" (1852), p. 314. "The cattle in bush re-acquire in many respects the habits of their wild progenitors; such is the habit of camping, and such, too, the manner in which, like the wild [feral] cattle of Chillingham Park in Northumberland, they march in single file to water, the bulls leading; so, too, when threatened, they take advantage of the inequalities of the ground and steal off in their hollows unperceived, the bulls, if attacked by dogs, bringing up the rear."

In the Swan River colony, both horses and horned cattle have gone completely wild, and buffaloes in the vicinity of Port Essington. *Vide* Leichardt, in "Journ. Roy. Geogr. Soc." xvi. 237.

(What are the wild cattle of Albania noticed by Count Karact in "Journ. Roy. Geogr. Soc." xii. 57? Also, what were those hunted by the ancient monarchs of Assyria, as represented in the Nineveh sculptures? What, indeed, were the Uri Sylvestres which haunted the great forests that surrounded London in the time of Fitzstephen—*i.e.*, about 1150 A.D.? The late Jonathan Couch remarked, in his "Cornish Fauna" (1838), that—"The ancient breed in the west of England was called "black cattle," from the very dark appearance of its coat, almost like velvet, circumstances in which it seems to have differed from the races of the north of England, which were white.")

‡ I refer more especially to the later or post-pliocene (pleistocene, or even

domestic cattle is generally diffused over the hotter parts of Africa, from east to west or ocean to ocean, and on the eastern side as

recent) type, the remains of which are found in almost modern lacustrine deposits, where likewise occur those of Bison europæus of the existing type, as distinguished from the wide-horned priscus type. This later form of primogenius (which is that originally so named by Bojanus) absolutely resembles the most finely developed examples of certain (unimproved) domestic races of large and very long-horned cattle, except that the size is fully one-third larger, as remarked by Professor Nilsson. In like manner, Mr. Hodgson notices, of the Indian buffalo, that—" The wild animals are fully a third larger than the largest tame breeds [in India], and measure from snout to vent 10½ feet and 6 to 6½ feet high at the shoulder." ("J. A. S.," xvi. 710). The older type of primogenius occurs in the pliocene drift, together with bison priscus; and (so far as I have seen) the size of the skull is smaller than in the other, but the horns are still larger, and curve round more towards each other at the tips ; moreover (if I mistake not), they are both thicker and longer in the bull than in the cow, whereas in the more modern type (as in domestic cylindrical-horned cattle, whether humped or humpless) they are thicker but shorter in the bull, longer and more slender in the ox and cow. With the exception of the Indian buffalo to some extent, I know of no other true bovine in which the horns are not both thicker and longer in the bull. In the old type of primogenius, the horn-cores are sometimes enormous. I have measured a pair which were 3 feet long and 19 inches round at base. Another of the same linear dimensions, but 18 inches in circumference at base, is noticed in the " Ann. Mag. N. H.," vol. ii. (1838), p. 163. I have drawings of a fine frontlet of perhaps a cow of this race, which was found in the gravel when digging the foundations of the Houses of Parliament. Of the later race, compare the noble Swedish bull-skull figured in " Ann. Mag. N. H.," second series, iv. 257, 259, with the superb Scottish cow-skull in the British Museum, figured in Prof. Owen's "British Fossil Mammals and Birds," 498, 507. The latter measures just 2½ feet from vertex to tips of intermaxillaries. Compare also Prof. Owen's figure of bison priscus with Prof. Nilsson's figure of the modern type of European bison from the Swedish peat (p. 490 and p. 415 of the same vols. respectively). Whether the latter has occurred in the British Islands I am unaware, but suspect that it does not, or at least that it has not been recognized hitherto.

Perhaps the latest (though vague) notice of the urus as an existing animal occurs in Bell's "Travels in Tartary," vol. i., ch. iii., p. 223: "Journey from Tomsky to Elimsky, in the country of the Tsuliam Tartars." It seems to me to refer more probably to the wild taurine urus than to the bison ; but in either case the notice is sufficiently remarkable. " On the hills and in the woods near this place are many sorts of wild beasts, particularly the urus or uhr-ox, one of the fiercest animals the world produces. Their force is such, that neither the wolf, bear, nor tiger dares to engage with them. In the same woods," Bell continnes, " is found another species of oxen, called bubul by the Tartars. It is not so large as the urus ; its body and limbs are very handsome ; it has a high shoulder and flowing with long hair growing from the rump to its extremity, like that of a horse. Those which I saw were tame and as tractable as other cattle." Certainly a remarkable notice of the yak, both wild and tame (as it would seem), in a region where that animal is at present unknown. The word bubul has probably its connection with bubulus.

The difference in the development of the wild and tame buffalo of India is equally observable where the two frequent the same pastures and commonly interbreed ; and I believe the main reason of it to be, that the tame calves are deprived of their due supply of milk. The importance of an ample supply of nourishment in early life, as bearing on the future development of any animal, cannot be over-estimated. A friend remarked to me that he had no idea of what a fine buffalo was till he saw those of Burmá. They are there, he states, far south as Natál, and throughout Madagascar ; the same being the only Taurine type known in Arabia,* though, curiously, in the essentially Arabian island of Socotra, the cattle are of the humpless European or N. Asiatic type.† Both humped and humpless cattle are represented in the old Egyptian paintings ; and the humpless reappear in S. Africa, in the remarkable indigenous (so far as known) Caffre cattle, and I have seen fossil remains of the same cylindrical-horned humpless type from the banks of a tributary of the Gariep river.‡ In Madagascar, also,

much larger than in Bengal, with splendid horns, and altogether a vastly superior animal. The Burmese never milk them, having the same strange prejudice against milk which the Chinese have, though otherwise both people are nearly omnivorous. There is a corresponding difference of development in the wild and tame races of yak, and of reindeer in Lapland, doubtless for the same reason.

* The humped cattle of Arabia generally are "of a very small and poor race, and are never, but with the greatest reluctance, killed for food." (Wallin, in "Journ. Roy. Geogr. Soc.," vol. xxiv. 148). Chesney remarks of them, that "bulls and cows take the next place to the buffalo, and, like those of India, they bear a hump, and are of small size ; some bullocks purchased at Suweideyah produced each only about 224 pounds of meat. Again, in his Appendix (vol. i. 279), he enumerates among the domestic animals of Arabia and Mesopotamia, "both the common bull and cow, and the bull and cow with hunch." In the province of Kerman, in Persia, Mr. Keith C. Abbot remarks that "the oxen of this part of the country are of a small humped kind, and are commonly used as beasts of burthen ; people also ride on them, seated on a soft pad, and a rope is passed through the nostril, by which they are guided." ("Journ. Roy. Geogr. Soc.," vol. xxv. 43.)

† *Vide* Wellsted in "Journ. Roy. Geogr. Soc.," vol. v. 200. On the confines of India, this European and also Tartar type of humpless cattle comes round evidently from the eastward into Butan. But the Chinese taurines (so far as I can learn) are mostly hybrid, being variously intermediate to the humped and humpless species, except, however, towards the north ; and huge herds of splendid Tartar cattle are pastured beyond the great wall of China, many of these, with vast troops of horses, &c., being the property of the emperor. (*Vide* Timkowski and others.) According to Major R. C. Tytler, a white breed of humpless (?) cattle is reared and highly prized by the natives of Dacca, who never turn them out to pasture. It has "little or no symptoms of a hump." "Ann. M. N. H.," second series, xiv. (1854), 177.

‡ *Vide* "Proc. Geol. Soc.," 1840, p. 152. Captain Speke observed some very fine humpless cattle on the N. W. shore of the Tanganyika lake, near the equator. "Very large cattle, bearing horns of stupendous size. They are of a uniform red colour, like our Devonshire breed, but attain a much greater height and size." Northward, again, on the shore of his grand Victoria Nyanza lake, he remarks that—"The cows, unlike the Tanganyika ones, are small and short-horned, and are of a variety of colours. They carry a hump, like the Brahmini bull, but give very little milk." *Vide* Blackwood's *Edinburgh Magazine*, No. dxxviii. (October, 1859), pp. 392, 398. A little further northward, in the Bari country, on the shores of the White Nile, between 4° and 5° N. lat., M. Ferdinand Werne tells us—"We remark, as usual among the light-coloured cows, many quite white, and few black or dapple. The bulls have the customary high and thick humps ; the cows, on the contrary, have exactly the appearance of those at Emmerich on the Rhine [?] ; their horns are twisted in a surprisingly handsome form, and set off with flaky hair, as well as the ears. They carry the latter erect, by which means the head,

where the tame cattle are all of the humped kind, a humpless wild race, not yet scientifically described, was long ago indicated by Flacourt, and since by the missionary Ellis; stated to resemble European cattle except in having longer limbs.* But to return to the humped cattle. These are now the ordinary Taurines of tropical and subtropical Asia, and, according to Kæmpfer, extend on to Japan. Though unknown in an aboriginally wild state, the species has relapsed into wildness in various parts of India, as especially in Oudh and Rohilkund, in Sháhabád, in Mysore, and even in Ceylon; a fact the more interesting, as proving (what had been doubted) that these humped cattle can maintain themselves,

and the lively eye acquire a brisk and intelligent expression." (Werne's "Narrative of Expedition to Discover the Sources of the White Nile, in the Years 1840, 1841," O'Reilly's translation, ii. 94.) It is not likely that the cows referred to should be entirely humpless, and the large lustrous eye is everywhere one of the many characteristics of the humped species, as is the lanceolate form of ear (which, I suppose, is referred to), as contrasted with the broad round ears of the humpless kind; and in hybrids of different degrees of admixture the proportion is more readily seen in the shape of the ear than in aught else. Moreover, it seems that, as in India, white or greyish-white humped cattle predominate, but the black tail-tuft is constant, except in the rare case of an albino. Between 6° and 7° N. lat., among the Kek or Kiak nation, we learn from the same authority that—"The cattle are generally of a light colour, of moderate size, and have long beautifully twisted horns, some of which are turned backwards (as also in India). The bulls have large speckled humps, such as are seen in the hieroglyphics; the cows, on the contrary, only a little elevation on the shoulders." (*Ibid.* i. 175.) As with the humped cow elsewhere; and when Col. Sykes mentions that this species of cattle, "when early trained to labour or to carriage, is nearly destitute of the hump" ("Proc. Zool. Soc." 1831, p. 105), he refers to cows and oxen only, for the labouring bull has always a well-developed hump, especially if well fed, and this has much to do with the filling out of the hump in oxen and cows; the fundamental structure is there invariably, and capable of development. The huge-horned Bornouese and Galla races of cattle are of the humped species, unlike the fine Tanganyika race "with stupendous horns." Indeed, cattle exceedingly like the African Galla race of Bruce and Salt are by no means very rare in India.

It is remarkable that the singular strepsicerine or Cretan breed of sheep exists in the country drained by the White Nile, modified, however, in its fleece by the locality. Thus, Werne tells us (ii. 18), that—"I purchased for a couple of miserable beads a little sheep, covered partly with wool and partly with hair, as the sheep here generally are, with a long mane under the throat, and horns twisted back. Selim Capitan says that a similar species (race) is found in Crete." Elsewhere (p. 97), he remarks—"Rams with horns twisted back and manes"—the latter of course under the throat, as mentioned in the preceding notice.

* "Horned cattle are numerous, both tame and wild; many of the latter resemble in shape and size the cattle of Europe." (Ellis's "History of Madagascar.") These wild animals abound in the province of Mena-bé which occupies much of the western portion of the island. In Mr. J. A. Lloyd's "Memoir on Madagascar," published in the 20th vol. of the "Royal Geographical Society's Journal," we read (p. 63) that "the northern part of Mena-bé contains great numbers of wild cattle; Radáma and his officers, in one of their warlike expeditions amongst the Sakalami, passing through this country, killed upwards of 340 [wild ?] oxen in one day for the use of his army, and two days afterwards 431 more were killed by the soldiers."

unaided by man, in regions inhabited by the tiger. The origin and history of the wild herds of the Sháhabád jungles, which still exist, are given by Dr. F. Buchanan Hamilton,* who remarks that—" In the woods of Jagadispur and Damraong are some wild cattle of the common breed; they resemble entirely in form and in variety of colours † those bred about the villages of this district, but are more active and very shy. The Rája of Bhojpur, and his kinsman Sáhebzádeh Singha [as of late Kumár Singha, the notable rebel], carefully preserve them from injury ; and say, that, owing to the encroachments of agriculture, the number is rapidly diminishing. Many of their neighbours, however, alleged that the devastation committed by these sacred herds was very ruinous, and every year occasioned more and more land to be deserted. The origin of these herds is well known. When the Ujayáni Rájputs incurred the displeasure of Kásim Ali, and for some years were compelled to abandon their habitations, some cattle were left in the woods without keepers; and on their owner's return had acquired the wild habits, which their offspring retain. Several calves had been caught; but it has been found impossible to rear them, their shyness and regret for the loss of liberty having always proved fatal. This shows what difficulties mankind must have encountered in first taming this most useful animal," &c. &c. The extreme wildness of the feral cattle of Oudh is noticed by Capt. (now Col. Sir T. Proby) Cautley, in " J. A. S.," ix. 623. " In the districts of Akhurpur and Doolpur, in the province of Oudh," he remarks, " large herds of black oxen are, or were, to be found in the wild uncultivated tracts, a fact to which I can bear testimony from my own personal observation, having, in 1820, come in contact with a very large herd of these beasts, of which we were only fortunate enough to kill one ; their excessive shyness and wildness preventing us from a near approach at any second opportunity." Another writer notices herds of these feral humped cattle on the road from Agra to Bareilly ; and, from all recent accounts, they seem to be on the increase rather than on the decrease.‡

---

* Montgomery Martin's compilation from the Buchanan Hamilton MSS., vol. i. 504.

† Major W. S. Sherwill, who has often shot over the now famous "Jugdespur jungle," by permission of the late Kumár (or Kooer) Singha, who allowed him to shoot what he pleased so long as he spared the wild cattle, informs me that, while of course respecting the Rája's injunction, he was curious about these cattle, and had opportunities of watching them somewhat closely. All he saw were rather of small size and of an earthy-brown colour, with shortish horns, and he thinks without the nil-gai markings on the feet (which are often seen in domestic humped cattle). Whether the Oudh herds tend to uniformity of colouring I am unaware. The feral herds of humpless cattle in S. America are, I believe, of various colours, like their domestic Spanish progenitors.

‡ In an article " On the Future of Oudh " (published in the *Morning Chronicle* for May 17, 1859), it is remarked that—" The forests, and notably among them

With this fact, therefore, to bear in mind, the excessive shyness and wildness of the feral herds known to be descended from domestic humped cattle, and also the fact (which I and others know from experience) of the extreme difficulty there is in subduing the wild propensities of the common Bengal Jungle-fowl (Gallus ferrugineus v. bankivus), from which wild species all the races of domestic poultry are as clearly derived as are those of tame ducks from the mallard, we are quite justified, I think, in

that of the Tarai, towards Nipal, serve as a shelter for innumerable wild cattle, which are admirably suited for artillery bullocks and other laborious purposes, besides affording excellent firewood and pasture for cattle, and also hunting-ground for the sportsman. In these forests and in the extensive jungles, are to be found the hides and horns of thousands of wild cattle, rotting, as it were, for want of hands to turn them to account, and which alone would prove a most remunerative branch of commerce, to judge from the success which the very few who have attempted to realize this branch of commerce, have met with. From the same source, tallow might be obtained in abundance, were there only a few speculators to inaugurate the trade, and to direct it into the natural channels for its development."

The making over of a considerable portion of the Tarai region to a Hindu Prince (Jung Bahádur), will of course tend to a further preservation of these feral cattle. Another and more remarkable locality where many beasts of the sort (and of various colours) are little molested, is the churr or alluvial island known as the Siddi churr, lying S.E. of Noacolly in the eastern Sundarbáns. On this churr there is no high tree-jungle, and scarcely brushwood enough to afford cover for tigers, which do not occur on the island.

It is probable that such feral herds occur also in Africa. Thus, in some "Notes on an Expedition down the Western Coast of Africa to 'the Bijuga Islands,' and the recently discovered river Kiddafing," by Col. L. Smyth O'Connor, C.B., F.R.G.S., communicated by the Colonial office to the Royal Geographical Society, and published in its Journal for 1859, p. 384, it appears that in the island of Ovanga "the finest oxen are wild in innumerable herds." In general, however, the notices of wild cattle in Africa refer either to—1. Bubaline species; 2. Gnus (Catoblepas), or "wilde beests" of the Dutch colonists; 3. Species of the Hartebeest group, as especially acronotus bubalis in N. Africa; 4. Even the leucoryx and kindred antelopes. As an illustration of this vague application of names, Capt. Lyon mentions a chain of mountains to the south of Fezzan, named Wadan, "on account of the immense number of buffaloes to be found there, and which are of three species—viz., the Wadan [ovis tragelaphus !], an animal of the size of an ass, having very large (or, as is elsewhere stated, very long, heavy) horns, and large bunches of hair hanging from the shoulder, to the length 18 inches or 2 feet; they have very large heads, and are very fierce. The bogua-el-weish [acronotus bubalis ?], which is a kind of buffalo, slow in its motion, having very large horns and being of the size of an ordinary cow; and the white buffalo [oryx leucoryx !], of a lighter and more active make, very shy and swift, and not easily procured. The calving-time of these animals is in April or May." ("Travels in N. Africa," pp. 76, 271.) Dr. Barth notices the ovis tragelaphus by the name Wadan. "Wild oxen" of some sort are stated to inhabit the country bordering on the river Koanza. ("Journ. Roy. Geog. Soc.," xxiv. 272.) Capt. Burton, also, in his recently published work, "The Lake Regions of Central Africa," notices that—"The park-lands of Duthumi, the jungles and forests of Ugogi and Mgunda Mk'hali, the barrens of Usukuma, and the tangled thickets of Ujiji, are full of noble game—lions and leopards, elephants and rhinoceroses, wild cattle (buffaloes?), giraffes, gnus, zebras, quaggas, and ostriches." Gnus, at least, being here discriminated.

withholding assent to the current opinion that the Gaour (Bos gaurus), or any kindred species, is incapable of domestication. From accounts of the savage nature of the wild Yak, the same might have been inferred of that species, which we know to be extensively domesticated ; or, if we were only acquainted with the wild reindeer as it exists in Arctic America, the varied applicability of the domestic herds of the corresponding regions of the major continent would scarcely have been predicated. So with the African elephant in modern times, as compared with the Asiatic elephant !* Civilized man, as a rule, exterminates but does not domesticate—has not hitherto done so, at least, whatever efforts may of late have been made (with but moderate result hitherto) by the Acclimation and different Zoological Societies. A cultivated country, however, is ill adapted for such experiments. Wild animals are rather to be won over, by degrees, in their indigenous haunts, where their habits of life are little changed by domestication, and their food continues to be that to which the race is accustomed : their subjugation being accordingly effected by human tenants of the same haunts, who can hardly have emerged from savagery, but are practically familiar with the habits of the creatures they seek to subdue. It is thus that the three species of known wild Asiatic Taurines with flattened horns have (each of them) been domesticated, to a greater or less extent, in their own wildernesses. A few calves may have originally been caught and tamed, and some stock established ; but how entire herds of full-grown wild animals may be won over and gradually domesticated, is thus told by Mr. McRae in "Lin. Tr." vii., 303 *et seq.*, the Gayál or Mit'hun (Gaveus frontalis) being the species referred to.

"The Kukis have a very simple method of training the wild Gayáls. It is as follows :—On discovering a herd of wild Gayáls in the jungles, they prepare a number of balls, of the size of a man's head, composed of a particular kind of earth, salt, and cotton ; they then drive their tame Gayáls towards the wild ones, when the two soon meet and assimilate into one herd, the males

---

* In a letter just received from Sir J. Emerson Tennent, I learn that the elephant of Ceylon is considered to be identical with that of Sumatra (!), which is adjudged to be a peculiar species (intermediate to the existing African and Indian elephants) by Prof. Schlegel and the late Prof. Temminck, as also by the late Prince of Canino. At all events the Sumatran elephant is described by three or four authors, to whom I have had access, to bear generally fine tusks (*i.e.*, the males), whereas a fine tusker is exceptional in the instance of the elephant of Ceylon. Sir J. E. Tennent's elaborate and most interesting series of chapters on the great proboscidian discloses certain facts, on the family resemblances of particular herds of elephants, which will not fail to interest the disciples of Mr. C. Darwin. How about the elephants of the Malayan Peninsula, if not also of the Indo-Chinese countries, as far at least as Cochin-China? I am trying to obtain grinders—*i.e.*, molar teeth, in the hope of coming soon to some understanding in the matter.

of the one attaching themselves to the females of the other, and *vice versâ.* The Kukis now scatter their balls over such parts of the jungle as they think the herd most likely to pass, and watch its motions. The Gayáls, on meeting these balls as they go along, are attracted by their appearance and smell, and begin to lick them with their tongues ; and relishing the taste of the salt and the particular earth composing them, they never quit the place until all the balls are destroyed. The Kukis having observed the Gayáls to have once tasted their balls, prepare what they consider a sufficient supply of them to answer the intended purpose, and as the Gayáls lick them up they throw down more ; and to prevent their being so readily destroyed, they mix the cotton with the earth and salt. This process generally goes on for three changes of the moon, or for a month and a half; during which time the tame and wild Gayáls are always together, licking the decoy balls ; and the Kuki, after the first day or two of their being so, makes his appearance at such a distance as not to alarm the wild ones. By degrees he approaches nearer and nearer, until at length the sight of him has become so familiar that he can advance to stroke his tame Gayáls on the back and neck without frightening away the wild ones. He next extends his hand to them, and caresses them also, at the same time giving them plenty of his decoy balls to lick ; and thus, in the short space of time mentioned, he is able to drive them along with his tame ones to his parrah or village, without the least exertion of force or compulsion ; and so attached do the Gayáls become to the parrah, that when the Kukis migrate from one place to another they always find it necessary to set fire to the huts they are about to abandon lest the Gayáls should return to them from the new grounds were they left standing. Experience has taught the Kuki the necessity of thus destroying his huts."

In at least some of the hill-ranges bordering the Bráhmaputra Valley on its left, where Gayáls are extensively domesticated by the mountaineers, they have been so far influenced as to vary considerably in colour, whatever may be the cause of such variation. Thus, amongst the Meris, Lieut. Dalton tells us that—" The Mit'hun (or Gayál) is the only species of horned cattle possessed by the Meris. It is rather a clumsy-looking animal in make ; but a group of Mit'huns grazing on the steep rocky declivities they seem to love, would be a noble study for Landseer ; some are milk-white, some nearly black, some black and white, and some red and white."* Elsewhere, the herds of tame Gayáls show generally a few individuals a little pied or splashed with white, with not uncommonly a white tail-tuft ; and they cannot be expected to vary much further than this, unless subjected to new influences, and above all to that of selection in breeding under human super-

* "J. A. S." xiv. 265.

intendence. In the Mishmi Hills wild Gayáls are still numerous,* but we know little of this species excepting on the outskirts of its range, where its native hills impinge on British territory.† The Rev. J. Barbe, R.C.M., who seems to have penetrated further into the interior of the Tipperá and Chátgaon (or "Chittagong") hills than any other European, even to the present time, remarks, in an account of his tour into the latter territory in 1844-45,‡ that "the Gayál, Bos frontalis, is found amongst the hills, particularly to the south of Sitacra; there are two species, differing in size and [a] little in colour; the large one is of a dark brown, and the male is nearly as high as a female elephant; the small one is of a reddish-brown; it is the Tenasserim "Bison," and the Arakanese call them by the same name as the Burmese do. These Gayáls are perfectly distinct from the Shio of the Kookies, which are smaller, have a projecting skin to their neck, and differ also by the form and direction of their horns." Now the Shio or Shiál of the Mughs is, for certain, the true Gayál (G. frontalis),§ as indeed indicated by the "projecting skin to their neck;" this species having the dewlap much more developed than in the Gaour (G. Gaurus) and Banteng or Tsoing (G. sondaicus), which last I believe to be M. Barbe's smaller species "of a reddish-brown," as I have ascertained his larger species to be the Gaour (which has hardly even a trace of dewlap). But the Gaour, and not the Banteng, is the "Bison" of Anglo-Indian sportsmen on both sides of the Bay of Bengal,‖ the Banteng being currently known as the "Wild Ox" of the Indo-Chinese countries. M. Barbe has there-

---

* "J. A. S." xiv. 495.

† The Gayál of Bishop Heber's Journal, which that much respected prelate saw in Barrackpore park, was, of course, the gavæus frontalis. But the figure and description given are monstrous, and were obviously got up from extremely vague recollection : the horns turn down instead of up, the space between them is narrow instead of being very broad, the heavy dewlap is not given, nor the white stockings; the tail is figured and described as "bushy," and as extending below the hocks, and the outline of the spinal ridge is utterly unlike what it should be. He says—"It is very much larger than the largest Indian cattle [he could not then have seen an ordnance bullock], but hardly, I think, equal to an English bull [!] : its tail is bushy [!], and its horns form almost a mass of white and solid bone to the centre of its forehead [!]" He could only have viewed the animal from a distance, and have mistaken the pale colour of the forehead for a continuation of the bases of the horns. Neither is it, as he remarks, "a native of Tibet and Nipal," nor even of Butan (*vide* Turner's Embassy). The second figure in the distance is meant, we can only suppose, to represent a large humped ox ; but here, again, the animal is furnished with a horse's tail, and is like nothing in nature ! Our utmost respect for the reverend Bishop can scarcely pardon him such outrageous caricatures, both of figure and description.—*Vide* Heber's "Journal," i. 31.

‡ "J. A. S." xiv. 386.

§ *Vide* "As. Res." viii. 488.

‖ In Orissa, the gaour is known to sportsmen and others as the "gayál;" although the natives of the province style and pronounce it goor, the names, of course, being branches or ramifications of the same root.

fore erroneously identified his *smaller* kind with the Tenasserim "Bison," and is also wrong in applying the name Bos frontalis to either of his species, as obviously so to both of them.

Soon after the publication of the foregoing notice, I had some conversation on the subject with M. Barbe, and have fortunately preserved a written memorandum of that conversation, intended for publication at the time, though it has not hitherto appeared in print. I did not then recognize the *third* species ; indeed, at that time, I had much less knowledge of the Banteng than I have at present ; but I now give the memo. as orginally written :—

"M. Barbe had informed me that, besides the common Gayál (Bos frontalis), the Kukis of the interior of the Chittagong hills had a very different species of Bos in a state of complete domestication, the exact species of which I could not satisfactorily make out from his description ; when, luckily, he remembered that he possessed a horn of one of those tame animals, and, to my very considerable surprise, it proved to be that of a Gaour, or (so-called) ' Bison ' of Anglo-Indian sportsmen, an animal which is commonly reputed to be untameable. The huge beasts are, however, stated to be most perfectly gentle and quiet, and they habitually pass the night and great part of the day beneath the raised habitations of their owners ; and M. Barbe further mentions that he was greatly astonished at the facility with which these enormous cattle ascended and descended heights so steep and precipitous, that, had he not witnessed the feat, he would scarcely have been inclined to credit it." The last observation points rather to the Gayál than to the Gaour !

As a rule, the proper habitat of the Gaour is an undulating grassy table-land intermixed with forest ; the heavy and buffalo-shaped Gayál being habitually much more of a climber, and also more exclusively affecting the dense craggy forest, where it browses in preference to grazing, the Gaour being much more of a grazer. Having possessed both species alive, I can testify to this difference in their feeding. The Gaour appears to be diffused throughout the Indo-Chinese countries, and all down the Malayan peninsula to the extreme south ; but has not been observed on any of the great islands of the archipelago. I have lately seen the skull with horns of an old bull from the mainland near Singapore; and in 1858 I purchased a live Gaour-calf that was brought from Singapore to Calcutta, together with a Malayan Tapir. This calf was in high health when I shipped him for England, and as tame and tractable as any domestic animal, yet full of life and frolic ; but he was suddenly taken ill when nearing the Cape, and died on the following or next day. He was very impatient of the sun, even at the height of the cold weather (so called) in Calcutta ; which rendered it difficult to secure a photograph of the animal, but a good one was taken, and copied in the *Illustrated London*

News; only the artist must needs improve upon nature by lengthening the tail beyond the hocks, which detracts from the *vraisemblance* of the wood-cut. The Gaour is the only species of the group which inhabits cis-Bráhmaputran India, in all suitable districts; extending formerly to Ceylon, where we recognize it as the Guavera of Knox; and in Johnson's "Indian Field Sports," it is familiarly referred to as "the Gour (a kind of wild bullock)" inhabiting, in about 1796, the hill-country bordering on the Dámudá, through which the Grand Trunk Road now runs from Ránigánj to Shergátti—a district from which it has been long since extirpated, or has retired some hundreds of miles further west. It is still numerous in various localities, and not always particularly shy where little persecuted; for instance, my late friend Capt. Crump (a distinguished sportsman, who fell most gallantly taking possession of a gun at Láknao,) found them so little shy towards the sources of the Nerbudda, that, on one occasion, a couple of young bulls came trotting fearlessly out of the forest, within easy gunshot of himself and companion on horseback, and continued for some time to trot alongside of them at that distance, till my friend's sporting (or destructive) propensities could brook it no longer. Others would have felt much greater pleasure in observing the noble animals thus fearlessly at liberty, and would have been loth to abuse their confidence.

In the catalogue of the specimens of mammalia in the India-house museum, published by the late veteran zoologist, Dr. Horsfield, in 1851, a Bos asseel is described as a new species, founded on a preserved head, with the skin on, in that collection. I have drawings of the identical specimen, which I pronounce, with confidence (as I did formerly in "J. A. S." xi. 445), to be that of a cow Gaour, with horns more slender and turning back more towards the tips than usual; but I have seen others like them, and of all intermediate grades between them and the ordinary type of female Gaour-horns, resembling those of the bull but more slender, and with always a greater amount of inclination backwards at the tips. The specimen in question is figured by Gen. Hardwicke in the "Zoological Journal," iii., pl. 7, together with a frontlet of a bull Gaour, and the two being by him also supposed to be distinct species.

Of the Banteng (G. sondaicus), or Tsoing of the Burmese (who designate the Gaour as the Pyoung), we possess two frontlets from Java—one of them particularly fine—also an imperfect skull with horns from Pegu, and a single horn from the Arakan side of the mountain range which separates that province from Pegu, both presented by Col. Phayre, together with a flat skin of a calf from Mergui, resembling in colour the Javanese calf figured by Dr. Salomon Müller, who has given four excellent coloured representations of this animal, of different sexes and ages, and profusely illustrated the skulls and horns. For this calf-skin, the Society is indebted to the late Major Berdmore. The species was long ago indicated in Pennant's " Hindustân," as a kind of wild ox "with white horns " inhabiting the Indo-Chinese countries; and our Peguan specimen has remarkably albescent horns, while the single horn from Arakan is darker, and resembles the Javanese examples in our museum. The next and more detailed notice which we can now refer, without hesitation, to this species, occurs in Herbert's " Gleanings in Science," iii. 61. It would appear that a skull and horns of this animal were presented to the Society at its meeting of February 2, 1831 ; * " with a descriptive notice by Mr. Maingy; by which it appears that, when full grown, it is about thirteen hands high, and of a most beautiful red colour, except under the belly, which is white. It has no hump, like the cow of India. Altogether, it resembles the red cow of England, but is a much handsomer animal. The bull is a large and fine animal, and, with the exception of having a white forehead, resembles the cow. Mr. Maingy has seen twenty or more of these animals in a herd, but it is a very difficult thing to get a shot at them, as they have a most acute sense of hearing and smelling; one or two appear to act as sentinels, while the others graze or drink. If, in snuffing the air, they find it tainted, off they fly in a moment, with a speed almost inconceivable, considering the form and bulk of the animal."

In the foregoing descriptions, the invariable great white patch on each buttock (whence the name leucoprymnos bestowed on the hybrid by MM. Quoy and Gaymard) is unnoticed, as also the dark colour of the old bull; but the alleged " white forehead " of the bull refers doubtlessly to the mass of thickened corneous substance between the horns, which, in our larger Javanese frontlet, is thick and solid enough to turn a musket-ball.† (*Vide* S. Müller's figure of the mature bull.) But, in a notice of " the Burmese wild Cow, or ' Sine Bar,' which appeared in the *Bengal Sporting Magazine* for 1841, p. 444, we are informed that " herds of thirty and forty frequent the open forest jungles [of the Tenasserim provinces]. They are noble-looking animals, with short curved horns, that admit of a beautiful polish. The cows

---

* These were not in the museum when I took charge of it in 1841 ; but only two frontlets from Java, presented by Prince William Henry of the Netherlands ("J. A. S." vi. 987), one of which has since been forwarded to the India-house museum.

† In our smaller Javanese frontlet (figured "J. A. S." xi. 490), a portion of this enormously thickened epidermis remains attached to the base of each horn, which led Mr. Hodgson to remark, when looking at these specimens as they hung up, that the horns were less approximated at base in the Peguan specimen. However, on close examination, the true base of the horn is seen to be well defined, and the supposed distinction disappears.

are red and white, and the bulls of a bluish colour. They are very timid, and not dangerous to approach. Their flesh is excellent. They are the only cows indigenous to the provinces ;" yet the preceding paragraph mentions "the Bison" or Gaour as "attaining a great size in the East."

Here the difference of colouring of the sexes observable in the Banteng (analogous to what is seen in the Nil-gai and Indian Antelope, and to a less extent in the Gayál) is noticed ; and Sir T. Stamford Raffles mentions, that (as also in the Nil-gai) "a remarkable change takes place in the appearance of this animal after castration, the colour in a few months becoming invariably red ;"*—*i.e.* reverting to the hue of the cow and immature bull. The horns cannot justly be termed *short* in an old bull ; but it is worthy of remark that, when full grown, they are flattened only towards the base, considerably less so than in the Gaour and Gayál, wherefore, when but half-grown, only the cylindrical portion of them appears, which has given rise to the reports of wild cattle with cylindrical horns inhabiting the Indo-Chinese territories. As shown by Prof. S. Müller's figures, the Banteng—though still very Gayál-like in general aspect—approximates more nearly in contour to the cylindrical horned humpless cattle of Europe and N. Asia, than is the case with its immediate congeners, the Gaour and Gayál ; and the increased amount of cylindricity of its horns adds to the resemblance. With much of the general aspect of the Gayál, it has longer limbs, and is less heavy and bubaline in its proportions   There is nothing exaggerated about its figure ; the spinal ridge is not more elevated than in B. Taurus, and the tail-tuft descends considerably below the hock-joint. Indeed, this animal has been compared to a Devonshire ox ; but it has nevertheless all the general features of the present group, and is true to the particular colouring, showing the white "stockings" (like the Gaour and the Gayál, and also not a few Indian buffaloes). The shoulder is a little high, with some appearance of the dorsal ridge behind the scapulæ, but this slopes off and gradually disappears behind ; the rump also is nearly as much squared as in European cattle ; dewlap moderate, with a different outline from that of the Gayál, more as in the B. Taurus ; colour of the calf bright chestnut, with a black tail-tuft, and also a black dorsal line commencing from where the ridge should terminate behind, † the white stockings having much rufous intermixture at this age. The cows are deeper-coloured, being of a rich light bay, and the old bulls are blackish; both, however, relieved by the white on the legs, buttocks, lips, and hair lining the ears, which last are scarcely so large as in the Gaour and Gayál, but of similar

---

* "History of Java," i. III.

† This black list is also conspicuous in the calves of both the gaour and the gayál, extending both over the dorsal ridge and behind it.

shape. The description here given is drawn up from Dr. S. Müller's elaborately careful coloured figures.

The Banteng inhabits Borneo, Jáva, and Báli, and I strongly incline to the opinion that the Gaour, Gayál, and Banteng alike inhabit the Malayan peninsula and Tenasserim provinces, the Gayál, probably, being confined to a certain altitude upon the mountains. Capt. (since General) Low distinctly indicates three species in the Malayan peninsula, besides the Buffalo, in " As. Res.," xviii. 159. He mentions :—" The bison [Gaour], which is found of a very large size in Thedda, the head [forehead] being of a fawn colour ; the wild ox [Gayál?] of the size of a large buffalo ; and also a species [Banteng?] resembling in every respect the domestic ox." There is, indeed, the skull of a bull Banteng divested of its horns, labelled " from the Keddah coast," in the London United Service Museum ;* and the considerable resemblance of this animal to the humpless domestic cattle of Europe has been mentioned repeatedly. Thus the late Major Berdmore, writing of it from the valley of the Sitang river, remarks :—" They are by no means so common here as they are to the south. I have often been in the midst of very large herds of them, and they appeared to me to be very like red domesticated cows." Helfer (no great authority yet) notices three species of wild cattle, besides the buffalo, in the Tenasserim provinces. He tells us that :—" The great Bos gaurus is rather rare, but Bison guodos [evidently a misprint for gavæus,†—*i.e.*, Bos gavæus of Colebrooke, or the Gayál,] very common ; besides another small kind of cow, called by the Burmese Fhain, of which I saw footprints, but never the living animal."‡ He does not mention the Gayál as domesticated in the provinces ; and I am not aware that any other writer has there noticed it at all. Still, I consider it highly probable that the Gayál, in addition to the Gaour and Banteng for certain, extends to the more elevated regions of the Malayan peninsula.§

The Banteng is the only species of the three which has been observed in certain of the great islands of the archipelago. The existence of a " wild ox " in Borneo was long ago noticed by Beckman, as cited by Pennant, who also recorded the occurrence of such an animal in Java, and had likewise (as we have seen)

* Figured in " J. A. S.," xi. 470, figs. 1, 2, and 3.
† The words may be written to look very much alike.
‡ " J. A. S." viii. 860.
§ The two species of Malayan wild cattle noticed as the sapi and the sapandang, in the " Journal of the Indian Archipelago," iv. 354 (as cited in " J. A. S.," xxi. 433), refer, as I am now satisfied, to the gaour and the wild buffalo. Dr. Cantor describes the gaour to be " numerous in the Malayan peninsula," where known as the sapi utan (literally " wild cow "), " J. A. S.," xv. 273. But he enumerates neither the gayál nor banteng in the peninsular fauna.

obtained intelligence of one "with white horns" in the Indo-Chinese countries. In Java, according to Raffles, "it is found chiefly in the forests eastward of Pásuran, and in Báli, though it also occurs in other parts of Java." Dr. S. Müller remarks that the Banteng is found in Java in territories which are seldom visited by man, as well in the forests of the plains and of the coast, as in those of the mountains up to 4,000 ft., where it is tolerably common. "We have likewise seen traces of it," he adds, "in Borneo, and have even received a calf from the Dyáks about a month old. According to Raffles, it is also found in Báli, but in Sumátra it does not appear to exist." In the N.E. peninsula of Borneo it would seem to be numerous. Thus, in a "Sketch of Borneo," published in Moor's "Notes of the Indian Archipelago," the writer remarks :—"During the wet season the rivers swell and overflow their adjacent shores, and run down with such continued rapidity that the water may be tasted fresh at sea at a distance of six or seven miles from their mouths. . . . . In the dry season the coast, from these overflowings, presents to the eye the richest enamelled fields of full-grown grass for miles around. It is at this season that whole herds of wild cattle range down from the mountains of the interior to fatten on the plains, but during the wet season they ascend to the hills." Hence we gather that the Banteng is essentially a grazer, like the Gaour, instead of being chiefly a browser like the Gayál, which never descends from its mountain forests.

Another writer in the same work states that, in Báli, "the breed of cattle is extremely fine, almost every one of these beasts being fat, plump, and good-looking ; you seldom, if ever, see a poor cow in Báli. It is a breed of a much larger size than the common run of [humped] cattle in Jáva, and is obtained from a cross with the wild cow [bull?] with the same animal. They are generally of a red colour, and all of them are white between the hind-legs and about the rump, so that I do not remember seeing one that was not white-breeched. The people have no land expressly devoted to grazing, but let their cattle eat their old stubble or fresh grass of the rice-fields after the crops have been taken off ; and while the rice is growing they let the cattle stray into the commons or woods, and pick up what they can get by the roadside. The rude plough is drawn by two abreast, which the plougher drives with one hand while he guides the plough with the other." This account pretty clearly indicates domesticated Bantengs, intermingled in blood, perhaps more or less, with the humped cattle, though there is nought to certify such intermixture in the notice quoted, but rather that—as in the case of the Gayál—both wild and tame exist and inter-breed occasionally. However, we have the authority of Professor Van der Hoëven that the Bos leucoprymnos of Quoy and Gamard is a hybrid Banteng; and there is a figure of a cow of this mixed race among the Hardwicke drawings in the British Museum which —as also in the instance of a hybrid Gayál that I saw alive—partook much more of the general aspect of what may be termed the jungle parent. These hybrid Bantengs are known as " Báli cattle " at Singapore.

The Rev. F. Mason, in his " Notes on the Fauna, Flora, &c., of the Tenasserim Provinces" (1852), remarks that "a small ox from the Shan country is brought down sometimes in considerable numbers, which resembles in its form the English rather than the Indian ox, but is probably derived from the wild race. Occasionally a young wild ox is domesticated, and brought under the yoke." This notice should have been more explicit. Crawford remarks :—" The ox is found wild in the Siamese forests, and exists very generally in the domestic state, particularly in the Southern provinces. Those we saw about the capital were shortlimbed, compactly made, and often without horns, being never of the white or grey colour so prevalent among the cattle of Hindustân. They also want the hump on the shoulders which characterizes the latter. They are used only in agricultural labour, and the slaughter of them, publicly at least, is forbidden even to strangers. Hence during our stay our servants were obliged to go three or four miles out of town and to slaughter the animals at night. The wild cattle—for the protection of religion does not extend to them—are shot by professed hunters, on account of their hides, horns, bones, and flesh, which last, converted into jerked beef, forms an article of commerce with China."*

* " Mission to Siam and Cochin China," p. 430.
The people of Laos "have a great many cattle, very small, which yield scarcely any milk, and which they never think of using. When we told them that in our country the milk of the cow was much esteemed, and that it formed a savoury food, they laughed, and only held our countrymen in contempt." (Grandjean, in the " Chinese Repository," as quoted by Sir J. Bowring). This prejudice against the milk of the cow seems to be common to all the Indo-Chinese nations, and prevails also in China, whilst the Mantchurian Tartars are great consumers of milk. Even the savages of the Nága hills, bordering on Asám, reject milk as food, in the belief that it is of excrementitious nature.
In Earl's " Voyage to the Molucca Islands and New Guinea," p. 361, we are informed that " Wild cattle are numerous in Timor Laut, of a brown colour, and size about the same as that of two-year old cattle in Holland. The natives catch them with rattan, and also shoot them with arrows."
The Tamarao of the island of Mindoro (one of the Philippines), as I was informed by Mr. Hugh Cuming, is a small bovine species, but fierce and dangerous to attack, of a dark colour, with horns rising at an angle of about 45° from the forehead." The nearly similar name Tambadao is applied in Borneo to the Banteng.
These various wild races and humpless tame races of S. E. Asia and its archipelago demand investigation; and though I have before published in the Society's Journal several of the notices here cited, it is convenient to bring them together, to save trouble in reference. What animal the following passage refers to, in Mrs. Graham's work in Ceylon, I am unable even to conjecture;

Are domesticated Bantengs here intended? The existence of hornless individuals is not more remarkable than that of hornless buffaloes and other domestic cattle, unless in the instance of a race little altered from the wild type. Thus the Italian race of buffaloes, in which hornless individuals sometimes occur (*vide* figure of the skull of one in Cuvier's "Ossemens Fossiles"), is considerably more removed from the aboriginally wild type of the species than are the domestic buffaloes of India, among which I am not aware that hornless individuals ever occur. But I have read of hornless Yaks; and instances have been known of hornless individuals of different species occurring even in the wild state: a tame Sprinkbok of this description was long in the possession of the Empress Josephine. By specially breeding from such animals, a race of them could be readily established.

In Sumátra, as in Jáva, the ordinary domestic Taurine cattle are humped, small, and of inferior quality; but, according to Sir T. Stamford Raffles—"There is a very fine breed of cattle peculiar to Sumátra, of which," he remarks, " I saw abundance at Menang Kabu, when I visited the capital of that country in 1818. They are short, compact, well-made animals, without a hump, and almost without exception of a light fawn colour, relieved with white. The eyes are large and fringed with long white lashes. The legs are delicate and well shaped. Among all that I saw I did not observe any that were not in excellent condition, in which respect they formed a striking contrast to the cattle generally met with in India [*i.e.*, S.E. Asia and its archipelago. India proper is styled "Western India" by Crawford.] They are universally used in agriculture, and are perfectly domesticated. This breed appears to be quite distinct from the Banteng of Jáva and the more eastern islands."* What, then, is it? The remark that these beasts are " perfectly domesticated " would hardly have been made of any race appertaining to the humped or to the ordinary humpless type, but seems to imply that the writer regarded it as a peculiar species, as does also his statement of its distinctness from the Banteng.

In the " Journal of the Indian Archipelago," ii. 831, is a notice of the existence of wild cattle in Celebes ; but I suspect that the

and certainly do not credit the existence of such a creature. At the Governor's house, this lady " saw, feeding by himself, an animal no less beautiful than terrible—the wild bull, whose milk-white hide is adorned with a black flowing mane !" The description is explicit enough, so far as it goes, but most assuredly no such animal is known to naturalists ; and with the example before us, of what a writer of Bishop Heber's stamp can make of the Gayál, we may cease to wonder at any amount of vagary of the kind on the part of unscientific observers ; though why people of education, who undertake to describe or notice an animal, however cursorily, should make such sorry use of their eyes is difficult to comprehend.

* " Lin. Trans. xiii. 267.

small Anoa Buffalo (Bubalus depressicornis) is intended. In an account of the province of Minahassa, it is there stated that— "Wild cows are also found here, principally in the higher parts of the mountains; but they bear little resemblance to the Banteng of Jáva, are below the middle size, yet possess notwithstanding an incredible strength." Just possibly an undescribed Taurine may be here indicated.

While illustrating the domesticability of all the flat-horned Taurine cattle indigenous to S.E. Asia, it is not disputed that some species of animals are more easily tameable than others; for instance, the American as compared with the European bison (by all accounts), or even the domestic humped bull as compared with the domestic European bull. It may be from more thorough rather association of mankind, from its youth continuously, but it seems from constitutional difference (still the result, perhaps, of countless ages of such complete domestication), but the fact is undeniable that the humped bull is far more gentle and tractable than his European compeer, being much more completely in subjection, and hardly (if at all) influenced by those paroxysms of sexual excitement which seem to be as irrepressible as ineradicable in the entire males of most other ruminants. It must be conceded, however, that the European bull is rarely subjected to like conditions—so much inured to constant handling, and governed by a cord passed through his septum narium. But the fact remains (as attested by daily observation) that, under existent respective conditions, the humped bull is—as a general rule—by far the more gentle, tractable, and inoffensive animal of the two.

XL.

NOTE BY GENERAL G. B. TREMENHEERE IN REFERENCE TO HIS PAPERS ON THE TIN OF MERGUI.

THE Chinese, from their settlement on our boundary river, the Pakchan, have for long periods exported tin to Pinang, Mergui and Rangoon. In 1868, fifty tons were reported, but the quantity was probably much more. Their surface washings for the ore are still carried on by this industrious people. It is believed a large quantity of tin is annually obtained, and that the working is profitable.

In about the same locality, some years ago, an English firm of

Rangoon prosecuted some stream works, but they did not pay expenses. There were also mining operations under skilled superintendence, " which had had to be abandoned owing to the scarcity of ore." "From the conformation of the ground good results were expected, but the lode died away," although at first it was extremely rich and produced solid lumps of tin ore.

There is no mention of any tin-mining in the neighbourhood of Mergui, where more than half a ton of clean ore was procured in 1842 from the Kahan Hill, and sent to England ; specimens of which are still in the Museum of Economic Geology in Jermyn Street, and in the Indian Museum. An analysis of these ores, communicated by Dr. Forbes Watson, gave the following results :—

	No. 1. Kahan tin ore. Per cent.		No. 2. Mergui. Per cent.		No 3. Tenasserim. Per cent.
Silica	27·55	...	10·91	...	7·99
Tin oxide	*55·18	...	*72·20	...	*65·54
Iron and aluminum oxide .	10·54	...	7·52	...	15·73
Calcium oxide . . .	3·82	...	7·76	...	10·27
Magnesium, &c. . . .	2·92	...	2·33	...	trace.
	100·01	...	100·72	...	99·53

These deposits occur on the same peninsula, and are similar to the ores from which the Banca and "Straits" tin is obtained. They are smelted at little cost, as charcoal to any quantity can be made in the forests, which cover nearly the whole of the province of Tenasserim. The climate is generally healthy ; the heavy periodical rains and perpetual verdure render the air cool and agreeable at all seasons. The Kahan Hill, which is eleven miles distant from Mergui by the river route, is 1,920 yards in circumference. Tin ore has been dug out on both sides of the hill. It is isolated, in an open plain, entirely free from jungle, and within a quarter of a mile of water communication by the Tenasserim where the river is a mile in breadth, leading to a sheltered roadstead off the town of Mergui, of from 9,000 to 10,000 inhabitants, from which steamers go periodically to Moulmein and Rangoon. Native vessels also ply frequently to Pinang and Singapore, and there is no scarcity of labour.

There are other small hills, like Kahan, similarly isolated in the same plain ; but excepting Yahmon, 20 miles south-east from Mergui, it is not known that they have yet been tested for tin ore.

In 1870 a correspondence commenced with the Chief Commissioner of British Burmah with regard to the terms upon which the Government of India might be disposed to lease out certain

---

* Metallic tin, 43·41 per cent., 56·80 per cent., 51·55 per cent.

tin mines in Tenasserim, or for collecting tin in the river-beds within that division ; and in 1871 a definite request for powers to work for tin at Kahan and other localities was made to the local authorities. The price of tin was then abnormally high in England, and soon had reached to more than £160 per ton, causing tin-mining in Cornwall to be pushed forward with unusual vigour. Inquiries were made in 1872 from merchants in London connected with the Indian trade, " whose attention had been more particularly directed to the valuable tin deposits in the hills called Kahan and Yahmon, near Mergui, as presenting ground in which mining operations could be at once commenced, and as furnishing a basis for the prosecution of further works," who entertained and expressed no doubt that, " under the grant of a lease on reasonable terms, a company could be at once formed to raise the necessary capital, and open mines at these places." The correspondence, however, was protracted, and it was not until May 1873 that it was notified that, " with the exception of the Malewoon township and the upper Tenasserim, the whole of the tin localities of the Mergui and Tavoy districts were available for mining purposes ; " and in 1874 the draft of the lease of a tract near Mergui was issued, defining the conditions upon which the sanction of the Government of India could be obtained.

Four years having elapsed since the subject was first mooted, and the price of tin in England in the meantime having fallen about £60 per ton, it was thought useless to attempt to procure capital in London for tin-mining in Mergui, and the project had therefore, for the time, to be abandoned.

The terms of lease then proposed by the Indian Government were, a yearly rent of 1,000 rupees, and a royalty of 10 per cent. of the value of metals and metallic ores raised, after the same shall have been dressed and made merchantable, either for smelting on the spot, or intended for exportation in an unprepared and unsmelted condition.

Also, if after the third year the aforesaid royalty should not exceed 1,000 rupees, then the rent for such year to be increased to 2,000 rupees.

It cannot be said that these terms are encouraging for mining, which of all enterprises is one of the most uncertain.

G. B. TREMENHEERE, *Major-Gen.*

SPRINGGROVE, ISLEWORTH, *Sept.* 11, 1885.

GENERAL INDEX.

INDEX OF VERNACULAR TERMS.

INDEX OF ZOOLOGICAL GENERA
AND SUB-GENERA

OCCURRING IN THE SECOND VOLUME.

—•◆•—

END OF VOL. II.

For Product Safety Concerns and Information please contact our EU representative GPSR@taylorandfrancis.com Taylor & Francis Verlag GmbH, Kaufingerstraße 24, 80331 München, Germany

Batch number: 08158917

Printed by Printforce, the Netherlands